# Environmental and Economic Impacts of Decarbonization

On December 12, 2015, at the United Nations Conference on Climate Change held in Paris, 195 countries adopted the first-ever universal and legally binding climate deal. They agreed to decarbonize the economy in order to hold the increase in the global average temperature to well below 2°C relative to the preindustrial levels. Although each country is free to design its own strategy on mitigation and adaptation, it will be bound to such a strategy and is supposed to implement the bulk of the adjustments by 2050.

Many questions arise from the Paris Agreement that points to a second Industrial Revolution. What are the required changes in the structure of production and in the patterns of consumption? What will be their impacts on emissions, employment and international trade? This book answers these questions from a variety of input-output models able to compute the impacts on specific sectors and regions. This volume has 17 chapters written by 52 co-authors who are specialists in input-output analysis and environmental sustainability. They come from 24 universities, research centers and international agencies all over the world, sharing their commitments to explain important and complex ideas in a way that is understandable to the non-experts and experts alike.

*Environmental and Economic Impacts of Decarbonization* is a very important read for those who study environmental economics, climate change and ecological economics.

**Óscar Dejuán** is Professor of Economics at University of Castilla, La Mancha, Spain.

**Manfred Lenzen** is Professor of Sustainability Research in the School of Physics at University of Sydney, Australia.

**María Ángeles Cadarso** is Associate Professor of Economics at University of Castilla, La Mancha, Spain.

# Routledge Explorations in Environmental Economics

Edited by Nick Hanley
*University of Stirling, UK*

For a full list of titles in this series, please visit www.routledge.com/series/REEE

# Environmental and Economic Impacts of Decarbonization

Input-Output Studies on the Consequences of the 2015 Paris Agreement

Edited by Óscar Dejuán,
Manfred Lenzen and
María-Ángeles Cadarso

Routledge
Taylor & Francis Group

LONDON AND NEW YORK

First published 2018
by Routledge

2 Park Square, Milton Park, Abingdon, Oxfordshire OX14 4RN
52 Vanderbilt Avenue, New York, NY 10017

*Routledge is an imprint of the Taylor & Francis Group, an informa business*

First issued in paperback 2019

*British Library Cataloguing-in-Publication Data*
A catalogue record for this book is available from the British Library

*Library of Congress Cataloging-in-Publication Data*
A catalog record for this book has been requested

ISBN: 978-0-415-78740-6 (hbk)
ISBN: 978-0-367-88722-3 (pbk)

Typeset in Times New Roman
by Apex CoVantage, LLC

# Contents

**PART IV**
**Policy tools** 271

# Figures

# Tables

# Contributors

**Guadalupe Arce,** Facultad de Ciencias Económicas y Empresariales, Universidad de Castilla-La Mancha, Spain.

**Giovanni Baiocchi,** Department of Geographical Sciences, University of Maryland, USA.

**Santacruz Banacloche,** Division of International Trade and Integration, Economic Commission for Latin America and the Caribbean, Chile.

**María Ángeles Cadarso,** Facultad de Ciencias Económicas y Empresariales, Universidad de Castilla-La Mancha, Spain.

**Natalia Caldés,** Energy Systems Analysis Unit, Energy Department, Centro de Investigaciones Energéticas, Medioambientales y tecnológicas (CIEMAT), Spain.

**José M. Cansino,** University of Seville (Spain). Universidad Autónoma de Chile, Chile.

**Javier Castañeda-León,** Facultad de Economía, Universidad Nacional Autónoma de México, México.

**Carmen Córcoles,** Facultad de Ciencias Económicas y Empresariales, Universidad de Castilla-La Mancha, Spain.

**Óscar Dejuán,** Facultad de Ciencias Económicas y Empresariales, Universidad de Castilla-La Mancha, Spain.

**Liang Dong,** Institute of Environmental Sciences, CML, Leiden University, the Netherlands. Center for Social and Environmental Systems Research, National Institute for Environmental Studies, Japan.

**Rosa Duarte,** Department of Economic Analysis, Faculty of Economics and Business Studies, University of Zaragoza, Spain.

**José Durán Lima,** Regional Integration Unit, Division of International Trade and Integration, Economic Commission for Latin America and the Caribbean, Chile.

**Kuishuang Feng,** Department of Geographical Sciences, University of Maryland, USA.

**Nuria Gómez,** Facultad de Ciencias Económicas y Empresariales, Universidad de Castilla-La Mancha, Spain.

**Stefanie Hellweg,** Institute for Environmental Engineering, ETH Zürich, Switzerland.

**Edgar Hertwich,** School of Forestry and Environmental Studies, Yale University, USA. Norwegian University of Science & Technology, Norway.

**Klaus Hubacek,** Department of Geographical Sciences, University of Maryland, USA.

**Shigemi Kagawa,** Faculty of Economics, Kyushu University, Japan.

**Alissa Kendall,** Department of Civil and Environmental Engineering, University of California, USA.

**Kurt Kratena,** Centre of Economic Scenario Analysis and Research (CESAR), Spain.

**Michael L. Lahr,** Bloustein School of Planning and Public Policy, USA.

**Manfred Lenzen**, School of Physics, University of Sydney, Australia.

**Soeren Lindner,** Radboud University, the Netherlands.

**Luis Antonio López,** Facultad de Ciencias Económicas y Empresariales, Universidad de Castilla-La Mancha, Spain.

**Fabio Monsalve,** Facultad de Ciencias Económicas y Empresariales, Universidad de Castilla-La Mancha, Spain.

**Eduardo Moreno-Reyes,** Facultad de Economía, Universidad Nacional Autónoma de México, México.

**Raúl Muñoz Castillo,** Department of Geographical Sciences, University of Maryland, USA. Interamerican Development Bank, USA.

**Keisuke Nansai,** Center for Material Cycles and Waste Management Research, National Institute for Environmental Studies, Japan.

**Manuel Ordóñez,** University of Seville, Spain.

**Jingzheng Ren,** Department of Industrial and Systems Engineering, the Hong Kong Polytechnic University, Hong Kong SAR, China.

**Jordi Roca,** Faculty of Economics and Business, University of Barcelona, Spain.

**Paola Rocchi,** European Commission, Joint Research Centre, Spain.

**João F. D. Rodrigues,** Institute of Environmental Sciences, CML, Leiden University, the Netherlands.

**Irene Rodríguez-Serrano,** Energy Systems Analysis Unit, Energy Department, Centro de Investigaciones Energéticas, Medioambientales y tecnológicas (CIEMAT), Spain.

**Rocío Román,** University of Seville, Spain. Universidad Autónoma de Chile, Chile.

**José-Manuel Rueda-Cantuche,** Institute for Prospective Technological Studies (IPTS), Spain.

**Pablo Ruiz-Nápoles,** Facultad de Economía, Universidad Nacional Autónoma de México, México.

**Julio Sánchez Chóliz,** Faculty of Economics and Business Studies, University of Zaragoza, Spain.

**Cristina Sarasa,** Faculty of Economics and Business Studies, University of Zaragoza, Spain.

**Mònica Serrano,** Faculty of Economics and Business, University of Barcelona, Spain.

**Yosuke Shigetomi,** Faculty of Environmental Science, Nagasaki University, Japan.

**Kayoko Shironitta,** Faculty of Economics, Kyushu University, Japan.

**Sangwon Suh,** Bren School of Environmental Science and Management. University of California, USA.

**Laixiang Sun,** Department of Geographical Sciences, University of Maryland, USA.

**María-Ángeles Tobarra,** Facultad de Ciencias Económicas y Empresariales, Universidad de Castilla-La Mancha, Spain.

**Arnold Tukker,** Institute of Environmental Sciences, CML, Leiden University, the Netherlands.

**Kirsten S. Wiebe,** Norwegian University of Science and Technology, Industrial Ecology Programme, Norway

**Thomas Wiedmann,** Sustainability Assessment Program (SAP), School of Civil and Environmental Engineering, UNSW, Australia. ISA, School of Physics A28, University of Sydney, Australia.

**Paul Wolfram,** Center for Industrial Ecology, School of Forestry & Environmental Studies, Yale University, USA.

**Richard Wood,** Norwegian University of Science and Technology. Industrial Ecology Programme, Norway.

**Jinjun Xue,** Graduate School of Economics, Nagoya University, Japan, and Hubei University of Economics, China.

**Jorge E. Zafrilla,** Facultad de Ciencias Económicas y Empresariales, Universidad de Castilla-La Mancha, Spain.

**Haiyan Zhang,** Johns Hopkins University-Nanjing University Center for Chinese and American Studies, Nanjing University, China.

# Introduction

*Óscar Dejuán, María-Ángeles Cadarso*
*and Manfred Lenzen*

## The long road to Paris

Paris, 12/12/2015, at 7:30 pm. "A historic agreement to combat climate change and unleash actions and investment towards a low carbon, resilient and sustainable future was agreed by 195 nations in Paris today" (Press release from the United Nations, (UNFCCC, 2015a)). The Paris agreement is, actually, the first universal and legally binding climate deal. It aims to prevent an increase in global temperature 2°C above the levels attained in the preindustrial era, and to pursue efforts to limit the temperature increase to 1.5°C. Extrapolating the current rhythm of global warming to 2,100, the average temperature could rise between 2.7 and 4°C relative to 1,800. This would trigger an irreversible climate change of catastrophic consequences for the ecosystem and mankind. All the parties of the United Nations Framework Convention for Climate Change (UNFCCC) understood the need to decarbonize the current systems of production and consumption.

Sixty-seven years earlier (1948), also in December and in Paris, the United Nations (UN) approved the Universal Declaration of Human Rights, a key column of the peace building process entrusted to the UN. Despite the obvious differences between the 1948 and 2015 agreements, they share a common message: People and governments are able to reach an international consensus on important issues concerning human rights and commit themselves to significant efforts, the beneficiaries of which may belong to remote countries or future generations.

Apart from promoting peace, the UN has also tried to prevent and solve humanitarian crises. In the last quarter of the 20th century climate change was considered one of them, not to say, the source of many of them. To tackle this issue, the UN created the *United Nations Environment Program* (UNEP) focused on developing countries and the *Intergovernmental Panel for Climate Change* (IPCC), a think tank. It has also promoted international conferences aimed at encouraging governments to prevent pollution and global warming.

The *Montreal Protocol* (1987) was the first climate deal fostered for the UN to protect the ozone layer. The success of this conference (both political and practical) encouraged 179 governments and 2,400 representatives of non-governmental organizations to attend the *Earth Summit of Rio de Janeiro* in1992. At this moment, the UNFCCC was created to check greenhouse gas (GHG) emissions that could cause undesirable climate change. The 195 countries of the UN plus the European Union (EU) and Palestine, became the "parties" of the UNFCCC. They have met annually since 1995 at the "Conferences of the Parties" (COP). The most important ones took place in Kyoto (1997) and Paris (2015).

The *Kyoto Protocol* was approved in 1997 but did not enter into force until 2005. The most striking measure was the *carbon emission trading*. The UNFCCC would decide the total of GHG emissions authorized by the industrial countries that ratified the treaty. An equivalent number of "permits" would be allocated among them. If a country needed more permits, it could buy them in the international carbon market. The least developed countries were exempted from legal obligations to avoid interfering with their development. Also to equilibrate the balance with advanced economies whose secular industrialization was based on fossil energy.

The Kyoto Protocol was less successful than expected. The first reason for its failure is that the two major polluting countries (China and the United States) were outside. China was considered a developing country. The United States signed the protocol, but the American Senate did not ratify it.

The second problem is related to the difficulty in accounting for the net transfers of emissions through international trade and global value chains. The extreme economic circumstances the protocol had to cope with is the third cause. In the first years, emissions soared everywhere due to the fact that business was booming while the prices of oil and coal fell at historical minima. During the economic crisis that followed the 2007 financial crash, the level of activity was so low that few countries or enterprises needed to buy emission permits. *Carbon emission trading* became at this time a complex and unnecessary mechanism.

The *Copenhagen Conference* (COP-15, 2009), aimed at finding a substitute to the Kyoto Protocol, was a complete failure. In the *Cancun Conference* (COP-16, 2010), the 2°C figure was written in an official document. The COP-17, held in *Durban* (South Africa) in 2011, envisaged a *Green Climate Fund* to distribute US$100 billion per year to help developing countries to adapt to climate change. The *Doha Conference* (COP-18, 2012) amended the Kyoto Protocol and extended it to 2020. The conditions were more demanding for advanced countries. Some of them did not ratify them. Canada withdrew from the protocol altogether.

During 2015, the staff of the UN worked hard to achieve a climate change consensus at the COP-21 to be held in Paris from 30 November to 11 December. On the 12 December 2015, a consensus was achieved among the 197 parties of the UNFCCC. A number of non-profit organizations and private corporations adhered to the agreement to show their commitment to the goals of the conference and the willingness to cooperate in its implementation.

The 29 articles of the agreement are preceded by a long declaration of intent or "explanatory memorandum", which is more detailed than the main text. The content of the climate deal can be summarized in the following sections: goals, tasks, implementation, finance and enforcement (UNFCCC, 2015b).

### (a) Goals (article 2)

The main goal is stated in the second article:

> To hold the increase in the global average temperature to well below 2°C above pre-industrial levels and to pursue efforts to limit the temperature increase to 1.5°C above pre-industrial levels, recognizing that this would significantly reduce the risk and impacts of climate change.

The "1.5" amendment shows the ambitious of the Paris Agreement over the previous conferences. The pressure of small islands threatened by the thermal expansion was decisive.

This goal should be compatible with the sustainable growth of the least developed countries, one of the problems inherited from previous conferences. These countries should cooperate to solve the global problem of climate change, but their efforts should be proportional to their means. Advanced countries should help them in the ways specified through the document.

### (b) Tasks

- *Mitigation* (articles 4, 5). The key strategy consists of the reduction of GHG emissions through a process of decarbonization. By midcentury, carbon dioxide equivalent ($CO_2$-eq) should be 80% below the level attained in 2009. By the end of the century, emissions should be reduced to the level that trees, soil and oceans can absorb naturally. "Parties should take action to conserve and enhance, as appropriate, sinks and reservoirs of greenhouse gases".
- *Adaptation* (article 7). It implies the transformation of infrastructures and buildings to resist the adverse impacts of climate change and to foster climate resilience.
- *Capacity building.* A country cannot mitigate or adapt to climate change without first having the capacity to do so. At the Conference of Durban (2011), this task was termed *capacity building*. It encompasses a variety of issues such as education, communications, greenhouse gas accounting and transfers of technology.

### (c) Implementation (articles 3, 4, 7, 9, 10, 11, 13, 14, 15)

Each party is supposed to prepare, communicate and maintain its *intended nationally determined contributions* (INDCs) to climate change. The INDCs group the national "pledges" for mitigation and adaptation. Governments are free to set their particular strategy and speed of adjustment, but they will be bound by them. They are supposed to report every five years about the advances. *Transparency* and *accountability* are the key words of the new way to implement international deals. The IPCC and other specialized organizations of the UN will offer the required assistance for the elaboration and verification of these plans.

The first INDCs were submitted to the COP-22 held in Marrakech in November 2016. The first "global stocktake", evaluating if the individual and collective efforts are consistent with the temperature target, is scheduled for 2023. Every five years, the parties should present a new INDC that is supposed to be even more demanding.

### (d)  Finance (article 9)

Mitigation and adaptation entail substantial investments. Rich countries can collect the required funds from their general tax system or from specific taxes on emissions. We can also expect the appearance of institutions and instruments that pave the way for the required transformation of production and consumption in rich countries.

Developing countries, on the contrary, need financial assistance from the developed world. International aid for mitigation and adaptation is supposed to compensate developing countries for their efforts in the conservation and sustainable management of forests and other natural resources. The Paris Agreement insists on this responsibility and creates the "Financial Mechanism of the Convention".

The explanatory memorandum of the Paris Agreement states, "The Conference shall set a new collective quantified goal from a floor of USD 100 billion per year, taking into account the needs and priorities of developing countries". This figure comes from Durban (2011), but had not been implemented yet. Although the time limit was set for 2025, there is a consensus that it should be extended and improved afterwards.

### (e)  Enforcement (articles 20, 21, 28)

The COP-21 produced the first UN universal and binding agreement on climate change. The time for ratification was set between 22 April 2016 and 21 April 2017. It would enter into force one month after the ratification by 55 countries representing at least 55% of worldwide emissions. This happened on 5 October 2016, after China and the United States ratified. The effective date of enforcement was, therefore, 4 November 2016. However, it is not until 2020 that the Paris Agreement will enter completely into force, replacing the Kyoto Protocol.

All the countries that have ratified the Paris Agreement are legally bound by its general statements and the particular commitments included in their INDCs. We know, however, that sovereign states have the right to denounce international contracts. Article 28.1 admits, "At any time after three years (of the ratification. . .) any Party may withdraw from this Agreement by giving written notification of the Depositary (UN)".

What would happen if a high emitter country withdraws and others follow suit? Certainly, the "shock" would shake the viability of the Paris Agreement; most of all it will cause a domino effect. Even if this is not the case, any withdrawal will squander the resources invested in projects that cannot be completed and cut the funds needed by developing countries. In our opinion, the success of the decarbonization process lies in the introduction of carrots and sticks, making withdrawals and free rides too expensive. They could be linked to broader carbon adjustments up to the limits admitted by the World Trade Organization, also part of the UN.[1]

## The data and some trends to be reversed

Underlying the Paris Agreement (and their surroundings: UNFCCC, IPCC, etc.) we find the following chain of arguments: (1) global warming may be dangerous for human life and the entire ecosystem when it surpasses a certain threshold; (2) the concentration of GHG in the atmosphere is one of the mayor causes of global warming; (3) the acceleration of such concentration is anthropogenic in the sense that the bulk of GHG emissions are related to an industrialization powered by fossil fuels; (4) the solution (decarbonization) depends upon us and should start as quickly as possible.

Today, the "global warming paradigm" is the prevalent one among scientists, economists and politicians. As we can expect, when an issue is so complex and sensitive, critics also abound. They can be classified in three groups: negationists, radicals and skeptics. The first group claims that "environmental alarmism" is not scientifically justified. What if the current global warming, they ask, is in compliance with natural forces? Decarbonization would be as expensive as useless. Radical ecologists believe the Paris proposals are insufficient and have arrived too late. Their alternative is to slow down economic growth. Skeptics are sympathetic with the Paris Agreement but cast doubt on its effectiveness: the UN lacks the authority to enforce such important changes to sovereign states and international companies.

No doubt, there is a grain of truth in these criticisms that should be considered by those concerned with checking global warming through decarbonization. But uncertainty (either scientific or political) does not justify inaction. The *precautionary principle*, already stated in the Earth Summit of Rio Janeiro, warns about this risk: "When there are threats of serious or irreversible damage, lack of full scientific certainty shall not be used as a reason from postponing cost-effective measures to prevent environmental degradation" (UN, 1992).

The scientific community should provide better data and stronger arguments. This book tries to contribute to this goal from an economic standpoint. To help the readers familiarize themselves with the economic and environmental issues dealt with in the book, we will present next the main data and trends of production, emissions and climate change.

Figure 0.1.A shows the most polluting sectors. By 2010, 70% of emissions stemmed from electricity generation, agriculture and forestry (fertilizers) and transport (petrol). These are the direct emissions that result from fossil fuel combustion. Industry (a conglomerate of sectors) and buildings are responsible for the indirect emissions that result when electrical devices are plugged in. The good news derived from this picture is that we can cut off 25% of emissions by shifting from fossil electricity (coal, petrol, gas) to renewable electricity (water, wind, sun

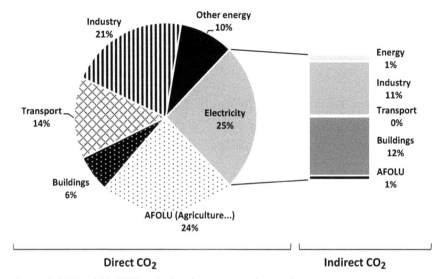

Direct CO$_2$                    Indirect CO$_2$

*Figure 0.1 (A and B)* GHG emissions by sectors and countries

*Figure 0.1.A* GHG Emissions by economic sector. 2010

Source: IPCC AR5 WG3. (2014). *Climate change 2014: Mitigation of climate change.* Berlin, Germany: Working Group III's contribution to the fifth assessment report of the intergovernmental panel on climate change.

## Global CO$_2$ emissions by countries (%)

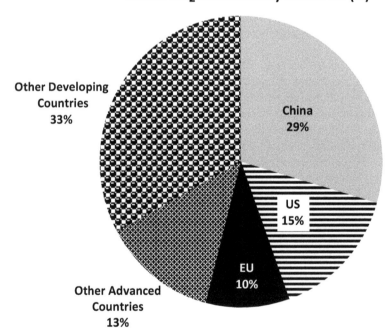

*Figure 0.1.B* Global CO$_2$ emissions by countries (%)

Source: CAIT Climate Data Explorer. 2017. Washington, DC: World Resources Institute. Available online at: http://cait.wri.org

and nuclear). This percentage would be augmented an additional 15%–20% when cars and heating systems are plugged into a clean electricity grid.

Figure 0.1.B shows the most polluting countries. Almost half of the emissions come from three regions: China, the United States and the EU. Emissions in China have increased by a factor of 4.5 over the last 25 years. If poor countries industrialize as fast as China and adopt the occidental patterns of life, the acceleration of the emissions would be unsustainable. The good news is that the EU and the United States have proved the possibility of decoupling, economic growth and emissions. In the EU, the flow of $CO_{02}$ eq emissions was 4.7 gigatonnes in 1990, 4.8 in 2000 and 4.2 in 2013 (CAIT, 2017). If this fossil-saving technology is transferred to developing countries and they adopt wiser patterns of life, emissions could be controlled.

A historical perspective of energy consumption and emissions teaches additional lessons. Figure 0.2.A shows the global energy consumption since 1800. Except for biofuels, energy consumption has been increasing steadily with industrialization and has replicated the long economic cycles. A coal-based industrial revolution started in England at the end of the 18th century. Coal only became globally significant in the last quarter of the 19th century when the rest of Europe and the United States joined the industrialization process. After 1920, petrol took the relay and became the dominant energy source by 1970. Gas energy grew in parallel but it did not become significant until the last decade of the 20th century. For a century, hydropower has represented a modest and relatively constant source of energy. Nuclear electricity started around 1960 and grew steadily until it found political opposition. Renewable energies based on wind and sun power started in the early years of the 21st century. They would be visible in Figure 0.2.A if it was extended until 2017.

The solid line in Figure 0.2.B shows $CO_2$ emissions (the bulk of GHG emissions). Notice that they replicate the path of fossil energy consumption and economic cycles. Energy consumption and emissions are accelerated in the long wave of prosperity that followed World War II and in the last boom (1995–2008).

A part of global GHG emission is absorbed by the ocean and the forests. Another is concentrated in the atmosphere, as appreciated in the discontinuous line of Figure 0.2.B. After 1850, the stock of $CO_2$ grew slowly but steadily. It accelerated after 1970 (a delayed reflection of the post war boom?). Today, it is approaching 350 ppm (parts per million) – the threshold that most scientists warn to avoid.

The preceding graphs suggest that the bulk of GHG emission are anthropogenic, in the sense that they are related to the global process of industrialization fueled with fossil energy. The next question is how important are the flows and stocks of GHG for global warming. To begin with, one should be aware that GHG is absolutely necessary for life on earth: it retains the heat coming from sunlight. However, when the concentration of GHG exceeds a certain level, it traps the sun's heat more effectively, and it may bring about a rise in the temperature in the atmosphere and the surfaces of land and oceans. There is a threshold that makes climate change irreversible and most scientists

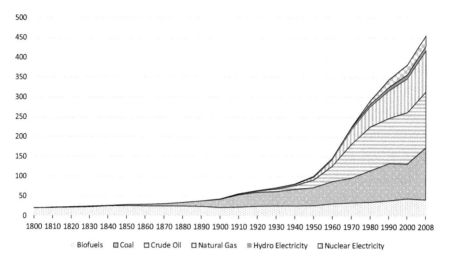

Biofuels    Coal    Crude Oil    Natural Gas    Hydro Electricity    Nuclear Electricity

*Figure 0.2 (A and B)*   Global energy consumption and emissions

*0.2.A*   Global energy consumption (exajoules)

Source: Our World in Data. (2017). *CO₂ and other greenouse gas emissions.* University of Oxford. Available online at: https://ourworldindata.org/.

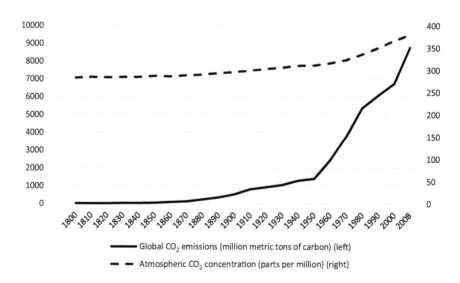

Global CO₂ emissions (million metric tons of carbon) (left)

Atmospheric CO₂ concentration (parts per million) (right)

*Figure 0.2.B*   Global emissions and $CO_2$ concentration

Source: Our World in Data. (2017). *CO₂ and other greenouse gas emissions.* University of Oxford. Available online at: https://ourworldindata.org/.

recommend not surpassing 2°C above the preindustrial level. As we know, the producers of the Paris Agreement suggested a reduction to 1.5°C and emissions to 85% by 2050.

Figure 0.3.A shows the temperature anomaly on Earth relative to the average of the period 1961–1990. We observe that it stayed relatively constant until 1910. Since then, it increased steadily, except for the period 1950–1970. Today, the current average temperature is 1°C above the level of the preindustrial era (15°C). An extrapolation of the current trend would imply an increase between 2.7°C and 4°C by the end of 21st century.

The impact of global warming on abnormal events is surrounded by many uncertainties. For this reason, scientists offer an arch of results and assign probabilities to each one. Some links between global warming and natural disasters are, however, obvious. The first one, exemplified in Figure 0.3.B, is the rise of the sea level derived from thermal expansion, in particular, the melting of the ice in glaciers and poles. The rise in the temperature of the surface of oceans seems to be part of the explanation of cyclones, tsunamis, hurricanes and storm surges. Global warming may also have contributed to the observed intermittence of heat waves and cold polar waves, as well as droughts and floods. These events are by no means new. The novelty is that they have become more extreme and frequent. Natural adaptation looks less plausible. The Paris Agreement is a coordinated attempt to tackle climate change before it becomes irreversible.

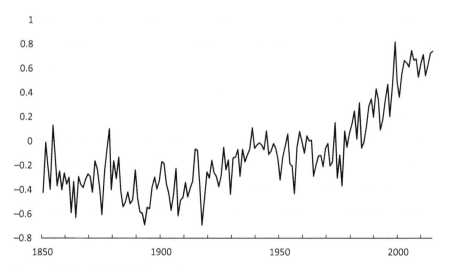

*Figure 0.3 (A and B)* Global warming

*Figure 0.3.A* Surface temperature anomalies (°C) relative to a 1961–1990 reference period

Source: HadCRUT3. Dataset CRUTEM3. Available online at: www.ipcc-data.org/observ/clim/ar4_global.html.

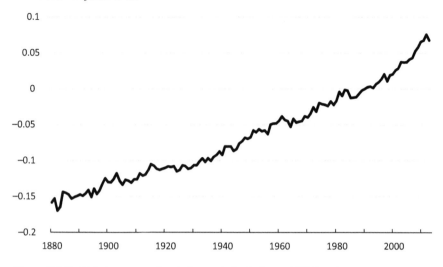

*Figure 0.3.B* Global mean sea level change (m) relative to 1990 level

Source: CSIRO (Commonwealth Scientific and Industrial Research Organisation) (2015).

## Input-output keys to open the environmental black box

The environment has been part of economics since its inception (Smith, [1776] 1979). "Land" (as it was labelled then) was one of the factors of production, jointly with labour and capital. Environmental issues played, however, a secondary role because natural resources were considered "free goods". Macroeconomic growth models, that became popular in the last quarter of the 20th century, marked a turning point. "The Report of the Club of Rome" on the "limits of growth" (Meadows et al., 1972) warned about the frailty of the postwar boom since natural resources could not afford the rate of expansion of demand. Some months later, the oil crisis confirmed this suspicion.

From a microeconomic standpoint, emissions have been treated as "externalities". They should be introduced in the production and investment functions via a rate of discount. A "prudent" rate would discourage the implementation of environmental "aggressive" investment projects, either public or private. The Stern's report remarks on the importance of the discount rate in environmental economics (Stern, 2006).

Input-output analysis (IOA) lies somehow between macroeconomics and microeconomics. "Messo-economics" could be a proper label. On the one hand, it is a comprehensive and systematic account of output and inputs, value added and final demand and employment, natural resources and emissions. On the other hand, it shows the interactions between productive sectors ("industries") and countries related through imports. "Externalities" can now be accounted for by indirect co-benefits, damages and costs and can be allocated to specific sectors and countries.

The potential of input-output methods on environmental analysis has been magnified in the last three decades thanks to the environmental annexes attached to the input-output tables (IOT) and to the multiregional presentation of most of the variables. World Input-Output Database (WIOD), EORA Multiregional database, Multi-regional Environmentally Extended Supply and Use, Input Output database (EXIOBASE) and Global Trade Analysis Project (GTAP) are examples of these environmentally extended, multiregional input-output (MRIO) databases.

To see the usefulness of a MRIO, consider the following example. The government in country A obliges (trough regulation) or stimulates (through the fiscal system) the use of electric radiators to heat buildings, both for businesses and households. This government might be proud to have reduced direct emissions in "buildings", but national emissions could continue at high levels if electricity continues to be generated by burning coal, gas or petrol. (In Figure 0.1.A, they appeared as "indirect emissions"). Even if fossil electricity is substituted by solar electricity, emissions could appear in country B, which produces and exports the radiators and the solar panels demanded by country A. The balance could become even more negative if these radiators and panels are shipped from a remote country. Who would be responsible for these emissions? Country B, which produces the radiators and solar panels, or country A, which demands them? Kyoto Protocol and the INDCs derived from the Paris Agreement charge these emissions to country B, according to the principle of "production-based (territorial) accounting". According to the principle of "consumption-based accounting", they should be charged to country A.

IOA is flexible enough to host a variety of techniques that may be combined in different ways. This will be made clear in this book. To help the reader, we can summarize the input-output models used nowadays for energy and environmental analysis. Most of them are presented in the textbook by (Miller and Blair, 2009). See also the two special issues of *Economic Systems Research* on MRIO tables, models and analysis (ESR 25/1, 2013 and 26/3, 2014, respectively; Tukker and Dietzenbacher, 2013).

(a) ***Impact analysis in environmental extended input-output models.*** Impact analysis through structural multipliers has been the typical input-output tool since the early studies of Leontief. (Leontief, 1936; Leontief, 1970). The development of *social accounting matrices* has permitted analysts to compute broader input-output multipliers that take into account the direct and indirect demand of both intermediate consumption by firms and final consumption by households (Pyatt and Round, 1979). Going back to the previous example, input-output multipliers would allow for the analysis of the impact on emissions derived from the construction of radiators and solar panels in one or several countries. In a Keynesian mood, these models assume that after such "shock", the economy adjusts via quantities, while prices remain constant. We could also represent the evolution of economic and environmental variables associated with different scenarios concerning the evolution of final demand – the driver.

(b) ***Input-output in macroeconometric models.*** They use econometrics to ascertain elasticities of demand and other parameters that are taken as a given in the traditional input-output model. These results are integrated in a *multisectoral macroeconomic model* that computes a new equilibrium after any shock.

The first combined models were *Inforum* of Maryland University (Almon, 1991) and the *Cambridge Growth Project*. The last one has evolved into the E3MG, where E3 refers to "economic, energy and environment" (Barker and Crawford-Brown, 2015). The subtitle of the book informs on its usefulness: "Assessing the Feasibility of Policies to Reduce GHG Emissions".

(c) *Dynamic input-output models.* Nowadays, most environmental input-output models use the "scenario approach". This can be considered the simplest way to dynamize a model. Complete dynamics requires the introduction of trends (instead of values) in the elements of autonomous demand (the multiplicand) and in the coefficients implicit in the multiplier. In our example, investment in solar panels would grow at an exogenous rate. Energy and emissions coefficients would shrink with investment, in particular, research and development (R&D) expenditure. An endogenous diffusion of technology across industries and regions could complete the dynamic model. The forerunners of dynamic disaggregated models were (von Neumann, 1945–46) and (Wassily Leontief, 1970/1986). See also (Kurz and Salvadori, 2000; Dejuán, 2006; Katrena and Sommer, 2014).

(d) *Computable general equilibrium models* (CGE). An IOT is embedded in a system of simultaneous, linear and non-linear equations. Some coefficients are calibrated from the original IOT, while others (like the capital/output ratio) are derive from the optimization process. The main advantage of the CGE model is the linkage, *à la Walras*, between prices and quantities (Ginsburgh and Keyzer, 2002). CGE are especially useful for analyzing the impact of a shock in prices – for instance, a tax on fossil electricity and a subsidy on renewable electricity or on electric radiators.

(e) *Integrated assessment models* (IAM). They belong to a broader category of "hybrid models" that mix physical and monetary variables. IAM combine the key elements of biophysical and economic systems into a single platform to address complex problems, including linkages and feedbacks among the social, economic and ecological systems. (For an overview, see Nordhaus, 2013; Kelly et al., 2013.) The substitution of fossil sources of electricity for renewable ones is a typical example of the use of IAM.

(f) *The environmental footprint* (EF). It is an overarching framework to quantify the total human pressure on the natural environment (Hoekstra and Wiedmann, 2014). During the past two decades, a wide range of footprints have been analyzed, both in relation to the nature of emitting agents (country, activity, product, institution, firm. . .) and in relation to the factors of production (land and other natural resources, water, materials, etc.). Land footprint, water footprint, carbon footprint emissions, etc., are recurrent titles in today's environmental literature. Typical striking questions that have contributed to popularized EF models are as follows: "How many planets would we need to sustain the current rhythm of land-intensive consumption?" "How many deserts would we need to replace the current fossil plants with solar power farms?"

(g) *Life-cycle assessment* (LCA). It assesses the environmental impacts of the emissions and resource absorption along the production, distribution, use and disposal of the product. From "cradle to the grave", is the catch-phrase. Going back to our example, apart from the emissions associated, directly and indirectly, with the production of the radiators, they compute the emissions stemming from the operation of the radiator during its lifetime and those generated in the moment of recycling or destroying it. LCA combines process analysis with IOT methods. The input-output part avoids any truncation error. Since it accounts for the inputs and the inputs of inputs. The process analysis methodology assesses the possible changes in consumer expenditure, income elasticities and cohort effects. (For a review of recent development of LCA, see (Hellweg and Milà i Canals, 2014.)

## Content of the book

There are multiple mitigation pathways for achieving the goals of the Paris Agreement and limiting warming to below 2°C relative to preindustrial levels. The 17 chapters of this book analyze some options and their respective effects. The chapters are based on the studies made by 52 researchers from 11 countries and 24 institutions, both universities and research institutes. This wide range of contributors reinforces the neutrality of the book and the advantages of viewing the same goal from different paths. Some chapters analyze decarbonization at the global level, while others focus on a specific country. Each chapter uses a particular database: national or international, traditional IOT or MRIO. Each chapter relies on any of the methods (or combination of methods) explained at the end of the previous section.

Table 0.1 offers an overview of this variety. Next, we summarize the main goals and conclusions of the 17 chapters grouped in 4 sections.

## Part I.  Electricity generation. Towards a cleaner mix

Part I chapters focus on the decarbonization of the electricity sector and the necessary increasing share of renewable energy. The subject that is obviously present all through the book is analyzed in this part, considering different sources of renewable energy and including the impact of the investments using slightly different approaches and focusing on different geographical locations in each chapter.

1    Decarbonizing electricity generation in Europe. Its impact on emissions and employment all over the world. Óscar Dejuán, Jorge Zafrilla, María Ángeles Tobarra, Fabio Monsalve and Carmen Córcoles.

This chapter explores the impact of a complete substitution of fossil-electricity by wind electricity in the EU during the period 2015–2050. They use broad multipliers and a multiplicand that includes the necessary investment in wind farms. The authors wonder whether the wind bet is a win-win strategy, in the sense that it can, simultaneously, slow down emissions and speed up employment. For the

Table 0.1 General overview of key aspects of book chapters

| | Country or Region | Specific Policy Measure | Model | Specific Energy Production | Databases | Scenarios | Impacts |
|---|---|---|---|---|---|---|---|
| **Chapter 1** Dejuán et al. | Europe 27, World | | MRIO – Broad structural multipliers | Wind | EXIOBASE | Yes | Carbon emissions and employment |
| **Chapter 2** Kratena | Europe 27 | Energy efficiency Renewables diffusion | Hybrid econometric input-output (IO) and CGE (Dynamic New Keynesian, DYNK) | Renewables | SUT, (Eurostat) others | Yes | Socioeconomic impact (GDP and employment) Carbon emissions |
| **Chapter 3** Wiebe | European Union/Germany | Technology diffusion | MRIO Dynamic energy-economy-environment model Technology change in renewable energy Learning curves | Photovoltaic wind | EXIOBASE | | Carbon emissions |
| **Chapter 4** Wolfram and Wiedmann | Australia | | Hybrid input output (LCA for renewable energy sources) | Renewable energy | EORA Ecoinvent 3.1 | Yes | Carbon GHG emissions-Carbon footprint |
| **Chapter 5** Hubacek et al. | | | MRIO | | Consumer expenditure surveys | | Carbon footprint |
| **Chapter 6** Rodríguez-Serrano and Caldes | Mexico | Renewable substitution | Integrated sustainability assessment | Solar termal Natural Gas Combined Cycle (NGCC) | WIOD SHSD Ecoinvent AusLCI | Yes | Economic social and environmental (14 impacts) |
| **Chapter 7** Zhang and Lahr | China | | SDA | | | | Household based $CO_2$ emissions |
| **Chapter 8** Duarte et al. | Spain | | Dynamic CGE | | | Yes | GHG emissions |
| **Chapter 9** Lindner et al. | | | MRIO SDA | | EXIOBASE | | GHG emissions/ carbon footprint |

| | | | | | | |
|---|---|---|---|---|---|---|
| **Chapter 10 Durán Lima and Banacloche** | South America, Colombia | | | South American IO Matrix (ECLAC/IPEA) and Mexico, Colombian EE-SUT DANE | | carbon footprint |
| **Chapter 11 Ruiz-Nápoles et al.** | China, the United States, India, Russia and Japan | Technological change | Structural IO analysis and EEIOA | | Yes | GHG emissions |
| **Chapter 12 Suh et al.** | | Efficiency technologies | Hybrid life-cycle analysis | | | |
| **Chapter 13 Arce et al.** | European Union | EU-Emission Trading System | MRIO | | | |
| **Chapter 14 Román et al.** | Chile | Carbon tax | Price model Social Accounting Matrix | | | GHG emissions tax structure Private welfare |
| **Chapter 15 Roca et al.** | European Union | Carbon border tax adjustment Carbon pricing – tax | | | | |
| **Chapter 16 Shigetomi et al.** | Japan | | | | | Carbon footprint |
| **Chapter 17 Dong et al.** | China | Fossil fuels subsidies removal | Hybrid physical input and monetary output model (HPIMO) Material and energy flow analysis (MEFA) and life-cycle analysis (LCA) | Chinese national IO table | Yes | Emissions ($CO_2$, $SO_2$ and $NO_x$) Employment Budget saving |

Source: Own elaboration

most probable scenario, the answer is negative due to the huge emissions accruing from the building of wind farms.

2    Indirect emissions and socio-economic impacts of energy efficiency improvements and renewable electricity in Europe. Kurt Kratena.

Two scenarios of European decarbonization policies are evaluated in this chapter: one based at improving energy efficiency and the other at increasing the renewable electricity share. It is assumed that fossil energy flows are substituted by capital, whose production is accompanied by indirect emissions. The modeling approach is a DYNK (disaggregated, dynamic new-Keynesian) input-output model. The overall result for emissions is in both scenarios almost fully determined by the emission reduction in the electricity sector.

3    Global renewable energy diffusion in an input-output framework. Kirsten S. Wiebe.

An important aspect of the Paris Agreement is the UNFCCC Technology Mechanism fostering the transfer of technologies from developed to developing countries. This chapter combines multiregional IOA, dynamic energy-economy-environment models and the literature on technological change in renewable energy technologies (RET) to model the impact of the global diffusion of RET on European consumption-based emissions. The author concludes that an explicit support of the diffusion RET is necessary to accelerate this development.

4    Potentials to decarbonize electricity consumption in Australia. Paul Wolfram and Thomas Wiedmann.

As part of the Paris Agreement, Australia intends to reduce total carbon emissions by 26%–28% by 2030 relative to 2005. This chapter assesses the potential contribution of the electricity sector towards Australia's intended emission reductions. A carbon footprint assessment of different renewable energy options based on hybrid LCA is performed to estimate all economy-wide carbon emissions related to a changing energy mix in electricity generation.

## Part II.  Household consumption and social well-being

Lifestyle and behavioural changes are among the key factors driving changes in GHG emissions. The chapters included in Part II pay special attention to the role of households in the economy under different perspectives: (a) lifestyles related to income levels, (b) social impact and risks assessment of increasing renewable energies in developing countries and (c) household energy use in different scenarios.

5    Global income inequality and carbon footprints: can we have the cake and eat it too? Klaus Hubacek, Giovann Baiocchi, Kuishuang Feng, Raul Munoz Castillo, Laixiang Sun, Jinjun Xue.

The UN has set targets to eradicate extreme poverty by 2030 and, in parallel, to keep warming below 2°C. However, the Paris Agreement does not prescribe how these goals are to be achieved in a compatible manner, nor how the burden or responsibility of achieving them may be shared. Clearly, lifestyles, consumption patterns and associated per capita carbon footprints differ enormously between rich and poor. To explore this issue, the authors use consumer expenditure surveys linked to a global multiregional input-output model.

6   The potential contribution of solar thermal electricity (STE) in Mexico in the light of the Paris Agreements. Irene Rodríguez-Serrano, Natalia Caldés.

In pursuing INDC emissions reduction targets, Mexican authorities give priority to energy technologies that simultaneously improve health and well-being – the co-benefits for the population. The goal of this chapter is to use the Framework for Integrated Sustainability Assessment to assess socio-economic, environmental and social impacts associated with an alternative future electricity mix scenario in Mexico where NGCC electricity generation is partially substituted by STE.

7   Peak carbon emission in China: a household energy use perspective. Haiyan Zhang, Michael L. Lahr.

China is now encouraging private consumption to boost its economy. In this chapter, the long-term trends of household $CO_2$ emission associated with the boom of consumption are explored. As China's households move up the consumption ladder, emissions will likely continue to rise for some time. Based on their results, the authors offer some policy suggestions for China to achieve its peak carbon emission target around 2030.

8   The road to Paris with energy-efficiency strategies and GHG emissions-reduction targets: the case of Spain. Rosa Duarte, Julio Sánchez Chóliz, Cristina Sarasa

Recent warnings about the impacts of climate change have led international climate negotiations to focus on the necessary global long-term goal (LTG) presented in the Paris Agreement. The aim is to achieve sustainable development with zero emissions by 2100, compatible with the achievement of poverty eradication and equity. The authors address the issue from a CGE model calibrated with Spanish data for 2010 and including GHG emissions and energy demands.

## Part III.  Key drivers in carbon emissions and improvements in energy efficiency

The chapters in this part are devoted to the understanding of key drivers of changes in carbon emissions, at the global level or for a particular region or country, as a necessary first step to inform an effective policy design and to determine the possibilities of energy efficiency.

9   Global drivers of change in GHG emissions from a consumption perspective. Carbon footprint accounting in a post-Paris world. Soeren Lindner, José-Manuel Rueda-Cantuche, Richard Wood.

The authors use a Global Multi-Region Input-Output Model in order to analyze the drivers of consumption-based GHG emissions. They conclude that a) efficiency effects have been historically successful, b) large growth in consumption per capita counteracts gains in efficiency and c) trade could allocate production to more efficient countries to reduce resource use and pollution, but historically, the effect of trade has been to increase energy and combustion GHG footprints in developed economies.

10   South America's global value chains and $CO_2$ emissions embodied in trade, an input-output approach. José Durán Lima, Santacruz Banacloche.

Using trade data recently produced in Colombia, the authors confirm the image that South America, as a region, is a net importer of environmentally sensitive products. Applying an environmentally extended input-output approach, the authors reveal that Colombia has turned from being a net producer of carbon dioxide in 2005 to being a net consumer in 2011. However, the overall carbon footprint of Colombia has increased as emissions embodied in imports have risen.

11   Structural analysis of the top-five most GHG emitting economies. Pablo Ruiz-Nápoles, Javier Castañeda-León, Eduardo Moreno-Reyes.

The authors analyze the economies of the five-most GHG emitting countries in 2011: China, the United States, India, Russia and Japan. They compare the expected trends of GHG emissions from 2011 to 2030 in relation with the targets set in the INDC derived to the Paris Agreement. Here are some conclusions: The United States, Russia and Japan established clear and feasible goals for 2030. China's targets seem too ambitious. To start reducing emissions after 2030, India should introduce energy-saving technical change.

12   Life-cycle environmental and natural resource implications of energy efficiency technologies. Sangwon Suh, Edgar Hertwich, Stefanie Hellweg, Alissa Kendall.

Meeting the ambitious target of the Paris Agreement would require a fundamental change in the way energy is transformed and utilized. In the effort to understand and improve this change, the International Resource Panel (IRP) of the UNEP has been working on two reports: one on low-carbon electricity generation technologies and the other on energy efficiency. This chapter summarizes the data and ideas that support these reports.

## Part IV. Policy tools

GHG emissions reductions can be obtained via regulation (prohibitions and obligations), via stimulation (taxes and subsidies) and via negotiation (through market-oriented mechanisms). Although policy strategies are present all over the book, the chapters included in this part focus on some of the policy tools used by some countries as part of their mitigation strategies – namely, trade emission markets, carbon taxes (at the border or not) and subsidies.

13 Carbon leakage risk criteria for improving INDC effectiveness. Guadalupe Arce, Luis Antonio López, María Ángeles Cadarso, Nuria Gómez.

The authors discuss the production-based accounting focus on mitigation policies. They claim that one of the two criteria of the EU Directive 2009/29/EC for identifying sectors presenting significant risks of carbon leakage fails because it does not include carbon content. The result is an underestimation of the number of sectors at risk of carbon leakage and in some cases their misidentification. The authors propose new criteria based on the consumption-based approach.

14 An assessment of the effects of the new carbon tax in Chile. Rocío Román, José M. Cansino, Manuel Ordóñez

The authors deal with the new tax on pollutant emissions to the atmosphere approved by the Chilean Parliament in 2014 in line with Chile's commitment in the Paris Agreement. A price model is conducted to assess the impact on prices, tax structure and private welfare. After introducing this new tax, private welfare decreases and GHG emissions fall around 1,800 Gg $CO_2$eq.

15 Paris-COP21 and carbon pricing: coordination challenges and carbon border measures. The case of the EU. Jordi Roca, Paola Rocchi, Mònica Serrano.

Since the Paris Agreement does not fix specific obligations, countries will likely implement different emissions reduction policies. The national policies could have a negative impact on competitiveness. The aim of this chapter is to shed some light on this issue by looking at carbon border adjustment measures as a possible solution. Through an exercise applied to the EU, the authors compare a system based on embodied emissions and a system based on what they call avoided emissions.

16 Revisiting Japanese carbon footprint studies. Yosuke Shigetomi, Keisuke Nansai, Kayoko Shironitta, Shigemi Kagawa.

Against the backdrop of the Paris Agreement and recent arguments for and against consumption-based accounting, this chapter provides a review of earlier IOA studies related to carbon footprints of Japanese consumption. The review emphasizes the importance for Japanese climate policy in considering carbon footprints to detect additional opportunities for mitigation of GHG emissions from the demand side. The chapter highlights the trade-offs between climate change mitigation, economic growth and resource consumption.

17   The socioeconomic and environmental impacts of fossil fuels subsidies reduction and renewable energy expansion in China. Liang Dong, Jingzheng Ren, João F. D. Rodrigues, Arnold Tukker.

In this chapter, the authors tackle the adoption by China's central government of an ambitious policy package that includes the reduction of fossil fuel subsidies (resulting in an expected expansion of renewables). They compiled a HPIMO. Three types of impacts are assessed: employment (societal), saving on budget (economic) and GHG mitigation (environmental). Considerable co-benefits can be expected in the three areas analyzed.

## Acknowledgment

This book is part of the research project PPII-2014–006-P, financed by the "Junta de Comunidades de Castilla-La Mancha" (Spain) and the EU regional funds. Our gratitude to the undergraduate student Ángela García-Alaminos, who helped in the editing tasks.

## Note

1  At the time of the last proofreading of this book (June 2017) all the countries of the world, except Syria and Nicaragua, had signed the Paris Agreement. On June 1st, United States President Donald Trump announced the withdrawal of the US. The EU and China answered that they were well prepared to lead the decarbonization process.

## References

Almon, C. (1991). The INFORUM Approach to Integrated Modelling. Economic Systems Research, 3(1), 1–8.

Barker, T., and Crawford-Brown, D. (2015). *Decarbonizing the world's economy: Assesing the feasibility of policies to reduce greenhouse gas emissions.* London: Imperial College Press.

CSIRO. (2015). Global mean sea level change. 2015 update to data originally published in: Church, J. A. and White, N. J. (2011). Sea-level rise from the late 19th to the early 21st century. *Surveys in Geophysics.* Retrieved from www.efuture.csiro.au/

Dejuán, Ó (2006). A dynamic model from a Classical-Keynesian-Schumpeterian approach. N. Salvadori (ed): *Economic growth and distribution. On the nature and causes of the wealth of nations.* Cheltenham, UK: Edward Elgar., 271–290.

Ginsburgh, V., and Keyzer, M. (2002). *The structure of applied general equilibrium models.* Cambridge, UK: Cambridge University Press.

Hellweg, S., and Milà i Canals, L. (2014). Emerging approaches, challenges and opportunities in life cycle assessment. *Science, 344*(6188), 1109–1113. doi: 10.1126/science.1248361

Hoekstra, A. Y., and Wiedmann, T. O. (2014). Humanity's unsustainable environmental footprint. *Science, 344*(6188), 1114–1117. doi: 10.1126/science.1248365

IPCC AR5 WG3. (2014). *Climate change 2014: Mitigation of climate change*. Berlin, Germany: Working Group III contribution to the fifth assessment report of the intergovernmental panel on climate change.

Kelly, R. A., Jakeman, A. J., Barreteau, O., Borsuk, M. E., ElSawah, S., Hamilton, S. H., . . . Voinov, A. A. (2013). Selecting among five common modelling approaches for integrated environmental assessment and management. *Environmental Modelling & Software, 47*, 159–181. doi: http://dx.doi.org/10.1016/j.envsoft.2013.05.005

Kurz, H. D., and Salvadori, N. (2000). The dynamic Leontief model and the theory of endogenous growth. *Economic Systems Research, 12*(2), 155–265.

Leontief, W. (1936). Quantitative input and output relations in the economic structure: an input-output approach. *Review of Economics and statistics, 52*(3), 262–271.

Leontief, W. (1970). Environmental repercussions and the economic structure: An input-output approach. *The Review of Economics and Statistics, 52*(3), 262–271.

Leontief, W. (1970/1986). The dynamic inverse. In W. Leontief (Ed.), *Input-output economics*. Oxford: Oxford University Press.

Meadows, D. H., Meadows, D. L., Randers, J., and Behrens, W. W. (1972). *The limits to growth: A report for the Club of Rome's project on the predicament of mankind*. Universe Books. New York

Miller, R. E., and Blair, P. D. (2009). *Input-output analysis: Foundations and extensions* (2nd ed.). Cambridge, UK; New York: Cambridge University Press.

Nordhaus, W. D. (2013). Integrated economic and climate modelling. In P. B. Dixon & D. W. Jorgenson (Eds.), *Handbook of computable general equilibrium*. North Holland: Elsevier.

Our World in Data. (2017). $CO_2$ *and other greenouse gas emissions*. University of Oxford. Retrieved from https://ourworldindata.org/co2-and-other-greeenhouse-gas-emissions

Pyatt, G., and Round, J. (1979). Accounting and fixed price multipliers in a social accounting matrix framework. *The Economic Journal, 89*, 850–873.

Smith, A. ([1776] 1979). *An enquiry into the nature and causes of the wealth of nations*. Oxford: Clarendon Press.

Stern, N. H. (2006). *Stern review on the economics of climate change*. London, UK: HM Treasury.

Tukker, A., and Dietzenbacher, E. (2013). Global multiregional input – output frameworks: An introduction and outlook. *Economic Systems Research, 25*(1), 1–19.

UN. (1992). Conference on environment and development – the earth summit. Rio de Janeiro.

UNFCCC. (2015a). Press release on the Paris Agreement [Press release].

UNFCCC. (2015b). *Text of the Paris Agreement*. Paris: UN.

von Neumann, J. (1945–46). A model of general economic equilibrium. *The Review of Economic Studies, 13*(1), 1–9.

World Resources Institute. (2017). *CAIT climate data explorer*. Washington, DC: World Resources Institute. Retrieved from http://cait.wri.org/.

# Part I

# Electricity generation. Towards a cleaner mix

# 1 Decarbonizing electricity generation in Europe

## Its impact on emissions and employment all over the world

*Óscar Dejuán, Jorge E. Zafrilla, María-Ángeles Tobarra, Fabio Monsalve and Carmen Córcoles*

## Introduction

Pollution and unemployment stand among the major economic problems and challenges of our times. On the one hand, the emission of $CO_2$ and other greenhouse gasses (GHG) is deteriorating our current life conditions and can cause an irreversible climate change of serious consequences. The second problem refers to the difficulty in employing the existing labour force. Young people in poor countries are forced to migrate to the first world with a serious risk of social exclusion if they do not find a job. The unemployment rate of young people in rich countries is also historically high despite their having received a good education.

"Europe 2020. A Strategy for Smart, Sustainable and Inclusive Growth" was the first strategy of the European Commission to solve jointly the environmental and employment problems (EC, 2010). By 2014, the EU had cut GHG emissions by 30% compared with the 1990 baseline – faster than expected. Wind parks represented 13.2% of total installed capacity to produce electricity, which was also faster than expected (EC, 2016). But the fear of a reversal in the next boom continues to be a threat since 42% of electricity generation is still produced by burning fossil fuels. The EU was the main supporter of the decarbonization proposed in the 2015 Paris Agreement for all the sectors and countries (UN, 2015). The "Energy Roadmap" approved by the European Commission a few months later committed EU countries to reduce GHG emissions by 40% in 2030 and by 80%–95% in 2050 (EC, 2016). These goals have inspired our chapter. More concretely, we want to explore the impacts all over the world of the European replacement of fossil-electricity by wind-electricity from 2015 to 2045.

The substitution of fossil-electricity for renewable primary inputs can be analyzed from different standpoints and methodologies.[1] Our approach is based on broad employment and emissions input-output multipliers. In the "multiplicand" (autonomous demand), we allocate the investment required to meet a growing permanent demand (this is the accelerator principle) and the investment required to build the wind-parks. Ours is a post-Keynesian model that emphasizes quantity changes over price changes, while technical change is embodied in investment goods.[2]

The computation of these broad multipliers is performed in the third section of this chapter. In section 2, we schedule the rhythm of substitution of fossil electricity for wind-electricity in the next 30 years, and we calculate the investment in wind-parks required to replace dirty fossil-electricity.

In section 4, we apply the model to figure out the impact on emissions and employment all over the world during the process of decarbonization. We analyze four possible scenarios which combine the economic rate of growth and the rhythm of substitution of fossil-electricity by wind-electricity. Our conclusions (in section 5) refer to the most probable scenario for the next 30 years – namely, an average rate of growth of 2.5%, a fast rhythm of substitution of fossil-energy by wind-electricity in the EU and a slow rhythm of substitution in the rest of the world.

## Building a dynamic energy model where the mix of sources for electricity production is changing

The main source of our data comes from EXIOBASE. It is a global, multi-regional, environmentally extended input-output table (Tukker et al., 2013; Wood et al., 2015).[3,4,5] It gives specific information for 48 countries/regions and 163 industries, although for our chapter, it has been aggregated to 41 sectors and 38 regions/countries – the 27 members of the European Union (EU), 7 additional major economies and 5 multi-country regions.[6] The main advantage of using EXIOBASE is the detail provided for energy sectors. It considers 12 ways of generating electricity (industries 96–107), apart from its transmission and distribution (industries 108–109). The technology of electricity depends on the main source of power used in its generation: coal, gas, nuclear, hydro, wind, petroleum, biomass, solar-photovoltaic, solar-thermal, tide wave, geothermal and nec. ("not elsewhere classified").

The purpose of this chapter is to simulate the impact of a change in the primary energy mix used to obtain electricity. More concretely, we represent the substitution of fossil-electricity by wind- electricity. This is a gradual dynamic process that obliges us to introduce a different IOT for each of the six-year periods considered: 2015–2020, 2021–2026, 2027–2032, 2033–2038 and 2039–2044. The increasing share of wind-electricity in the EU is done at the expense of fossil-electricity that diminishes 20% in points every six years. By 2045, electricity produced by burning coal, gas and petrol will be almost entirely replaced by wind-electricity. This rhythm of decarbonization refers to the EU. The rest of the world (RoW) is supposed to start later or to advance at a slower pace, as it has been the case so far.[7]

The process of substitution of fossil by wind-electricity requires a huge investment in wind-parks. We assume that they are produced during the six-year period that precedes year $t$ when a change in the electricity mix is registered. Once we know the wind-electricity power required after $t$, we compute how many parks have to be built in the six years preceding $t$. The required investment will be introduced in the autonomous demand vector. The data for this purpose has been found in Eurostat (EC, 2012) and IDAE (IDAE, 2016).[8]

EXIOBASE provides additional information about total GHG emissions in terms of its carbon dioxide equivalent ($CO_2$eq). In the original sources, they are expressed in kilograms (Kg) of $CO_2$eq We transform them into gigatons (GT) and present them in a vector $E$ of total emissions – a vector disaggregated by industries and by regions. Dividing by total output, we get the emission coefficients – i.e. emissions per unit of total output (row vector $e'$). The same information can be obtained for the total hours of labour ($L$) employed in each industry of each country and the corresponding vector of labour coefficients ($l'$).

## A multiplier-accelerator model

A horizontal reading of the world IOT shows the quantity system. It is summarized in a column vector of total output per industry ($x$) that results from the sum of the intermediate consumption matrix ($Zm$) and final demand ($y$).[9] The last one results from adding the column vectors of final consumption ($yc$) and final investment ($yh$) (see equation 1.1).[10]

$$x = Zm + y = Zm + yc + yh \tag{1.1}$$
$$x = Zm + c + c_a + h + h_a \tag{1.2}$$
$$x = \left(Zm + Zc + Zh\right) + c_a + h_a = Z + c_a + h_a \tag{1.3}$$

Equation (1.2) separates induced and autonomous elements of final consumption and final investment. Equation (1.3) endogenizes the parts of final consumption and investment that can be considered "induced" because they depend on current production or on its expected growth.

The column vector of autonomous consumption ($c_a$) gathers non-capital expenditures of non-profit organizations and the government. The remaining part ($c$) is considered induced consumption.[11] In a post-Keynesian mood, we assume that most of induced consumption stems from wages (Kalecki, 1971; Lavoie, 2014). This justifies distributing the figure in each cell of $c$ among industries according to their share in wages. This way, we obtain a matrix $Zc$ of the same dimensions as the transactions matrix ($Zm$). The typical element of the new matrix is $c_{ij} = c_i (W_j/W)$.

The final investment is also split into induced and autonomous expenditure. We consider autonomous all public investment, residential investment and "modernization investment" of firms here related to R&D expenditure.[12] In the vector of autonomous investment, we also include the investment associated with the wind-parks and related infrastructure.

Induced investment is identified with the productive investment by firms that try to expand capacity in order to meet efficiently a higher permanent demand. This is the principle of acceleration that post-Keynesian economists have presented both in aggregate and disaggregated terms.[13] It can be computed with this equation: $I_I = g \cdot <k> \cdot x = h \cdot x$, where $g$ is the expected growth of permanent demand; $k$ is the optimal capital/output ratio per industry/region. This justifies the distribution of each cell of $yh$ among industries according to their shares in the stock of capital.

This way, we obtain a matrix *Zh* of the same order as the transactions matrix (*Zm*). The typical element of the matrix of induced investment is $h_{ij} = h_i(K_j/K)$[14]

The addition of *Zm* and *Zc* makes $Z^+$. The addition of *Zm*, *Zc* and *Zh* makes *Z\**. Dividing each column by the total output of the industry, we obtain the matrices of coefficients. They refer to intermediate consumptions ($A = Zm·<x>^{-1}$), or to intermediate plus final induced consumption ($A^+ = Z^+·<x>^{-1}$) or to total induced expenditure ($A^* = Z^*·<x>^{-1}$). Notice that any *Z* and *A* matrix is linked to a different type of autonomous demand: *Zm* and *A* to final demand (*y*); $Z^+$ and $A^+$ to autonomous demand ($y_a$); and *Z\** and *A\** to proper autonomous demand ($y_{aa}$) that excludes productive investment of the expansionary type.

Now we are prepared to derive total output as a multiple of demand. It can be done in different ways:

$$x = A·x + y = [I - A]^{-1}·y = Mx·y \tag{1.4}$$

$$x = A^+·x + y_a = [I - A^+]^{-1}·y_a = Mx^+·y_a \tag{1.5}$$

$$x = A^*·x + y_{aa} = [I - A^*]^{-1}·y_{aa} = Mx^*·y_{aa} \tag{1.6}$$

The technological multiplier of total output (*Mx*) is identified with the typical Leontief inverse: $[I - A]^{-1}$. It captures the induced intermediate consumption generated in the production of final demand. ($Mx^+$) is the economic multiplier (or Keynesian multiplier applied to total output instead of final income). It is represented by $[I - A^+]^{-1}$. The multiplier-accelerator (or "supermultiplier") captures, besides induced consumption, "induced" investment: $Mx^* = [I - A^*]^{-1}$.

We can derive the employment multiplier by premultiplying the previous expressions (that appear as a matrix) by the row vector of labour coefficients (*l'*). In each country, total labour by industry would be *L'* (the apostrophe indicates that it is a row vector). It can be computed in three alternative ways:

$$L' = [l'·Mx]·\hat{y} = Ml'\hat{y} \tag{1.7}$$

$$L' = [l'·Mx^+]·\hat{y}_a = Ml'^+·\hat{y}_a \tag{1.8}$$

$$L' = [l'·Mx^*]·\hat{y}_{aa} = Ml'^*·\hat{y}_{aa} \tag{1.9}$$

The multipliers of emissions of $CO_2$eq are obtained by premultiplying output multipliers by the row vector of emission coefficients (*e'*). Total emissions by industry would be *E'*. A row vector than can be obtained in three alternative ways:

$$E' = [e'·Mx]·\hat{y} = Me'·\hat{y} \tag{1.10}$$

$$E' = [e'·Mx^+]·\hat{y}_a = Me'^+·\hat{y}_a \tag{1.11}$$

$$E' = [e'·Mx^*]·\hat{y}_{aa} = Me'^*·\hat{y}_{aa} \tag{1.12}$$

Tables 1.1 and 1.2 show the employment and emissions multipliers associated with the production of one additional unit of electricity (worth 1 million euros),

Table 1.1 Multipliers in the generation of electricity

| | 14 coal | 15 gas | 16 nuclear | 17 hydro | 18 wind | 19 petrol | 20 biomass | 21 solar PH | 22 solar TH | 23 tide, wave | 24 geothermal | 25 nec |
|---|---|---|---|---|---|---|---|---|---|---|---|---|
| Multipliers of total output | | | | | | | | | | | | |
| Mx' | 2.33 | 2.51 | 1.41 | 1.74 | 1.87 | 2.67 | 2.43 | 1.55 | 1.04 | 1.05 | 1.39 | 1.93 |
| Mx'+ | 4.76 | 4.89 | 3.19 | 4.25 | 4.30 | 5.04 | 4.93 | 3.10 | 1.20 | 1.15 | 2.17 | 3.68 |
| Mx'* | 5.90 | 5.98 | 4.04 | 5.45 | 5.45 | 6.11 | 6.09 | 3.81 | 1.28 | 1.19 | 2.52 | 4.50 |
| Multipliers of employment | | | | | | | | | | | | |
| MI' | 0.06 | 0.05 | 0.03 | 0.03 | 0.04 | 0.05 | 0.08 | 0.01 | 0.00 | 0.00 | 0.01 | 0.03 |
| MI'+ | 0.18 | 0.18 | 0.12 | 0.15 | 0.14 | 0.16 | 0.19 | 0.08 | 0.00 | 0.01 | 0.05 | 0.12 |
| MI'* | 0.23 | 0.23 | 0.16 | 0.20 | 0.19 | 0.20 | 0.24 | 0.11 | 0.01 | 0.01 | 0.06 | 0.15 |
| Multipliers of emissions | | | | | | | | | | | | |
| Me' | 21.75 | 8.63 | 0.23 | 0.41 | 0.53 | 11.50 | 5.63 | 0.27 | 0.02 | 0.03 | 0.27 | 0.77 |
| Me'+ | 27.96 | 11.69 | 1.32 | 1.92 | 1.98 | 15.03 | 7.26 | 1.14 | 0.10 | 0.09 | 0.76 | 1.95 |
| Me'* | 28.58 | 12.29 | 1.79 | 2.56 | 2.59 | 15.61 | 7.88 | 1.52 | 0.14 | 0.12 | 0.95 | 2.41 |

Source: Authors' calculations with data from EXIOBASE

Table 1.2 Economic multipliers of labour and emissions in selected countries

| | Employment multiplier | | | | Emissions multiplier | | | |
|---|---|---|---|---|---|---|---|---|
| | Electricity by coal | Electricity by gas | Electricity by petrol | Electricity by wind | Electricity by coal | Electricity by gas | Electricity by petrol | Electricity by wind |
| EU | 0.12 | 0.15 | 0.13 | 0.08 | 20.52 | 8.72 | 11.38 | 1.65 |
| RoW | 0.30 | 0.24 | 0.21 | 0.27 | 44.09 | 18.13 | 22.96 | 2.70 |
| France | 0.22 | 0.36 | 0.32 | 0.07 | 13.48 | 5.62 | 6.99 | 1.59 |
| Germany | 0.10 | 0.09 | 0.09 | 0.07 | 19.00 | 9.34 | 12.02 | 1.42 |
| Italy | 0.15 | 0.45 | 0.26 | 0.08 | 17.01 | 6.99 | 8.65 | 1.58 |
| Spain | 0.19 | 0.42 | 0.16 | 0.09 | 18.15 | 8.52 | 12.41 | 1.98 |
| UK | 0.14 | 0.09 | 0.09 | 0.09 | 24.44 | 6.58 | 8.63 | 2.07 |
| USA | 0.08 | 0.09 | 0.09 | 0.08 | 38.81 | 20.23 | 32.64 | 1.80 |
| Japan | 0.12 | 0.09 | 0.09 | 0.07 | 15.31 | 12.78 | 12.12 | 1.22 |
| China | 0.31 | 0.27 | 0.28 | 0.26 | 25.06 | 30.33 | 19.46 | 2.75 |

Source: Authors' calculations with data from EXIOBASE

according to the sources of primary energy used. Some comments seem in order here:

(1) Fossil energies are among the most pollutant and the most labour intensive. Wind energy is among the least. In principle, a shift from fossil-electricity towards wind-electricity is supposed to reduce emissions and employment. Yet the necessary building of the wind-parks may change the result, as we shall see in the next section.
(2) Emissions increase considerably when we skip from the technological multipliers to the economic ones – our main tool for impact analysis. On average, they double. The progression is also verified (although less pronounced) in the employment multipliers. This result recommends the use of broad multipliers, as we are going to do.
(3) Regional differences are also significant. To simplify our analysis at this stage, we can focus on the cells corresponding to petrol and wind in the first two rows of Table 1.2. The $CO_2$eq emissions in the production of one million euros of petrol electricity in the EU are half the emissions resulting from the same production in the RoW (11.38/22.96 = 0.5). A similar ratio results in wind-electricity (1.65/2.7 = 0.61). Regarding employment, we observe that the EU requires less labour for the same effort: 0.62 (= 0.13/0.21) and 0.3 (= 0.08/0.027). This observation tells us that the international impact of decarbonization depends on the region that takes the lead. In this chapter, we assume that the leader is the EU.

## Simulations of the impacts of the decarbonization of electricity generation

The main goal of this chapter is to compute the impact on employment and emissions all over the world resulting from the decarbonization of electricity generation in the EU. The answer depends on the macroeconomic scenarios considered. In this section, we shall refer to four scenarios plus the baseline or *bau* (business as usual). They result from different combinations of two variables: the growth of the economy ($g$) and the rhythm ($r$) of decarbonization of electricity production – i.e. the speed of the substitution of fossil sources by wind. The $g$ and $r$ will be complemented with the subindex "e" for the EU and the subindex "w" for the RoW.

Regarding economic growth, we shall contemplate three possible scenarios for the EU: (1) Stagnation ($g_e$ = 0); (2) Moderate growth ($g_e$ = 2.5%) and Boom ($g_e$ = 5%). For the rest of the world, we assume a constant average growth of $g_w$ = 2.5%.

Regarding the rhythm of decarbonization, we assume that the EU holds its commitment to decarbonize entirely electricity production by the mid-century. After 2021, the share of wind-electricity is supposed to increase an additional 20% in points while fossil-electricity falls in the same proportion. These results correspond to the rhythm $r_e$ = 20. Since most of the non-European countries have not started the process of decarbonization and/or are not so much committed to it, we introduce a delay until 2050 (which implies $r_w = 0$) or a slower rhythm ($r_w = 10$). The last assumption implies that by the mid-century, fossil-electricity would represent half the total production of electricity.

Table 1.3 summarizes the possible combinations and identifies the scenarios that will be analyzed in this section.

Table 1.4 shows the evolution of employment in four different scenarios (always with respect to the *bau*) in four years (2015; 2021, 2033 and 2045). Table 1.5 offers the information with respect to GHG emissions.

*Table 1.3* Scenarios to be analyzed

|  | *Rhythm of decarbonization (r)* | *Growth of the economy (g)* |
| --- | --- | --- |
| Scenario 0, *baseline, bau* | $r_e = 0$; $r_w = 0$ | $g_e = 2.5\%$; $g_w = 2.5\%$ |
| Scenario 1 | $r_e = 20$; $r_w = 0$ | $g_e = 0\%$; $g_w = 2.5\%$ |
| Scenario 2 | $r_e = 20$; $r_w = 0$ | $g_e = 2.5\%$; $g_w = 2.5\%$ |
| Scenario 3 | $r_e = 20$; $r_w = 0$ | $g_e = 5\%$; $g_w = 2.5\%$ |
| Scenario 4 | $r_e = 20$; $r_w = 10$ | $g_e = 2.5\%$; $g_w = 2.5\%$ |

*Note*: Subindex "e" refers to the EU and subindex "w" to the RoW

Source: Authors' calculations

*Table 1.4* Evolution of employment in different scenarios, % change respect to baseline

|  | *EU* | | | *RoW* | | |
| --- | --- | --- | --- | --- | --- | --- |
|  | *2021* | *2033* | *2045* | *2021* | *2033* | *2045* |
| Scenario 1 | −11% | −26% | −37% | −2% | −4% | −6% |
| Scenario 2 | 0% | 0% | 1% | 0% | −1% | −1% |
| Scenario 3 | 12% | 40% | 76% | 1% | 5% | 9% |
| Scenario 4 | 16% | 49% | 72% | 11% | 36% | 53% |

Source: Author's calculations

*Table 1.5* Evolution of $CO_2$eq emissions in different scenarios, % change respect to baseline

|  | *EU* | | | *RoW* | | |
| --- | --- | --- | --- | --- | --- | --- |
|  | *2021* | *2033* | *2045* | *2021* | *2033* | *2045* |
| Scenario 1 | −15% | −41% | −52% | −2% | −5% | −7% |
| Scenario 2 | −6% | −24% | −30% | 0% | −1% | −1% |
| Scenario 3 | 4% | 1% | 15% | 2% | 5% | 11% |
| Scenario 4 | 12% | 20% | 31% | 12% | 25% | 25% |

Source: Authors' calculations

## Impact on employment

If the world economy continues its historical trend ($g = 2.5\%$), without either technical improvements or a special effort to decarbonize, production and employment will double in the 30 years that elapse between 2015 and 2045. If we accept a decrease of labour coefficients at the rhythm of the two decades previous to the 2008 crisis (2%), the increase in employment would be just 16%. We do not need, however, to introduce new variables and uncertainties since our interest is just to compare the deviations of the variables in the new scenarios in comparison with the baseline. The only technological alteration is the shift to an electrical mix that is less labour intensive and less pollutant.

Scenario 1 locates the European decarbonization effort in a long recession, while nothing changes in the RoW. The growth of employment decelerates. The number of jobs in 2045 would be 37% lower than in the baseline. Three forces are at play: (1) The recession. (2) Electricity production in the EU has shifted towards a technology based on wind that is less labour intensive and has lower employment multipliers. (3) New jobs are required to build the wind-farms and associated infrastructures in the EU. Looking at the results, we can conclude that the last force is not big enough to compensate the negative impact on employment stemming from the other two.

Scenario 2 is similar to the previous one but decarbonization is introduced in a "normal" economic expansion with $g_e = 2.5\%$. Now the difference with the baseline scenario is minimal. This implies that the increase in jobs linked to the normal economic growth plus the jobs created in the building of wind-parks amount, more or less, to the employment destroyed by the higher technological efficiency of wind-electricity.

If the European economy experiences a long boom (scenario 3), the number of European jobs in 2045 would be 76% bigger than in the baseline for the EU and 9% bigger for the RoW. This is a typical result of the Keynesian model, where the main determinant of employment is the level of production and its rate of growth.

Scenario 4 considers a middle international economic expansion ($g = 2.5\%$) together with an international decarbonization effort that is faster in the EU than in the RoW. The result is a strong increase in employment with reference to the baseline: 72% in the EU and 53% in the RoW. This shows the importance of the spillover effects embodied in our interregional multipliers. Most of the materials directly and indirectly required to build wind-farms in the RoW are purchased in the EU. The same happens with a part of the consumption goods demanded by the direct and indirect labour employed in the production of wind-farms.

## Impact on emissions

In 2015, GHG emissions amounted to 36.64 Gt (4.24 in the EU and 32.40 in the RoW). In the baseline scenario, emissions would double in 30 years (2015–2045) if the world economy is expanding at an accumulated rate of 2.5% without any effort of decarbonization. Contrasted to this baseline, emissions in 2045 would be

52% and 30% lower in scenarios 1 and 2, and 15% and 31% higher in scenarios 3 and 4. These results confirm that GHG emissions are positively correlated to (1) the growth of the economy, (2) the share of fossil-electricity and (3) the rhythm of wind-farms construction.

Figures 1.1 to 1.5 clarify the outcomes of each scenario. Here we consider the trends of the absolute level of emissions in Gt/a of $CO_2$eq, where "a" is an index of the emissions-saving-technical change. a>1 implies that there has been a reduction of energy use per unit of output and/or emissions per unit of energy. We do not need to calibrate this new variable, full of uncertainties. What matters for our purposes is the distance between the trends corresponding to the scenario under scrutiny and the baseline, both for the EU and the RoW. We know that the baseline (*business as usual scenario*) causes a dangerous concentration of $CO_2$eq enough to raise global warming more than 2°C above the preindustrial level. New scenarios whose emissions supersede the baseline (cutting them from below), should be considered even more dangerous.

Scenario 1, Figure 1.1. If the EU economy enters a protracted recession, emissions in the EU will keep roughly constant until 2045 and will retreat afterwards, once the building of wind-farms has been completed. In the RoW, that is growing at $g_w = 2.5\%$, emissions slow down after 2045 due to the smaller spillover effects stemming from the EU.

Scenario 2 is seen in Figure 1.2. What would happen if the EU starts growing at a more "normal" rate, $g_e = 2.5\%$? In the EU, GHG emissions increase but at a

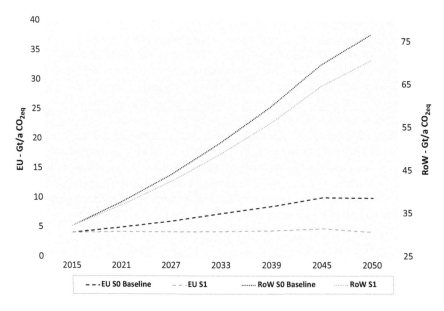

*Figure 1.1* Evolution of GHG emissions in the EU and the RoW (2015–2050): scenario 1

Note: (ge = 0; gw = 2.5%; re = 20; rw = 0) versus baseline (g = 2.5%; r = 0)

Source: Authors' calculations

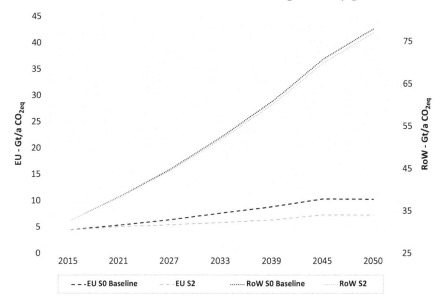

*Figure 1.2* Evolution of GHG emissions in the EU and the RoW (2015–2050): scenario 2

Note: (ge = 2.5%; gw = 2.5%; re = 20; rw=0) versus baseline (g = 2.5%; r = 0)

Source: Authors' calculations

slower pace than in the baseline scenario. After 2045, they stabilize. For the RoW, the gap between the new scenario and the baseline is negligible.

Scenario 3 is seen in Figure 1.3. What if the EU enters a long wave of prosperity with $g_e$ = 5%? GHG emissions expand closer to the baseline scenario for a time. After 2039, they overcome it. This result makes clear that the substitution of fossil with wind electricity in the EU is not big enough to reduce $CO_2$eq in boom periods. Other ancillary measures have to be implemented to check emissions.

Scenario 4 is shown in Figure 1.4. Arguably, this is the most realistic scenario and deserves special attention. The international economy (both the EU and the RoW) is growing at a moderate rate ($g$ = 2.5%) that can be considered the normal one as the average in long periods of time. Decarbonization is undertaken all over the world, although it advances faster in the EU than in the RoW ($r_e$ = 20, $r_w$ = 10). Figure 1.4 shows that both the EU and the RoW emit more GHG than in the baseline scenario during the whole period of 2015–2045. Only after 2045 can we expect stable emissions in the EU, when the building of wind-farms has been completed. In the RoW, we observe a deceleration of emission after 2045, when fossil substitution is halfway.

The investment necessary to substitute fossil with wind-electricity is so big that GHG emissions could surpass the baseline that leads to increases in global warming above 2°C. These results do not discredit our goal of changing the mix of primary energy in electricity production. They only remind us of the need to introduce complementary measures.

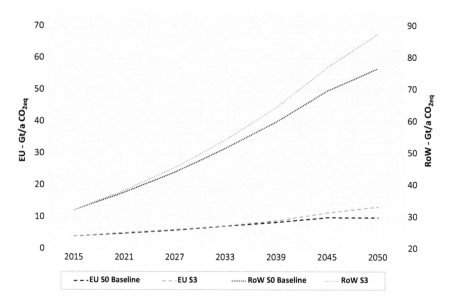

*Figure 1.3* Evolution of GHG emissions in the EU and the RoW (2015–2050): scenario 3

Note: (ge = 5%; gw = 2.5%; re = 20; rw = 0) versus baseline (g = 2.5%; r = 0)

Source: Authors' calculations

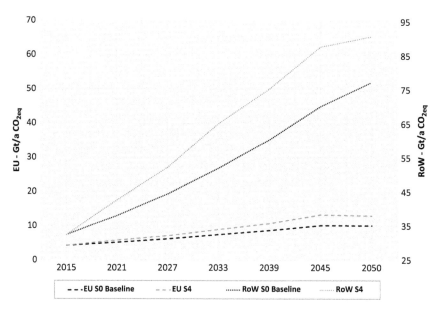

*Figure 1.4* Evolution of GHG emissions in the EU and the RoW (2015–2050): scenario 4

Note: (ge = 2.5%; gw = 2.5%; re = 20; rw = 10) versus baseline (g = 2.5%; r = 0)

Source: Authors' calculations

## Conclusions

The 2015 Paris Agreement urges a decarbonization of the economy that should be well advanced by the mid-century. Arguably, the first and most important measure is a cleaner mix of primary sources of energy in the production of electricity. In this chapter, we have explored the substitution of fossil-electricity with wind-electricity. In the EU, the process would be completed in the 30 years that elapse between 2015 and 2045. This implies a huge effort in building the required wind plants and related infrastructure. We assume that the rest of the world starts later or at a slower pace.

What will be the impacts on employment and GHG emissions of the decarbonization process led by the EU? Will it be a win-win strategy in the sense that it solves simultaneously our two goals (a reduction of GHG emissions and an increase in employment)?

To answer these questions, we have computed and applied broad input-output multipliers on employment and emissions. In addition to the direct and indirect intermediate consumption by firms (accounted by the typical Leontief's inverse), we have computed the direct and indirect induced final consumption of households. In the multiplicand (autonomous demand), we have included (1) the "induced" investment required to meet the expected growth of permanent aggregate demand (acceleration principle) and (2) the investment in the wind-parks required for the new electricity mix.

Our conclusions are derived from a typical "scenario approach". Arguably, the fourth scenario is the closest to the real world. It considers an average real rate of growth of 2.5% both in the EU and in the RoW for the period of 2015–2050. The rhythm of substitution is faster in the EU than in the RoW, as it has been the case so far. By the mid-century, fossil-electricity will be negligible in the EU, while it will still amount to 50% in the RoW. The results are contrasted with the baseline scenario (*bau*) where the international economy grows at 2.5% and electricity is produced using the 2015 mix.

In 2045, employment in the EU would be 31% above the baseline and 25% in the RoW. The key employer is the industry building wind-farms and wind infrastructure. Once the adaptation has been completed, this industry will grow at the average rate of the economy and will provide new permanent jobs only for the operation and maintenance of the wind-farms. Many jobs will disappear and should wait until another industry takes up the relay as an employment driver.

GHG emissions in the EU are supposed to grow until 2045 and stabilize afterwards in our scenario 4. For the RoW, emissions will continue growing after this date but at a slower pace. The distance with respect to the baseline is bound to increase if the economy speeds up. These results may jeopardize the Paris Agreement to keep global warming well below 2°C with respect to preindustrial levels. Emissions associated with the huge investment in wind-farms might reach dangerous levels before society starts enjoying the benefits of a decarbonized economy.

Our conclusion does not discredit the commitment to decarbonize electricity generation. It only reminds us of the need to search for complementary measures as electric cars and heating systems. They will be less polluting when they can be plugged into wind-electricity.

## Acknowledgement

This chapter was written within the research project PPII-2014–006-P, supported by the Junta Comunidades de Castilla-La Mancha and the European Union (European Fund for Regional Development), and within the project ECO2016–78939-R, supported by the Spanish Ministry of Economy, Industry and Competitiveness.

## Notes

1  See Barker and Crawford-Brown, 2015; IEA, 2010, Berril et al. (2016), Gambhir et al. (2017); Peters et al. (2017).
2  Antecedents of structural multiplier can be traced back to Goodwin (1949), Barker et al. (2006), Dejuán (2006), Dejuán et al. (2013) and Portella-Carbo (2016).
3  EXIOBASE is produced by a consortium of European universities and research centres specialized in natural resources and the environment: NTNU (Norway), TNO (the Netherlands), SERI, Leiden University and Wien University.
4  The main problem faced by input-output scholars is the long delay in data publication. In our case, the problem is somehow minimized since we extract from IOT just the technical coefficients and certain expenditure propensities that tend to evolve slowly. In addition, the projections of these coefficients until 2050 do not appear in absolute terms but as a divergence from the baseline (i.e. with the 2015 mix of primary energy to produce electricity). The divergence would be similar whether all technical coefficients remain constant or they decrease x%.
5  Those not familiar with multiregional IOA can consider that products are differentiated according to the country of origin. Despite serving for the same purposes, the electricity generated in Spain is a different product from the electricity generated in France, for example. The number of rows and columns of our interindustry transaction table ($Z$) amounts to 1556 (41 industries times 38 regions). By the same token, the column vector of autonomous demand has 1556 cells.
6  The six non-EU big regions are the United States of America (US), Japan, China, Brazil, India, Russia and the United Kingdom (UK). Since our simulations start after 2020, it seems reasonable to exclude the UK from the EU.
7  The Paris Agreement allows for a minimum of fossil-electricity that is convenient when the wind does not blow strong enough and can be neutralized by natural sinks such as forests. Alternatively, we could complement wind-electricity with other renewable sources that do not depend on weather conditions, like nuclear plants.
8  Each wind turbine produces 2.5 MW (at 100% load). A typical wind park of 20 turbines produces 50 MW and costs 65 million euros.
9  Remember that in a MRIO, the total and final output are represented by two column vectors ($x$ and $y = yc+yh$) of 1558 cells each one (41 industries times 38 regions). Column $yc$ gathers the domestic purchase of consumption goods and the purchases of consumption goods in the remaining 37 regions. Exports of region $r$ do not appear explicitly in the macroeconomic equilibrium. They can be figured out by adding the imports from other regions to $r$.
10  As it is usual in input-output studies, matrices are represented by uppercase bold letters, vectors by lowercase bold letters and an apostrophe is added when they represent a row vector. As an exception, the total labour employed per industry and total emissions per industry are represented by L and E. Diagonal matrices are indicated by a

circumflex (^) or angular brackets (< >). I stands for the identity matrix. When it refers to a column vector of investment we will add a subindex, for instance $I_1$ and $I_2$.
11 Usually, the consumption of pensioners is treated as autonomous because pensions are not a fixed proportion of current income. By endogenizing it, we are assuming that the ratio "pensions/income" is quite stable and pensions are systematically consumed.
12 From the database of the OECD and World Bank, we have obtained the shares in GCF of public investment, residential investment and R&D expenditure. See OECD (2015, 2016, 2016b) and WB (2016).
13 Bortis (1997), Dejuán (2006), Dejuán et al. (2013), Lavoie (2014) Portella-Carbo (2016).
14 The matrix of capital stocks by sector has been obtained from the WIOD database.

## References

Barker, T., Pan, H., Köhler, J., Warren, R., and Winne, S. (2006). Decarbonising the global economy with induced technological change: Scenarios to 2100 using E3MG. *The Energy Journal, 27*, 143–160.
Barker, T., and Crawford-Brown, D. (2015). *Decarbonizing the world's economy. Assessing the feasibility of policies to reduce greenhouse gas emissions.* London: Imperial College Press.
Berril, P., Anderds, A., Schulz, Y., Gils, H.C., Herwich, E.G. (2016). Environmental impacts of high penetration renewable energy scenarios for Europe. *Environmental Research Letters*, 11, 1–10.
Bortis, H. (1997). *Institutions, behaviour and economic theory: A contribution to Classical-Keynesian political economy.* Cambridge, UK: Cambridge University Press.
Dejuán, Ó. (2006). A dynamic AGE model from a Classical-Keynesian-Schumpeterian approach. In N. Salvadori (Ed.), *Economic growth and distribution: On the nature and causes of the wealth of nations.* Cheltenham: Edward Elgar.
Dejuán, Ó., López, L.-A., Tobarra, M.-Á., and Zafrilla, J. (2013). A post-Keynesian AGE model to forecast energy demand in Spain. *Economic Systems Research, 25*(3), 1–20. doi: JCR, 2.429
EC. (2010). *Europe 2020: A strategy for smart, sustainable and inclusive growth.* Brussels: European Commission.
EC. (2012). *Energy in figures – statistical pocket book.* Brussels: European Commission.
EC. (2016). *EU energy in figures: Statistical pocketbook 2016.* Luxembourg: Publications Office of the European Union.
Gambhir, A., Drouet, L., McCollum, D., Napp, T., and Lowe, J. (2017). Assessing the feasibility of global long-term mitigation scenarios. *Energies*, 10(1), 89–99.
Goodwin, R. M. (1949). The multiplier as matrix. *Economic Journal, 59*, 537–555.
IDAE. (2016). *Plan de energías renovables 2011–2020.* IDAE. Retrieved from www.idae.es
IEA. (2010). *Scenarios and strategies to 2050.* World Energy Outlook
Kalecki, M. (1971). *Selected essays in the dynamics of the capitalist economy (1933–1970).* Cambridge: Cambridge University Press.
Lavoie, M. (2014). *Post-Keynesian economics: New foundations.* Cheltenham: Edward Elgar.
OECD. (2015). Pensions at a glance 2015: OECD and G20 indicators. Paris: OECD.
OECD. (2016). OECD Data. Aggregate National Accounts. (Indicators. Investment (GFCF) by asset (dwellings), Investment (GFCF) by sector (general government)).
OECD. (2016b). *OECD data. Research and Development (R&D). Indicator: Gross domestic spending on R&D.* Paris: OECD.

Peters, G.P., Andrew, R.M. and Nakicenovic, N. (2017) Key indicators to track current progress and future ambition of the Paris Agreement. *Nature Climate Change*, 7(2), 118–122.

Portella-Carbo, F. (2016). Effects of international trade on domestic employment: An application of a global multiregional input-output supermultiplier model (1995–2011). *Economic Systems Research, 28*, 95–117.

Tukker, A., de Koning, A., Wood, R., Hawkins, T., Lutter, S., Acosta, J., . . . Kuenen, J. (2013). Exiopol – development and illustrative analyses of a detailed global MR EE SUT/IOT. *Economic Systems Research, 25*(1), 50–70. doi: 10.1080/09535314.2012.761952

UN. (2015). Report of the Conference of the Parties on its twenty-first session, held in Paris from 30 November to 13 December 2015. Paris: United Nations.

WB. (2016). *World bank data base – world development indicators*. World Bank. Retrieved from http://data.worldbank.org

Wood, R., Stadler, K., Bulavskaya, T., Lutter, S., Giljum, S., de Koning, A., . . . Tukker, A. (2015). Global sustainability accounting-developing EXIOBASE for multi-regional footprint analysis. *Sustainability (Switzerland)*, 7(1), 138–163. doi: 10.3390/su7010138

# 2 Indirect emissions and socio-economic impacts of energy efficiency and renewable electricity in Europe

*Kurt Kratena*

## Introduction

Since the Conference of the Parties (COP 3) climate conference (Kyoto), the European climate policy aims at decarbonization via increasing energy efficiency and the support of carbon-free technologies in electricity generation. The latest conference (COP21) in Paris in 2015 brought some new features in international climate negotiations: a legally binding 2° C target and submissions of climate action pledges labelled "Intended Nationally Determined Contributions" (INDCs) by most countries. Within this policy framework, the European climate policy is characterized by taking on a long-run perspective (up to 2050) with short-term emission reduction targets for the years 2020 and 2030. By aiming at the binding 2° C target, a deep decarbonization of the European economy will be a prerequisite. Already, the EU Roadmap for GHG emission reduction emphasizes a combination of higher energy efficiency with pure decarbonization measures for the electricity sector such as nuclear energy, renewables and Carbon Capture and Storage (CCS). Several studies for Europe have highlighted the role of energy efficiency improvement (for example, Ifeu and Prognos, 2011) for achieving the targets of GHG emission reduction. Besides market-oriented policies ($CO_2$ pricing), other measures can be used to increase energy efficiency and the share of renewables. Usually, the instruments for these measures include market-oriented policies (subsidies) as well, and their main mechanism of action is a change in the structure and nature of capital stocks that – in turn – induces a significant and long-term increase in investment (IEA, 2012). This investment might have macroeconomic impacts depending on the economic situation (unemployment, capacity utilization) and produce indirect emissions. The emission reduction path, therefore, depends on the timing of the change in the capital stock and the efficiency increase achieved. The more efficient capital stock reduces emissions after being installed, depending on the lifetime. On the other hand, indirect emissions from producing this capital stock compensate partly or completely ("cannibalism") the emission reduction at the beginning of the implementation of the measure. For renewables, this aspect has been researched and traced back to the low 'Energy Return on Energy Investment', EROEI (Fagnart and Germain, 2016).

In general, we find different patterns of mechanisms of direct and indirect emissions reductions, depending on the sector of energy use and the instrument for efficiency improvement. We analyze two different alternative scenarios (compared to a "BASE" scenario) until 2050. One scenario assumes considerable energy efficiency improvements (scenario "EFF") via scrappage policies for vehicles and electrical appliances with ambitious conditions for energy efficiency of new purchases and refurbishment of buildings. The scrappage policies lead to a reduction in lifetime of these durable household goods. For vehicles, it has been shown that shortening the lifetime without any additional requirement for energy efficiency of new purchases (i.e. only allowing for the trend in technical progress) does not reduce overall emissions (Kagawa et al., 2009). Therefore, in this scenario, it is assumed that the direct effect of the scrappage policy is that on average, new purchases are 25% more energy efficient than actual new purchases (for vehicles) and 50% more energy efficient (for electric appliances). This policy is in place until 2030 and therefore does not lead to a permanent decrease in direct emissions. After the fading out of the measure, consumers switch back to less energy-efficient durables in their new purchases. For building refurbishment, due to the long lifetime of buildings, the direct emission reduction is long lasting. Indirect emissions (both domestic and imported) also decrease only until 2030; then the emission effects are slightly reduced until 2050. The production of durable goods leads to higher indirect emissions until 2030, which partly compensate the emission reduction in the energy-producing sectors (coal, oil products and natural gas). Imported indirect emissions are continuously reduced, but at a slower pace, until 2030 due to the foreign production of durables imported in the EU 27. The total reduction of indirect emissions is mainly driven by the large decrease of emissions in electricity generation.

The other scenario assumes much higher diffusion of renewables in European electricity generation (scenario "RENEW"), mainly crowding out generation from coal Again, as in the scenario with energy efficiency improvements ("EFF"), no explicit policy is simulated, but the faster diffusion of renewables is assumed. As in the scenario "EFF", this policy is in place until 2030 and leads to an increase in the renewable share with a stabilization afterwards. Contrary to the results in scenario "EFF", the effect on capital demand is permanent due to the higher capital intensity and lower capital lifetime of renewable energy generation. In the model, that leads to higher costs of electricity generation and thereby to higher electricity prices. This feedback can be seen as the equivalent of the costs of such a policy that otherwise might be implemented via subsidies or other support schemes. In order to be able to analyze this scenario in a consistent way, the Dynamic New Keynesian (DYNK) model used in this study is disaggregated to bottom-up information (as in Daly et al., 2015 and Schumacher and Sands, 2007) of the electricity sector. The production model (Translog) for this sector in the DYNK model is therefore substituted by a structure, where the aggregate factor demand depends on the electricity generation mix. In the case of this study, this mix is fixed and changed exogenously, but could otherwise be determined by some partial model of the electricity sector, such as TIMES (Daly et al., 2015).

The main result for indirect emissions in this scenario is similar to the one in scenario "EFF": total reduction of indirect emissions is completely driven by emissions reduction in electricity generation. For imported indirect emissions, the higher emissions of a more capital-intensive electricity sector in Europe are balanced by lower emissions from energy production in the rest of the world (due to lower energy demand in Europe). This gives an overall sight reduction of imported indirect emissions. In the case of domestic indirect emissions, the higher indirect emissions from the production of capital goods more than compensates for the emission reduction in the energy-producing sectors (coal, oil products and natural gas).

The chapter is organized as follows: section 2 describes the methodology and the modelling framework with special emphasis on direct and indirect emissions. In section 3, the main assumptions for both emission reduction scenarios ("EFF" and "RENEW"), their sources and the way of implementation in the model are revealed. The simulation results are presented in section 4, and section 5 concludes the chapter. A detailed model description with an emphasis on consumption, production and trade can be found in the Appendix.

## Methodology and data

The *DYNK (DY*namic *N*ew *K*eynesian) model approach applied in this study is a hybrid between an econometric IO and a CGE model, and is characterized by the integration of rigidities and institutional frictions. These rigidities include liquidity constraints for consumers (deviation from the permanent income hypothesis) and wage bargaining (deviation from the competitive labor market). In the long run, the model works similarly to a CGE model and explicitly describes an adjustment path towards a long-run equilibrium. The model describes the inter-linkages between 59 industries as well as the consumption of five household-income groups by 47 consumption categories and covers the EU 27 (as one economy).

The IO core of the model is based on supply-use tables for Europe (EUROSTAT), and intermediate demand is split into domestic and imported commodities. Instead of deriving a technical coefficient matrix (inputs of intermediate commodities per unit of industry output) from the use matrix, this modelling step is split into two parts in the DYNK model. First, vectors of total input coefficients per unit of industry output for domestic and imported commodities ($v_D$ and $v_M$) are defined. The commodity structure below this level is then in a second step defined by use structure matrices $S^m$ and $S^d$ with a column sum equal to unity. A further distinction within the use matrix is between non-energy and energy commodities. The commodity balance for non-energy commodities is then defined by applying the use structure matrices $S_{NE}^m$ and $S_{NE}^d$, as well as the diagonal matrices of the factor shares defined earlier: $\hat{V}_D$ and $\hat{V}_M$. Multiplying the use structure matrix with the corresponding factor share matrix and with the column vector of output in current prices gives the sum of intermediate demand by commodity. The procedure for energy commodities is the same, with use structure matrices $S_E^m$ and $S_E^d$ (where the column sum over both matrices yields one), and diagonal matrix $\hat{V}_E$.

The full commodity balance is given by adding the column vectors of domestic consumption ($\mathbf{c}^d$), capital formation ($\mathbf{cf}^d$) and public consumption ($\mathbf{cg}^d$). Capital formation is endogenous as well and derived from capital demand by industry in the Translog model, applying the capital formation matrix (for details, see the Appendix). The (column vector) of the domestic output of commodities in current prices, $\mathbf{p}^D\mathbf{q}^D$, is transformed into the (column vector) of output in current prices, $\mathbf{p}_Q\mathbf{q}$ by applying the market-shares matrix, $\mathbf{C}$ (industries * commodities), with column sum equal to one:

$$\mathbf{p}^D\mathbf{q}^D = \left[\hat{\mathbf{V}}_D\mathbf{S}_{NE}^d\right]\mathbf{p}_Q\mathbf{q} + \left[\hat{\mathbf{V}}_E\mathbf{S}_E^d\right]\mathbf{p}_Q\mathbf{q} + \mathbf{c}^d + \mathbf{cf}^d + \mathbf{ex}^d + \mathbf{st}^d + \mathbf{cg}^d \qquad (2.1)$$

$$\mathbf{p}_Q\mathbf{q} = \mathbf{C}\mathbf{p}_D\mathbf{q}_D \qquad (2.2)$$

These two equations describe the core IO model of the system and can be solved in a loop for equilibrium values of output ($\mathbf{p}_Q\mathbf{q}$ and $\mathbf{p}^D\mathbf{q}^D$) once final demand categories ($\mathbf{c}^d$, $\mathbf{cf}^d$, $\mathbf{ex}^d$, $\mathbf{st}^d$ and $\mathbf{cg}^d$) and matrices ($\hat{\mathbf{V}}_D$, $\hat{\mathbf{V}}_E$, $\mathbf{S}_{NE}^d$ and $\mathbf{S}_E^d$) are given.

The final demand categories ($\mathbf{c}^d$, $\mathbf{cf}^d$, $\mathbf{ex}^d$, $\mathbf{st}^d$ and $\mathbf{cg}^d$) comprise energy and non-energy commodities, are all in current prices and are all – except stock changes ($\mathbf{st}^d$) – endogenous. The export vector $\mathbf{ex}^d$ is modelled via linear functions of demand in the rest of the world (RoW), where the different commodities in $\mathbf{ex}^d$ reveal different elasticities with respect to total demand in RoW. Additionally, commodity exports depend on prices and are calibrated with price elasticity of unity for all commodities. The vector of public consumption $\mathbf{cg}^d$ is determined in the public sector block of the model in order to close the model with a predetermined public deficit.

### Household demand and direct GHG emissions of households

*Total consumption and energy demand of households*

The consumption block differentiates between different stages and separability is assumed between these stages. The separability assumption in that context also implies that the dynamic decision process is disentangled as outlined in Attanasio and Weber (1995). At the first stage, the demand for durables (real estate property and vehicles) is modelled in a way consistent with the version of the buffer-stock model described in Luengo-Prado (2006). Further, total nondurable demand is also specified in a way consistent with the main properties of the buffer-stock model (excessive smoothing, excess sensitivity). All model parameters are based on dynamic estimation of panel data for Europe (1995–2011) in the first stage for 14 EU countries (Belgium, Czech Republic, Denmark, Germany, France, Italy, Cyprus, Lithuania, Austria, Poland, Portugal, Romania, Slovakia, Finland). The data for the estimation of consumption demand functions are mainly taken from EUROSTAT's National Accounts. The capital stock of housing property was estimated for one year based on the Household Financial and Consumption Survey (HFCS) of the European Central Bank (ECB). By applying property prices from the Bank of International Settlement (BIS) and EUROSTAT population data, a time series of owned houses was constructed for the 14 EU countries. A crucial variable at this first stage of consumers' demand is the down payment for durable purchases (see the Appendix for details). Once the full model is set up with the integrated consumption block, the property of "excess sensitivity" can be tested. Excess sensitivity describes the empirical fact that the growth rate of consumption – partly – reacts to the lagged growth rate of disposable (or labour) income. The full model presented here is run until 2050 so that endogenous disposable household income is generated. Then excess sensitivity is tested by regressing the growth rates for durable ($C_{dur,t}$) and nondurable consumption ($C_{nondur,t}$) for each quintile ($q$) on lagged disposable income growth (without profit income) for each quintile generated by the full model. Profit income is not included, because it is endogenous and depends on equity built up, which in turn is a result of the intertemporal optimization. Luengo-Prado (2006) also carries out excess sensitivity tests with her calibrated model, based on US household survey data, and confronts these results with US stylized macroeconomic facts. The excess sensitivity coefficients – i.e. the marginal propensity of consumption (MPC) with respect to lagged income change – found by Luengo-Prado (2006) are 0.16 (nondurables) and 0.26 (durables). The results from the model solution until 2050 clearly reveal that, for the fifth and partly for the fourth quintile, durable and nondurable consumption do not statistically significantly depend on transitory income shocks.

The MPC is higher in general for lower income households and for situations with higher liquidity constraints (higher down payment $\theta$). The "low $\theta$ scenario" corresponds to a financial regime, where the relationship debt to durable stock does not significantly decrease – i.e. no major debt deleveraging by households occurs. The "high $\theta$ scenario" corresponds to debt deleveraging so that the relationship debt to durable stock in the long-run decreases to its values before 2002 – i.e. before the main expansion of household debt began. The multiplier of policies that influence income is therefore not constant, but depends on the financial market environment (liquidity constraints) and the income groups that are most affected.

At the second stage, energy consumption, disaggregated into heating, electricity and fuels for transport, and is modeled as a service demand in terms of utilization of the capital (durable) stock. Therefore, it links energy demand (in monetary and physical units) to the durable stock (houses, vehicles, appliances). An important variable is the average energy efficiency of the corresponding durable stocks (dwelling for heating, vehicles for fuels for transport, and appliances for electricity). The transport part allows for substitution between public transport services and private car transport. For this second stage, the model parameters are based on estimations with an EU 27 country panel (1995–2011). The energy expenditure of households is based on EUROSTAT, the Energy Accounts from the WIOD database, as well as IEA Energy Prices. Energy efficiency for electricity and for heating is calculated from the ODYSSEE database. Efficiency of the car fleet is taken from a revised version of the GAINS project database. All equations have been estimated in a dynamic autoregressive distributed lag (ADL) specification.

Table 2.1 Excess sensitivity of consumption w.r.t. lagged disposable income (without profit income)

| Sensitivity, low q | 1st quintile | | 2nd quintile | | 3rd quintile | | 4th quintile | | 5th quintile |
|---|---|---|---|---|---|---|---|---|---|
| dlog($C_{dur}$) | 0.45 | *** | 0.38 | *** | 0.30 | ** | 0.21 | | 0.14 |
| | (0.15) | | (0.16) | | (0.16) | | (0.16) | | (0.16) |
| dlog($C_{nondur}$) | 0.94 | *** | 0.76 | *** | 0.58 | *** | 0.38 | *** | −0.03 |
| | (0.41) | | (0.20) | | (0.15) | | (0.12) | | (0.13) |

| Sensitivity, high q | 1st quintile | | 2nd quintile | | 3rd quintile | | 4th quintile | | 5th quintile |
|---|---|---|---|---|---|---|---|---|---|
| dlog($C_{dur}$) | 0.44 | *** | 0.40 | *** | 0.33 | *** | 0.26 | ** | 0.20 |
| | (0.13) | | (0.14) | | (0.14) | | (0.14) | | (0.14) |
| dlog($C_{nondur}$) | 1.02 | *** | 0.86 | *** | 0.69 | *** | 0.49 | *** | 0.09 |
| | (0.37) | | (0.18) | | (0.14) | | (0.12) | | (0.09) |

Note: * and ** indicate significance at the 10% and 5% level, respectively

The price elasticity values found here for heating, transport fuel and electricity (around –0.8) are outside the range established by the existing literature for the energy price elasticity. That can be explained by two factors. First, the elasticity values presented here measure the service price elasticity and the reaction of service demand to both price changes and improvements of energy efficiency in the durable stock. Service price has been almost constant in the sample period used for estimation due to energy efficiency improvements, whereas demand has increased considerably. This is consistent with part of the literature on the (price) rebound effect that finds rebound effects of 100% in some cases. Second, the elasticity values calculated here are conditional on the stock of durables thereby implicitly assuming a unitary elasticity of energy demand to the durable stock as a strong driving force of demand.

Finally, the third stage contains the model of non-energy nondurable consumption, modeled in a flexible demand system (AIDS model). This third step is again split into two nests: (i) an aggregate level of eight categories, described in an AIDS model and (ii) a detailed model of 47 COICOP categories, explained by sub-shares of the aggregate categories that change over time and can be changed exogenously for model simulation purposes. The econometric estimation has been carried out for an EU 27 country panel (1995–2009) from EUROSTAT National Accounts, as well as for data from the household survey 20004/2005 for six EU countries: Austria, France, Italy, Slovakia, Spain and the United Kingdom (Salotti et al., 2015). For the cross-section model, no price variance across time is available and therefore the AIDS model only estimates the expenditure term. The main results of the estimation of the demand system for non-energy nondurables are the expenditure elasticity from both models (panel and cross section) and the price

*Table 2.2* Commodity demand and direct $CO_2$ emissions of households

| *Nondurable* | *own price* | *expenditure elasticity* | |
| --- | --- | --- | --- |
| *Consumption* | *elasticity* | *Time series* | *Cross section* |
| Food | −0.14 | 0.85 | 0.61 |
| Clothing | −0.64 | 1.04 | 1.28 |
| Furniture/equipment | −1.06 | 1.11 | 1.46 |
| Health | −0.83 | 0.98 | 1.20 |
| Communication | −0.89 | 0.96 | 0.68 |
| Recreation/accomodation | −0.50 | 1.08 | 1.27 |
| Financial Services | −0.94 | 1.33 | 1.00 |
| Other | −0.68 | 1.09 | 1.00 |

| *Energy* | *own price* | *durable stock* |
| --- | --- | --- |
| *Consumption* | *elasticity* | *elasticity* |
| Transport fuel | −0.77 | 1.00 |
| Heating | −0.87 | 1.00 |
| Electricity | −0.81 | 1.00 |

elasticity from the panel data model. The price elasticity shows considerable heterogeneity across categories. For the expenditure elasticity values, the results of both models differ considerably. While the expenditure elasticity of the panel data model is mainly distributed around unity, the expenditure elasticity of the cross-section model differs largely between categories.

The first stage yields (column) vectors of total nondurable consumption $(\mathbf{c}_{nondur})$ and of investment in owned houses $(\mathbf{c}_{hous})$ and in vehicles $(\mathbf{c}_{veh})$ by quintile $(q)$. From the second stage, one derives (column) vectors of fuel, heat and electricity consumption, again by quintile $(q)$: $\mathbf{c}_{fuel}$, $\mathbf{c}_{heat}$ and $\mathbf{c}_{el}$.

Nondurable non-energy consumption (the vector by quintiles) is then given by

$$\mathbf{c}_{NE} = \mathbf{c}_{nondur} - \mathbf{c}_{fuel} - \mathbf{c}_{heat} - \mathbf{c}_{el}. \tag{2.3}$$

The matrix of commodities of non-energy consumption by quintiles $(\mathbf{C}_j)$ is in a next step derived from multiplying the matrix of budget shares by quintiles, $\mathbf{W}$ (for details, see the Appendix), with the vector of nondurable non-energy consumption (converted into a diagonal matrix):

$$\mathbf{C}_j = \mathbf{W}\left[\hat{\mathbf{c}}_{NE}\right], \tag{2.4}$$

where $j = 1 \ldots 8$ are the eight non-energy consumption commodities. The final result of this procedure is a matrix of durable, energy and non-energy consumption by quintiles $(\mathbf{C}_C)$:

$$\mathbf{C}_C = \begin{bmatrix} c_{hous,1} & \cdot & \cdot & \cdot & c_{hous,5} \\ c_{veh,1} & \cdot & \cdot & \cdot & c_{veh,5} \\ c_{fuel,1} & \cdot & \cdot & \cdot & c_{fuel,5} \\ c_{heat,1} & \cdot & \cdot & \cdot & c_{heat,5} \\ c_{el,1} & \cdot & \cdot & \cdot & c_{el,5} \\ \cdot\cdot & \cdot\cdot & \cdot\cdot & \cdot\cdot & \cdot\cdot \\ c_{j,1} & \cdot & \cdot & \cdot & c_{j,5} \\ \cdot\cdot & \cdot\cdot & \cdot\cdot & \cdot\cdot & \cdot\cdot \end{bmatrix}.$$

This matrix is then transformed into a consumption matrix by commodities of the input-output core in the DYNK model and quintiles in purchaser prices, $\mathbf{C}_{pp}$, by applying the bridge matrix, $\mathbf{B}_C$:

$$\mathbf{C}_{pp} = \mathbf{B}_C \mathbf{C}_C. \tag{2.5}$$

The bridge matrix links the classification of consumption commodities (COICOP) to the industry classification of the DYNK model. The consumption vector in purchaser prices and industry classification is derived by summing up over $\mathbf{C}_{pp}$: $\mathbf{c}_{pp} = \mathbf{C}_{pp}e$ with $e$ as the diagonal matrix (per quintiles) of the unity vector.

This vector is then split up into a domestic and imported part for each commodity and converted into producer prices by reallocating trade and transport margins to the corresponding industries and subtracting taxes less subsidies. That yields the vectors of total domestic ($\mathbf{c}^d$) and imported ($\mathbf{c}^m$) consumption, with $\mathbf{c} = \mathbf{c}^d + \mathbf{c}^m$ all valued at producer prices. For this converting, a matrix of net tax rates (with identical tax rates on domestic and imported commodities) is applied.

The two directly emission relevant energy categories (fuel and heating) of the model of energy consumption need to be directly linked to the energy accounts by user (59 industries plus households) and detailed fuel category (26) in physical units. This is done in two several steps. First, the vector $\begin{bmatrix} c_{fuel} \\ c_{heat} \end{bmatrix}$ is deflated by aggregate prices of fuels and heating, where these energy prices are not specified as deflators, but as monetary values per physical energy unit (TJ). Then the deflated categories, in energy units, are allocated to the 26 energy types ($e$) of the model by applying fixed sub-shares, $s_{ef}$. The aggregate prices used for the first step (for fuel and heating, $p_f$) are defined by the exogenous prices by energy type ($p_e$) and the corresponding sub-shares: $p_f = \sum_e s_{ef} p_e$. This gives a matrix of direct energy consumption of households by type of energy ($e$) and quintile ($q$), whose elements are defined as $c_{e,q} = s_{ef,q} \dfrac{c_{f,q}}{p_f}$ :

$$\mathbf{C}_e = \begin{bmatrix} c_{e1,1} & .. & .. & .. & c_{e1,5} \\ .. & .. & .. & .. & .. \\ .. & .. & .. & .. & .. \\ c_{e26,1} & .. & .. & .. & c_{e26,5} \end{bmatrix}.$$

Applying a (row) vector of fixed $CO_2$ emission factors per unit of energy type ($\mathbf{em}_{GHG,e}$) to the physical energy consumption by energy type and quintile finally yields the (row) vector of *direct* $CO_2$ emissions of household consumption by quintile $\mathbf{EM}_{GHG,q}$:

$$\mathbf{EM}_{GHG,q} = \mathbf{em}_{GHG,e} [\mathbf{C}_e]. \tag{2.6}$$

### Production, trade and the indirect GHG emissions of households

*The translog model of production*

The model of production links the above described commodity balances of the IO core model (Leontief technologies) of 59 domestic and imported inputs to a Translog model with $K$, $L$, $E$, $M^m$ (imports) and $M^d$ (domestic) factors (for details see the Appendix). The aggregate $E$ comprises five (aggregate) energy commodities, $f$, which are determined in a Translog model of inter-fuel substitution (see the

Appendix for details). This sub-model also determines the bundle price of energy. The *f* aggregate categories of energy (coal, oil, gas, renewable, electricity/heat) are further split up into 26 (*k*) types of energy, from which carbon emissions of production are derived, a part of which constitutes the domestic indirect carbon emissions of households. The imported indirect carbon emissions of households are taken from simulation results with a MRIO model (Arto et al., 2014).

The Translog specification assumes constant returns to scale and perfect competition and incorporates autonomous technical change for all input factors (i.e. the factor biases) as well as total factor productivity (TFP). All data for the production system are derived from the *World Input Output Database* (WIOD) dataset, which contains World Input Output Tables (WIOT) in current and previous years' prices, Environmental Accounts (EA) and Socioeconomic Accounts (SEA). For energy inputs, the data in physical units (TJ) by energy type and user are used. Energy prices by energy type are exogenous, like in the household block of the model. The systems of output price and factor demand equation by industry across the EU 27 have been estimated applying the Seemingly Unrelated Regression (SUR) estimator for the balanced panel under cross-section fixed effects. The estimation results yield values for the own and cross-price elasticity for capital, labour, energy, and imported intermediates, respectively. The average (un-weighted) own price elasticity of labour as well as of energy is about −0.5, while the own price elasticity of imported intermediates (−0.75) and capital (−0.95) is considerably higher.

For energy-intensive industries, their own price elasticity of energy is lower, but the substitution elasticity between energy and capital is slightly higher than the average. Though, also on average, capital and energy are substitutes (though in several sectors complementary). The rate of factor bias in general is very low, and technical progress slightly energy using and labour saving.

*Table 2.3* Parameters for factor demand (price elasticity, factor bias) and wage function

| Production | own price elasticity | cross price elasticity, E/K | rate of factor bias |
|---|---|---|---|
| K, all industries | −0.95 | | 0.00 |
| L, all industries | −0.51 | | −0.01 |
| E, all industries | −0.53 | | 0.02 |
| E, energy intensive | −0.37 | 0.20 | 0.00 |
| all industries | | 0.15 | |
| M(m) | −0.75 | | 0.02 |

| Wage curve | long−run elasticity |
|---|---|
| Consumer price | 0.82 |
| Productivity | 0.27 |
| Unemployment rate | −0.06 |

The labor market is characterized by wage bargaining, formalized in wage curves by industry. These wage curves are specified as the employee's gross wage rate per hour by industry. The labor price (index) of the Translog model is then defined by adding the employers' social security contribution to that. Wage data including hours worked are taken from WIOD Sectoral Accounts and are complemented by labor force data from EUROSTAT. The wage equations have been estimated for the full EU 27 panel. Combining the *meta-analysis* of Folmer (2009) on the empirical wage curve literature with a basic wage bargaining model from Boeters and Savard (2013) gives a specification for the sectoral hourly wages. The un-weighted average of the long-run unemployment elasticity of wages across industries is −0.06. The long-run productivity elasticity of wages is only about 0.3, whereas the consumer price elasticity is close to unity (0.8).

*Energy flows and indirect emissions of final demand*

The set of five energy categories ($f$) of the model of inter-fuel substitution needs to be directly linked to two parts of the model: (i) the energy accounts by industry and detailed fuel category $k$ (26) in physical units (TJ) and (ii) the energy commodities and industries of the use table (NACE/CPA 10, 11, 23, 40) in monetary units. The first link is carried out in the same way as described above for households – i.e. by deflating with a price per unit of physical input (TJ) and applying sub-shares in physical terms. The second link is carried out by applying changes in the structure of the five energy inputs to the use structure matrix of the factor $E$.

The GHG emissions by industry are therefore derived in a similar way as in the case of households. One main difference is that the GHG emissions by industry do not only comprise $CO_2$ emissions stemming from energy input but also $CH_4$ and $N_2O$ emissions (both measured in carbon equivalent). These emissions are directly linked via a (row) vector of fixed emission factors per unit of output ($\mathbf{em}_{GHG,j}$) to the gross output in constant prices of the industries. The data source for these emissions is the EA of the WIOD database.

A matrix of energy input in physical units by industry is further constructed, whose elements represent the energy costs in each industry $j$, ($v_{E,kj}E_j$) divided by given energy prices $p_{E,k}$ and multiplied by the corresponding sub-shares $s_{kj}$, $s_{ekj}\dfrac{v_{E,kj}E_j}{p_{E,k}}$. Applying the same (row) vector of fixed $CO_2$ emission factors per unit of energy type ($\mathbf{em}_{GHG,e}$) as in the consumption block to this energy matrix and the (row) vector of fixed emission factors per unit of output ($\mathbf{em}_{GHG,j}$) yields the (row) vector of domestic $CO_2$ emissions by industry $\mathbf{EM}_{GHG,j}$:

$$\mathbf{EM}_{GHG,j} = \mathbf{em}_{GHG,e}^{d}\left[\mathbf{E}_e\right] + \mathbf{em}_{GHG}^{d}\mathbf{q}. \tag{2.7}$$

Imports by commodity are in this model determined by the sum of final and intermediate demand by commodity. For this purpose, an import shares matrix for final demand $\mathbf{M}^f$ is introduced and applied to the total final demand matrix,

**F** (consisting of the columns of final demand, **c, cf, ex, st, cg**). The elements of matrix $\mathbf{M^f}$ are treated as constant and could alternatively be modelled via the Armington elasticity. Note that the major part of imports (i.e. intermediate goods) is variable and reacts upon prices. Total imports by commodities **IM** are in this framework given by imports of final demand, both energy and non-energy commodities imports and of intermediate inputs (energy), as well as non-energy (the symbol $\otimes$ represents element-by-element multiplication of two matrices.):

$$\mathbf{IM} = \mathbf{M^f} \otimes \mathbf{F} + \left[\hat{\mathbf{V}}_M \mathbf{S}^m_{NE}\right]\mathbf{p}_Q\mathbf{Q} + \left[\hat{\mathbf{V}}_E \mathbf{S}^m_E\right]\mathbf{p}_Q\mathbf{Q}. \tag{2.8}$$

The GHG emissions of imports (in the rest of the world) by import commodity *i* are given by a (row) vector of average coefficients of GHG emissions by one unit of import in the EU27 ($\mathbf{em}^m_{GHG}$) derived from a MRIO (multi-regional input-output) model (Arto et al., 2014).[1] The total imported *indirect* carbon footprint of the economy is therefore given as

$$\mathbf{EM}^m_{GHG} = \mathbf{em}^m_{GHG}\mathbf{IM}. \tag{2.9}$$

*Factor demand in the electricity sector: a bottom-up approach*

In the electricity sector, the Translog function and the inter-fuel substitution model described earlier have been substituted by a bottom-up approach. This approach is based on the link between the energy accounts data for the electricity sector (26 fuel categories in physical units (TJ)) and the column corresponding to the electricity sector of the use table (in monetary units). This link works via prices, defined as monetary values per physical energy unit (TJ). The bottom-up approach based on the energy balance data has the same energy commodities structure as the DYNK model (5 aggregate energy inputs ($f$) and 26 fuel categories ($k$)). This could in principle be extended towards a link to a bottom-up model (such as TIMES) that further disaggregates $k$ into the dimension of different technologies $p$ (in our case, based on the energy balance $p = f$). The main identity for the link of both frameworks is the identity that the factor share for the K,L,E,M factors in the electricity sector are given as the weighted sum of the corresponding factor share (input-output coefficient in monetary terms) of technology $p$ multiplied with the production share of this technology. In the case of the energy share ($v_E$),

$$v_E = \sum_p w_E(p,q) v_E(p). \tag{2.10}$$

The production share of each technology ($w_E(p,q)$) is taken from the energy balance that reports electricity output and fuel input by fuel category. Assuming only one production price for electricity, the physical technology shares ($w_E(p,q)$) can be applied to the electricity output in monetary units as well. The inter-fuel substitution model block of DYNK defines the sub-shares of fuels ($v_{E,f}$) in the total aggregate $E$. Therefore, the relationship between $w_E(p,q)$ and $v_{E,f}$ has to be additionally considered in order to implement the bottom-up data into DYNK. This relationship is defined via the following identity:

$$w_E(p,q) = v_{E,f} \eta(p) v_E. \tag{2.11}$$

Endogeneity problems are avoided by approximating the aggregate energy cost share in (2,11) by its lagged value. The sub-shares ($v_{E,f}$) and the production shares ($w_E(p,q)$) are mainly linked by the efficiency of the corresponding technology, $\eta(p)$. The other term in identity (2.10) – i.e. the cost shares by technology (in equation (10) $v_E(p)$) – is taken from IEA (2015), where the cost categories capital, fuel input and operation and management costs are differentiated. IEA (2015) contains cost data in US\$/MWh for different generation technologies, which have been used to calculate absolute costs (in €) and cost shares of generation technologies in the EU 27 in the base year (2005). This is simply carried out by multiplying the specific cost (US\$/MWh) with the corresponding electricity output (derived from applying $w_E(p,q)$), considering the exchange rate.

The model is then calibrated in order to fulfill identity (ten). Another statistical problem is that the electricity sector in the use table includes distribution of electricity and therefore also includes an input of electricity. This input is considered in intermediate inputs, therefore, and not in the energy aggregate $E$. The fuel shares in Table 2.4 do not include electricity, therefore, and reflect the database of the energy balance. If data from a bottom-up model (TIMES) were available, the number of technologies could be extended accordingly. The cost shares for energy and capital by technology reveal the largest heterogeneity across generation technologies; those for labour and intermediates are within a narrower range.

## Emission reduction scenarios

Two alternative scenarios have been designed and compared to the baseline scenario ("BASE") for Europe until 2050. The scenario "BASE" is characterized by a continuation of trends and in some cases constant variables. The development of output and prices by industry is mainly driven by exogenous import prices and world energy prices, as well as sectoral TFP growth. This in turn drives export demand, which is

*Table 2.4* Production and cost shares by technology, electricity sector (2005)

|  | *Coal* | *Gas* | *Renewables* | *Oil* | *Total Sector* |
|---|---|---|---|---|---|
| Fuel shares* | 0.566 | 0.316 | 0.046 | 0.072 | 1 |
| Energy cost share | 0.371 | 0.470 | 0 | 0.470 | 0.392 |
| Capital cost share | 0.156 | 0.071 | 0.697 | 0.071 | 0.148 |
| Labour cost share | 0.120 | 0.055 | 0.213 | 0.055 | 0.099 |
| Intermediates cost share | 0.034 | 0.016 | 0.061 | 0.016 | 0.028 |

Note: * shares in total energy input, excluding electricity

the main exogenous final demand component. Public consumption is endogenous, as the deficit share in GDP is set exogenously according to the European fiscal policy plans (see the Appendix for details). Technical progress that is relevant for energy demand (efficiency of households' durables, factor bias for energy and fuels in production) is extrapolated according to historical trends. In the scenario "BASE". total energy demand rises slightly and $CO_2$ emissions are constant until 2050.

The scenario "EFF" contains measures for improving energy efficiency in the durable stock of households (buildings, vehicles, electric appliances). For the efficiency scenario, the following assumptions have been made, based on policy simulations for Germany (Ifeu and Prognos, 2011): A scrappage policy is in place for electric appliances and vehicles that reduces the lifetime by two years (vehicles) and five years (appliances). No specific policy is assumed, but some subsidizing scheme is implicitly in place that compensates households so that the path of the capital stock is the same as in the baseline. There are very stringent conditions for entering the scrappage policy in place. As a result, it is assumed that the new purchases of cars of the average household exhibit an energy intensity of 25% below the one in the scenario "BASE". For appliances, the new purchases are 50% less energy intensive (Figure 2.1).

The scrappage policy is in place until 2030 and reduces average energy intensity of the durable stock significantly. After 2030, households start buying less efficient vehicles and appliances again so that – given the relative short lifetime – the gains in energy efficiency are partly lost and the energy intensity of the stocks converges to the same values as in the scenario "BASE" until 2050. Building refurbishment leads to an investment-induced improvement of energy efficiency that lasts until 2050 due to the longer lifetime of buildings. The energy intensity of buildings increases by 35% compared to 2015 by the policy.

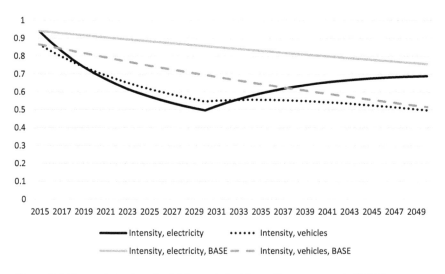

*Figure 2.1* Energy intensity of vehicles and electric appliances, scenario "EFF"

As mentioned earlier, the scenario is based on assumptions and does not model a consistent policy. Real policy analysis needed to incorporate issues such as the financing of the policy and a sub-model of choice that shows the impact of certain scrappage instruments on the energy efficiency of new purchases.

The scenario "RENEW" consists of significantly higher diffusion of renewables in electricity generation at the expense of generation from coal. This scenario consists of defining an alternative path of fuel shares in the bottom-up model of the electricity sector described in the bottom-up approach.

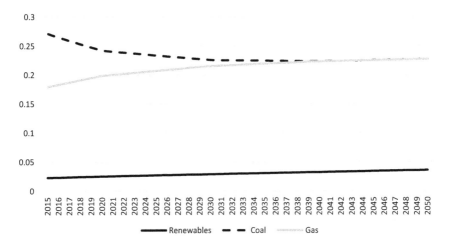

*Figure 2.2* Production shares in electricity production, scenario "BASE"

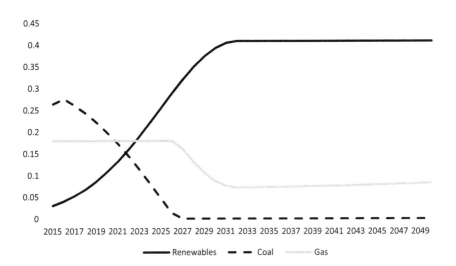

*Figure 2.3* Production shares in electricity production, scenario "RENEW"

In the scenario "BASE", the share of renewables increases continuously, but is still insignificant in 2050. The shares of coal (27% in 2015) and gas (18% in 2015) both converge towards a value between 20 and 25% until 2050. For the scenario "RENEW", it has been assumed that through – not specified and modelled support measures – a higher diffusion of renewables takes place. The share of renewables ($v_{E,R,t}$) develops according to the following logistic curve in this scenario: $v_{E,R,t} = (1 + c + bt)v_{E,R,t-1}$ with parameterization $c = 0.35$ and $b = -0.02$. From 2033 on ($t = 18$), the growth rate of this formula would become negative, and the share therefore has been kept constant from this year on.

Another assumption is that this high diffusion of renewables is achieved at the expense of generation form coal and partly also from gas. Shortly before 2030, electricity generation from coal therefore drops to zero in this scenario.

## Model simulation results

### *The socio-economic impact*

The macroeconomic impact of the scenario "EFF" is characterized by significant positive effects on GDP and employment, driven by higher durable purchases of households. This in turn leads to an increase in the gross output of sectors producing these goods as well as sectors such as basic metal industry and non-metallic minerals that are vertically integrated with the investment goods sectors.

Private consumption (new purchases of durables) and private investment (building refurbishment) are the two final demand categories that drive the development. The increase in income and output triggers higher tax revenues which – for a given deficit target (in % of GDP) – allow for higher public consumption as well. The positive output stimulus also increases labor productivity, which is not fully compensated by wage increases; therefore, price competitiveness and

*Table 2.5* Macroeconomic impact of scenario "EFF" (difference to "BASE" in %)

|  | 2015 | 2020 | 2030 | 2050 |
|---|---|---|---|---|
| GDP, const. prices | 0.20 | 2.36 | 7.83 | 6.33 |
| Private Consumption, const. prices | 0.18 | 2.23 | 5.65 | 4.30 |
| Public Consumption, const. prices | 0.27 | 1.72 | 6.45 | 3.08 |
| Capital formation, const. prices | 0.24 | 1.09 | 4.40 | 4.26 |
| Exports, const. prices | 0.02 | 0.80 | 3.95 | 4.81 |
| Imports, const. prices | 0.11 | −1.14 | −7.92 | −37.12 |
| Employment (persons) | 0.19 | 1.41 | 4.80 | 3.37 |
| Unemployment rate (% points) | −0.15 | −1.10 | −4.07 | 0.00 |
| GHG emissions, households | −0.69 | −6.96 | −16.34 | −12.32 |
| GHG emissions, production | −0.10 | −1.19 | −1.69 | −0.44 |
| GHG emissions, imports | 0.09 | −0.20 | −0.46 | −0.71 |
| GHG emissions, total | −0.09 | −1.44 | −2.59 | −1.47 |

exports are increased as well. At the same, imports decrease due to lower energy demand mainly.

Private consumption of durables as well as of nondurables increases, though consumption of energy goods drops by about 30% (compared to the scenario "BASE") until 2030. During the period the scrappage policy is in place, the impact on real disposable income is higher for the two quintiles at the top of the income distribution than for those at the bottom.

The macroeconomic impact of the scenario "RENEW" reveals considerably smaller positive impacts on GDP and employment than in the scenario "EFF". In the latter, the shorter lifetime of durables and the investment in refurbishing of buildings lead to higher costs, for which households are compensated via the scrappage policies. Therefore, these measures lead to additional consumption expenditure. This kind of additional demand effect is absent in the scenario "RENEW". The stimulus in this scenario stems from higher capital intensity of

*Table 2.6* Impact of scenario "EFF" on households (difference to "BASE" in %)

|  | 2015 | 2020 | 2030 | 2050 |
|---|---|---|---|---|
| Durable consumption, const. prices | 0.92 | 3.14 | 5.23 | 2.79 |
| Nondurable consumption, const. prices | 0.05 | 2.25 | 6.20 | 4.73 |
| Energy, const. prices | −0.98 | −8.93 | −19.93 | −16.67 |
| *Real disposable income, const. prices* | *2015* | *2020* | *2030* | *2050* |
| Total | 0.14 | 2.05 | 5.32 | 4.65 |
| 1st quintile | 0.07 | 1.26 | 3.27 | 4.59 |
| 2nd quintile | 0.14 | 1.92 | 4.65 | 4.53 |
| 3rd quintile | 0.15 | 2.05 | 5.04 | 4.53 |
| 4th quintile | 0.16 | 2.16 | 5.44 | 4.57 |
| 5th quintile | 0.14 | 2.15 | 5.79 | 4.76 |

*Table 2.7* Macroeconomic impact of scenario "RENEW" (difference to "BASE" in %)

|  | 2015 | 2020 | 2030 | 2050 |
|---|---|---|---|---|
| GDP, const. prices | 0.03 | 0.39 | 1.68 | 2.52 |
| Private Consumption, const. prices | 0.00 | 0.06 | 0.48 | 1.56 |
| Public Consumption, const. prices | 0.03 | 0.36 | 1.59 | 2.25 |
| Capital formation, const. prices | 0.10 | 0.73 | 2.14 | 2.56 |
| Exports, const. prices | 0.00 | 0.11 | 0.69 | 1.43 |
| Imports, const. prices | −0.01 | −0.36 | −2.21 | −11.00 |
| Employment (persons) | 0.01 | 0.14 | 0.60 | 1.13 |
| Unemployment rate (% points) | −0.01 | −0.11 | −0.51 | 0.00 |
| GHG emissions, households | 0.00 | 0.00 | 0.05 | 0.31 |
| GHG emissions, production | −0.48 | −6.20 | −21.08 | −17.00 |
| GHG emissions, imports | 0.00 | −0.32 | −1.04 | −0.23 |
| GHG emissions, total | −0.19 | −2.45 | −7.42 | −4.55 |

renewable electricity generation, partly due to higher investment cost per installed capacity (MWh), partly due to lower lifetime (higher user costs of capital). Private investment, therefore, is the final demand component with the highest positive impact in this scenario and via higher tax revenues also boosts public consumption, as well as private consumption via income effects. Exports and imports behave in a similar way, as in the "EFF" scenario, due to productivity and price dampening effects and lower energy imports.

During the period the policy is in place increases the renewables share in the electricity sector (2030), the impact on real disposable income is considerably higher for top than for bottom incomes. Income and consumption are increased much less than in the other scenario and due to an income rebound effect consumption for energy goods also increases (Figure 2.4).

*Table 2.8* Impact of scenario "RENEW" on households (difference to "BASE" in %)

|  | 2015 | 2020 | 2030 | 2050 |
| --- | --- | --- | --- | --- |
| Durable consumption, const. prices | 0.00 | 0.05 | 0.34 | 0.88 |
| Nondurable consumption, const. prices | 0.00 | 0.06 | 0.50 | 1.64 |
| Energy, const. prices | 0.00 | 0.00 | 0.04 | 0.28 |
| *Real disposable income, const. prices* | *2015* | *2020* | *2030* | *2030* |
| Total | 0.02 | 0.20 | 0.88 | 1.96 |
| 1st quintile | 0.01 | 0.06 | 0.42 | 1.71 |
| 2nd quintile | 0.01 | 0.14 | 0.64 | 1.73 |
| 3rd quintile | 0.01 | 0.17 | 0.73 | 1.77 |
| 4th quintile | 0.02 | 0.19 | 0.82 | 1.81 |
| 5th quintile | 0.02 | 0.24 | 1.09 | 2.17 |

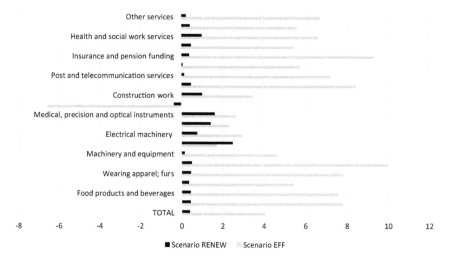

*Figure 2.4* Gross output impact of scenarios (difference to "BASE" in %)

The much higher macroeconomic impact in scenario "EFF" also leads to higher output effects in almost all sectors. The only exception is the sector "office machinery". The electricity sector decreases its output strongly in the "EFF" scenario due to higher efficiency of household appliances. In scenario "RENEW", this sector also exhibits a negative impact on output due to higher costs of electricity generation from renewables, which lead to higher output prices of the sector. All investment goods sectors show above average output effects in scenario "RENEW", as the macroeconomic impact is driven by investment in this scenario. In the scenario "EFF", service sectors and consumer goods also exhibit high output impacts.

### *The impact on $CO_2$ emissions*

The general result is that in scenario "EFF", almost only emissions of households are reduced, whereas indirect emissions (from domestic production and imports) are only reduced by a small amount. In the case of scenario "RENEW", it is mainly the emissions in production that are reduced, while the emissions of households even increase slightly due to an income rebound effect. The overall reduction in emissions – including imported emissions – in both scenarios is between 3% and 7%, and emission reductions are partly compensated by higher indirect emissions (Figure 2.5).

In scenario "EFF", indirect domestic emissions from investment related industries (Other non-metallic mineral products, basic metals, metal products, machinery and equipment, office machinery, electrical machinery, radio/television/communication equipment, medical, precision and optical instruments, motor vehicles, other transport equipment and construction) increase until 2030 and in general compensate half of the emission reduction in energy producing sectors, especially in coke/refined petroleum products/nuclear fuels (Figure 2.6).

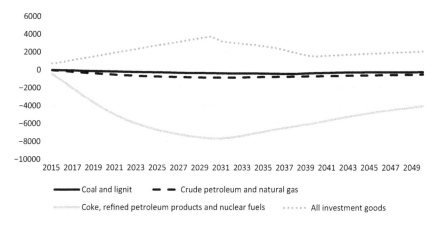

*Figure 2.5* $CO_2$ emission reduction in selected industries (compared to "BASE", kt), scenario "EFF"

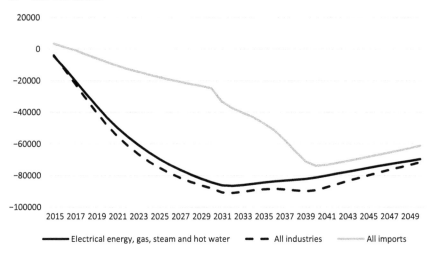

*Figure 2.6* $CO_2$ emission reduction in electricity sector and total (compared to "BASE", kt), scenario "EFF"

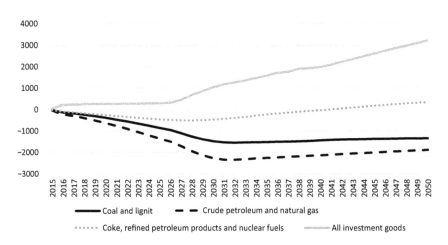

*Figure 2.7* $CO_2$ emission reduction in selected industries (compared to "BASE", kt), scenario "RENEW"

The total domestic indirect emission reduction is mainly determined by the reduction in the electricity sector in scenario "EFF" and slightly decreases after the policy is abandoned (2030). Imported indirect emissions decrease less in the beginning due to positive indirect emission effects from imported investment related activities (basic metals, etc.), and the emission reduction effect also decreases after 2040 (Figure 2.7).

In scenario "RENEW" the indirect emissions from domestic investment related activities increase continuously and almost fully compensate the domestic indirect

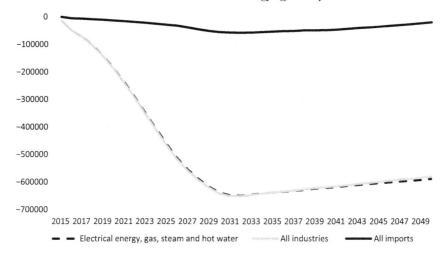

*Figure 2.8* $CO_2$ emission reduction in electricity sector and total (compared to "BASE", kt), scenario "RENEW"

emission reduction from energy sectors (crude petroleum and natural gas, coal and lignite). In this scenario, the total domestic indirect emission reduction is much bigger than in the other scenario and completely determined by emissions reduction in the electricity sector. Due to this high impact of this sector, the reduction in imported indirect emissions that has the same dimension as in scenario "EFF" contributes much less to the total emissions effect (Figure 2.8).

## Conclusions

In aiming for the binding 2° C target, as accorded at the COP21 in Paris in 2015, a deep decarbonization of the European economy will be a prerequisite. Within this policy framework, the European climate policy is characterized by taking on a long-run perspective (up to 2050) with short-term emission reduction targets for the years 2020 and 2030.

This study analyzes two different alternative scenarios of decarbonization (compared to a "BASE" scenario) until 2050. Scenario "EFF" assumes extremely ambitious energy efficiency improvements via scrappage policies for vehicles and electrical appliances as well as investment in the refurbishment of buildings. The other scenario (scenario "RENEW") assumes much higher diffusion of renewables in European electricity generation, mainly crowding out generation from coal.

One aim of the study is to quantify the macroeconomic impacts and indirect emissions of policies that reduce emissions via an increase of capital stocks. The more efficient or less carbon-intensive capital stock reduces emissions after being installed and induces indirect emissions that compensate partly the emission reduction of the measure. In scenario "EFF", the production of the durable goods leads to higher indirect emissions, which partly compensate the emission reduction in the energy producing sectors (coal, oil products and natural gas). Imported indirect emissions are continuously reduced as well. In scenario "RENEW", the higher indirect emissions from the production of capital goods more than compensates the emission reduction in the energy producing sectors (coal, oil products and natural gas). Both scenarios exhibit positive macroeconomic impacts and favor top income households more than those at the bottom of the income distribution. This distributional effect is only derived from the model feedbacks in the scenarios and is not based on the impact of certain financing schemes for the underlying policies (scrappage policy and support scheme for renewables). In both scenarios, an important reduction in indirect emissions stems from the large decrease of emissions in electricity generation. This might be due to the assumption that high efficiency gains can be achieved by scrappage policies in the "EFF" scenario, especially for electrical appliances, and that renewables crowd out the fuel with the highest $CO_2$ emission coefficient (coal). These assumptions are inspired by the literature, but not fully based on a technological bottom-up study. Future research, therefore, should aim at a combined technological bottom-up and top-down model studies. As far as scenarios are concerned, full policy scenarios with the implementation of instruments and their potential economic impacts (financing, etc.) shall be analyzed.

# Appendix

## The DYNK Model

### Household behaviour and private consumption

#### *Durable demand and total nondurables*

Starting point for determining total private consumption is the buffer-stock model developed by Deaton (1991) and Carroll (1997). We apply a specification, where buffer-stock saving is not motivated by income uncertainty but by down payments for purchase of durables, as laid down in Luengo-Prado (2006). Consumers maximize the present discounted value of expected utility from consumption of nondurable commodity and from the service provided by the stocks of durable commodity:

$$\max_{(C_t, K_t)} V = E_0 \left\{ \sum_{t=0}^{\infty} \beta^t U\left(C_t, K_t\right) \right\}. \tag{2.A.1}$$

Specifying a Constant Relative Risk Aversion- (CRRA) utility function and a budget constraint the model can be solved in terms of first order conditions, but not in terms of explicit demand functions. The budget constraint in this model without adjustment costs for the durables stock is given by the definition of assets, $A_t$:

$$A_t = \left(1+r\right)\left(1-t_r\right)A_{t-1} + YD_t - C_t - \left(K_t - \left(1-\delta\right)K_{t-1}\right). \tag{2.A.2}$$

In (A2), the sum of $C_t$ and $\left(K_t - \left(1-\delta\right)K_{t-1}\right)$ represents total consumption – i.e. the sum of nondurable and durable expenditure (with depreciation rate of the durable stock, $\delta$). The gross profit income $rA_{t-1}$ (with interest rate $r$) is taxed with tax rate $t_r$. Disposable household income excluding profit income, $YD_t$, is given as the balance of net wages $\left(1-t_S - t_Y\right)w_t H_t$ and net operating surplus accruing to households $\left(1-t_Y\right)\Pi_{h,t}$, plus transfers $Tr_t$:

$$YD_t = \left(1-t_S - t_Y\right)w_t H_t + \left(1-t_Y\right)\Pi_{h,t} + Tr_t. \tag{2.A.3}$$

The following taxes are charged on household income: social security contributions with tax rate $t_S$, which can be further decomposed into an employee and an employer's tax rate $(t_{wL}$ and $t_L)$ and income taxes with tax rate $t_Y$. The wage rate

$w_t$ is the wage per hour and $H_t$ are total hours demanded by firms. Wage bargaining between firms and unions takes place over the employee's gross wage, i.e. $w_t (1 - t_L)$.

All the income categories are modelled at the level of quintiles $q$ of household incomes ($q = 1 \ldots 5$):

$$YD_t = \sum_q \left[ \left( 1 - t_{S,q} - t_{Y,q} \right) w_{t,q} H_{t,q} + (1 - t_{Y,q}) \Pi_{t,q} + Tr_{t,q} \right]. \tag{2.A.4}$$

Financial assets of households are built up by saving after durable purchasing has been financed, and the constraint for lending is

$$A_t + (1 - \theta) K_t \geq 0. \tag{2.A.5}$$

This term represents voluntary equity holding, as the equivalent of the other part of the durable stock ($\theta K_t$) needs to be held as equity. The consideration of the collateralized constraint is operationalized in a down payment requirement parameter $\theta$, which represents the fraction of durables purchases that a household is not allowed to finance. One main variable in the buffer-stock model of consumption is "cash on hand", $X_t$, measuring the household's total resources: $X_t = (1 + r_t)(1 - t_t)A_{t-1} + (1 - \delta)K_{t-1} + YD_t$. The model is specified here in the form of demand functions that are consistent with the model properties. These comprise non-linear consumption functions for durables, which are based on the concave shape of the policy functions for consumption in Luengo-Prado (2006), and where with higher levels of durables per household ($K_t/h_t$) the marginal propensity of investment in durables, $C_{Kt}$ with respect to $X_t$, decreases. The down payment parameter $\theta$ in Luengo-Prado (2006) represents a long-term constraint between the liabilities stock and the durable stock of households and is specified here by imposing limits to the down payment for durable purchases. Durables in this model are owned houses (dwelling investment) and vehicles. The long-run demand functions for the two durable categories ($C_{dur,t}$) is a function of "cash on hand" ($X_t$), the down payment for durable purchases ($\theta_{Ct}$) and static user costs of durables, $p_{dur,t}(r_t + \delta)$.

$$\log C_{dur,t} = \log C_{dur,t} \left[ \log X_t, \theta_{Ct}, \log \left( p_{dur,t}(r_t + \delta) \right), \log \left( K_{t-1}/h_{t-1} \right) \right] \tag{2.A.6}$$

The long-run demand function for total nondurable consumption is a function of "cash on hand" and down payments for durable purchases ($\theta_{Ct} \log C_{dur,t}$):

$$\log C_{nondur,t} = \log C_{nondur,t} \left[ \log X_t, \theta_{Ct} \log C_{dur,t} \right]. \tag{2.A.7}$$

The latter considers that households need to finance down payments, and will not do so by savings in the same period but will smooth nondurable consumption accordingly. The estimation is carried out as error correction panel data estimation and the results are used to calibrate the model at the level of the 5 quintiles of income, which are characterized by different values for the durable stocks per household. Therefore, the model contains growth rates for $C_{dur,t}$ and $C_{nondur,t}$ for each quintile ($q$).

### *Energy demand*

The energy demand of households comprises fuel for transport, electricity and heating. These demands are part of total nondurable consumption and separability from non-energy nondurable consumption is assumed. In line with the literature on the rebound effect (Khazzoom, 1989), the energy demand is modelled as (nominal) service demand, and the service aspect is dealt with via service prices. The durable stock of households (vehicles, houses, appliances) embodies the efficiency of converting an energy flow into a service level $S = \eta_{ES} E$, where $E$ is the energy demand for a certain fuel and S is the demand for a service inversely linked by the efficiency parameter ($\eta_{ES}$) of converting the corresponding fuel into a certain service. For a given conversion efficiency, a service price, $p_S$, (marginal cost of service) can be derived, which is a function of the energy price and the efficiency parameter: $p_S = p_E/\eta_{ES}$. Any increase in efficiency leads to a decrease in the service price and thereby to an increase in service demand ("rebound effect").

For transport demand of private households, we take substitution between public ($C_{pub}$) and private transport ($C_{fuel}$) into account. The price for fuels, $pc_{S,fuel}$, is defined as a service price. Total transport demand of households depends on the composite price of private and public transport, as well as on total nondurable expenditure. The demand for transport fuels is linked to the vehicle stock and depends on the service price of fuels as well as on the endowment of vehicles of the population. The latter term is important because the second car of the household usually is used less in terms of miles driven than the first.

$$\log\left(\frac{C_{fuel,t}}{K_{veh,t}}\right) = \mu_{fuel} + \gamma_{fuel} \log\left(\frac{p_{fuel,t}}{\eta_{fuel,t}}\right) + \xi_{fuel} \log\left(\frac{K_{veh,t}}{h_t}\right) \qquad (2.A.8)$$

In (A8) $\mu_{fuel}$ is a constant or a cross-section fixed effect and $\gamma_{fuel}$ is the price elasticity under the condition that there is a unitary elasticity of fuel demand to the vehicle stock.

The equations for heating and electricity demand are analogous to equation (A8) and have the following form:

$$\log\left(\frac{C_{heat,t}}{K_{hous,t}}\right) = \mu_{heat} + \gamma_{heat} \log\left(\frac{p_{heat,t}}{\eta_{heat,t}}\right) + \xi_{heat} \log\left(dd_{heat}\right), \qquad (2.A.9)$$

$$\log\left(\frac{C_{el,t}}{K_{app,t}}\right) = \mu_{el} + \gamma_{el} \log\left(\frac{p_{el,t}}{\eta_{el,t}}\right) + \xi_{el} \log\left(dd_{heat}\right). \qquad (2.A.10)$$

In both equations, the variable heating degree days, $dd_{heat}$, is added. The durable stocks used are the total housing stock ($K_{hous,t}$) and the appliance stock ($K_{app,t}$).

The latter is accumulated from consumption of appliances, $C_{app}$, which in turn is explained in a log linear specification like total transport demand.

### Nondurable (non-energy) demand

The non-energy demand of nondurables is treated in a demand system. The one applied in this DYNK model is the Almost Ideal Demand System (AIDS), starting from the cost function for $C(u, p_i)$, describing the expenditure function (for C) as a function of a given level of utility $u$ and prices of consumer goods, $p_i$ (Deaton and Muellbauer, 1980). The AIDS model is represented by the budget share equations for the $i$ nondurable goods in each period:

$$w_i = \alpha_i + \sum_j \gamma_{ij} \log p_j + \beta_i \log\left(\frac{C}{P}\right); i = 1 \ldots n, j = 1 \ldots k, \qquad (2.A.11)$$

with price index, $P_t$, defined by $\log P_t = \alpha_0 + \sum_i \alpha_i \log p_{it} + 0.5 \sum_i \sum_j \gamma_{ij} \log p_{it}$
$\log p_{jt}$, often approached by the Stone price index: $\log P_t^* = \sum_k w_{it} \log p_{it}$. The expressions for expenditure ($\eta_i$) and compensated price elasticities ($\varepsilon_{ij}^C$) within the AIDS model for the quantity of each consumption category $C_i$ can be written as (the details of the derivation can be found in Green, and Alston, 1990)[2]:

$$\eta_i = \frac{\partial \log C_i}{\partial \log C} = \frac{\beta_i}{w_i} + 1, \qquad (2.A.12)$$

$$\varepsilon_{ij}^C = \frac{\partial \log C_i}{\partial \log p_j} = \frac{\gamma_{ij} - \beta_i w_j}{w_i} - \delta_{ij} + \varepsilon_i w_j. \qquad (2.A.13)$$

In (2.A.13), $\delta_{ij}$ is the Kronecker delta with $\delta_{ij} = 0$ for $i \neq j$ and $\delta_{ij} = 1$ for $i = j$.

The commodity classification $i = 1 \ldots n$ in this model comprises the $n$ non-energy nondurables: (i) food and beverages, tobacco, (ii) clothing and footwear, (iii) furniture and household equipment, (iv) health, (v) communication, (vi) recreation and accommodation, (vii) financial services and (viii) other commodities and services.

## Firm behaviour and production structure

### Substitution in a K,L,E,M^m,M^d model

The model is set up with inputs of capital ($K$), labor ($L$), energy ($E$), imported ($M^m$) and domestic non-energy materials ($M^d$) and their corresponding input prices $p_K$,

$p_L$, $p_E$, $p_{Mm}$ and $p_{Md}$. Each industry faces a unit cost function for the price ($p_Q$) of output $Q$, with constant returns to scale:

$$\log p_Q = \alpha_0 + \sum_i \alpha_i \log(p_i) + \frac{1}{2}\sum_i \gamma_{ii}\left(\log(p_i)\right)^2 + \sum_{i,j}\gamma_{ij}\log(p_i)$$

$$\log(p_j) + \alpha_t t + \frac{1}{2}\alpha_{tt}t^2 + \sum_i \rho_{ti}t\log(p_i), \tag{2.A.14}$$

where $p_Q$ is the output price (unit cost); $p_i$, $p_j$ are the input prices for input quantities $x_i$, $x_j$ and $t$ is the deterministic time trend, TFP is measured by $\alpha_t$; and $\alpha_{tt}$. Shepard's Lemma yields the cost share equations in the Translog case, which in this case of five inputs can be written as

$$v_K = \left[\alpha_K + \gamma_{KK}\log(p_K/p_{Md}) + \gamma_{KL}\log(p_L/p_{Md}) + \gamma_{KE}\log(p_E/p_{Md})\right.$$
$$\left. + \gamma_{KM}\log(p_{Mm}/p_{Md}) + \rho_{tK}t\right]$$

$$v_L = \left[\alpha_L + \gamma_{LL}\log(p_L/p_{Md}) + \gamma_{KL}\log(p_K/p_{Md}) + \gamma_{LE}\log(p_E/p_{Md})\right.$$
$$\left. + \gamma_{LM}\log(p_{Mm}/p_{Md}) + \rho_{tL}t\right]$$

$$v_E = \left[\alpha_E + \gamma_{EE}\log(p_E/p_{Md}) + \gamma_{KE}\log(p_K/p_{Md}) + \gamma_{LE}\log(p_L/p_{Md})\right.$$
$$\left. + \gamma_{EM}\log(p_{Mm}/p_{Md}) + \rho_{tE}t\right]$$

$$v_M = \left[\alpha_M + \gamma_{MM}\log(p_{Mm}/p_{Md}) + \gamma_{KM}\log(p_K/p_{Md}) + \gamma_{LM}\log(p_L/p_{Md})\right.$$
$$\left. + \gamma_{EM}\log(p_E/p_{Md}) + \rho_{tM}t\right]. \tag{2.A.15}$$

The homogeneity restriction for the price parameters $\sum_i \gamma_{ij} = 0$, $\sum_j \gamma_{ij} = 0$ has already been imposed in (A15) so that the terms for the price of domestic intermediates $p_{Md}$ have been omitted. The immediate *ceteris paribus* reaction to price changes is given by the own and cross-price elasticity. These own- and cross-price elasticities for changes in input quantity $x_i$ are given as

$$\varepsilon_{ii} = \frac{\partial \log x_i}{\partial \log p_i} = \frac{v_i^2 - v_i + \gamma_{ii}}{v_i} \tag{2.A.16}$$

$$\varepsilon_{ij} = \frac{\partial \log x_i}{\partial \log p_j} = \frac{v_i v_j + \gamma_{ij}}{v_i}. \tag{2.A.17}$$

Here the $v_i$ represent the factor shares in equation (A15) and the $\gamma_{ij}$ the cross-price parameters. The rate of factor bias, i.e. the impact of $t$ on factor $x_i$ without considering TFP is given by

$$\frac{d \log x_i}{dt} = \frac{\rho_{ti}}{v_i}. \tag{2.A.18}$$

Factor prices are exogenous for the derivation of factor demand, but are endogenous in the system of supply and demand. Some factor prices are directly linked to the output prices $p_Q$, which are determined in the same system. All user prices are the weighted sum of the domestic price $p^d$ and the import price, $p^m$. The import price of commodity $i$ in country $s$ is given as the weighted sum of the commodity prices of the $k$ sending countries ($p^{d,k}$). Once the (user-specific) import prices for intermediate goods are given, the price vectors of total domestic ($\mathbf{p}_{Md}$) and imported ($\mathbf{p}_{Mm}$) intermediate inputs by industry can be calculated. Within the bundle of intermediate inputs ($M^m$ and $M^d$), which comprises 55 non-energy industries/commodities, Leontief technology is assumed. These bundles are defined by the "use structure matrices" ($\mathbf{S}_{NE}^m$ and $\mathbf{S}_{NE}^d$) with column sum of unity.

$$\mathbf{p}_{Mm} = \mathbf{p}^m \mathbf{S}_{NE}^m \qquad \mathbf{p}_{Md} = \mathbf{p}^d \mathbf{S}_{NE}^d \qquad (2.A.19)$$

The price of capital is based on the user cost of capital: $u_K = p_{CF}(r + \delta)$, with $p_{CF}$ as the price of investment goods an industry is buying, $r$ as the deflated benchmark interest rate and $\delta$ as the aggregate depreciation rate of the capital stock $K$. The investment goods price $p_{CF}$ can be defined as a function of the domestic commodity prices and import prices, given the input structures for investment, derived from the capital formation matrix for domestic ($\mathbf{B}_K^d$) and imported ($\mathbf{B}_K^m$) investment demand:

$$\mathbf{p}_{CF} = \mathbf{p}^m \mathbf{B}_K^m + \mathbf{p}^d \mathbf{B}_K^d. \qquad (2.A.20)$$

The price of labor is endogenous as well and determined in the labor market. The prices of energy types are assumed to be determined at world markets for energy and are therefore treated as exogenous. A specific feature of capital is that two prices of this input can be formulated: (i) the *ex post* rate of return to $K$ (derived from operating surplus) and (ii) the *ex ante* rate of return to $K$ – i.e. the user cost. In economic terms, that represents an imperfect capital market, which can be in disequilibrium. It is assumed that after the base year, this adjustment takes place instantaneously.

### Energy inputs in production and the domestic indirect carbon footprint of households

The aggregate $E$ comprises five energy industries/commodities. In a second nest, the factor $E$ is split up into $f$ aggregate categories of energy (coal, oil, gas, renewable, electricity/heat) in a Translog model. The unit cost function of this model determines the bundle price of energy, $p_E$, and the cost shares of the five aggregate energy types ($i = f$):

$$\log p_E = \alpha_0 + \sum_i \alpha_{E,i} \log(p_{E,i}) + \frac{1}{2} \sum_i \gamma_{E,ii} \left( \log(p_{E,i}) \right)^2$$
$$+ \sum_{i,j} \gamma_{E,ij} \log(p_i) \log(p_j) + \sum_i \rho_{tE,i} t \log(p_{E,i}), \qquad (2.A.21)$$

$$v_{E,i} = \left[ \alpha_{E,i} + \sum_{i,j} \gamma_{E,ij} \log(p_{E,i}) + \rho_{tE,i} t \right].$$    (2.A.22)

In some cases, the elasticity of inter-fuel substitution is very close to zero, but most industries show a value of straying around −0.5. The cross-price elasticity also shows negative signs in a large number of industries, indicating complementarity between fuels.

### Government and model closure

The public sector balances close the model and show the main interactions between households, firms and the general government. Taxes from households and firms are endogenized via tax rates and the path of the deficit per GDP share according to the EU stability programs is included as a restriction. Wage income of households is taxed with social security contributions (tax rates $t_{wL}$ and $t_L$) and wage income plus operating surplus accruing to households are taxed with income taxes (tax rate $t_y$). Additionally, households' gross profit income is taxed with tax rate $t_r$. Taxes less subsidies are not only levied on private consumption, but also on the other final demand components in purchaser prices ($\mathbf{f}_{pp}$, comprising capital formation, changes in stocks, exports and public consumption), as well as on gross output. The expenditure side of government is made up of transfers to households ($Tr$), public investment ($cf_{gov}$) and public consumption ($cg$). Additionally, the government pays interest with interest rate $r_{gov}$ on the stock of public debt, $D_{gov}$.

The model is closed by further fixing the public budget constraint, which defines the future path of government net lending to GDP ($p_yY$). Linking public investment with a fixed ratio ($w_{cf}$) to public consumption and introducing the net lending to GDP constraint, public consumption is then derived as the endogenous variable that closes the model:

$$cg\left(1 + w_{cf}\right) = \Delta D_{gov,t} / p_y Y - r_{gov,t} D_{gov,t-1} - Tr + \left(t_{wL} + t_L\right) w_t H_t$$
$$+ t_Y \left(w_t H_t + \Pi_{h,t}\right) + t_r r_t A_{t-1} + \hat{\mathbf{T}}_N \left[ \mathbf{c}_{pp,t} + \mathbf{f}_{pp,t} + \mathbf{p}_{Q,t} \mathbf{Q}_t \right].$$    (2.A.23)

### Notes

1  We are indebted to Iñaki Arto for providing us with the aggregate results of his work for the EU27.
2  The derivation of the budget share with respect to log ($C$) and log ($p_j$) is given by $\beta_i$ and $\gamma_{ij} - \beta_i$ (log(P)), respectively. Applying Shephard's Lemma and using the Stone price approximation, the elasticity formulae can then be derived.

### References

Arto, I., Rueda-Cantuche, J. M., and Peters, G. P. (2014). Comparing the GTAP-MRIO and WIOD databases for carbon footprint analysis. *Economic Systems Research*, 26(3), 327–353.

Attanasio, O. P., and Weber, G. (1995). Is consumption growth consistent with intertemporal optimization? Evidence from the consumer expenditure survey. *Journal of Political Economy, 103*(6), 1121–1157.

Boeters, S., and Savard, L. (2013). The labor market in computable general equilibrium models. In P. Dixon & D. W. Jorgenson (Eds.), *Handbook of CGE modeling* (Vol. 1, pp. 1645–1718). Elsevier, Amsterdam.

Carroll, C. D. (1997). Buffer-stock saving and the life cycle/permanent income hypothesis. *The Quarterly Journal of Economics, 112*(1), 1–55.

Daly, H. E., Scott, K., Strachan, N., and Barrett, J. (2015). Indirect $CO_2$ emission implications of energy system pathways: Linking IO and TIMES models for the UK. *Environmental Science & Technology, 49*(17), 10701–10709.

Deaton, A. (1991). Saving and liquidity constraints. *Econometrica, 59*(5), 1221–1248. doi: 10.2307/2938366

Deaton, A., and Muellbauer, J. (1980). An almost ideal demand system. *The American Economic Review, 70*(3), 312–326.

Fagnart, J.-F., and Germain, M. (2016). Net energy ratio, EROEI and the macroeconomy. *Structural Change and Economic Dynamics, 37*, 121–126.

Folmer, K. (2009). *Why do macro wage elasticities diverge: A meta analysis.* Central Planning Bureau (CPB) Discussion Paper(122).

Green, R., and Alston, J. M. (1990). Elasticities in AIDS models. *American Journal of Agricultural Economics, 72*(2), 442–445.

IEA. (2012). *World Energy Outlook 2012.* Paris, France: IEA.

IEA. (2015). *Projected costs of generating electricity* (2015 ed.). Paris, France: IEA.

Ifeu, F. I., and Prognos, G. (2011). Energieeffizienz: Potenziale, volkswirtschaftliche Effekte und innovative Handlungs-und Förderfelder für die Nationale Klimaschutzinitiative. *Endbericht des Projektes „Wissenschaftliche Begleitforschung zu übergreifenden technischen, ökologischen, ökonomischen und strategischen Aspekten des nationalen Teils der Klimaschutzinitiative",* Heidelberg, Karlsruhe, Berlin, Osnabrück, Freiburg.

Kagawa, S., Nansai, K., and Kudoh, Y. (2009). Does product lifetime extension increase our income at the expense of energy consumption? *Energy Economics, 31*(2), 197–210.

Khazzoom, J. D. (1989). Energy savings from more efficient appliances: a rejoinder. *The Energy Journal, 10*(1), 157–166.

Luengo-Prado, M. J. (2006). Durables, nondurables, down payments and consumption excesses. *Journal of Monetary Economics, 53*(7), 1509–1539.

Salotti, S., Montinari, L., Amores, A. F., and Rueda-Cantuche, J. M. (2015). *Total expenditure elasticity of non-durable consumption of European households.* Joint Research Centre/IPTS, Seville.

Schumacher, K., and Sands, R. D. (2007). Where are the industrial technologies in energy – economy models? An innovative CGE approach for steel production in Germany. *Energy Economics, 29*(4), 799–825.

# 3 Global renewable energy diffusion in an input-output framework

*Kirsten S. Wiebe*

## Introduction: emissions and technology diffusion

> Affordable, scalable solutions are now available to enable countries to leapfrog to cleaner, more resilient economies. The pace of change is quickening as more people are turning to renewable energy and a range of other measures that will reduce emissions and increase adaptation efforts.

> But climate change is a global challenge that does not respect national borders. Emissions anywhere affect people everywhere. It is an issue that requires solutions that need to be coordinated at the international level and it requires international cooperation to help developing countries move toward a low-carbon economy. SDG Goal 13: Take urgent action to combat climate change and its impacts

> (UN, 2016)

> Existing clean technologies, if implemented in our daily lives, could cut our energy consumption by half. Action does not need to come in the form of mega projects, either. Simple things, such as installing LED lights, properly insulating homes, building with lightweight materials and using electric vehicles are all examples of where consumers and businesses can make a difference. We need to get our head around the fact that lower greenhouse gas emissions and less waste mean having a healthier planet.

> Bertrand Piccard, Initiator, Chairman, and Pilot of Solar Impulse and UNEP Goodwill Ambassador

> (Piccard, 2016)

The Paris Agreement adopted in December 2015 represents the consensus of 195 nations in the world that the increase of anthropogenic GHG emissions in the atmosphere needs to be radically slowed in the short term and reversed in the medium and long terms. The breadth of the consensus and the ambition of the target are unprecedented. It is a major step toward a new era of international collaboration in climate change mitigation.

One of the most controversially discussed topics during the negotiations was the financing of climate change mitigation and adaptation in developing countries.

Developed countries are expected to significantly contribute to the financing of the corresponding technologies in developing countries. A wide spectrum of technologies is required to deal with mitigation and adaptation, and while mitigation technologies are readily available, technologies supporting adaptation to climate change still need to be developed and tailored to the specific (though uncertain) circumstances brought about by a changing climate. An important tool in the Paris Agreement to achieve a global diffusion of clean technologies is the UNF-CCC Technology Mechanism (CTCN, 2013; UNFCCC, 2015) – a mechanism that supports the transfer of technologies from developed countries to developing countries. This transfer is to be facilitated through two bodies: i) the Technology Executive Committee (TEC) and ii) and the Climate Technology Centre and Network (CTCN). Established in 2010 at COP16 (UNFCCC, 2011) ¡, and operational since 2014 the CTCN, provides a platform by which countries are able to express demand for transfers. But it is not yet used widely enough to build networks between the recipient and source countries to facilitate technology transfer to a significant extent (De Coninck and Sagar, 2015). As Shimada and Kennedy (2015, p. 5) state, "The Technology Mechanism is responding to developing countries' climate technology needs, bridging gap between planning of climate technology actions and implementation, and supporting developing countries to scale-up and replicate climate technology actions".

Using a different perspective on emissions – i.e. emissions embodied in final consumption goods (consumption-based or final-product-based emissions) rather than production-based emissions – can induce technology transfers for two reasons:

1   Policymakers in the EU are trying to find a way to reduce consumption-based emissions (projects for the European Commission DG RESEARCH (Carbon-CAP 2013; Schanes et al., 2016) and DG CLIMA (Wiebe et al., 2016)). Directly influencing policies abroad, to decrease emissions during production abroad, is almost impossible. Plus, public institutions are inert, especially when it comes to international collaboration. But renewable power generation technologies have been employed on an increasing scale globally, the more the costs of these technologies decreased. Following the learning concept from technology diffusion literature, costs decrease with increasing capacity installations. Hence the EU can indirectly influence capacity installations elsewhere in the world by increasing deployment of renewable power generation technologies within the EU. This will then decrease the EU's consumption-based emissions.

2   Data on the emissions embodied in final products produced by industries can reduce the psychological distance of producers to the climate change problem, making them increasingly aware of how their actions and choices influence emissions in other parts of the world. This knowledge may then further increase competition by giving final products producers the opportunity to compare their environmental global supply chain management with the industry averages in their country and other countries. By reducing these two psychological barriers to climate change mitigation (Stoknes, 2014, 2015),

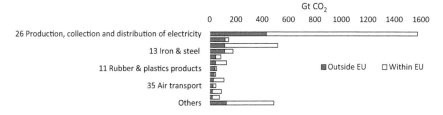

*Figure 3.1* Industries emitting $CO_2$ emissions embedded in goods consumed in the EU28 in 2010 in Mt $CO_2$ according to origin (emitted within EU28 or outside EU28)

Note: These figures exclude direct emissions from final demand, such as private road transport and other emissions directly produced by final consumption of fossil fuels. These are produced and "consumed" domestically and not traded internationally, thus not changing the amount of emissions embodied in imports.

Source: Own calculations based on the GRAM model

firms can be motivated to actively engage in technology transfers to reduce emissions in their upstream production processes.

Data on consumption-based emissions show that the major part of emissions embodied in final consumption goods imported from outside the EU occurred during electricity production (see Figure 3.1). These numbers clearly show that decarbonizing the electricity industry globally is essential for decreasing emissions embodied in imports into the EU. The IEA envisages that about 40% of investments into energy efficiency and low carbon technology will need to go into decarbonizing the power sector and the remaining $8.3 trillion into the transport, buildings and industry sectors (IEA, 2015a, 2015b).

The remainder of this chapter is organized as follows: first, modelling technological change regarding renewable power generation technologies in input-output systems will be explained. Section 3 analyzes European consumption-based $CO_2$ emissions with and without technology diffusion. Section 4 then introduces an idea of how to further use the data generated from MRIO analysis to reduce the psychological distance of producers to climate change and for determining possible destinations for technology transfer. Section 5 concludes the chapter.

## Modelling technological change in forward looking input-output models

The literature on technology advancements in an economy differentiates between different stages of technological change: invention, innovation and diffusion. Given the meso-economic (industry level) perspective of IOA, the analysis of technological change in the context of IO models focuses on the diffusion stage of technological advancements of an economy. Thus the new product has been invented (i.e. someone came up with the idea) and innovated (the new product/process can be produced/implemented at a marketable scale). This means that the production recipe of the new product is known – i.e. which intermediate products/ processes are necessary and how much.

Technology in IO models is represented in the intermediate input coefficient matrix **A**. This matrix is calculated by dividing the entries of intermediate flow matrix **Z** with the corresponding industry output in vector **x**:

$$A = Z\hat{x}^{-1}. \tag{3.1}$$

Depending on whether it is a product by product or industry by industry symmetric input-output table, column $j$ of **A** gives the average technology by which products of product group $j$ or the products produced by industry $j$ are produced. Thus, the technology in input-output models is represented not at the product level, but only at the level of industries or product groups. In the following, we will focus on industry-by-industry tables, but the same methodology can be applied to product-by-product symmetric IOTs or product-by-industry supply-and-use tables (SUTs).

If technologies, such as renewable power generation technologies (RPGTs), are increasingly diffused around the world, different parts of the input-output tables are changing. First, there is investment in the new technologies, and they need to be produced. To identify the change in the IOT, the industry that produces the new technology needs to be identified. A new production technology is an investment in gross capital formation (GCF) – i.e. increased investment spending on products of that industry (IOT change 1: GCF of technology production). If that industry then produces more of that technology compared to other products, the input coefficients change (IOT change 2: input coefficients of technology production). Then the use of the new technology in the production of products might change intermediate inputs of the industry where it is used (IOT change 3: input coefficients of technology use). For example, using more RPGTs in electricity generation reduces the input of coal and gas into the electricity industry. Then, the last change, and the most crucial one in terms of climate change impacts, is the effect of the use of the new technology on the carbon emissions associated with the industry using the new technology (IOT change 4: emission intensity of technology use). If more RPGTs are used and less coal and gas, the emissions of the electricity industry decrease per unit of electricity produced (in physical and monetary terms). Figure 3.2 shows where the changes occur for the diffusion of wind energy in a schematic representation of an input-output system.

In the base year (usually the last year for which data is available), some initial values need to be calculated from the system. The most important additional information that is necessary is the share of the new technology in the technology producing industry $S$, the intermediate input coefficients of the technology and the current investment into that technology. Given the row and column balance in IOTs, the share $S$ can be calculated from the current investment into the technology (considering exports of that technology as well and assuming that the new technology is recorded as an investment good in the IOT, not as an intermediate good).

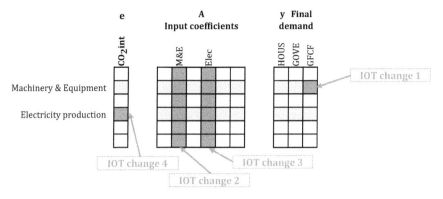

*Figure 3.2* Technology diffusion related changes in an environmentally extended input-output framework: the example of wind turbines

Note: Wind turbines are produced by the "Machinery & Equipment" industry (M&E). Thus an increased diffusion of wind turbines is reflected through a change in the investment in M&E (IOT change 1), changing intermediate input coefficients due to the increased share of wind turbines in the total production of the M&E industry (IOT change 2). Then, more wind turbines are used for electricity production (Elec), thus less coal and gas is needed, changing the input coefficients of the electricity industry (IOT change 3). This in turn reduces the $CO_2$ intensity ($CO_2$int) of the electricity industry.

Source: Own illustration

The necessary changes in the IOT are explained using the example of wind turbines, which are produced by the machinery and equipment (M&E) industry (ISIC Rev. 3 D29 and ISIC Rev. 4 C28).

*IOT change 1*: For estimating the wind turbine related spending on investment in M&E, one needs the additional capacity installations in MW and the costs per MW of RPGT installed in the base year. If these are known, the share $S_0$ of wind turbines in total output of the industry can be calculated for the base year (0). Then, for modelling the development in the future, the additional capacity installations and their price can be used to project the investment in wind turbines and the general projection model will be used to project the development of investments in products of the remaining M&E industry. Thus giving share $S_t$ for year $t$.

*IOT change 2*: The current technology representation of the M&E industry is given by column $j$ of the intermediate coefficient matrix $\mathbf{a}_{.j}$. To separate wind turbines from this, the share $S$ of wind turbines in total output of the industry is necessary. The input coefficients for wind turbines are given in $\mathbf{a}_{WIND}$. The input coefficients of industry M&E excluding wind can be calculated as $\mathbf{a}_{.M\&E} = \dfrac{1}{(1-s_0)}\left[\mathbf{a}_{.j} + s_0\,\mathbf{a}_{.WIND}\right]$. In the projections, the share $S$ changes over time depending on the relative development of investments in wind and demand for products by M&E, excluding wind turbines. The total input coefficient vector in year $t$ can be calculated as $\mathbf{a}_{.j,t} = (1 - s_t) \mathbf{a}_{.M\&E} + s_t \mathbf{a}_{.WIND}$.

*IOT change 3*: This change depends on the exact structure of the IOT and what kind of model is used to do the projections in the future. But the general assumption should be that all installed RPGTs should be used for electricity production. Then, depending on the country's policy, other power generation technologies are used: Nuclear power stations are also used to full capacity, while coal and gas fired power plants are easier to adjust to actual power demand. For the results presented in the next section, the energy industry was represented in detail using the IEA's energy balances (IEA, 2015d). Electricity demand was calculated from the macro-economic projection model and electricity production was adjusted accordingly, using the hierarchy mentioned earlier.

*IOT change 4*: The emission intensity coefficient of the electricity coefficient was then calculated using constant $CO_2$ emission factors, the physical use of energy carriers and the monetary demand for electricity from the macro-economic model.

If, as for example in EXIOBASE (Tukker et al., 2013), the electricity industry in the IOTs is split according to energy carriers, IOT changes 3 and 4 need to be modelled slightly differently: e.g. the D-tour using the energy balances is not necessary. However, if the changes are to be introduced in IOTs with one aggregated electricity industry such as GRAM (Wiebe et al., 2012), which is used for the results in the next section, the OECD ICIO (Wiebe and Yamano, 2016) or WIOD (Timmer et al., 2014), a more detailed representation of the electricity industry is necessary outside the IOT.

All of these changes are applied to the individual countries' input-output tables. These can then be reorganized into a multi-regional input-output table using trade data. Using the basic Leontief inverse equation and its environmentally extended form (of the global MRIO system) and assuming that economic development is demand driven, both industry output $\mathbf{x}$ and associated environmental pollution $\mathbf{P}$ can be calculated by

$$\mathbf{x} = (\mathbf{I} - \mathbf{A})^{-1} \mathbf{y}, \tag{3.2}$$

$$\mathbf{P} = \hat{\mathbf{e}} (\mathbf{I} - \mathbf{A})^{-1} \mathbf{y}. \tag{3.3}$$

As there is no exogenous output or value added data available for the projections, no balancing of the IOTs after applying the different changes to the structure is necessary.

## Endogenous technological change and technology diffusion

Technological change, here the diffusion of technologies, can be modelled using the concept of learning curves. Learning curves relate the cost of a technology to the cumulative amount that has been produced by a technology (learning-by-doing, first introduced by Arrow, 1962) and, in case of a two-factor learning curve, to the cumulative research efforts that have gone into the technology (learning-by-(re)searching; Cohen and Levinthal, 1989). The theory is that the more of the technology is produced, the lower the costs are due to learning (increased efficiency of the production process) and economies of scale. Kahouli-Brahmi (2008) surveyed learning-by-doing and learning-by-(re)searching rates estimated in different energy-environment-economy models between 1974 and 2007. The learning-by-doing rates for photovoltaic (PV) are found to be 20% on average, while those for wind are about 11% on average. This means that for every doubling of the amount of PV or Wind capacity installed (i.e. the technology produced), costs for the technology are have decreased by 20% and 11%, respectively. The learning rates estimated here, based on data by Bloomberg New Energy Finance (2012) (for global capacity and world average prices per MW) and OECD and IEA (2013) (for RD&D), are slightly more conservative: 17% for PV and 3.8% for Wind (Wiebe and Lutz, 2016).

These estimates are implemented in the renewable power generation module of the energy-economy-environment model GINFORS_E.[1] This module endogenizes technology diffusion in the global input-output system, by closing the circle between global cost reduction in PV and wind technologies and respective capacity installations: Country-specific investment costs for these technologies depend on global cost development. With decreasing costs, more PV and wind capacity is installed in all countries. In addition, capacity installations also depend on the general macro-economic development of the countries and possibly on the saturation of the electricity industry with renewable power (resembling the s-curve of technology diffusion). The exact relationship between decreasing costs and increasing capacity installation is econometrically estimated for each of the countries.

The costs of the technologies also depend on the costs of the raw materials used in the technologies. In the case of wind turbines and PV modules, specific raw materials such as rare earths are needed. As the name "rare" indicates, there might at one point be a shortage of supply of these materials, which can result in price increases breaking the link between capacity increase and cost decrease. However, according to Exner et al. (2016), only in the case of very little technological progress and very high global demand, will a shortage of rare earths used for PV modules and wind turbines (such Gallium and Neodym) occur. Given the conservative learning rates used in this model and the medium term horizon for the projection, the projected development will most likely not overestimate the decreases in costs.

Global capacity is the sum of the capacity installed in all the countries. The new capacity installed in each country multiplied with the installation costs gives the necessary investment into the new technologies (*IOT change 1*). From this, the share in production in the respective industry (machinery and equipment for wind, electrical machinery and apparatus) can be calculated. Using this together with the input-coefficient vectors for the RPGTs estimated by Lehr et al. (2011), the new input coefficient vector for the industry are approximated (*IOT change 2*).

The capacity installations are converted into GWh of electricity produced using country-specific average load factors – i.e. GWh electricity produced annually per MW installed capacity. It is important to use country-specific factors for that as sun and wind are available to different extends in different countries. The electricity demand in the projections is determined by the macro-economic development in the input-output system of the country models in GINFORS_E. As explained above in *IOT change 3*, the amount of coal and gas needed to satisfy the electricity consumption are determined as residuals between total electricity needed and the use of nuclear and renewable power to full capacity (as shown in the energy balance). This change is then implemented in the IOTs in GINFORS_E as a reduction in coal and gas inputs into the electricity industry, i.e. a change in the corresponding input coefficients. Furthermore, the reduced use in gas and coal has a direct implication in the $CO_2$ intensity of electricity production, thus the $CO_2$ emission coefficient of the electricity industry is reduced accordingly (*IOT change 4*).

Wiebe (2016) uses this approach to show how European consumption-based emissions develop with and without the technology diffusion. To this end, the MRIO system was applied to four different combinations of input data:

1) Using data for 2010 for final demand, input structure and emission intensities (2010);
2) Using data for 2020 for final demand, input structure and emission intensities projected with GINFORS_E for global renewable energy diffusion (2020 RE diffusion);
3) Using data for final demand from 2010 and for the technology (input structure and emission intensity) from 2020 (2020 technology and 2010 final demand); and
4) Using data for final demand from 2020 and for the technology (input structure and emission intensity) from 2010 (2010 technology and 2020 final demand).

   The latter two provide insights into

3) What would be the level of EU consumption-based emissions in 2010 if the technology of 2020 – i.e. high penetration of PV and wind – were used?
4) What would be the level of EU consumption-based emissions in 2020 if the "current" 2010 technology were used?

Figure 3.3 (bottom panel) shows that total emissions embedded in EU final demand (EU consumption-based emissions) increased between 2010 and 2020 RE diffusion. While emissions originating from Europe decreased, emissions originating from outside the EU remained constant due to increasing import demand from the EU. If the final demand structure did not change, emissions embodied in EU final consumption would decrease outside the EU as well (2020 technology 2010 final demand).

Looking at the individual industries emitting $CO_2$ (top panel of Figure 3.3) shows that that through the technology diffusion (comparing "2010" and "2010

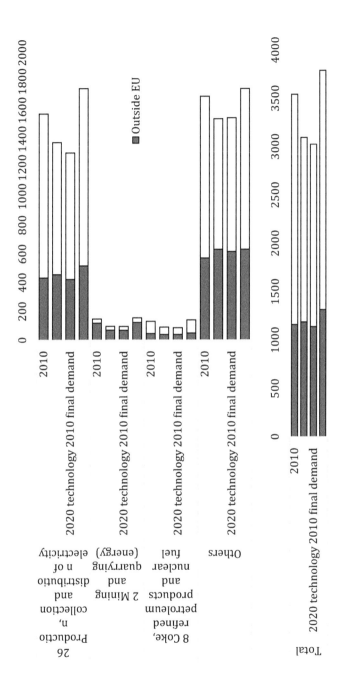

*Figure 3.3* Industries emitting CO$_2$ emissions embedded in goods consumed in the EU28 in Mt CO$_2$ according to origin (emitted within EU28 or outside EU28)

Note: These figures exclude direct emissions from final demand such as private road transport and other emissions directly produced by final consumption of fossil fuels. These are produced and "consumed" domestically and not traded internationally, thus not changing the amount of emissions embodied in imports.

Source: Own calculations based on the GRAM model

technology 2020 final demand" with "2020 RE diffusion" and "2020 technology 2010 final demand") $CO_2$ emissions decrease not only in the electricity industry but also in the two most important industries upstream from fossil fuel based electricity: mining and quarrying (energy) and coke and refined petroleum products. The notable difference between these two industries is that, emissions are mostly reduced outside the EU during mining and quarrying activities and within the EU for coke and refined petroleum products (i.e. that industry within the EU using less intermediate inputs from the mining and quarrying (energy) industry outside the EU).

Figure 3.4 shows the shares of the different world regions in cumulative installed capacity of wind and PV electricity generating technologies. The large share of EU28 suggests that capacity installations in Europe itself have indeed been a large driving force in the observed cost reductions of the technologies. Thus a continuously high deployment of RPGT in Europe still has a large impact on overall cost reductions of the technologies (following the learning concept). By supporting and possibly even accelerating capacity installations within the EU, global prices drop, making these technologies affordable in more and more countries. If the technologies are also deployed outside the EU on an increasing scale (as can be witnessed in Figure 3.4), cost reductions are enhanced, thus further accelerating the diffusion.

By giving the initial impulse in decreasing costs through enhanced capacity installations, the EU can indirectly influence capacity installations abroad and, with that, decrease their consumption-based carbon emissions. In the 2020 RE diffusion scenario, the increases in import demand almost offset the decrease in $CO_2$ intensity of the electricity industry abroad. This indirect market-based mechanism

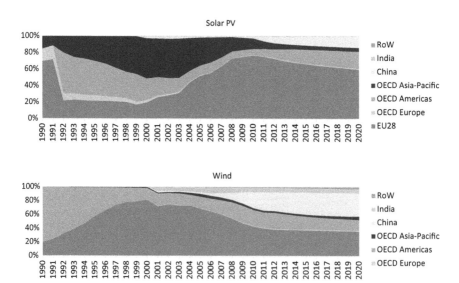

*Figure 3.4* Capacity installed of wind and photovoltaic (PV) by world region

Source: Data from Bloomberg (2012) up to 2012, own estimations 2013–2020

may not be sufficient enough. Thus more efforts for decreasing the $CO_2$ intensity, also in industries other than the electricity industry, need to be initiated.

## Accelerating technology diffusion through active technology transfer

A slightly different concept of consumption-based emissions are final-product-based emissions. That is, the emissions are allocated to the country/industry producing and selling the final product. Given that the final demand matrix has the dimensions "number of industries times number of countries" by "number of countries", the final goods and services produced by a certain industry in a certain country can be calculated as the row sum of that matrix's row corresponding to that industry/country. Let's denote the vector calculated as the row sum of the final demand matrix as **y** and correspondingly $\hat{\mathbf{y}}$ as the diagonalized matrix form of vector **y**. Final product-based emissions can then be calculated as the column sum of the matrix $\mathbf{P}_{FP}$, which is defined as

$$\mathbf{P}_{FP} = \hat{\mathbf{e}}(\mathbf{I} - \mathbf{A})^{-1}\hat{\mathbf{y}}. \tag{3.4}$$

Knowledge about final product-based $CO_2$ emissions raises the awareness of the link between final goods produced by industries and the environmental pollution caused by upstream production processes. Producers of final products learn where in the world $CO_2$ was emitted along the upstream production chain. This reduces the psychological distance to the climate change problem. This is one of the five psychological barriers to active climate change mitigation efforts identified by (Stoknes, 2014, 2015).

In addition, the data can give benchmarks against which establishments in that industry can compare their performance. Such benchmarking can increase pressure on firms to produce more cleanly, and, hence, an effective means to overcome one of the other psychological barriers (Stoknes, 2015). The effect of enhancing environmentally friendly behaviour across related economic agents has been thoroughly researched; a prominent focus has been the effect of informing households about their energy consumption vis-à-vis social norms (Allcott, 2011).

This knowledge about "emission hotspots" (countries/industries where a bulk of the upstream emissions occur) can then be used for well-targeted technology transfers from $CO_2$-consuming to $CO_2$-emitting countries. If industries care about the $CO_2$ footprints of their final products, these technology transfers can provide a cost-effective way of reducing their footprint – cost effective because of two reasons: First, no new technology has to be invented when engaging in technology transfer. Technology transfer aims at helping countries/industries to catch up with the technology frontier. The country/industry initiating the transfer is already much closer to the technological frontier. Further upgrading technology close to the frontier involves heavy research spending. Second, the new technology will require less fossil energy, thus decreasing operating costs.

Figure 3.5 presents estimates of the origin of emissions embodied in the final products sold by Germany's motor vehicle industry (i.e. those sold in Germany

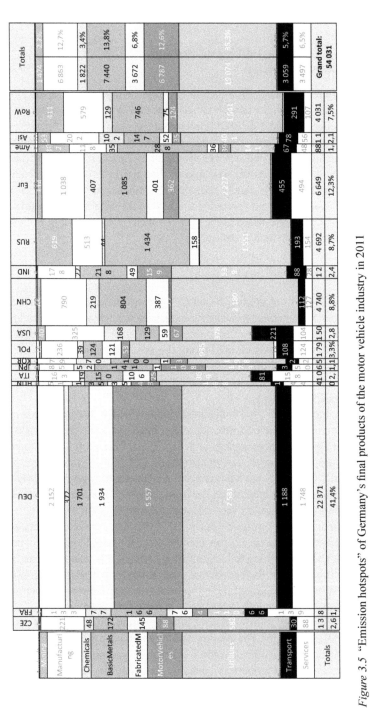

*Figure 3.5* "Emission hotspots" of the motor vehicle industry in 2011

Source: Own calculations based on IEA CO$_2$ emission from fuel combustion (IEA, 2015a) and OECD ICIO (OECD, 2015, Wiebe and Yamano, 2016)

and those exported). The countries with high shares in the origin of emissions are the Czech Republic, Poland, USA, China, India and Russia (wide columns in the figure). The "emission hotspot" industries are chemicals; basic metals; fabricated metal products; the motor vehicle industry itself; electricity, gas and water supply (utilities); and transport (boxes with large areas).

The emission hotspots are determined by the share of that country's industry in the total upstream production processes and the emission intensity of the production in that country's industry. Important country-industry combinations in terms of value added may not show up in these graphs if their emission intensities are low. France, Italy and the United Kingdom, for example, are major trading partners of Germany and have high shares of value added (VA) embodied in Germany's final demand for or final products from the motor vehicle industry.[2] But they have equally low or even lower emission intensities, so that in embodied $CO_2$ terms, these countries do not rank high. Figure 3.6 shows that Germany's emission intensities in the emission hotspot industries are substantially lower than those of the emission hotspot countries. The main difference may not only derive from the employment of different technologies but also from different product mixes manufactured by those industries. For example, per unit of weight, the production of aluminium is much more carbon intense than is steel production.

The differences also come about from the use of different energy carriers during the production processes. The energy mix used in three of the emission hotspot industries is displayed in Figure 3.7. Generally speaking, Germany's energy mix (based on data from the IEA (2015d)) of the "hotspot industries" is less $CO_2$-intense, relying less on coal or oil than in Germany's emission hotspot countries. Therefore, Germany's $CO_2$ emission intensities – i.e., $CO_2$ emissions per unit of output – in these industries are lower. The iron and stel industry in both Germany and the USA, for example, has much lower $CO_2$ emission intensity than does its equivalent in China. This is because China still uses the more carbon intense process of basic oxygen furnaces (BOF) to produce iron, while Germany and USA have largely converted to electric arc furnaces (EAF). The latter requires substantial amounts of electricity, so in those two countries at least it seems the iron and steel has simply "outsourced" its emissions to another industry. The overall effect on emissions depends on the energy mix of the electricity production.

The underlying reasons why Germany uses a less $CO_2$ intense energy mix than its "hotspot" trading partners in global value chains are due to its different national policies and technology stock. For engaging in technology transfer, it is necessary to analyse both the actual nature of the products produced by the hotspot industry, the exact technology used by the industry, as well as country-specific factors, like labor costs and resource availability. Regarding the exact technology used, just looking, for example, at the shares of BOF and EAF used in iron and steel production is insufficient. While EAF is generally considered to be less emission intense than BOF, there are different types of EAF technologies. India, for example, uses coal-based Direct Reduced Iron (coal-based DRI) for EAF and this technology is extremely emission intense, having perhaps the highest intensity steel production technologies (Newman, 2010). This results in

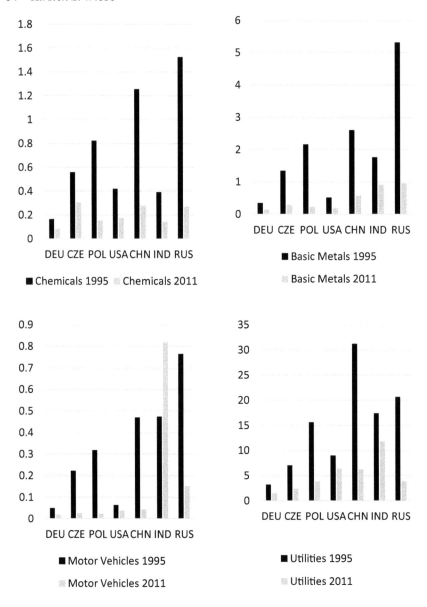

*Figure 3.6* Emission intensities of Germany's emission hotspots in 1995 and 2011

Source: Own calculations based on IEA CO₂ emission from fuel combustion(IEA, 2015a) and OECD ICIO (OECD, 2015, Wiebe and Yamano, 2016)

India having a higher $CO_2$ emission intensity in the iron and steel industry than Germany even though the share of steelmaking via BOF is lower in India than it is in Germany. In this case, the current technology in India can be changed to a less polluting alternative DRI technologies. In other countries such as Russia, the

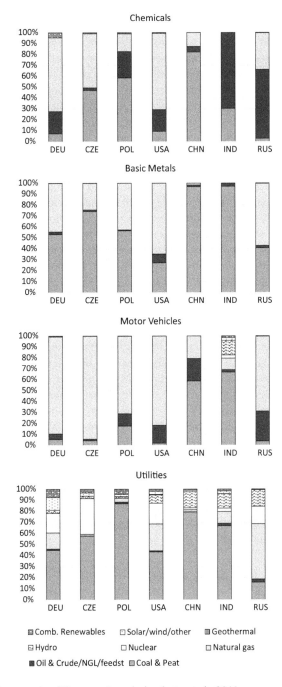

*Figure 3.7* Energy mix of Germany's emission hotspots in 2011

Source: IEA Energy Balances (IEA, 2015d)

currently dominating technology of steel production (open hearth furnace – OHF) represents more of a technological lock-in, where huge investments are required to change the current capital stock of steel producing plants. For other highly energy-intense products, such as aluminum, country-specific factors can play an important role: While in Iceland aluminium production is almost carbon free due to the abundance of geothermal power, aluminium production in other countries may be among the most carbon-intensive production processes.

This shows a limitation of the data available from this analysis for finding technology transfer target industries and countries: Technology transfer possibilities depend on the exact basket of goods and services produced by an industry, while here it only is industry averages, and on local circumstances, which are exogenously determined, e.g. natural resources. In addition, policies providing an enabling environment for technology transfer and preventing emission-intense technological lock-ins or supporting escaping those lock-ins, are necessary.

The necessary subsequent analysis of different technologies, country-specific factors as well as policy influence is the same as in conventional production-based or territorial cross-country comparisons of $CO_2$ emissions; see, for example, the collection of data and literature for ODYSSEE project since the 1990s (Bosseboeuf et al., 1997; ODYSSEE-MURE, 2016) or the IEA Energy technology perspectives and related analyses published annually since 2006 (IEA, 2006, 2015c, 2016a). Thus when countries or industries have analyzed their "emission hotspots" they can base their actions on existing analysis and only need to do little additional research on how and why there may be differences in the emission intensity and what technologies could possibly be transferred.

German car manufactures have already taken initial steps to tackle upstream energy use and emissions: BMW has reduced its energy consumption per vehicle produced by 36% between 2006 and 2016, by applying state-of-the-art process technologies not only in Germany but also in China, where, for example, in one plants painting a car body uses just a third of the energy that was spent ten years ago (BMW Group, 2016). BMW, Daimler and Volkswagen as well as other European car manufacturers that are part of the European Automotive Working Group on Supply Chain Sustainability,[3] are developing standards for more sustainable supply chain management. They are also organizing training seminars for their suppliers with a similar aim.

## Conclusions for technology transfer

The IEA (2016b) and the WRI (2016) emphasize the importance of collaborative action of the public and private sector across countries. They are now focusing on the deployment and transfer of technologies. The term technology transfer encompasses not only the sourcing of hardware by countries with advanced technologies to those countries using technologies that pollute more or that require more energy, but it also involves R&D support and collaboration, energy conservation and related management practices as well as other innovation strategies (De Coninck and Sagar, 2015). In essence, it is anything that enables technology adaptation and deployment.

Wurlod and Eaton (2015) find that for poor countries to gain from productivity increases from technology transfer, a certain level of education is a prerequisite as well as sound public policies and the openness of the economy. Given these prerequisites, factors such as substantial investments in public R&D and effective IPR policies can become important too. For example, a variety of factors contributed to Germany's decarbonization of its electricity industry. *Inter alia*, over a long period of time it took a fairly consistent mix of policies encouraging innovation, changes in energy resources, and heightening concern about climate change to reach different actors in different industries and governance levels before the first version of the renewable energies act was implemented in 2000 (Rogge and Reichardt, 2015).

Some countries, for example, the United Kingdom, already use consumption-based accounting to monitor the development of $CO_2$ emissions associated with their economic activities in an effort to account for potential "leakage". Recent research projects (for the European Commission DG RESEARCH (Carbon-CAP; Schanes et al., 2016) and DG CLIMA (Wiebe et al., 2016)), have started looking into policies that should reduce consumption-based emissions, but the implementation of policies that directly reduce emissions abroad is not straight forward and more research is necessary.

The considerations presented here can be used concurrently with existing technology transfer mechanisms of the UNFCCC or IEA. Data on consumption-based or final-product-based emissions can first be used to reduce the psychological distance to climate change (more research on this is still necessary). Second, for those countries/industries that want to do more than legally obligated, the data can be used to identify "emission hotspots", which should be targeted by technology transfers. The advantages for these countries are obvious: First, technology transfers are a cost-effective way of reducing the $CO_2$ emission footprints of upstream production processes. Second, they can profit from other countries using their technologies. Over time, the indirect impact of the direct technology transfers and, hence, technology diffusion are decreasing costs due to learning and scale effects. This will make technologies more affordable and economically viable, indirectly contributing to a further diffusion.

The results of the scenario analysis further show that both quantity of final demand as well as the technologies (emission intensity and input coefficients) used along global production chain matter for the level of consumption-based carbon emissions. With globally increasing capacity installed of wind power and PV, EU consumption-based emissions decrease, while consumption itself in nominal terms continues to increase. When looking at the differences between the scenarios in greater detail, it becomes clear that differences in the technology (higher share of PV and wind in electricity production) have a higher contribution (−15% and −20%) to consumption-based emissions than differences in final demand (+7%, +2.5%). This confirms that a decarbonization of the electricity sector abroad is inevitable for reducing consumption-based emissions.

Clean technologies can contribute to structural change, new industrialization patterns and hence an enhanced economic development (Günther and Alcorta,

88   *Kirsten S. Wiebe*

2011; Mathews and Tan, 2014, 2016). These additional indirect effects can also be analyzed using the MRIO approach.

## Notes

1 GINFORS_E is a version of the GINFORS (Global INterindustry FORecasting System) model (Lutz et al., 2009) tailored to fit the MRIO GRAM (Wiebe et al. 2012). It is based on the exact same historical database as GRAM (OECD input-output tables and bilateral trade data as well as IEA energy balances) and thus covers the exact same industries (48 industries in ISIC Rev. 3 classifications) and countries. Those countries, for which no IOTs exist, are represented in GINFORS_E by simple macro-economic models projecting the main components of GDP as well as the key labor market indicators (Wolter et al., 2014). Therefore, for these countries, the same information is available for the projections as is available for the historical MRIO analysis. Projecting GRAM is then simply taking the projected data from GINFORS_E and populating the full MRIO.
2 See relatively large shares of France (FRA), Italy (ITA) and the UK (GBR) in the figure at http://oecd-icio.cloudapp.net:3838/icioapp2015/ with parameter selection Year = 2011, Subject = TiVA, Demand Data = Final Demand (excl. Inventories), Result Dimension = Source Country and Source Industry, Demand Industry = C34, Product Origin Country (or Region) = World, Demand Country/Region = DEU.
3 www.csreurope.org/european-automotive-working-group-supply-chain-sustainability-1

## References

Allcott, H. (2011). Social norms and energy conservation. *Journal of Public Economics*, *95*(9), 1082–1095.
Arrow, K. J. (1962). The economic implications of learning by doing. *The Review of Economic Studies*, *29*, 155–173.
Bloomberg New Energy Finance. (2012). *The great renewable energy race*. Retrieved April 5, 2013, from http://go.bloomberg.com/multimedia/the-great-renewable-energy-race/
BMW Group. (2016). Sustainability factbook. Retrieved from https://www.bmwgroup.com/content/dam/bmw-group-websites/bmwgroup_com/responsibility/sustainable-value-report/e_101101_BMW%20Sustainability%20fact%20book%202016.pdf
Bosseboeuf, D., Chateau, B., and Lapillonne, B. (1997). Cross-country comparison on energy efficiency indicators: The on-going European effort towards a common methodology. *Energy Policy*, *25*(7–9), 673–682.
Carbon-CAP (2013). Consumption-based Accounting and Policy-An EU FP7 funded research project under grant agreement No 603386.
Cohen, W. M., and Levinthal, D. A. (1989). Innovation and learning: The two faces of R & D. *The Economic Journal*, *99*(397), 569–596.
CTCN. (2013). *Introducing the CTCN*. Copenhagen, Climate Technology Centre and Network.
De Coninck, H., and Sagar, A. (2015). Technology in the 2015 Paris climate agreement and beyond. *ICTSD Programme on Innovation, Technology and Intellectual Property Issue Paper* (42).
Exner, M. A., Held, M., and Kümmerer, K. (2016). Einführung: Kritische Metalle in der Großen Transformation. In Kritische Metalle in der Großen Transformation (pp. 1–16). Berlin, Springer-Verlag.
Günther, T., and Alcorta, L. (2011). *Industrial policy for prosperity: Reasoning and approach*. Vienna, United Nations Industrial Development Organization (UNIDO).

IEA. (2006). *Energy technology perspectives 2006: Scenarios and strategies to 2050.* Paris, France: IEA.

IEA. (2015a). *CO$_2$ emissions from fuel combustion.* Paris, France: IEA.

IEA. (2015b). *Energy and climate – world energy outlook special briefing for COP21.* Paris, France: IEA.

IEA. (2015c). *Energy technology perspectives 2015: Mobilising innovation to accelerate climate action.* Paris, France: IEA.

IEA. (2015d). *World energy balances: Database documentation* (2015 rev. ed.). Paris, France: IEA.

IEA. (2016a). *Energy technology perspectives website.* Retrieved September 9, 2016, from www.iea.org/etp/publications/

IEA. (2016b). *IEA Technology Collaboration Programmes: Follow-up from 18 September meeting and IEA ministerial mandate.* Paris, France: IEA.

Kahouli-Brahmi, S. (2008). Technological learning in energy – environment – economy modelling: A survey. *Energy Policy, 36*(1), 138–162.

Lehr, U., Lutz, C., Edler, D., O'Sullivan, M., Nienhaus, K., Nitsch, J., . . . Ottmüller, M. (2011). *Kurz-und langfristige Auswirkungen des Ausbaus erneuerbarer Energien auf den deutschen Arbeitsmarkt.* Osnabruck, GWS mbH.

Lutz, C., Meyer, B., and Wolter, M. I. (2009). The global multisector/multicountry 3-E model GINFORS: A description of the model and a baseline forecast for global energy demand and CO$_2$ emissions. *International Journal of Global Environmental Issues, 10*(1–2), 25–45.

Mathews, J. A., and Tan, H. (2016). Circular economy: Lessons from China. *Nature, 531*(7595), 440–442.

Newman, J. (2010). *Climate change policy and iron and steel industry.* O. DSTI/SU/ SC(2010)17, 1–45. Paris: OECD.

ODYSSEE-MURE. (2016). *Introduction to the Odyssee-Mure project.* Retrieved September 9, 2016, from www.odyssee-mure.eu/project.html

OECD. (2015). *OECD Inter-Country Input-Output (ICIO) Tables.* Retrieved February 2, 2016, http://oe.cd/icio.

OECD and IEA. (2013). RD&D Budget, IEA Energy Technology R&D Statistics. Paris: OECD.

Piccard, B. (2016). How clean technologies can improve health worldwideUNEP at medium.com: A guest post from Bertrand Piccard, Initiator, Chairman, and Pilot of Solar Impulse and UNEP Goodwill Ambassador. Retrieved from https://medium.com/ @UNEnvironment/how-clean-technologies-can-improve-health-worldwide-3b9940cb d3ec#.yhys12vau

Rogge, K., and Reichardt, K. (2015). Going beyond instrument interactions: Towards a more comprehensive policy mix conceptualization for environmental technological change.

Schanes, K., Giljum, S., and Hertwich, E. (2016). Low carbon lifestyles: A framework to structure consumption strategies and options to reduce carbon footprints. *Journal of Cleaner Production, 139*, 1033–1043.

Shimada, K., and Kennedy, M. (2015). Potential role of the technology mechanism in implementing the Paris agreement. UN Nations Framework Convention on Climate Change. Retrieved from http://unfccc.int/ttclear/misc_/StaticFiles/gnwoerk_static/ events_SE-TEC-CTCN-COP21/d093a44fa4b34caabe125562e66b80b9/0595db8c40d3 4226be9b58999e59ba78.pdf

Stoknes, P. E. (2014). Rethinking climate communications and the "psychological climate paradox". *Energy Research & Social Science, 1*, 161–170.

Stoknes, P. E. (2015). *What we think about when we try not to think about global warming: toward a new psychology of climate action.* Vermont, Chelsea Green Publishing.

Timmer, M. P., Erumban, A. A., Los, B., Stehrer, R., and de Vries, G. J. (2014). Slicing up global value chains. *The Journal of Economic Perspectives, 28*(2), 99–118.

Tukker, A., de Koning, A., Wood, R., Hawkins, T., Lutter, S., Acosta, J., . . . Drosdowski, T. (2013). EXIOPOL – development and illustrative analyses of a detailed global MR EE SUT/IOT. *Economic Systems Research, 25*(1), 50–70.

UN. (2016). *SDG Goal 13: Take urgent action to combat climate change and its impacts.* Retrieved from www.un.org/sustainabledevelopment/climate-change-2/.

UNFCCC. (2011). Report of the Conference of the Parties on its sixteenth session: Proceedings. FCCC/CP/2010/7.Cancún, UN.

UNFCCC. (2015). Technology mechanism – enhancing climate technology development and transfer. UN. http://unfccc.int/ttclear/tec

Wiebe, K. S. (2016). The impact of renewable energy diffusion on European consumption-based emissions. *Economic Systems Research, 28*(2), 133–150.

Wiebe, K. S., Bruckner, M., Giljum, S., and Lutz, C. (2012). Calculating energy-related $CO_2$ emissions embodied in international trade using a global input – output model. *Economic Systems Research, 24*(2), 113–139.

Wiebe, K. S., Gandy, S., and Lutz, C. (2016). Policies and consumption-based carbon emissions from a top-down and a bottom-up perspective. *Low Carbon Economy, 7*(01), 21.

Wiebe, K. S., and Lutz, C. (2016). Endogenous technological change and the policy mix in renewable power generation. *Renewable and Sustainable Energy Reviews, 60,* 739–751.

Wiebe, K. S., and Yamano, N. (2016). Estimating $CO_2$ emissions embodied in final demand and trade using the OECD ICIO 2015.

Wolter, M. I., Großmann, A., Mönnig, A., and Wiebe, K. S. (2014). *TINFORGE-trade for the interindustry forecasting Germany model.* Osnabruck, GWS-Institute of Economic Structures Research.

WRI. (2016). *After COP21: 7 key tasks to implement the Paris agreement.* World Resources Institute. Retrieved from www.wri.org/blog/2016/03/after-cop21-7-key-tasks-imple ment-paris-agreement?utm_campaign=socialmedia&utm_source=facebook.com&utm_ medium=wri-page

Wurlod, J.-D., and Eaton, D. (2015). Technology diffusion and its problematics: The case of global agriculture.Research Paper 37, Center for International Environmental Studies, Geneva.

# 4 Potentials to decarbonize electricity consumption in Australia

*Paul Wolfram and Thomas Wiedmann*

## Introduction

At the twenty-first Conference of the Parties in Paris, national governments agreed to restrict global warming to well below 2°C and to undertake efforts to aim for 1.5°C (UNFCCC, 2015). The vast majority of countries submitted Intended Nationally Determined Contributions to reduce national greenhouse gas (GHG) emissions. Australia pledged for a 26%–28% economy-wide reduction of GHG emissions below 2005 levels by 2030 (DFAT, 2015). In order to stay below a global warming of 2°C, the total amount of globally emitted GHG emissions must be restricted to around 1,000 Gt between 1990 and 2050, which is also referred to as the global carbon budget (Meinshausen et al., 2009). Australia can be assigned an (unofficial) national carbon budget of around 18 Gt, of which 12 Gt have been used already between 1990 and 2012. This leaves a remainder of around 6 Gt for the period 2013 to 2100, assuming zero emissions post-2100 (Ecofys, 2013).

According to ClimateWorks et al. (2014), electricity generation is the largest GHG emitting industry in Australia, with a share of 35% of total national GHG emissions. This is mainly caused by the high share of fossil fuels (e.g. 64% coal and 20% natural gas in 2012–2013) and the relatively high electricity demand (249 TWh in 2012–2013)[1] in Australia's main electricity grid, the National Electricity Market (BREE, 2014) Thus, decarbonization of the electricity sector will play an important role in the question whether Australia will achieve the intended carbon reduction goals and whether Australia will stay within the national carbon budget.

Even with deep reductions of direct electricity emissions, e.g. through large-scale penetration of renewable energy, electricity generation is not completely free of GHG emissions as all economic activity requires the input of energy and material flows, and thus indirect emissions. Therefore, this chapter investigates questions such as the following:

1   How big are potential GHG emission reductions in Australia under different decarbonization scenarios in the electricity sector, even when considering indirect emissions from electricity generation?

2   Can Australia achieve the stated climate goals and/or stay within the national carbon budget given these GHG emission reductions in the electricity sector (without any reductions in other economic sectors)?

In order to answer these questions, we employ a novel scenario-based approach to hybrid life cycle assessment (LCA) to evaluate a range of different renewable electricity scenarios. The focus metric of this analysis is the total carbon footprint of electricity as a final product. The carbon footprint is an indicator that quantifies both direct and indirect GHG emissions of a product, process, activity or entity (Thomas O. Wiedmann and Minx, 2008). It is therefore well suited to identify the indirect (embodied) GHG emissions of electricity provision, even if all electricity is produced with renewable electricity. This work is the first to apply a full life-cycle approach to scenario analysis of electricity generation in Australia.

## Overview of recent energy and greenhouse gas scenario analyses

Hatfield-Dodds et al. (2015) utilize an integrated multi-model framework that represents the world economy with a spatial focus on Australia. The study explores several scenarios until 2050 and, while indirect emissions are not considered, a wide range of indicators such as territorial GHG emissions, ecosystem services, water stress and material extraction are applied. The study finds that – under certain policy settings – energy and food production and water extraction can increase in Australia and globally while environmental pressures such as GHG emissions, water stress and ecosystem loss can decrease (and "decouple" from economic growth), without outsourcing environmental impacts to other nations.

Schandl et al. (2016) assess the potential for decoupling in 13 regions and globally in a hybridized multi-region input-output model. The authors apply three scenarios out to 2050: a business-as-usual case, a scenario with a high carbon price and high resource efficiency and a medium case. It is found that developed countries can reduce future GHG emissions and material use with little impact on economic growth, and developing countries could increase economic welfare at much lower environmental cost as is the case nowadays. Consequently, global reduction efforts have negligible effects on the world economy.

In a response to the two papers noted earlier, Lenzen et al. (2016) use IOA to perform a structural decomposition analysis of GHG emissions in Australia between 1976 and 2050. For their work, the scholars use historical data as well as the scenario data generated by the aforementioned papers. The study suggests that affluence and population growth are the main drivers of GHG emissions in Australia. It is therefore concluded that emission efficiency in Australia and globally will need to improve dramatically in order to reduce GHG emissions.

Hong et al. (2014) compare and evaluate 11 existing low-carbon and renewable electricity scenarios for Australia using multi-criteria decision analysis. They apply eight sustainability criteria including GHG emissions, land use, safety and cost of electricity production, each with an equal weight. As a result of their work, CSIRO's e-future default scenario,[2] which explores a mix of conventional and renewable electricity, scores worst with a relatively high impact score of 4.51 out of 8. At the same time, CSIRO's e-future scenario with some renewable energy and maximum nuclear energy penetration yields the lowest impact score (1.46 out of 8), with an average life-cycle GHG emissions below 27 g $CO_2$e per kWh by 2050.

Berrill et al. (2016) assess 44 electricity scenarios for the European Union through to 2050 in an integrated hybrid LCA modelling framework. A novelty of this work is that it captures material and energy requirements of electricity transmission, distribution and storage, which often has been underrepresented in earlier LCAs. The research concludes that the cumulative amount of GHG emissions can be cut by a factor of ten in a renewable electricity scenario with wind and solar power compared to a scenario with predominantly electricity from natural gas, even when additional infrastructure needs for renewable energy are considered.

While the potential of renewable energy for decarbonization has been demonstrated repeatedly, concerns arose whether a large-scale deployment of renewables is able to deploy sufficient power during supply peaks. Hearps and Wright (2010) published a study that proposes an ambitious transition to 100% renewable energy in Australia within only ten years. Demand is assumed to increase up to 325 TWh per year by 2020, which is 40% higher compared to 2010. The study suggests that a combination of wind power and concentrated solar power (CSP), supported by minimal energy backup by biomass, can guarantee a reliable energy supply, resulting in a near-zero, GHG-emitting electricity sector by 2020.

Not only forms of renewable energy generation are discussed but also fossil-fuel based low-carbon technologies such as carbon capture and storage (CCS) systems. Singh et al. (2015) perform a scenario-based, life-cycle material use analysis of CCS systems. The authors find that life-cycle $CO_2$ emissions can be reduced by 83% in a scenario with CCS-equipped coal power plants relative to a scenario without CCS. However, CCS also increases land and water requirements, as well as usage of coal and limestone, copper, steel and selected chemicals, and thereby posing additional pressures on the environment.

## Data

The two main data types for this assessment are top-down economic data and bottom-up engineering-type data, which are typically combined to form the basis for hybrid LCA. The combination of the two facilitates a comprehensive accounting framework which, on the one hand, captures all economic activities and their related environmental impacts, and on the other hand provides greater detail for the modelling of specific processes that are of most interest (here, all processes related to electricity generation).

### *Top-down data*

Aggregate economic data in the form of a 2008–2009 national supply-and-use table (SUT) is taken from the Australian Bureau of Statistics (ABS, 2012b). This initial SUT consists of 112 industries and 112 commodities (according to the input-output product classification, IOPC), representing all financial flows within the Australian economy. In order to gain a more detailed SUT, we further disaggregate the initial SUT using the Industrial Ecology Virtual Laboratory (IELab) (Lenzen et al., 2014). The IELab's automated aggregation/disaggregation process offers full flexibility on the desired dimensions of the final SUT. We choose to work with a final SUT with 215 industries and 215 commodities. The additional 103 sectors provide a better representation of processes specifically related to electricity generation. In addition, we add a second region to the SUT representing international trade between Australia and the rest of the world (RoW) (Figure 4.1). This step allows for distinction of domestic and foreign carbon intensity of production. Respective data is taken from the Eora database (Lenzen et al., 2012; Lenzen et al., 2013).

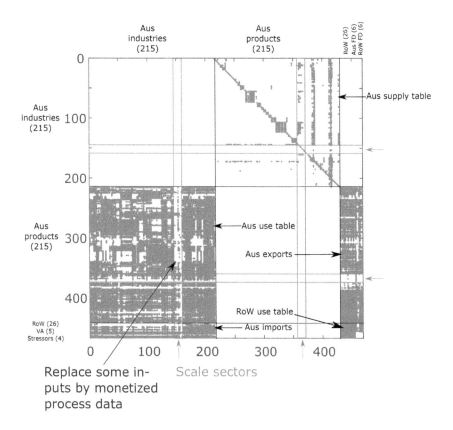

*Figure 4.1* Graphical representation of the two-region supply-and-use table and the hybridization process.

Note: Numbers in brackets refer to the amount of rows and columns of each element in the input-output framework. Aus = Australia; RoW = rest of world; FD = final demand; VA = value added

***Bottom-up data***

Detailed life-cycle inventories for onshore and offshore wind power, run-of river and reservoir hydro power, geothermal power and photovoltaics are obtained from the Ecoinvent 3.1 database (Ecoinvent, 2014). Life-cycle data for CSP is taken from Burkhardt et al. (2011). The inventories include all material and energy requirements during raw material mining, transportation of materials and parts, power plant construction, operation and maintenance, and disposal at the end of life. We adjust the initial life-cycle inventories with regionally specific data from AusLCI, an Australian life-cycle database (ALCAS, 2011).

Bottom-up life-cycle data is typically available in physical units, whereas top-down economic data is obtained in monetary units. In order to facilitate the combination (or hybridization) of the two data types, we convert all physical data into monetary data. Therefore, we collect price data for all processes taken from Ecoinvent. This step is not as straight-forward as desired as the Australian Bureau of Statistics does not publish prices for products and raw materials. Therefore, we determine the price $\mathbf{p}_j$ of a product j according to

$$\mathbf{p}_j = \mathbf{x}_j \left( \mathbf{q}_j \mathbf{c}_j \right)^{-1}, \tag{4.1}$$

where $\mathbf{x}_j$ is the total output of the selling sector $j$ in monetary values and $\mathbf{q}_j$ is the total sectoral production in physical units. Furthermore, prices are assumed to be

*Table 4.1* Selected input processes, their assigned IOPC sectors and estimated prices

| Process according to Ecoinvent | Economic sector according to IOPC | $x_j$ (in $10^3$ AUD) | $q_j$ (in $10^3$) | $c_j$ | $c_j$ |
|---|---|---|---|---|---|
| Concrete | Cement, lime and ready-mixed Concrete Manufacturing | 5,047,091 | 23,896 m³ | 1.2133 | 174 AUD m⁻³ |
| Cement, Portland | Cement (incl. hydraulic and Portland, excl. adhesive or refractory) | 1,445,000 | 9,108 t | 1.2133 | 0.13 AUD kg⁻¹ |
| Gravel | Gravel | 205,000 | 12,403 t | 1.5110 | 0.01 AUD kg⁻¹ |
| Styrene-acrylonitrite copolymer | Styrene | 94,000 | 48 t | 1.2759 | 1.53 AUD kg⁻¹ |
| Reinforcing steel | Reinforcing steel rods or bars | 1,141,000 | 1,452 t | 1.0776 | 0.73 AUD kg⁻¹ |
| Copper | Copper (incl. brass) primary and secondary recovery (excl. from purchased scrap) | 2,552,000 | 446 t | 1.0406 | 5.62 AUD kg⁻¹ |

purchaser's prices ($\mathbf{pp}_j$), which include margins. To receive factory-gate prices, or basic prices ($\mathbf{bp}_j$), conversion ratios obtainable from ABS (2015, Table 4.1) are applied as in $\mathbf{c}_j = \mathbf{pp}_j \, \mathbf{bp}_j^{-1}$. In total, 102 prices are estimated. See Table 4.1 for selected examples.

To estimate $\mathbf{p}_j$, we collect specific $\mathbf{q}_j$ for Australia for the year 2009 whenever available. If this is not possible, we use averaged prices from other countries and/or other years, excluding outliers beforehand. Respective data sources include ABS (2007, 2010, 2011, 2012a, 2014) ABARE (2003), World Steel Association (2014), the World Bureau of Metal Statistics, USGS (2009), BREE (2011), AEMO (2014), Lenzen (1999), and UNSD (2015), which alone comprises 25 publically available databases.

## Methods

### *Carbon footprint calculations using input-output-based hybrid life-cycle assessment*

The carbon footprint (CF) measures GHG emissions associated with the consumption of goods and services (Thomas O. Wiedmann and Minx, 2008). Two fundamental methods for calculating CFs have been described in the literature: (1) IOA, based on top-down economic data (see section 3.1), and (2) process analysis, based on bottom-up process data (see section 3.2.) (Suh, S., Lenzen, M., Treloar, G. J., Hondo, H., Horvath, A., Huppes, G., . . . Moriguchi, Y. (2004). System boundary selection in life-cycle inventories using hybrid approaches. Environmental Science & Technology, 38(3), 657–664. Wiedmann, T. O., Suh, S., Feng, K., Lenzen, M., Acquaye, A., Scott, K., and Barrett, J. R. (2011). Application of hybrid life cycle approaches to emerging energy technologies the case of wind power in the UK. Environmental Science & Technology, 45(13), 5900–5907. Wiedmann et al., 2011). Process analysis facilitates a detailed assessment of specific processes due to usage of physical data. This makes process analysis suitable at a lower product-level scale. However, it is often difficult to capture all processes that are involved in the full life cycle of an object (Majeau-Bettez, G., Strømman, A. H., and Hertwich, E. G. (2011). Evaluation of process-and input output-based life cycle inventory data with regard to truncation and aggregation issues. Environmental Science & Technology, 45(23), 10170–10177. Majeau-Bettez et al., 2011). IOA has a lower relative precision since all processes are described at a higher and more aggregate level. But IOA can ensure a complete description of an object due to the inclusion of a representation of the whole economy (Minx, J. C., Wiedmann, T., Wood, R., Peters, G. P., Lenzen, M., Owen, A., . . . Baiocchi, G. (2009). Input output analysis and carbon footprinting: an overview of applications. Economic Systems Research, 21(3), 187–216. Minx et al., 2009). The combination of both methods in a hybrid LCA has emerged as the state-of-the-art approach in order to utilize the individual strengths of both methods (Suh, S., Lenzen, M., Treloar, G. J., Hondo, H., Horvath, A., Huppes,

G., ... Moriguchi, Y. (2004). System boundary selection in life-cycle inventories using hybrid approaches. Environmental Science & Technology, 38(3), 657–664. Suh et al., 2004).

We make use of an input-output table that is extended with an additional environmental satellite account (often referred to as environmentally extended IOA), including the direct greenhouse gas emissions $CO_2$, $CH_4$ and $N_2O$ of all industries. Following the standard input-output calculus, we can decompose a total carbon footprint $CF_{ij}$ of a product j, which has embodied emissions originating from industry i, according to T. O. Wiedmann et al. (2015).

$$\mathbf{CF}_{ij} = \widehat{\left(\mathbf{E}_i \mathbf{x}_i^{-1}\right)}\left(\mathbf{I} - \mathbf{A}\right)^{-1} \hat{\mathbf{y}}_j, \tag{4.2}$$

where

$\widehat{\left(\mathbf{E}_i \mathbf{x}_i^{-1}\right)}$ is a diagonalized vector of industry emission intensities. $\mathbf{E}_i$ is the environmental satellite account in matrix form, and $\mathbf{x}_i$ is a vector of total industry outputs of sector i. The hat symbol indicates diagonalization of the vector.

$\mathbf{I}$ is the identity matrix, which is characterized by, and $i_{ij} = 0 \, \forall \, i \neq j$ – i.e. all diagonal elements of $\mathbf{I}$ are ones and all off-diagonal elements are zeros.

$\mathbf{A}$ is the technology matrix of the same size as $\mathbf{I}$. The elements $a_{ji}$ of $\mathbf{A}$ are derived using $a_{ji} = x_{ji} \, x_i^{-1}$, where $x_{ji}$ is the input from sector j to sector i in order for sector i to realize its own production, and $x_i$ is the total output of sector i.

The results of (2) are total carbon footprints of final demand for each electricity type j expressed in Mt $CO_2$e. The relative carbon footprint intensity $cf_{ij}$ for each electricity product j, expressed in g $CO_2$e per kWh, is then obtained as $cf_{ij} = CF_{ij} z^{-1}$, where z is the actual final demand for electricity in physical units obtained from ABS (2011).

In our hybrid LCA approach, we disaggregate the electricity rows and columns in the SUT (top-down section). The disaggregation process facilitates a more detailed representation of electricity generation from different renewable and fossil fuel feedstocks. The original SUT obtained from the Australian Bureau of Statistics includes three electricity sectors (fossil fuels, hydropower, non-hydro renewable electricity). These three sectors are disaggregated into a total of 16 subsectors. Fossil fuels are broken down into black coal, black coal combined with CCS, lignite, direct-injection coal engine, natural gas and natural gas combined with CCS. Hydropower remains as one sector. Non-hydro renewable electricity is broken down into biomass, wind onshore, wind offshore, solar photovoltaics, concentrated solar power, wave power and geothermal power.[3] All sectors are broken down according to the technologies' actual shares in total electricity generation in Australia in 2008–2009. These shares are applied to both the supply and the use table and to both the columns and the rows. After disaggregation, we insert the monetized physical process data (bottom-up section) into the electricity sector columns of the use table. This way, some of the original input-output-based cell values are replaced by the new converted process values (see first step in Figure 4.1), leading to updated elements $x_{ij}^*$ in the use table columns. This leads to a new input vector $\mathbf{x}^*$ and a new technology matrix $\mathbf{A}^*$. In a final adjustment step, we update direct emissions from each electricity sector with available process-level data, leading to a new stressor matrix $\mathbf{E}^*$.

### Scenario analysis

We apply scenario analysis to introduce changes to certain parameters, such as total electricity generation and total final demand for electricity. Scenario-based IOA is particularly suggestive for this task because changes in demand for consumer goods (here, electricity generated from different fossil and renewable sources) and the resulting structural changes in the economy can be modelled. This type of approach is sometimes referred to as prospective or consequential LCA, which is increasingly used to evaluate effects of such systemic changes (Finnveden et al., 2009; Plevin et al., 2014; Weidema, 2000).

Two scenarios are taken from the literature which are assumed to explore feasible pathways of the Australian electricity sector. The business-as-usual (BAU) scenario, or S1, is based on the default case of the e-future web tool of the Commonwealth Scientific and Industrial Research Organisation (CSIRO, 2015). This scenario forecasts a growing electricity demand from 229 TWh up to 353 TWh in the period between 2015 and 2050. During the same time period, the share of electricity generated from renewable sources increases up to 36%. CCS is expected to reach large-scale penetration from around 2040. Wind power grows in the mid-term, but is assumed to be more costly than solar power and therefore declines after 2040 (Figure 4.2a).

The second scenario, S2, is based on ClimateWorks et al. (2014), who present a deep decarbonization pathway of the Australian economy, including the sectors electricity, transportation and buildings. However, we only consider the electricity sector in this work. Electricity demand is projected to grow from 264 TWh to 607 TWh between 2015 and 2050. Electricity generation from renewable sources increases up to a share of 96%, whereby grid-electricity is 100% renewable, and only a small fraction of off-grid electricity generation is fossil (Figure 4.2b). Scenario S3, the best-case scenario, combines the lower electricity demand of scenario S1 and the high share of renewable electricity generation of scenario S2 (Figure 4.2c). In scenario S4, the worst-case scenario, we assume the opposite – namely, higher electricity demand and lower renewables shares (Figure 4.2d).

Both original scenarios, S1 and S2, are based on CSIRO's Energy Sector Model (CESM). CESM is an economic model, which determines emission abatement activities as a response to the carbon price (ClimateWorks et al., 2014). Although the carbon tax has been repealed in 2014 (BBC, 2014), the modeling results from CSIRO and ClimateWorks et al. are used nevertheless, as we are unaware of future studies that already include effects of the abolished carbon tax.

### Matrix balancing

The changes in electricity demand, as obtained from the scenarios outlined above, are introduced into the initial 2009 supply-and-use table (see second step in

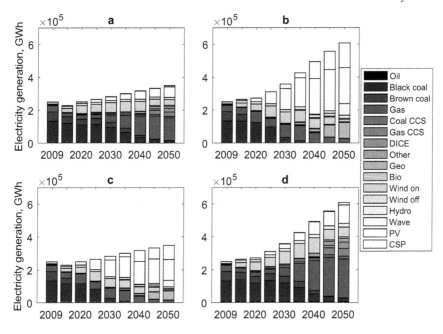

*Figure 4.2* Electricity generation shares in scenarios (a) S1-BAU, (b) S2-100% RE, (c) S3-best case, (d) S4-worst case.

Figure 4.1). This is done in five-year intervals, producing updated SUTs for 2015, 2020, 2025 and so on until 2050. Interjacent years are linearly interpolated. The described changes initially disturb the balance of the SUT and thus, lead to an imbalanced SUT. This means that $\sum_{i=1}^{m} x_i \neq \sum_{j=1}^{n} x_j$ – i.e. total row sums are unequal to total column sums. These imbalances can be ignored in cases when the exogenous changes are small, but this is not the case here. Thus, in order to rebalance the table, we make use of the "analytical approach" proposed by Malik et al. (2014, p. 86). The rebalancing method is an iterative process which endogenously forces input values to match the new scenario-generated output values. Thus, after we manually alternate final demand for electricity $\tilde{y}$ in each period t, we calculate the new corresponding output $\tilde{x}$ according to

$$\tilde{\mathbf{x}}_t = \left( \mathbf{I} - \mathbf{A}^* \right)^{-1} \tilde{\mathbf{y}}_t \qquad (4.3)$$

as well as the new use table $\tilde{\mathbf{T}}$ according to

$$\tilde{\mathbf{T}}_t = \mathbf{A}^* \hat{\tilde{\mathbf{x}}}_t. \qquad (4.4)$$

During the balancing process, the production recipes in $\mathbf{A}^*$ remain constant for all technologies except for the electricity product rows. Only the total levels of inputs are adjusted as a consequence of changes in total sectoral outputs. New direct GHG emissions of all industry sectors in the scenario economy can be calculated using

$$\tilde{E}_t = \tilde{x}_t \left( E^* x^{*-1} \right).$$ (4.5)

We assume that the emissions intensity of industries other than electricity has not changed over time. This means that all industries other than electricity remain at constant carbon intensities. This is a deliberate assumption since it is not within the scope of this work to assess potential carbon efficiency improvements of all sectors. In addition, the sole focus on the electricity sector allows for an impact analysis of electricity in isolation.

## Results

### Scenario results

Overall, our results show that a shift to a stronger usage of electricity from renewable sources and a simultaneous decrease in electricity generation from fossil fuels can save the majority of GHG emissions of Australia's electricity sector as well as a considerable fraction of Australia's overall GHG emissions.

In particular, total carbon footprints of final demand for electricity decrease in all four scenarios. As expected, the strongest reduction is achieved in the best-case scenario, S3, with a reduction of 96% from 47 Mt $CO_2$e in 2009 down to 2 Mt $CO_2$e in 2050 (Figure 4.3c). With 26%, the lowest reduction is achieved in the worst-case scenario, S4, resulting in 35 Mt $CO_2$e in 2050 (Figure 4.3d). Note that also direct GHG emissions from electricity generation decrease in the scenarios but remain at a constantly higher level than CF emissions (not shown in Figure 4.3). For example, direct GHG emissions reduce from 156 Mt $CO_2$e down to 4 Mt $CO_2$e in scenario S3 during the same period. In S4, direct emissions reduce to 102 Mt by 2050.

The reason why electricity-related carbon footprints are lower than direct electricity emissions is that only households consume electricity as a final product. All other industrial consumers, such as the agricultural sector, as well as private and commercial sectors, consume electricity as an intermediate product (or input) to realize the production of their own goods and services. Footprint calculations are consumption oriented and therefore emissions associated with this intermediate demand are allocated to the final product in the form of embodied emissions. For example, electricity-related emissions from metal production are allocated to the purchase of a passenger vehicle.

We assumed that, while there are carbon emission reductions in the electricity sector, other industries do not undertake decarbonization efforts. This way, we can evaluate the potential individual contribution of the electricity industry to Australia's carbon emission reduction goals: 26%–28% by 2030 as laid out in the Paris Agreement. In the best-case scenario, S3, total economy-wide emissions

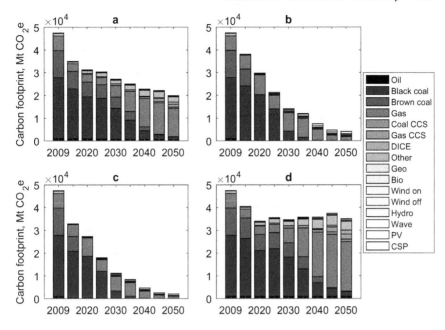

*Figure 4.3* Carbon footprint time series of finally demanded electricity in scenarios (a) S1-BAU, (b) S2-100% RE, (c) S3-best case, (d) S4-worst case

reduce by 12% from 495 Mt $CO_2$e in 2009 down to 435 Mt in 2030. By 2050, a 19% reduction is achieved, arriving at 403 Mt. It is obvious that even in the best-case scenario actual emission reductions clearly fall short of the stated goals. In the worst-case scenario, S4, total carbon emissions even increase by 2% up to 505 Mt in the period from 2009 and 2050, illustrating that efficiency gains in GHG emissions cannot outweigh increased electricity consumption in this case.

In the light of the carbon budget approach, above results concede an interesting insight. As laid out in the introduction, Australia can be assigned an (unofficial) national carbon budget of roughly 6 Gt for the period 2013–2100, assuming zero emissions thereafter (Ecofys, 2013). Cumulative economy-wide GHG emissions exceed 6 Gt well before the end of 2024 under the scenarios S1, S2 and S4. Even in the best-case scenario, the budget is used up early in 2025. This clearly shows that decarbonization efforts in the electricity sector alone are by far not sufficient to achieve GHG emission levels commensurate with a 2°C warming. The underlying assumption for these figures is that per-capita GHG emissions of all countries converge to an equal level at some point in the future and then decrease to zero altogether by 2100, which is known as the contraction and convergence principle (GCI, 2008; Schellnhuber et al., 2009). It is obvious that, if Australia and other countries were to make efforts to aim at a warming in the region of 1.5°C as laid out in the Paris Agreement, their national carbon budgets would be even smaller, requiring an even deeper decarbonization in order to avoid "carbon bankruptcy" (Kartha, 2016).

*Carbon footprint intensities*

The higher-level findings reported in the previous section are based on detailed carbon footprint intensities of the different renewable electricity technologies. Hybrid LCA results are shown in Figure 4.4. Hybrid LCA adds further economy-wide upstream emissions that are not considered in pure process analysis, leading to considerably higher CF intensities (Figure 4.5). Geothermal electricity has the highest carbon footprint intensity (92 g $CO_2$e $kWh^{-1}$). Run-of river hydropower lies on the other end of the range with only 37 g $CO_2$e $kWh^{-1}$. For further results, see Wolfram (2015) and Wolfram et al. (2016).

Electricity inputs generally cause the highest contribution to the overall impact, ranging from 32% for CSP up to 62% for hydropower. This includes electricity use by all processes along the whole life cycle – for example, electricity usage during the production of plastics, metals, etc. While this is captured by process data to some degree, the higher results from hybrid LCA reflect the extended system boundary as well as the specific GHG intensities of Australia's industries. Thus, also Australia's electricity grid mix, dominated by coal and natural gas, influences the results.

In the course of the four scenarios, the individual CF intensities decrease as well as a consequence of increasing decarbonization efforts in the electricity sector. Yet the magnitude in the reduction potentials differ. For example, the steepest reduction in CF intensity is observed for reservoir hydropower, falling from 49 g $CO_2$e $kWh^{-1}$ in 2009 down to 10 g $CO_2$e $kWh^{-1}$ in 2050 (hybrid LCA results in scenario S3). The lowest CF intensity reduction is achieved for geothermal power, decreasing from 92 g $CO_2$e $kWh^{-1}$ to 33 g $CO_2$e $kWh^{-1}$ (S3, hybrid LCA). This is

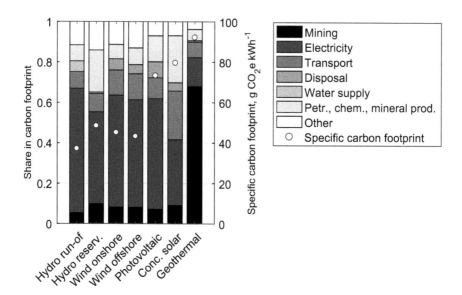

*Figure 4.4* Carbon footprint intensities of different renewable electricity generation types and relative contribution of different economic sectors calculated with hybrid LCA

mainly due to the relatively low contribution of electricity as a share of the total CF intensity of geothermal power.

## Discussion and conclusions

### *Comparison with other studies*

In general, the carbon footprint intensities found in this chapter fall within the range of estimates of other studies. Compared to an extensive harmonization and review study by Asdrubali et al. (2015), our findings are at the higher end of previously reported ranges of CF intensities (Figure 4.5). This is due to two main reasons: (1) We apply hybrid LCA and therefore capture indirect upstream emissions, and (2) we consider Australia's economy as a background system, accounting for the country's relatively high carbon intensity of production, in particular electricity production. This comparison of results demonstrates that electricity carbon footprints from purely process-based LCA are often underestimated. This emphasizes the usefulness of hybrid approaches. However, there are some limitations inherent to hybrid LCA as well.

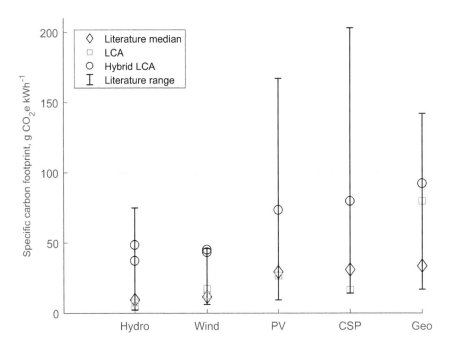

*Figure 4.5* Literature review of the carbon footprints of different renewable electricity types (Asdrubali et al., 2015) compared to the results of this article

Note: Diamonds show median values from the literature. Error bars indicate the range of CFs from the literature. Circles represent hybrid LCA results and squares represent process-based LCA results from this work. For hydro, the lower circle/square represents run-of river; for wind, the lower circle represents offshore, the lower square represents onshore.

*Limitations of the presented method*

As we apply input-output analysis, the methodology's usual assumptions and constraints apply. These are homogeneity and non-elasticity of prices, as well as proportionality between the price of a commodity and its environmental impact (Miller and Blair, 2009).

The two-region input-output framework used in this work accounts for the environmental repercussions of trade between Australia and the rest of the world. The RoW table combines all countries outside of Australia and distinguishes only 26 sectors. A more detailed representation of the rest of the world is desirable for a more detailed accounting of trade-related environmental impacts and may be a subject to future research efforts. Ideally, the trade tables will have the same resolution as the technology matrix, which is 215 by 215 sectors. In addition, several distinct country tables may be constructed to capture the real-world trade situation between Australia and other countries more adequately.

By using Malik et al.'s "analytical approach" (Malik et al., 2014) for our scenario analysis, we also adopt the major assumption that use table column proportions (production recipes) of industries other than electricity do not change over time. Only their level of input and sales proportions do change. Changes in production output and carbon intensity of other important sectors may be a future research avenue.

There is an ongoing discussion among scholars whether attributional or consequential LCA should be the preferred method (and what exactly characterizes a consequential LCA). Plevin et al. (2014) argue that the static character of attributional LCA is insufficient to inform policymaking. On the other hand, Yang (2016) proposes that the attributional framework is in fact suitable to address change-oriented questions under the premise that assumptions are discussed thoroughly and limitations are recognized. Our scenario analysis based on input-output hybrid LCA can be seen as an approach to integrate scenario changes into an attributional framework, which is sometimes referred to as consequential or prospective LCA (Finnveden et al., 2009; Plevin et al., 2014; Weidema, 2000). Even though the method will likely be subject to future improvements, we regard our proposed input-output based scenario analysis as particularly useful for change-oriented questions as alterations in production can be modelled as a consequence of changes in final demand.

*Final remarks*

Critics argued that not only is Australia's intended 26%–28% GHG emission reduction by 2030 little ambitious, implying that other nations would have to take proportionately stronger actions in order to ensure a global warming to below 2°C (Gerholdt and Ge, 2015). However, even these unpretentious targets will be hard to meet given Australia's current climate policies (Pears, 2015). Our chapter makes a valuable contribution to that discussion in that it shows that decarbonization efforts in the electricity sector alone are likely to be insufficient to reach Australia's climate goals or to stay within the national carbon budget. It is obvious that, if the global community was to make efforts to aim at a warming of around 1.5°C as laid out in the Paris Agreement, the global carbon budget would be smaller, requiring an even deeper decarbonization in order to avoid "carbon bankruptcy".

This work is the first to apply a full life-cycle approach to scenario analysis of electricity generation in Australia. We present a scenario-based hybrid LCA that builds on and extends an analytical solution based on input-output analysis, facilitating appropriate modelling of economy-wide effects of changes in technology and demand and accounting of embodied emissions in the supply chain of the electricity industry. We find that the vast majority of electricity-related greenhouse gas emissions can be saved by shifting towards an increased renewable power deployment, even when taking into account all life-cycle emissions. However, further reductions in other carbon-intensive sectors such as agriculture, extracting industries, and transportation will be necessary in the future. Our presented modelling framework, and the results obtained from it, can help informing policymakers in that it can be used to evaluate specific policy scenarios aimed at decarbonizing the economy. While this study focusses on the electricity industry, changes in any other industry can be modelled with equal rigour. Those changes may include carbon efficiency improvements, technological advancements and changes in final demand.

## Acknowledgements

This work was financially supported by the German Academic Exchange Service, the European Institute of Technology and UNSW Australia. IELab development was funded by the Australian government under the National eResearch Collaboration Tools and Resources project (NeCTAR, code VL201). IELab data feeds and routines written by Manfred Lenzen, Arne Geschke, Joe Lane and Hazel Rowley were used to create data for this study. Further scenario data were provided by Thomas Brinsmead from CSIRO and Rob Kelly from ClimateWorks.

This book chapter is based on Wolfram, P., T. Wiedmann and M. Diesendorf (2016) Carbon Footprint Scenarios of Renewable Electricity in Australia. *Journal of Cleaner Production*, 124, 236–245, http://dx.doi.org/10.1016/j.jclepro.2016.02.080; and Wolfram (2015) *Carbon Footprint Scenarios of Renewable Electricity: A Greenhouse Gas Assessment for Australia*. AV Akademikerverlag, Saarbrücken. ISBN: 978-3-639-87143-2.

## Notes

1 Compare to, for example, Germany where annual electricity generation was about 2.5 times higher (602 TWh in 2011) but the population is about 4 times higher. In Germany, 45% of total electricity was generated by coal and 14% by natural gas (as of 2011) (IEA, 2013).
2 CSIRO's e-future default scenario is also used for scenario analysis in this work
3 Biomass, wave power and fossil-based electricity are modelled with less rigour as these forms are outside the scope of this chapter.

## References

ABARE. (2003). *Australian commodity statistics 2002*. Canberra, Australia: Australian Bureau of Agricultural and Resource Economics.

ABS. (2007). *8226.0 – electricity, gas, water and waste services, Australia*. Canberra, Australia: Australian Bureau of Statistics. Retrieved from www.abs.gov.au/AUSSTATS/abs@.nsf/DetailsPage/8226.02006-07.

ABS. (2010). *8301.0.55.001 – Manufacturing Production, Australia*. Canberra, Australia: Australian Bureau of Statistics. Retrieved from www.abs.gov.au/ausstats/abs@.nsf/mf/8301.0.55.001

ABS. (2011). *4604.0 – energy account, Australia, 2011–12*. Canberra, Australia: Australian Bureau of Statistics. Retrieved from http://abs.gov.au/ausstats/abs@.nsf/Lookup/4604.0main+features42011-12

ABS. (2012a). *1301.0 – year book 2012*. Canberra, Australia: Australian Bureau of Statistics. Retrieved from www.abs.gov.au/ausstats/abs@.nsf/Lookup/by%20Subject/1301.0~2012~Main%20Features~Downloads~96

ABS. (2012b). *5215.0.55.001 – Australian national accounts: Input-output tables (Product details) 2008–09*. Canberra, Australia: Australian Bureau of Statistics. Retrieved from www.abs.gov.au/AUSSTATS/abs@.nsf/Lookup/5215.0.55.001Main+Features12008-09?OpenDocument

ABS. (2014). *8301.0 – production of selected construction materials*. Canberra, Australia: Australian Bureau of Statistics. Retrieved from www.abs.gov.au/ausstats/abs@.nsf/mf/8301.0

ABS. (2015). *5209.0.55.001 – Australian national accounts: Input-output tables, 2012–13*. Canberra, Australia: Australian Bureau of Statistics. www.abs.gov.au/AUSSTATS/abs@.nsf/DetailsPage/5209.0.55.0012012-13?OpenDocument.

AEMO. (2014). *Electricity data: Price and demand*. Australia: Australian Energy Market Operator. Retrieved from http://aemo.com.au/Electricity/Data/Price-and-Demand

ALCAS. (2011). *AusLCI-The Australian Life Cycle Inventory database initiative*. Australian Life Cycle Assessment Society. Retrieved from http://alcas.asn.au/AusLCI/

Asdrubali, F., Baldinelli, G., D'Alessandro, F., and Scrucca, F. (2015). Life cycle assessment of electricity production from renewable energies: Review and results harmonization. *Renewable and Sustainable Energy Reviews, 42*, 1113–1122.

BBC (2014). *Australia votes to repeal carbon tax*. Retrieved from www.bbc.com/news/world-asia-28339663

Berrill, P., Arvesen, A., Scholz, Y., Gils, H. C., and Hertwich, E. G. (2016). Environmental impacts of high penetration renewable energy scenarios for Europe. *Environmental Research Letters, 11*(1), art. 014012.

BREE. (2011). *Resources and energy statistics 2011*. Canberra, Australia: Bureau of Resources and Energy Economics. Retrieved from www.industry.gov.au/Office-of-the-Chief-Economist/Publications/Pages/Resources-and-energy-statistics.aspx

BREE. (2014). *Energy in Australia 2014*. Canberra, Australia: Bureau of Resources and Energy Economics.

Bureau of Metal Statistics. *World bureau of metals database*. United Kingdom: Ware. Retrieved from www.world-bureau.com/index.html.

Burkhardt, J. J., Heath, G. A., and Turchi, C. S. (2011). Life cycle assessment of a parabolic trough concentrating solar power plant and the impacts of key design alternatives. *Environmental Science & Technology, 45*(6), 2457–2464.

ClimateWorks, ANU, CSIRO, and CoPS. (2014). Pathways to deep decarbonisation in 2050: How Australia can prosper in a low carbon world. Technical report. Melbourne, Australia: ClimateWorks Australia.

CSIRO. (2015). *eFuture*. Retrieved from www.efuture.csiro.au/

DFAT. (2015). *Australia's climate action*. Retrieved from http://dfat.gov.au/international-relations/themes/climate-change/Pages/australias-climate-action.aspx

Ecofys. (2013). *Australia's carbon budget based on global effort sharing*. Technical report. Cologne, Germany: Ecofys.

Ecoinvent. (2014). *Ecoinvent database.* Zurich, Switzerland: Swiss Centre for Life Cycle Inventories. Retrieved from www.ecoinvent.org

Finnveden, G., Hauschild, M. Z., Ekvall, T., Guinée, J., Heijungs, R., Hellweg, S., . . . Suh, S. (2009). Recent developments in life cycle assessment. *Journal of Environmental Management, 91*(1), 1–21.

GCI. (2008). Contraction and convergence: A global solution to a global problem. Retrieved from www.gci.org.uk/contconv/cc.html

Gerholdt, R., and Ge, M. (2015). Australia offers lackluster 2030 climate target. Retrieved from http://www.wri.org/blog/2015/08/australia-offers-lackluster-2030-climate-target

Hatfield-Dodds, S., Schandl, H., Adams, P. D., Baynes, T. M., Brinsmead, T. S., Bryan, B. A., . . . Harwood, T. (2015). Australia is "free to choose" economic growth and falling environmental pressures. *Nature, 527*(7576), 49–53.

Hearps, P., and Wright, M. (2010). *Australian sustainable energy: Zero carbon Australia stationary energy plan.* Melbourne, Australia: Beyond Zero Emissions and University of Melbourne Energy Research Institute.

Hong, S., Bradshaw, C. J., and Brook, B. W. (2014). Nuclear power can reduce emissions and maintain a strong economy: Rating Australia's optimal future electricity-generation mix by technologies and policies. *Applied Energy, 136,* 712–725.

IEA. (2013). *Energy policies of IEA countries – Germany 2013 review.* Paris, France: IEA.

Kartha, S. (2016). Implications for Australia of a 1.5 C future. Working Paper 2016-09. Stockholm, Sweden: Stockholm Environment Institute.

Lenzen, M. (1999). Total requirements of energy and greenhouse gases for Australian transport. *Transportation Research Part D: Transport and Environment, 4*(4), 265–290.

Lenzen, M., Kanemoto, K., Moran, D., and Geschke, A. (2012). Mapping the structure of the world economy. *Environmental Science & Technology, 46*(15), 8374–8381.

Lenzen, M., Geschke, A., Wiedmann, T., Lane, J., Anderson, N., Baynes, T., . . . Fry, J. (2014). Compiling and using input – output frameworks through collaborative virtual laboratories. *Science of the Total Environment, 485,* 241–251.

Lenzen, M., Malik, A., and Foran, B. (2016). Reply to Schandl et al., 2016, JCLEPRO and Hatfield-Dodds et al., 2015, Nature: How challenging is decoupling for Australia? Reply to: Schandl H., Hatfield-Dodds S., Wiedmann T., Geschke A., Cai Y., West J., Newth D., Baynes T., Lenzen M. and Owen A.(2016). Decoupling global environmental pressure and economic growth: Scenarios for energy use, materials use and carbon emissions. *Journal of Cleaner Production, 132,* 45–56.

Lenzen, M., Moran, D., Kanemoto, K., and Geschke, A. (2013). Building Eora: A global multi-region input – output database at high country and sector resolution. *Economic Systems Research, 25*(1), 20–49.

Majeau-Bettez, G., Strømman, A. H., and Hertwich, E. G. (2011). Evaluation of process- and input – output-based life cycle inventory data with regard to truncation and aggregation issues. *Environmental Science & Technology, 45*(23), 10170–10177.

Malik, A., Lenzen, M., Ely, R. N., and Dietzenbacher, E. (2014). Simulating the impact of new industries on the economy: The case of biorefining in Australia. *Ecological Economics, 107,* 84–93.

Meinshausen, M., Meinshausen, N., Hare, W., Raper, S. C., Frieler, K., Knutti, R., . . . Allen, M. R. (2009). Greenhouse-gas emission targets for limiting global warming to 2 C. *Nature, 458*(7242), 1158–1162.

Miller, R. E., and Blair, P. D. (2009). *Input-output analysis: Foundations and extensions* (2nd ed.). Cambridge: Cambridge University Press.

Minx, J. C., Wiedmann, T., Wood, R., Peters, G. P., Lenzen, M., Owen, A., . . . Baiocchi, G. (2009). Input – output analysis and carbon footprinting: An overview of applications. *Economic Systems Research, 21*(3), 187–216.

Pears, A. (2015). Even Abbott's weak emissions target will be hard work to meet. *Renew Magazine.*

Plevin, R. J., Delucchi, M. A., and Creutzig, F. (2014). Using attributional life cycle assessment to estimate climate-change mitigation benefits misleads policy makers. *Journal of Industrial Ecology, 18*(1), 73–83.

Schandl, H., Hatfield-Dodds, S., Wiedmann, T., Geschke, A., Cai, Y., West, J., . . . Owen, A. (2016). Decoupling global environmental pressure and economic growth: Scenarios for energy use, materials use and carbon emissions. *Journal of Cleaner Production, 132*, 45–56.

Schellnhuber, H., Messner, D., Leggewie, C., Leinfelder, R., Nakicenovic, N., Rahmstorf, S., . . . Schubert, R. (2009). Solving the climate dilemma: The budget approach (Special Report 2009) Berlin, Germany: German Advisory Council on Global Change (WBGU).

Singh, B., Bouman, E. A., Strømman, A. H., and Hertwich, E. G. (2015). Material use for electricity generation with carbon dioxide capture and storage: Extending life cycle analysis indices for material accounting. *Resources, Conservation and Recycling, 100*, 49–57.

Suh, S., Lenzen, M., Treloar, G. J., Hondo, H., Horvath, A., Huppes, G., . . . Moriguchi, Y. (2004). System boundary selection in life-cycle inventories using hybrid approaches. *Environmental Science & Technology, 38*(3), 657–664.

UNFCCC. (2015). Adoption of the Paris agreement – Proposal by the President. Bonn, Germany: United Nations framework convention on climate change.

UNSD. (2015). *UNdata v0.14.6 beta.* United Nations Statistics Division. Retrieved from http://data.un.org/Explorer.aspx?d=CLINO

USGS. (2009). *2009 minerals yearbook: Australia.* Washington, DC: US Geological Survey.

Weidema, B. (2000). Avoiding co-product allocation in life-cycle assessment. *Journal of Industrial Ecology, 4*(3), 11–33.

Wiedmann, T. O., Chen, G., and Barrett, J. (2015). The concept of city carbon maps: A case study of Melbourne, Australia. *Journal of Industrial Ecology, 20*, 676–691.

Wiedmann, T. O., and Minx, J. (2008). A definition of "carbon footprint". *Ecological Economics Research Trends, 1*, 1–11.

Wiedmann, T. O., Suh, S., Feng, K., Lenzen, M., Acquaye, A., Scott, K., and Barrett, J. R. (2011). Application of hybrid life cycle approaches to emerging energy technologies – the case of wind power in the UK. *Environmental Science & Technology, 45*(13), 5900–5907.

Wolfram, P. (2015). *Carbon footprint scenarios of renewable electricity: A Greenhouse Gas assessment for Australia.* Saarbrücken, Germany: AV Akademikerverlag.

Wolfram, P., Wiedmann, T., and Diesendorf, M. (2016). Carbon footprint scenarios for renewable electricity in Australia. *Journal of Cleaner Production, 124*, 236–245.

World Steel Association. (2014). *Online database.* Brussels, Belgium: World Steel Association. Retrieved from www.worldsteel.org/

Yang, Y. (2016). Two sides of the same coin: Consequential life cycle assessment based on the attributional framework. *Journal of Cleaner Production, 127*, 274–281.

# Part II

# Household consumption and social well-being

# 5 Global income inequality and carbon footprints

## Can we have the cake and eat it too?

*Klaus Hubacek, Giovanni Baiocchi, Kuishuang Feng, Raúl Muñoz Castillo, Laixiang Sun and Jinjun Xue*

## Introduction

In November 2016, in the Paris Agreement within the United Nations Framework Convention on Climate Change, 195 countries agreed

> to strengthen the global response to the threat of climate change, in the context of sustainable development and efforts to eradicate poverty, including by holding the increase in the global average temperature to well below 2°C above pre-industrial levels in the long term.
>
> (UNFCCC, 2015)

The new chair of the United Nations Intergovernmental Panel on Climate Change (IPCC) Hoesung Lee, in charge of the 6th Climate Change Assessment Report, has stressed the joint importance of economic development *and* poverty reduction when addressing climate change. Ending poverty and sustainable growth are also two key Sustainable Development Goals (SDGs) of the new sustainable development agenda adopted by the UN's General Assembly in September of 2015 (UN, 2014, 2017). However, these agreements do not prescribe how this ambitious goal can be achieved nor if these goals are mutually compatible. These issues must be considered within the context of global economic and 'carbon inequality' characterized by a historical responsibility with developed countries being responsible for most of cumulative GHG emissions (Baumert et al., 2005) and close to one billion people still living in extreme poverty. According to a recent Oxfam report, the wealth of the world is divided in two: almost half is going to the richest 1%; the other half is going to the remaining 99% (Hardoon, 2015). When we look at the extreme ends of the distribution, we find that the wealth possessed by the richest 80 individuals is equal to the wealth of the poorest half (i.e. some 3.7 billion people!) of the global population (Hardoon, 2015). While these estimates are not to be taken at face value, they do provide a powerful narrative about the extent of global inequality.

The global community has responded with numerous policy goals to address the issue of extreme poverty. "End poverty in all its forms everywhere" is the first of the UN development goals and "Poverty eradication is seen as the greatest global challenge facing the world today." Sustainable Development requires the meeting of the twin objective of 1) ensuring that all people have the resources needed, such as food, water, access to health care and energy, and 2) ensuring that humanity's use of natural resources does not stress critical earth system processes.

Similar high-level activities have been under way in the climate arena, astutely aware of the interactions between poverty and climate change, culminating in the targets set by the recent Paris Agreement and earlier by the Cancun UNFCCC meeting. Achieving the Cancun and Paris climate target of staying within a 2°C increase would require aggressive decarbonization in rich countries but is also seen as limiting aspirations of poor countries given the fact that GHG emissions are highly coupled with poverty alleviation and the climate target permits little room for energy growth (Steckel et al., 2013).

Two broad approaches have been pursued hitherto in international negotiations: 'top-down' international agreements, such as the so-called Kyoto Protocol, and 'bottom-up' (voluntary) contributions by nations, cities, companies and other entities. The top-down approach has made little progress so far due to the open access problem of global atmospheric sinks (Raupach et al., 2014), but the approach can nevertheless provide an important framework within which voluntary contributions can take place. The equity focused contraction and convergence argument allocates emissions based on equal rights to pollute or utilize these commons for every individual (i.e. per capita) (Baer et al., 2000). This would require knowledge about per capita carbon footprints across income groups and countries. In this chapter, we attempt to address this important issue by providing important groundwork for the ongoing discussion and negotiations of GHG mitigation targets and on how to allocate emission rights between and within countries.

The key question we try to address is as follows. What are the differences in carbon footprints for different income categories in different countries and globally? To address this question, we will assess the relative contribution to total carbon emissions of the extreme poor, the global middle class and the global elites, and examine if there is a convergence of consumption patterns and carbon footprints of people with increasing income across countries (although here we will focus on the 90 poorest countries). These assessments would enable us to develop scenarios and quantify the carbon implications of important likely or potential socio-economic change so that we can answer the following questions: What are the carbon implications of moving hundreds of millions of people out of poverty? What are the carbon implications of urbanization and associated lifestyle and income changes in the most populous countries, India and China, given current trends? To answer these questions, we present our compilation of consumption patterns for different income categories from consumer expenditure surveys for most countries of the world. We then link these consumption patterns to a global multi-regional input-output model (MRIO) and to calculate carbon footprints for different income categories, globally. (For more detail see Hubacek, Baiocchi, Feng, Munoz Castillo, et al. (2017) Hubacek, Baiocchi, Feng, and Padwardhan (2017)).

## Methods and Data

In this study, we use environmentally extended MRIO to estimate carbon footprints of different household groups in 90 developing countries and 28 developed countries. The global MRIO table is collected from the Eora database (http://worldmrio.com/). Eora is a multi-region IO database that provides a time series of high-resolution input-output tables (IOA) with matching environmental and social satellite accounts for 186 countries (Lenzen et al., 2012; Lenzen et al., 2013). The MRIO tables from Eora contain trade flows, production, consumption and intermediate use of commodities and services for 26 sectors, both within and between 186 countries. This study focuses on 2010 to accommodate the compiled Global Consumer Expenditure Database provided by the World Bank.

In a MRIO framework, different regions are connected through inter-regional trade, $T^{rs}$ and $T^{sr}$. The technical coefficient sub-matrix $A^{rs}$ consisting of $\{a_{ij}^{rs}\}$ is given by $a_{ij}^{rs} = T_{ij}^{rs} / x_j^s$, in which $T_{ij}^{rs}$ is the inter-sector monetary flow from sector $i$ in region $r$ to sector $j$ in region $s$; $x_j^s$ is the total output of sector $j$ in region $s$. The final demand matrix is $\{y_i^{rs}\}$, where $y_i^{rs}$ is the final demand of region $s$ for goods of sector $i$ from region $r$. Using matrix notation and dropping the subscripts, we have

$$A = \begin{bmatrix} A^{11} & A^{12} & \cdots & A^{1n} \\ A^{21} & A^{22} & \cdots & A^{2n} \\ \vdots & \vdots & \ddots & \vdots \\ A^{n1} & A^{n2} & \cdots & A^{nn} \end{bmatrix}; Y = \begin{bmatrix} y^{11} & y^{12} & \cdots & y^{1n} \\ y^{21} & y^{22} & \cdots & y^{2n} \\ \vdots & \vdots & \ddots & \vdots \\ y^{n1} & y^{n2} & \cdots & y^{nn} \end{bmatrix}; x = \begin{bmatrix} x^1 \\ x^2 \\ \vdots \\ x^n \end{bmatrix}.$$

Consequently, the MRIO framework can be written as

$$x = (I - A)^{-1} y, \tag{5.1}$$

where $(I - A)^{-1}$ is the Leontief inverse matrix which captures both direct and direct economic inputs to satisfy one unit of final demand in monetary value; $I$ is the identity matrix with ones on the diagonal and zeros on the off-diagonal.

To calculate the consumption-based greenhouse gas emissions (GHG), we extend the MRIO table with a vector of sectoral $CO_2$ emission coefficients for all regions, $k = \begin{bmatrix} k_1 & k_2 & \cdots & k_n \end{bmatrix}$.

Thus, the total consumption-based $CO_2$ emissions for all regions can be calculated by

$$GHG = k (I - A)^{-1} y, \tag{5.2}$$

where GHG is a vector of the total greenhouse gas emissions embodied in goods and services used for the final demand of all regions; $k$ is a vector of GHG emissions per unit of economic output for all economic sectors in all regions.

In the World Bank's Global Consumption Database (The World Bank, 2015), households in developing countries were categorized in four consumption segments: lowest, low, middle and higher. They are based on global income distribution data, which rank the global population by income per capita. The lowest consumption segment (below $2.97 per capita a day) corresponds to the bottom half of the global distribution, or the 50th percentile and below, the low consumption segment (between $2.97 and $8.44 per capita a day) to the 51th–75th percentiles, the middle consumption segment (between $8.44 and $23.03 per capita a day) to the 76th–90th percentiles and the higher consumption segment (above $23.03 per capita a day) to the 91st percentile and above.

Population data for different consumer groups were collected from the World Bank Povcalnet (http://iresearch.worldbank.org/PovcalNet/). According to the World Bank PovcalNet database, developed countries only have a share of about 1% of the global population in the lowest and low-income groups. In terms of global middle income, developed countries' share in this group account for about 19%, while their share of the global high-income group is 89%. Therefore, we use the World Bank's 90 developing countries' consumption data to estimate per capita carbon footprint for the lowest and the low-income groups. To calculate the footprint for the middle and high-income group, we use the consumption expenditure data of these consumer groups of the 90 developing countries in the World Bank's consumption database and consumer expenditure surveys from the United States and EU to represent consumption patterns in developed countries.

## Current distribution of income and associated carbon emissions

Lifestyles, consumption patterns and associated per capita carbon footprints differ enormously (see Figure 5.1). According to our calculations, the top 10% cause

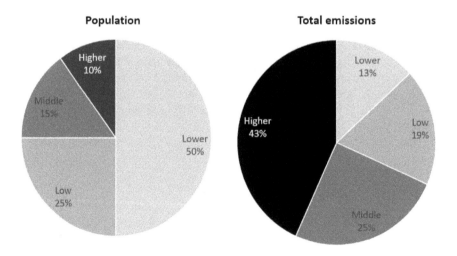

*Figure 5.1* Shares of population and associated carbon emissions

almost half of global GHG emissions, whereas the bottom 50% are responsible for only 13% of global emissions.

The average carbon footprint starts at 1.7t for the lowest income category, then quickly increases to 4.7t and 10.6t for the two middle income categories and finally to an average of 27.5t for the highest income category. In order words, the average carbon footprint of the global elites is about 16 times as high as the carbon footprint of the lowest expenditure group. When disaggregating the various groups further, to potentially account for the global top 1% and the extreme poor, these differences would become much more pronounced.

These differences between global expenditure groups hide potentially starker differences within countries in terms of expenditure patterns and associated carbon footprints, and this is especially true for poorer countries with a majority of the population living in poverty.

When looking at poor countries with the lowest carbon footprints (see Figure 5.2), we can see large disparity between the poor and rich in these countries. The lowest income category has a carbon footprint of close to zero, whereas the elites in some of these countries have footprints larger than the global average in the richest category. Especially in Africa we find countries with more than 90% of the population falling in the less-than-$2.97-income-per-day category explaining

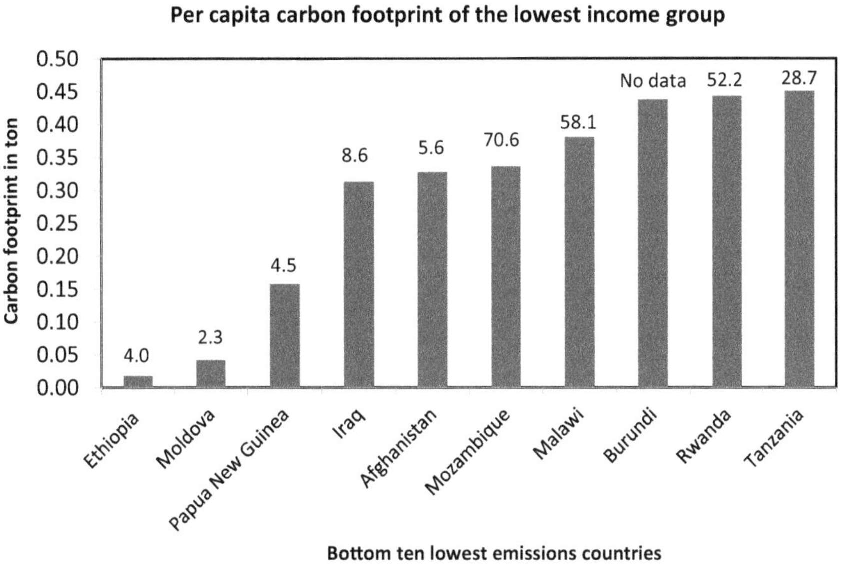

*Figure 5.2* Carbon footprints of lowest and highest income in low-income countries

Note: The size of the bar reflects the per capita carbon footprint of the lowest income group for each country, whereas the numbers on top of each bar indicates the carbon footprint in the highest expenditure group in each country.

some of the disparity and low overall carbon footprint despite the outliers provided by the respective elites.

In Figure 5.3, we explore how carbon disparity changes with increasing income. We have ranked the countries from lowest to highest income and plotted the various footprints for each income category of each country. We can see huge variation on the left of the figure and a declining range of carbon

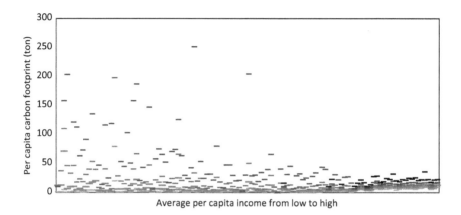

*Figure 5.3* Carbon footprints per income category for 90 ranked by per capita income, from lowest income on the left to highest incomes on the right (see the Appendix for complete list)

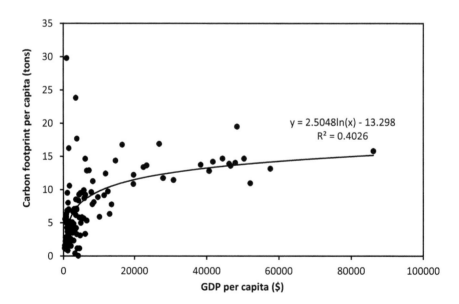

*Figure 5.4* Carbon footprints per GDP per capita

footprints within a country with increasing income. In other words, the intra-country disparity in carbon footprints is declining with per capita income, but at the same time, the average carbon footprint is increasing with increasing income (see Figure 5.4).

## What about the elephant in the room?

There are, in fact, two elephants in the room: China and India. Together they represent more than 36.5% of the global population, and their economies are growing quickly, although China's economic growth has slowed somewhat recently. Nevertheless, China's economy has been doubling on average every 7 years over the last 35 years (excluding recent slower growth). In other words, China's economy is now more than 30 times the size it was in 1980. At the same time, both countries have large segments of the population that live in incredible poverty. As of 2010, in China, there were still more than 500 million people living with less than three dollars purchasing power parity (PPP) a day. While we find a sizeable middle class in China, most people in India (more than one billion people) fall in the lowest income category without any significant middle class or sizeable high income earners (see Figure 5.5).

Given the differences in the demographics of these two countries, it is not surprising to see that most of the carbon emissions in China are caused by its middle class (78%), whereas in India, it is the poorest category contributing 63% to the carbon total. The elites contribute 9% in China and only about 0.5% in India (Figure 5.6).

These differences are mainly due to the population size in each category. When looking at the respective per capita carbon footprints in each category, we see that the national average is fairly low for both countries, despite of a sizeable

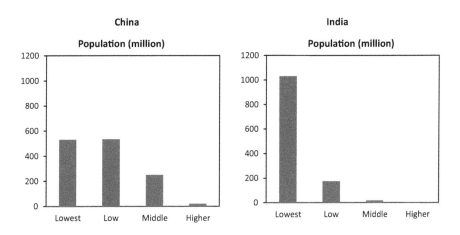

*Figure 5.5* Population in China and India per income category

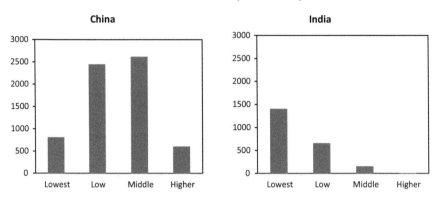

*Figure 5.6* Total carbon emissions in China and India per income category

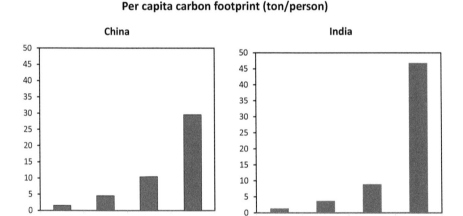

*Figure 5.7* Per capita carbon footprints in India and China for each income category and the national average

difference, with 4.8t in China and 1.7t for India due to the income distribution in these two countries. Striking is the difference in average carbon consumption of the elites with 29.5t in China and 48.6t in India (Figure 5.7).

## Some simple scenarios

The compiled data set allows us to assess some important questions such as what are the carbon implications of moving the poorest people out of poverty. When looking specifically at India and China (see Figure 5.8), we find that global carbon emissions would increase by 4% and 6%, respectively.

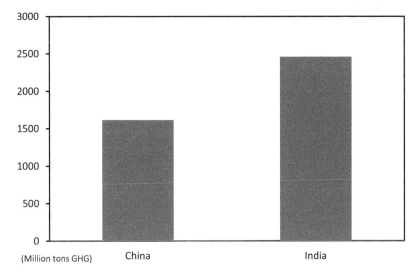

*Figure 5.8* Global carbon implications of moving

We did a similar exercise by moving the lowest income category to the next income level until 2050. The IPCC reported that the remaining carbon emissions quota associated with a 66% of probability of keeping warming below 2°C is estimated to be 1,200 Gt $CO_2$ (Friedlingstein et al., 2014). In this study, we compare this to the required carbon to lift the lowest household group or the lowest 50% of world population out of poverty (i.e. to the next income level). We found that by moving the global poor into the next income category we require 66% of available cumulative carbon emissions that are not available for other uses or need to be taken out of the atmosphere in order for the global community to remain on track towards to two-degree goal. The temperature increase of this scenario was considerable during this time period, whereas a scenario of lifting people out of extreme poverty had less of an impact due to the extremely low carbon footprint of that group. (For more detail, see Hubacek, Baiocchi, Feng, and Padwardhan (2017)).

## Conclusions

Our results show that when focusing on countries and averages we miss lots of interesting information. There are huge differences in carbon footprints between as well as within countries. There are interesting differences between countries. When looking at poor countries, we tend to find larger disparities between the carbon footprint of the rich versus the poor. For some very poor countries, the disparity is more than one order of magnitude.

A general finding is that the higher the income the higher the carbon footprint. There seems to be no leveling off. Higher incomes generate higher carbon footprints although at a declining growth rate within our sample of 90 poor countries. The global elites – i.e. the top 10% of world population – are the main contributors to global carbon emissions, followed by global middle class, together accounting for about 87% of the global household carbon footprint. Thus it is not surprising that adding to the middle class by moving people out of poverty adds significantly to global carbon emissions and makes global targets for mitigating GHGs more difficult to achieve given the pace of technological progress, fossil fuel dependence and generally increasing carbon emissions with higher income. Decarbonization efforts, as suggested by the Paris Agreement, can help ameliorate global emission growth from household consumption, but lifestyles and economic growth need to be part of the global discourse on mitigating climate change.

# Appendix

**Countries in figure 5.1 ranked according to income from lowest to highest**

*Table 5.A.1* Countries in figure 5.1 ranked according to income from lowest to highest

| | |
|---|---|
| 1 | Madagascar |
| 2 | Burundi |
| 3 | Congo, Dem. Rep. |
| 4 | Tanzania |
| 5 | Nicaragua |
| 6 | Burkina Faso |
| 7 | Mozambique |
| 8 | Rwanda |
| 9 | Malawi |
| 10 | Niger |
| 11 | Benin |
| 12 | Mali |
| 13 | Togo |
| 14 | India |
| 15 | Bangladesh |
| 16 | Uganda |
| 17 | Pakistan |
| 18 | Ethiopia |
| 19 | Guinea |
| 20 | Liberia |
| 21 | Zambia |
| 22 | Nigeria |
| 23 | Gambia, The |
| 24 | Nepal |
| 25 | Cameroon |
| 26 | Chad |
| 27 | Vietnam |
| 28 | Kenya |
| 29 | Senegal |
| 30 | Swaziland |
| 31 | Afghanistan |

(*Continued*)

*Table 5.A.1*  (Continued)

| | |
|---|---|
| 32 | Indonesia |
| 33 | Lao PDR |
| 34 | Cambodia |
| 35 | Kyrgyz Republic |
| 36 | Tajikistan |
| 37 | Ghana |
| 38 | Lesotho |
| 39 | Sierra Leone |
| 40 | Egypt, Arab Rep. |
| 41 | Mauritania |
| 42 | Philippines |
| 43 | Mongolia |
| 44 | Bhutan |
| 45 | Cote d'Ivoire |
| 46 | Armenia |
| 47 | El Salvador |
| 48 | Sri Lanka |
| 49 | Honduras |
| 50 | Yemen, Rep. |
| 51 | Congo, Rep. |
| 52 | Bolivia |
| 53 | Djibouti |
| 54 | Namibia |
| 55 | Azerbaijan |
| 56 | China |
| 57 | Morocco |
| 58 | Ukraine |
| 59 | Moldova |
| 60 | Fiji |
| 61 | Mauritius |
| 62 | Maldives |
| 63 | Thailand |
| 64 | Peru |
| 65 | Albania |
| 66 | Guatemala |
| 67 | Mexico |
| 68 | Kazakhstan |
| 69 | Iraq |
| 70 | Belarus |
| 71 | Jamaica |
| 72 | Macedonia FYR |
| 73 | Gabon |
| 74 | Romania |
| 75 | Papua New Guinea |
| 76 | Cabo Verde |
| 77 | Macedonia, FYR |
| 78 | Colombia |
| 79 | Jordan |
| 80 | Bulgaria |
| 81 | Serbia |
| 82 | Turkey |
| 83 | Sao Tome and Principe |

| | |
|---|---|
| 84 | Lithuania |
| 85 | South Africa |
| 86 | Bulgaria |
| 87 | Montenegro |
| 88 | Montenegro |
| 89 | Russian Federation |
| 90 | Romania |
| 91 | Latvia |
| 92 | Brazil |
| 93 | Bosnia and Herzegovina |
| 94 | Turkey |
| 95 | Latvia |
| 96 | Lithuania |
| 97 | Poland |
| 98 | Hungary |
| 99 | Croatia |
| 100 | Estonia |
| 101 | Slovakia |
| 102 | Malta |
| 103 | Czech Republic |
| 104 | Portugal |
| 105 | Slovenia |
| 106 | Greece |
| 107 | Cyprus |
| 108 | Spain |
| 109 | United Kingdom |
| 110 | France |
| 111 | Germany |
| 112 | Belgium |
| 113 | Finland |
| 114 | Austria |
| 115 | Ireland |
| 116 | United States |
| 117 | Netherlands |
| 118 | Sweden |
| 119 | Denmark |
| 120 | Norway |

## References

Baer, P., Harte, J., Haya, B., Herzog, A. V., Holdren, J., Hultman, N. E., . . . Raymond, L. (2000). Equity and greenhouse gas responsibility. *Science, 289*(5488), 2287–2287.

Baumert, K. A., Herzog, T., and Pershing, J. (2005). *Navigating the numbers: Greenhouse gases and international climate change agreements.* World Resources Institute. Washington, D.C.

Friedlingstein, P., Andrew, R. M., Rogelj, J., Peters, G. P., Canadell, J. G., Knutti, R., . . . Van Vuuren, D. (2014). Persistent growth of $CO_2$ emissions and implications for reaching climate targets. *Nature Geoscience, 7*(10), 709–715.

Hardoon, D. (2015). *Wealth: Having it all and wanting more.* Oxford: Oxfam GB, Oxfam House.

Hubacek, K., Baiocchi, G., Feng, K., Munoz Castillo, R., Sun, L., and Xue, J. (In Press). Global carbon inequality. *Energy, Ecology* and *Environment*.

Hubacek, K., Baiocchi, G., Feng, K., and Padwardhan, A. (2017). Poverty eradication in a carbon constrained world. *Nature Communications*.

Lenzen, M., Kanemoto, K., Moran, D., and Geschke, A. (2012). Mapping the structure of the world economy. *Environmental Science & Technology*, *46*(15), 8374–8381.

Lenzen, M., Moran, D., Kanemoto, K., and Geschke, A. (2013). Building Eora: A global multi-region input – output database at high country and sector resolution. *Economic Systems Research*, *25*(1), 20–49.

Raupach, M. R., Davis, S. J., Peters, G. P., Andrew, R. M., Canadell, J. G., Ciais, P., . . . Le Quere, C. (2014). Sharing a quota on cumulative carbon emissions. *Nature Climate Change*, *4*(10), 873–879.

Steckel, J. C., Brecha, R. J., Jakob, M., Strefler, J., and Luderer, G. (2013). Development without energy? Assessing future scenarios of energy consumption in developing countries. *Ecological Economics*, *90*, 53–67.

United Nations (2015). Transforming our world: the 2030 Agenda for Sustainable Development. Resolution adopted by the General Assembly on 25 September 2015. A/RES/70/1.

UNFCCC. (2015). Historic Paris agreement on climate change – 195 nations set path to keep temperature rise well below 2 degrees Celsius [Press release]. Retrieved from http://newsroom.unfccc.int/unfccc-newsroom/finale-cop21/

The World Bank. (2015). *Global consumption database*. The World Bank. Retrieved from http://datatopics.worldbank.org/consumption/

The World Bank. (2017). PovcalNet. *World Bank's Poverty database* Retrieved from http://iresearch.worldbank.org/PovcalNet/

# 6 The potential contribution of solar thermal electricity (STE) in Mexico in the light of the Paris Agreements

*Irene Rodríguez-Serrano, Natalia Caldés*

## Introduction

Mexico is undoubtedly committed to address climate change as demonstrated by the mitigation and adaptation measures set over the last few years as well as the financial resources devoted to such efforts. Proof of that is that since 2000, Mexico has published three National Strategies on Climate Change. In 2012, and as part of the National Strategy for Climate Change, the General Law of Climate Change was published in order to promote renewables energies, setting the target of 35% of the electricity generation from clean energy technologies by 2024 (Secretaría General, 2012). Additionally, Mexico´s Special Program on Climate change and Mexico´s Intended Nationally Determined Contributions (INDC) set the target to reduce 22% of greenhouse gases (GHG) emissions by the year 2030 with respect to the year 2013 (SERMANAT, 2015).

To achieve the aforementioned GHG emission reductions, Mexico has to progressively substitute fossil fuel technologies with renewables. Nevertheless, despite its large renewables potential (Secretaría de Economía de Mexico, 2015), the total installed capacity of renewables in 2015 was somehow limited, amounting 17 GW and representing 21% of the total electricity installed capacity, mainly from hydropower (INERE, 2015). To reverse this situation, the National Energy Secretariat (SENER) expects an increase of renewables installed capacity by 21 GW from 2012 to 2026 (Secretaría de Economía de Mexico, 2013). Such estimates are in line with IRENA, which estimates that by 2030 renewable energies could reach up to 21% of the total final energy consumption in Mexico (IRENA and SENER, 2015).

According to national energy plans, renewable energies technologies such as wind onshore, geothermal, photovoltaics and biomass are expected to contribute to the future Mexican electricity mix (INERE, 2015; IRENA and SENER, 2015; Secretaría de Economía de Mexico, 2013; SENER, 2014, 2015a). However, according to the governmental institution Proméxico, Solar Thermal Electricity (STE) is only expected to play a minimal role, with only 30 MW by 2026 (Secretaría de Economía de Mexico, 2013). This is a surprising fact, given the remarkable solar potential in Mexico, especially in the North Western of the country with more than 2,500 kWh/m2 of Direct Normal Irradiation (DNI) (Arancibia-Bulnes et al., 2014; Greenpeace et al., 2016; Romero-Hernández et al., 2012). Moreover, this technology presents a remarkable advantage over other renewable technologies due to its energy storage capacity (Greenpeace et al., 2016). In this sense, the ability to control the output of a Concentrating Solar Power (CSP) plant via the use of its Thermal Energy Storage (TES) creates the opportunity to maximize its value to the grid, particularly with larger shares of other variable renewable technologies. Additionally, despite its higher electricity generation cost compared to other technologies, large cost reductions are expected as result of a progressive market growth (SolarPaces et al., 2016).

Besides contributing to the international efforts and commitments to mitigate climate change, there exist additional reasons why Mexico is advocating for a more sustainable and low carbon energy mix. Being one of the top-ten oil producer countries, Mexico is largely dependent and vulnerable to oil price fluctuations and is largely dependent on natural gas imports (U.S. Energy Information Agency, 2014), which represents a cornerstone in the Mexican Economy. In 2014, domestic demand of natural gas represented 43% of the total primary fuels and imported natural gas represented 30% of national production. Most natural gas imports come from United States (around 70%) and the rest correspond to liquefied natural gas mainly from Peru, Trinidad and Tobago, Nigeria, Indonesia and Qatar (SENER, 2015b). Electricity production from natural gas represented 57% of the electricity mix in 2014, having increased from 43% in 2004 mainly due to decrease from fuel oil (SENER, 2015c).

In this context, making balanced energy investment decisions that consider environmental, social and economic concerns is a challenging task as the three pillars involve different types of values that are not easily commensurable with each other. Moreover, non-industrialized countries face important pressures to exploit their environmental resources as their economies rely heavily on them and they have laxer social and environmental protection laws (Lehman, 1999). Consequently, their rapid economic growth often comes at the expense of irreversible environmental and social damages. Furthermore, globalization has increased the complexity of supply chains as products and services consumed in developed countries are often produced in developing countries, sometimes resulting in not only environmental impacts but also social abuses due to weaker social protection measures (Alsamawi et al., 2014; Wilshaw, 2013).

The Mexican government has indicated to follow a sustainable development pathway in a way that the associated impacts across the three sustainability pillars should be identified, characterized and valued so that the required prevention and mitigation measures can be put in place (SERMANAT, 2015). In this respect, while some methodologies that were originally designed to capture macroeconomic impacts of investments (such as input-output analysis (IOA)) have been extended and hybridized to include environmental effects (Lenzen, 1998; Wiedmann et al., 2007), the incorporation of the social perspective in this type of study has mostly been limited to job creation (Alsamawi et al., 2014; Thornley et al., 2008), and the inclusion of additional social impacts is still very incipient in this framework (Papong et al., 2015). One of the challenges is that most social impacts are based on qualitative results from surveys or field visits, and they cannot be straightforwardly converted to quantifiable results and integrated with traditional economic or environmental methodologies. Also, qualitative data is more subjective and more locally specific than quantitative values (UNEP et al., 2009).

In the light of the aforementioned challenges, the Framework for Integrated Sustainability Assessment (FISA), described in detail in Rodríguez-Serrano et al. (2016) and used in this work, broadens the existing body of literature and helps to fill the social gap by integrating the social pillar into the sustainability assessment (Rodríguez-Serrano et al., 2016). Based on a multiregional input output (MRIO) integrated with a social risk database, FISA allows for the assessment of different sustainability impacts by relating the economic stimulation results associated to the studied investment projects with environmental, socioeconomic and social risk data. Additionally, it is possible to distinguish and compare between direct, indirect and domestic and international effects caused by different projects.

In this sense, this work aims to apply the FISA framework to estimate the potential sustainability impacts associated to a larger deployment of STE technology in Mexico. To evaluate such a potential contribution, the net impacts of an alternative scenario are assessed. Such scenario is defined by a gradual penetration of three 100 MW STE power plants in Mexico to 2030, which substitute the equivalent electricity produced by the Natural Gas Combined Cycle (NGCC). The results obtained could potentially help decision makers reconsider the role that STE could play in the future Mexican electricity system as well as to identify the necessary measures needed to minimize the potential harmful effects while fostering the positive effects of such an alternative scenario, both in Mexico as well as in other parts of the world.

## Methodology

### *Multiregional input output (MRIO)*

Input-output (IO) methodology allows to analyze trade relationships of economic sectors through the use of input-output tables (IOTs) (Leontief, 1936). IOTs describe, in columns, the monetary value of those products that a sector needs from the rest of the sectors to obtain its total production (inputs), whereas rows show the distribution in monetary values of the production of a sector over the rest of sectors (outputs) (Wiedmann et al., 2007). When considering various regions or countries, it is possible to estimate the economic stimulation produced in other regions due to a change in the demand of goods and services (G&S) of one region by the use of multiregional input-output tables (MRIOTs) (Ten Raa, 2006). The monetary value of products that one sector needs from the rest of sectors to obtain one monetary unit of production is represented by technical coefficients, which are gathered within the technical coefficient matrix or A matrix (Miller and Blair, 2009).

The total G&S produced by a specific demand can be estimated as shown in Eq. (6.1).

$$x = (I - A)^{-1}y \tag{6.1},$$

where x is the total production of goods and services (total effects); A is the technical coefficient matrix; $(I - A)^{-1}$ is the inverse of Leontief, which represents direct and indirect effects; and y is the required demand.

Estimation of total effects include direct and indirect effects, being direct effects related to the demand requirements for the project and indirect effects those inputs necessary to satisfy the direct demand. The multiplier effect gives information about the total stimulation produced from direct effects (Caldés et al., 2009).

IO analysis allows for estimating other impacts (e.g. working hours, $CO_2$ emissions), by extending the methodology with vectors describing specific impacts per monetary unit produced in each economic sector. These impacts can be calculated by Eq. (6.2).

$$z_t = z_t (I - A)^{-1} y, \tag{6.2}$$

where $z_t$ is the total socioeconomic or environmental effects and $z_i$ is the environmental or socioeconomic vector

MRIO analysis in this work is based on the World Input Output Database (WIOD), which is the result of a European Commission funded project within the seventh Framework Programme (Timmer et al., 2015). It contains the time-series of world IOTs from 1995 to 2011, including 40 countries with 35 economic sectors plus a rest of the world (RoW) region. It also contains a time-series of socioeconomic and environmental data (e.g. employment, working hours, energy use, air emissions or water consumption). One of the advantages of this database is that it is publicly accessible, and its IOTs are based on supply-use tables from national statistics that are later integrated with bilateral trade statistics, reaching more accuracy between resulting information and national statistical (Jones et al., 2014). Nevertheless, it has fewer sectorial disaggregation and less country data than other exiting databases, especially from the aggregation of countries within the RoW region (Tukker and Dietzenbacher, 2013).

### *Adding the social pillar: framework for integrated sustainability assessment*

To achieve the integrated sustainability assessment previously described, the social pillar is covered by adding a social risk database named Social Hotspot Database (SHDB). Developed by New Earth in 2011, it contains information of an ample variety of social indicators classified in 22 social themes and 5 impact categories (SHDB, 2016).

The social indicators values are obtained from numerous social databases such as International Labor Organization (ILO) or World Bank (WB). These indicators

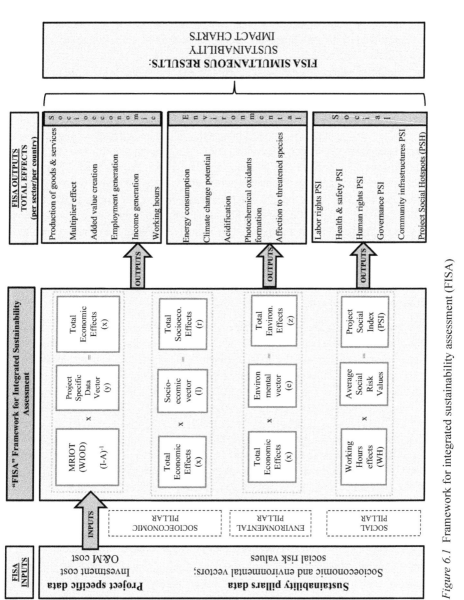

*Figure 6.1* Framework for integrated sustainability assessment (FISA)

are transformed into social risk values, which represent the degree of different social threats occurring in the various economic sectors (Benoît Norris et al., 2012). The transformation process is mainly based on the distribution of data (e.g. quartiles) (Franze, 2013), and the social risks obtained are classified into a one to four quantitative scale in which one represents low risks and four represents very high risk. Detailed information about social risks and the underlying data can be found in New Earth (2013).

The methodological link between the SHDB and the MRIO is possible by relating sectorial social risks values according to WIOD classification with MRIO working hours resulted from a project. Such a linkage is done in the so called Project Social Index (PSI) (Rodríguez-Serrano et al., 2016). In this sense, an economic sector with a high PSI value indicates that it has been highly stimulated by the analyzed project (in terms of working hours) and that this sector has some sort of social risks. The highest PSI values help identify the Project Social Hotspots (PSH), which raise an alert about the potential largest social risks associated to the studied project. Based on the PSH results, it is recommended that a more detailed analysis of the corresponding social risks within sectors at the local level is conducted to corroborate the results and identify potential measures needed to minimize such problems. Figure 6.1 shows the structure of the FISA framework and its methodological steps (Rodríguez-Serrano et al., 2016).

## Data and assumptions

In this work, two electricity generation scenarios have been considered and compared in terms of GHG emissions and other 14 sustainability impacts. In the first considered scenario, named the NGCC scenario, the electricity generation projections from 2013 to 2030 according to the Mexican Energy Secretariat (SENER) have been considered. Under this scenario, the total generation of NGCC for the studied period amounts of 3,527 TWh, starting with 127 TWh in 2013 and 259 TWh in 2030 (SENER, 2015b).

The second scenario, named NGCC + STE scenario, considers that three 100 MW STE tower plants with molten salt technology and five hours of storage will be installed and operated during the same period. Under the NGCC+STE scenario, it is assumed that the electricity produced by STE would generate 9.5 TWh and substitute the equivalent electricity produced by NGCC. A brief description of the prototype plant is described in Table 6.1 (Rodríguez-Serrano, et al., 2017).

The construction of each one of the three STE plants is assumed to last two years starting in 2017, 2021 and 2025, and the total electricity produced by the three plants throughout the whole period would amount to 9.5 TWh. Figure 6.2 illustrates the assumed timeline of the STE three plants.

The considered amount of STE represents a substitution of 0.27% of the electricity produced with NGCC in the analyzed period. However, the different nature of both technologies implies that their sustainability performance of the two alternative technologies throughout the studied period could have significant differences, including GHG emissions. To assess such differences, the associated GHG

*Table 6.1* Description of the 100 MW plant prototype (Rodríguez-Serrano et al., 2017)

**Characteristics of the 100 MW STE plant**

| | |
|---|---|
| **Construction time** | 2 years |
| **Operational time** | 30 years |
| **Yearly production (GWh)** | 395.7 |
| **Occupied land area (ha)** | 728.4 |
| **Technology** | Molten salts central receiver |
| **Tower height (m)** | 205 |
| **Storage hours** | 5 |
| **Salts composition** | 60% NaNO3, 40% KNO3 |
| **Power cycle technology** | Steam Rankine |

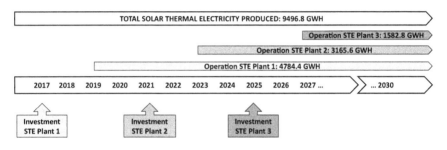

*Figure 6.2* Timeline of the investment and operation phases of the three STE plants

emissions under the two scenarios (NGCC and NGCC+STE) will be assessed together with other environmental, economic and social risks impacts.

STE investment and operation and maintenance (O&M) cost data has been provided by the European Solar Thermal Energy Association and cost breakdown has been adapted following different literature review (Rodríguez-Serrano et al., 2017). As for the NGCC cost data, it has been adapted from the Mexican Electricity Federation Commission (CFE, 2012) and the investment cost breakdown has followed Batelle (1982) (Rodríguez-Serrano et al., forthcoming). Tables 6.2 and 6.3 show the assumed investment and O&M cost breakdown for both technologies (Rodríguez-Serrano et al., forthcoming).

Imports considered in this case study are mostly related to plant components within the investment phase. For the STE plant, molten salts are imported from the Netherlands and the receiver and solar field control systems are imported from the United States (Rodríguez-Serrano et al., 2017). As for NGCC, the gas turbine is imported from the United States. Additionally, both technologies import the steam turbine and the generator from Germany. Table 6.4 shows the share of imports from investment costs as well as from the total costs (Rodríguez-Serrano et al., forthcoming).

After having applied the proposed FISA framework (Rodríguez-Serrano et al., 2016) under the aforementioned costs assumptions, Table 6.5 shows

*Table 6.2* Investment cost breakdown for STE and NGCC prototypes (Rodríguez-Serrano et al., forthcoming)

| STE investment cost breakdown | STE investment costs (US$/MWh) | NGCC investment cost breakdown | NGCC investment costs (US$/MWh) |
|---|---|---|---|
| **Site improvements** | 1.30 | Site improvements | 0.02 |
| **Heliostat field** | 11.95 | Earth work and piling | 0.23 |
| **Tower costs** | 1.69 | Circulating water system | 0.52 |
| **Receiver** | 5.05 | Heat recovery boilers, gas turbine | 2.57 |
| **Thermal Energy Storage** | 2.42 | Steam turbines and generator | 0.88 |
| **Balance of plant** | 3.10 | Other mechanical Equipment, buildings and construction | 3.22 |
| **Power block** | 9.69 | Piping | 0.57 |
|  |  | Electrical equipment | 0.69 |
| **Tax** | 1.51 | Substation and electrical distribution | 0.35 |
| **Engineering, procurement and construction contracts and owner costs** | 4.14 | Architect/engineer services and other non-manual staff salaries | 2.35 |
| **Land costs** | 1.52 | Land costs | 1.05 |
| **Contingency** | 2.46 | Contingency | 1.55 |
| **Total** | **44.84** | **Total** | **14.00** |

*Table 6.3* O&M costs for STE and NGCC (Rodríguez-Serrano et al., forthcoming)

| STE O&M cost breakdown | STE O&M costs (US$/MWh) | NGCC O&M costs (US$/MWh) |
|---|---|---|
| **Spare parts and replacement** | 1.75 | 0.53 |
| **Insurances** | 1.26 | 0.87 |
| **Water** | 0.17 | 0.17 |
| **Regular labor maintenance** | 2.19 | 1.69 |
| **Annual labor maintenance** | 2.02 | 1.58 |
| **Financial costs** | 16.29 | 2.66 |
| **Fuel costs** | – | 36.85 |
| **Total** | 23.68 | 44.04 |

the sustainability impacts per unit of electricity produced for NGCC and STE (Rodríguez-Serrano et al., forthcoming) which will be considered to evaluate the sustainability performance of the two studied scenarios. In the first columns, impacts are displayed distinguishing between the total effects that would take

*Table 6.4* Share of imported components in STE and NGCC projects (Rodríguez-Serrano et al., forthcoming)

| Country | STE imports (%) | | NGCC imports (%) | |
|---|---|---|---|---|
| | Investment costs | Total costs | Investment costs | Total costs |
| **Germany** | 11% | 8% | 6% | 3% |
| **Mexico** | 63% | 74% | 91% | 95% |
| **Netherlands** | 2% | 1% | – | – |
| **United States** | 25% | 17% | 3% | 2% |

*Table 6.5* Sustainability impacts for NGCC and STE (Rodríguez-Serrano et al., forthcoming)

| Sustainability dimension | Indicators | Total impacts | | Mexico impacts | |
|---|---|---|---|---|---|
| | | STE | NGCC | STE | NGCC |
| **Environmental** | Climate change potential ($gCO_2eq/kWh$) | 634 | 24 | 13 | 591 |
| | Energy consumption (MJ/kWh) | 0.5 | 11.7 | 0.2 | 11.0 |
| | Acidification ($gSO_2eq/kWh$) | 0.08 | 1.63 | 0.04 | 1.58 |
| | Photochemical oxidants formation (gNMVOCeq/kWh) | 0.14 | 2.17 | 0.08 | 2.08 |
| | Affection to threatened species (% of affection) | 0.002% | 0.030% | 0.001% | 0.029% |
| **Socioeconomic** | Production of goods and services ($/MWh) | 114 | 120 | 66 | 85 |
| | Added value creation ($/MWh) | 61 | 51 | 40 | 39 |
| | Employments (jobs/GWh) | 2.1 | 2.2 | 1.5 | 1.7 |
| | Working hours (WH/GWh) | 2,809 | 2,861 | 2,209 | 2,407 |
| | Wages ($/GWh) | 18,691 | 14,997 | 8,676 | 9,574 |
| **Social** | Labor risks (PSI/GWh) | 6,121 | 6,078 | 4,871 | 5,126 |
| | Health and safety risks (PSI/GWh) | 6,648 | 6,751 | 5,063 | 5,517 |
| | Human rights risks (PSI/GWh) | 5,054 | 5,189 | 3,884 | 4,270 |
| | Governance risks (PSI/GWh) | 8,101 | 8,478 | 6,940 | 7,561 |
| | Community infrastructures risks (PSI/GWh) | 4,412 | 4,511 | 3,470 | 3,780 |

place globally from those that would take place in Mexico, taking into account the import shares and only looking at the economic, social and environmental effects that would occur in Mexico.

# Results

## *Environmental impacts*

### $CO_2eq$ emissions

According to the INDC of Mexico, when 2013 is set as the reference point, the GHG reduction target is set at 22% in 2030 from the business-as-usual (BAU) scenario. Within the BAU scenario, the projected $CO_2eq$ emissions are 792 Mt $CO_2eq$ for 2020, 888 Mt $CO_2eq$ for 2025 and 973 Mt $CO_2eq$ for 2030 (SER-MANAT, 2015). Consequently, the amount of GHG emissions to be reduced by 2030 is 214 Mt $CO_2eq$. According to the Mexican Low Emission Development Program (MLED), the electricity sector has a potential GHG reduction contribution of 17% (USAID and MLED, 2013). Thus, according to these estimations, the total amount of emissions to be reduced by the electricity sector in 2030 would be 36.4 Mt $CO_2eq$. Figure 6.3 shows the projected $CO_2eq$ emissions in Mexico from the period 2013 to 2030 as well as the estimated emissions reduction from the 22% target and the reduction contribution of the electricity sector.

As displayed in Figure 6.3, by the end of the period, around 3,250 Mton $CO_2eq$ are estimated to be reduced, from which the electricity sector can contribute with 553 Mton $CO_2eq$.

When applying the GHG emissions factors displayed in Table 6.5 to the NGCC scenario, the associated $CO_2eq$ emissions of this scenario amounts to 2,236 Mt $CO_2eq$. In the case of the NGCC+STE scenario, results amount to 2,230 Mt $CO_2eq$ from NGCC electricity and 0.2 Mt $CO_2eq$ from STE. According to these figures, the total reduction from STE integration amounts to 5.8 Mt $CO_2eq$, which represent 0.2% of the total amount to be reduced by the INDC and 1.05% from the emissions to be reduced by the electricity sector.

As for the specific impact in Mexico, the national emission factor from MRIO results is 13 g/kWh for STE and 591 g/kWh for NGCC (Table 6.5). Under the NGCC Scenario, emissions in Mexico amount to 2,084 Mt $CO_2eq$, while under

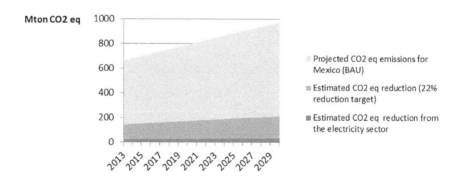

*Figure 6.3* Projected $CO_2eq$ emissions, national reduction target and contribution of the electricity sector

the NGCC+STE scenario, emissions result in 2,078 from NGCC and 0.1 from STE. The difference between the scenarios amounts to 5.5 Mt avoided emissions in Mexico as a result of the penetration of STE, which represents 0.2% of total emissions to be reduced from the national target and 1.0% reduction from the electricity sector. To put this figure in perspective, this 5.5 Mt $CO_2$eq is equivalent to the total emission from the Mexican metal sector in 2010, or five times the emissions from the chemical sector in the same year (SENER, 2015b).

*Other environmental impacts*

Beyond GHG emissions reductions, there are other relevant environmental impacts associated to the introduction of STE in Mexico such as energy consumption, acid-ification, photochemical oxidants formation and affection to threatened species.

Following the same FISA framework used to estimate the $CO_2$eq emissions, Table 6.6 displays the associated impacts of the two considered alternative sce-narios and the resulting net impacts from the substitution of NGCC electricity by STE. Again, these figures distinguish the global effects from those occurring in Mexico when taking into account the embedded effects of international trade.

Table 6.6 shows, according to the results, all environmental impacts that would be reduced when integrating STE. More than 102,000 TJ of energy consump-tion would be avoided mainly from the substitution of natural gas as fuel. In the same way, acidification and formation of photochemical oxidants impacts would decrease in more than 14,500 and 19,000 ton of $SO_2$eq and NMVOC eq, respec-tively. Regarding affection to threatened species, more than 1,000 threatened spe-cies would be affected in both scenarios, affecting only around three fewer species with STE integration.

The contribution of economic sectors to environmental impacts is displayed in Figure 6.4.

For the NGCC technology, the Mexican electricity and gas supply sector is the largest responsible sector in all categories, with more than 89% contribution in all impacts. This is mainly related to the natural gas used as fuel for the electricity production. Regarding STE, the Mexican electricity and gas sectors also have the largest contribution in all impacts, with more than 13% contribution and specially achieving a 32% contribution in the affection to threatened species category. This is related to the large stimulation of this sector and the relevant share of fossil fuel technologies within the Mexican electricity mix. Other relevant sectors for STE are the non-metallic minerals and the metal sectors in Mexico, as a result of the activities within the investment phase such as manufacturing of concrete needed for the tower and other infrastructures and the metal needed also for the infra-structures and plant components. When accounting for international trade, these sectors also have a significant contribution in the United States due to the manu-facturing of imported components. In the case of the threatened species category, the Chinese electricity sector shows a remarkable contribution due to its stimula-tion by indirect trade relationships and the large impact that this sector causes to the ecosystems and to biodiversity in many different ways.

Table 6.6 Environmental impacts from the two scenarios including international trade (total impacts) and national impacts only (Mexico)

| Environmental impacts | Total | | | Mexico | | |
|---|---|---|---|---|---|---|
| | NGCC | NGCC+STE | Net impact | NGCC | NGCC+STE | Net impact |
| **Energy consumption (1000TJ)** | 41,262 | 41,156 | −106.4 | 38,894 | 38,792 | −102.6 |
| **Acidification (ton SO₂ eq)** | 5,748,497 | 5,733,777 | −14,720.0 | 5,556,336 | 5,541,742 | −14,595 |
| **Photochemical oxidants formation (ton NMVOC eq)** | 7,652,908 | 7,633,629 | −19,278.5 | 7,332,102 | 7,313,078 | −19,024 |
| **Threatened species (Number of threatened species affected)** | 1,058 | 1,055 | −2.7 | 1,023 | 1,020 | −2.6 |

**Contribution of economic sectors to environmental impacts**

| Country | Economic sector | Energy Use (%) | | Climate change (%) | | Acidification (%) | | Photochemical oxidants (%) | | Total species threatened (%) | |
|---|---|---|---|---|---|---|---|---|---|---|---|
| | | NGCC | STE | NGCC | STE | NGCC | STE | NGCC | STE | NGCC | STE |
| CHN | Electricity, Gas and Water Supply | 0% | 2% | 0% | 4% | 0% | 7% | 0% | 0% | 1% | 14% |
| MEX | Coke, Refined Petroleum, Nuclear Fuel | 2% | 8% | 0% | 0% | 0% | 0% | 5% | 10% | 0% | 0% |
| MEX | Other Non-Metallic Mineral | 0% | 7% | 0% | 17% | 0% | 14% | 0% | 15% | 0% | 0% |
| MEX | Basic Metals and Fabricated Metal | 0% | 8% | 0% | 10% | 0% | 5% | 0% | 8% | 0% | 0% |
| MEX | Electricity, Gas and Water Supply | 93% | 13% | 97% | 1% | 95% | 15% | 89% | 5% | 97% | 32% |
| MEX | Construction | 0% | 0% | 0% | 0% | 0% | 0% | 0% | 3% | 0% | 8% |
| MEX | Renting of M&Eq and Other B.A. | 0% | 0% | 0% | 2% | 0% | 0% | 0% | 0% | 0% | 14% |
| USA | Coke, Refined Petroleum, Nuclear Fuel | 2% | 9% | 0% | 0% | 0% | 2% | 0% | 0% | 0% | 0% |
| USA | Basic Metals and Fabricated Metal | 0% | 5% | 0% | 6% | 0% | 5% | 0% | 5% | 0% | 0% |
| USA | Electricity, Gas and Water Supply | 0% | 4% | 0% | 4% | 0% | 4% | 0% | 0% | 0% | 6% |
| Total contribution | | 98% | 61% | 98% | 63% | 98% | 61% | 97% | 59% | 99% | 87% |

*Figure 6.4* Contribution of economic sectors to environmental impacts Rodriguez-Serrano et al., forthcoming

*Socioeconomic impacts*

Socioeconomic impacts accounted by the FISA framework include economic stimulation (production of goods and services (PG&S)), added value (AV) creation, job creation, working hours (WH) and income generation.

As displayed in the earlier section, Table 6.7 shows the socioeconomic impacts derived from the two alternative scenarios taking into account the whole supply chain as well as international trade distinguishing between the effects that occurred globally and those that occurred in Mexico.

When accounting for total impacts, the economy is less stimulated in the NGCC+STE scenario by $57 million due to the decrease in production of goods and services along natural gas supply chain activities. However, with respect to added value (AV) creation, sectors with large AV creation are more stimulated as a consequence of STE integration by $87 million. As for the employment, job creation decreased by 285 employees due to the reduction of natural gas supply chain activities. Similarly, working hours decrease by 0.5 million. Nevertheless, with regard to incomes, an additional $35 million are generated as a result of STE activities, which reflects better employment conditions associated to this technology compared to NGCC.

Focusing on those impacts occurring in Mexico, results show that the stimulation of the national economy (demand of goods and services) would decrease as a result of the STE integration by $185 million due to the importance of natural gas market in the Mexican economy and the relevance of STE imports. However, STE economic stimulation is larger in some key sectors with high AV creation (as shown in Figure 6.5), amounting to $7 million. In terms of employment, 2,000 fewer jobs are created as a result of STE integration due to manufacturing of imported STE components outside Mexico and the current development of the NGCC market in the country. This fact is also responsible for a decrease of $2 million WH and $8.5 million of income generated.

With regard to the sectorial contribution, Figure 6.5 shows main economic sectors responsible for socioeconomic impacts.

As for NGCC, the Mexican electricity and gas supply sector has the largest contribution, with more than 26% in all categories, mainly from the natural gas supply and electricity generation. Other relevant sectors include renting of machinery and other business activities sector in Mexico, especially in terms of job creation (9%) and WH (12%) categories. With regard to STE technology, the financial sector in Mexico appears to be a remarkable sector in terms of production of goods and services, AV creation and income-generation categories, with 24%, 31% and 34% contribution, respectively. This can be explained by increase in the financial activities required by the investment of the project. Additionally, the Mexican renting of machinery and other business activities sector also shows a significant contribution, mainly from engineering activities, especially in the job creation and WH, with 17% and 24%, respectively. Another sector worth mentioning is the Mexican construction sector that is responsible for 6% and 7% of the total Mexican job creation and WH contribution, respectively, whereas income generation

Table 6.7 Socioeconomic impacts from both scenarios including international trade and impacts in Mexico

| Socioeconomic impacts | Total | | | Mexico | | |
|---|---|---|---|---|---|---|
| | NGCC | NGCC+STE | Net impact | NGCC | NGCC+STE | Net impact |
| **Production of goods and services (Million $)** | 423,202 | 423,145 | 57.0 | 299,768 | 299,583 | 185.2 |
| **Added value creation (million $)** | 180,919 | 181,006 | -87.4 | 137,541 | 137,547 | -6.6 |
| **Employments** | 7,617,641 | 7,617,356 | 284.9 | 6,024,181 | 6,022,165 | 2,015.8 |
| **Working hours (million)** | 10,090 | 10,089 | 0.5 | 8,489 | 8,487 | 1.9 |
| **Wages (million $)** | 52,888.29 | 52,923.38 | -35.1 | 33,764 | 33,755.78 | 8.5 |

| | | Contribution of economic sectors to socioeconomic impacts | | | | | | | | | |
|---|---|---|---|---|---|---|---|---|---|---|---|
| | | G&S (%) | | AV (%) | | Jobs (%) | | WH (%) | | Wages (%) | |
| Country | Economic sector | NGCC | STE | NGCC | STE | NGCC | STE | NGCC | STE | NGCC | STE |
| MEX | Electrical and Optical Equipment | 0% | 2% | 0% | 0% | 3% | 7% | 0% | 2% | 0% | 1% |
| MEX | Electricity, Gas and Water Supply | 39% | 0% | 30% | 0% | 30% | 0% | 26% | 0% | 30% | 0% |
| MEX | Construction | 0% | 2% | 0% | 2% | 5% | 6% | 5% | 7% | 0% | 3% |
| MEX | Retail Trade, Except Motor Vehicles | 2% | 0% | 4% | 0% | 7% | 2% | 11% | 4% | 3% | 0% |
| MEX | Financial Intermediation | 7% | 24% | 10% | 31% | 4% | 11% | 5% | 16% | 8% | 34% |
| MEX | Renting M&Eq,Other Business Act. | 4% | 8% | 6% | 11% | 9% | 17% | 12% | 24% | 7% | 11% |
| USA | Basic Metals and Fabricated Metal | 0% | 6% | 0% | 4% | 0% | 3% | 0% | 2% | 0% | 8% |
| USA | Electrical and Optical Equipment | 0% | 5% | 0% | 6% | 0% | 0% | 0% | 0% | 0% | 18% |

*Figure 6.5* Economic sectors responsible for larger socioeconomic impacts

Table 6.8 PSI values from both scenarios including international trade and impacts in Mexico

| Social risks | Total | | | Mexico | | |
|---|---|---|---|---|---|---|
| | NGCC | NGCC+STE | Net impacts | NGCC | NGCC+STE | Net impacts |
| **Labor risks (million PSI)** | 21,436 | 21,437 | 0.4 | 18,079 | 18,076 | −2.4 |
| **Health and safety risks (million PSI)** | 23,809 | 23,808 | −1.0 | 19,456 | 19,452 | −4.3 |
| **Human rights risks (million PSI)** | 18,300 | 18,299 | −1.3 | 15,060 | 15,056 | −3.7 |
| **Governance risks (million PSI)** | 29,900 | 29,897 | −3.6 | 26,664 | 26,658 | −5.9 |
| **Community infrastructures risks (million PSI)** | 15,910 | 15,908.85 | −0.9 | 13,332 | 13,329 | −2.9 |

contributes with only 3% in this sector. Finally, it is needed to highlight the large income generation figures in the electrical and optical equipment US sector, with an 18% contribution. These results are consistent with the fact that that some Mexican sectors have jobs with large working hours but much lower salaries than some jobs outside Mexico (such as the ones in the United States).

### Social impacts

As for the social impacts, those are represented by PSI values, which are calculated from the combination of WH stimulation results and social risks figures. Table 6.8 shows the PSI values from both scenarios occurring in Mexico as well as when accounting for international trade.

When comparing the results from both scenarios, it can be concluded that all social risks would decrease as a result of the penetration of STE in substitution of NGCC, with the exception of labour risks when accounting for international trade. This latter result can be explained by the indirect activities involved within the investment phase, most of which take place outside of Mexico (for example, the manufacturing of concrete needed for the tower, the manufacturing of different plant components made of metal and other indirect activities which provide goods and services to these activities).

Furthermore, PSI results allow to identify the PSH associated with the two technologies (Rodríguez-Serrano et al., 2016). In this sense, special attention should be paid to the Mexican electricity and gas supply sector, as it is responsible, according to the PSH results, for the main social risks associated to NGCC activities, contributing to more than 24% in all social categories. In the case of the STE technology, the PSH results indicate that renting of machinery and other activities sector is the highest contributor to social risks, accounting for more than 23% in all social categories. From the results, it could be recommended that social risks within these two sectors should be particularly monitored along the whole supply chain of the electricity generation with both technologies.

## Conclusions

The FISA aims at informing decision makers about the different impacts that alternative technologies have in the three sustainability pillars. In the light of the Paris Agreement, this work has evaluated the potential contribution of STE in the Mexican decarbonization process by assessing the sustainability impacts associated to the construction and operation of three 100 MW STE plants in substitution to the equivalent electricity generated by NGCC technology.

Applying the FISA framework, results shows that during the 2013–2030 period, around 6 Mton of $CO_2$ equivalent could be avoided by substituting NGCC electricity with STE. Additionally, other negative environmental impacts would be reduced such as energy consumption, acidification, creation of photochemical oxidants and threatened species affected. Furthermore, socioeconomic impacts show that the integration of STE would increase AV creation as well as the quality of employment by reducing the required working hours figures and providing higher wages. On the other side, the total demand of Mexican goods and services as well as job creation would decrease due to the important role that the natural gas market plays in the Mexican economy and the large share of imported STE components. Finally, as for the social impacts, the social risks in the five assessed categories would be reduced as a result of the introduction of STE in the Mexican electricity mix.

Summarizing, results show that STE could play a relevant role in the reduction of GHG emissions and other local emissions and environmental burdens, becoming a potential climate change mitigation technology option. Additionally, STE could also contribute to fostering gross domestic product creation, improving the quality of employments and decreasing existing social risks.

## References

Alsamawi, A., Murray, J., and Lenzen, M. (2014). The employment footprints of nations. *Journal of Industrial Ecology*, *18*(1), 59–70. doi: 10.1111/jiec.12104

Arancibia-Bulnes, C., Peón-Anaya, R., Riveros-Rosas, D., Quiñones, J., Cabanillas, R., and Estrada, C. (2014). Beam solar irradiation assessment for Sonora, Mexico. *Energy Procedia*, 49, 2290–2296.

Battelle (1982). Natural Gas-Fired Combined-Cycle Power Plant Alternative for the Railbelt Region of Alaska. Vol. XIII. Battelle, Pacific Northwest Laboratories, Alaska; 1982.

Benoît Norris, C., Aulisio, D., and Norris, G. A. (2012). Working with the social hotspots database-methodology and findings from 7 social scoping assessments. Conference Paper. 19th CIRP International Conference on Life Cycle Engineering, Berkeley (USA) DOI: 10.1007/978-3-642-29069-5_98

Caldés, N., Varela, M., Santamaría, M., and Sáez, R. (2009). Economic impact of solar thermal electricity deployment in Spain. *Energy Policy*, 37(5), 1628–1636.

CFE (2012). Costos y parámetros de referencia para la formulación de proyectos de inversión del sector eléctrico. Edición 32. Comisión Federal de Electricidad. México DF.

Franze, J. (2013). *Working with the social hotspots database in OpenLCA*. Greendelta, April 2013

Greenpeace, ESTELA, and SolarPACES. (2016). *Solar thermal electricity global outlook 2016*. Executive summary. Abu Dhabi, United Arab Emirates.

INERE. (2015). *Inventario Nacio de Energias Removables*. México. Retrieved March 28, 2016, from Gobierno de Mexico: http://inere.energia.gob.mx/version4.5.

IRENA, and SENER. (2015). *REmap 2030. Renewable energy prospects: Mexico*. Abu Dhabi: United Arab Emirates.

Jones, L., Wang, Z., Xin, L., and Degain, C. (2014). *The similarities and differences among three major inter-country input-output databases and their implications for trade in value added estimates. Office of Economics* Working Paper No. 2014-12B. U.S. International Trade Commission, Washington, DC.

Lehman, G. (1999). Disclosing new worlds: A role for social and environmental accounting and auditing. *Accounting, Organizations and society*, 24(3), 217–241.

Lenzen, M. (1998). Primary energy and greenhouse gases embodied in Australian final consumption: an input – output analysis. *Energy Policy*, 26(6), 495–506.

Leontief, W. W. (1936). Quantitative input and output relations in the economic systems of the United States. *The Review of Economic Statistics*, 18(3), 105–125.

Miller, R. E., and Blair, P. D. (2009). *Input-output analysis: Foundations and extensions* (2nd ed.). Cambridge: Cambridge University Press.

New Earth. (2013). Social hotspots database supporting documentation. New Earth. United States.

Papong, S., Itsubo, N., Malakul, P., and Shukuya, M. (2015). Development of the Social Inventory Database in Thailand using input – output analysis. *Sustainability*, *7*(6), 7684–7713.

Rodríguez-Serrano, I., Caldés, N., De la Rúa, C., and Lechón, Y. (2017). Assessing the three sustainability pillars through the Framework for Integrated Sustainability Assessment (FISA): Case study of a Solar Thermal Electricity project in Mexico. *Journal of Cleaner Production* 149, 1127–1143.

Rodríguez-Serrano, I., Caldés, N., De la Rúa, C., and Lechón, Y. (forthcoming). Integrated sustainability impact assessment of alternative solar thermal and natural gas combined cycle for electricity production in Mexico. *Energy for Sustainable Development*.

Rodríguez-Serrano, I., Caldés, N., De La Rúa, C., Lechón, Y., and Garrido, A. (2016). Using the Framework for Integrated Sustainability Assessment (FISA) to expand the multiregional input – output analysis to account for the three pillars of sustainability. *Environment, Development and Sustainability*, 1–17. DOI:10.1007/s10668-016-9839-y

Romero-Hernández, S., Duarte Rodríguez-Granada, B., Romero-Hernández, O., and Duncan, W. (2012). *Solar energy potential in Mexico's Northern border states*. Woodrow Wilson International Center for Scholars, Mexico Institute, Washington DC, U.S.

Secretaría de Economía de Mexico. (2013). *ProMéxico. Inversión y Comercio. Energías renovables*. Mexico DF, Mexico: Gobierno de Mexico.

Secretaría de Economía de Mexico. (2015). *Industria de Energías Renovables Prospectiva y Oportunidades de Negocio en México*. Mexico DF, Mexico: Gobierno de Mexico.

Secretaría General. (2012). *Ley general de cambio climático DOF 06–06–2012*. Mexico DF, Mexico: Gobierno de Mexico.

SENER. (2014). *Prospectiva del Sector Eléctrico 2014–2028*. Mexico DF, Mexico: Secretaría de Energía, Gobierno de México.

SENER. (2015a). *Programa de Desarrollo del Sistema Eléctrico Nacional 2015–2029*. Mexico DF, Mexico: Secretaría de Energía, Gobierno de México.

SENER. (2015b). *Prospectiva del Gas Natural y Gas L.P. 2015–2029, Documento nacional*. Mexico DF, Mexico: Secretaría de Energía, Gobierno de México.

SENER. (2015c). *Prospectiva del Sector Eléctrico 2015–2029*. Mexico DF, Mexico: Secretaría de Energía, Gobierno de México.

SERMANAT. (2015). *Contribución Prevista y Determinada a Nivel Nacional de México*. Mexico D.F., Mexico: Secretaria de Medio Ambiente y Recursos Naturales. Gobierno de México.

SHDB. (2016). *Social hotspots database*. Retrieved March 28, 2016, from http://social-hotspot.org/

SolarPaces, Greenpeace, and ESTELA. (2016). *Solar thermal electricity global outlook 2016*. Executive summary. SolarPaces Secretariate, Greenpeace International and ESTELA.

Ten Raa, T. (2006). *The economics of input-output analysis*. Cambridge: Cambridge University Press.

Thornley, P., Rogers, J., and Huang, Y. (2008). Quantification of employment from biomass power plants. *Renewable Energy*, *33*(8), 1922–1927.

Timmer, M. P., Dietzenbacher, E., Los, B., Stehrer, R., and de Vries, G. J. (2015). An illustrated user guide to the world input – output database: The case of global automotive production. *Review of International Economics*, *23*(3), 575–605.

Tukker, A., and Dietzenbacher, E. (2013). Global multiregional input – output frameworks: An introduction and outlook. *Economic Systems Research*, *25*(1), 1–19.

U.S. Energy Information Agency. (2014). *Mexico energy report*. Washington, DC: U.S. Government.

UNEP, SETAC, and Life Cycle Iniciative. (2009). *Guidelines for social life cycle assessment of products, management*. United Nations Environment Programme. Belgium.

USAID, and MLED. (2013). *Análisis actualizado de la línea base de emisiones de GEI de México, curva de costo marginal de reducción y cartera de proyectos*. Mexico DF, Mexico: United States Agenciy for International Development. Mexico Low Emissions Development Programme.

Wiedmann, T., Lenzen, M., Turner, K., and Barrett, J. (2007). Examining the global environmental impact of regional consumption activities – Part 2: Review of input – output models for the assessment of environmental impacts embodied in trade. *Ecological Economics*, *61*(1), 15–26.

Wilshaw, R. (2013). *Exploring the links between international business and poverty reduction: Bouquets and beans from Kenya*, Oxford: Oxfam GB.

# 7 Peak carbon emission in China

## A household energy use perspective

*Haiyan Zhang, Michael L. Lahr*

## Introduction

The Paris Agreement, which was engaged in November 2016, is ambitious. It is designed to strengthen a worldwide resolve to the threat of climate change. The hope is that the relationships and agreement established through it will restrict global temperature rises below 2° C through 2100. Main threats to positions and limits that were set out in the Paris Agreement are fast-growing economies that rely on carbon-based fuels as energy resources. Over the past 15 years, annualized energy consumption has been fastest in such countries as China, India, Egypt, and Brazil (Enerdata, 2016). Of these, the targets developed by China and India are prime threats to the Paris Agreement since their total levels of consumption are already rather high-ranking, first and third worldwide, while their energy consumption per capita appear comparatively low when juxtaposed with equivalents for developed nations. In essence, this suggests that there is every reason to believe that developing nations will extend their increases in the consumption of energy at a strong pace for some time into the future.

There are, of course, some mitigating factors to the above expectations for developing nations. First, it may be that they burn energy at unsustainable levels due to their use of old, affordable technology that is likely to be replaced as energy costs rise or if the nations enforce their Paris Agreement targets. That is, if their energy intensities (energy consumption/gross domestic product (GDP)) are presently high, adjustments through technology transfer could make compliance with their aspects of the Paris Agreement possible. Another is that these particular countries could experience unexpected slowdowns in population growth. And, finally, expectations on growth in energy consumption depend on the trajectory of their residents' lifestyles. This arises since standards of energy consumption differ substantially across developed countries – for example, in 2015 the United States consumed twice as much energy per capita (6.83 tonnes) compared to Japan (3.42 tonnes) or the European Union (3.09 tonnes). Thus, if the leading developing nations can somehow encourage their people manage their energy consumption by modeling their behavior on that of, say, a typical Italian (2.49 tonnes) than of a typical American, the goals of the Paris accord will be met more readily.

China's energy consumption grew 0.9% from 2014 to 2015 (Enerdata, 2016). This was far below the average annualized growth rate from 2000–2015 that China experienced (6.6%). This slowdown shows some promise, not only for a greener China but as a possible pathway for other countries. As part of the Paris Agreement, China promised to peak carbon dioxide emissions around 2030 by lowering carbon dioxide emission per unit of GDP by 60% to 65% from the 2005 level (Xinhua News, 2015). Green and Stern (2017) recently hazarded that the nation's greenhouse gas emissions will peak before 2025. Herein, we proffer that such targets may be overly ambitious, after examining the trajectory of Chinese lifestyles.

Due to its emphasis on capital investment and an export orientation, China's share of household consumption in GDP has remained quite low – in 2015, just 37.0% compared to 68.1% in USA and 59.6% in India (The World Bank, 2016b). Nonetheless, China's households have experienced fairly radical lifestyle changes during the past three decades. Prior to the 1970s, most of China's population lived in abject poverty; now, households aspire toward western living standards (Hubacek et al., 2011). From 1962 to 2015, China's gross national income skyrocketed at an average annual rate of around 9.3%, with its fastest rates of change occurring more recently – from 2005 to 2015 – the average annual rate of change was 16.2% (The World Bank, 2016a). Household incomes have benefitted much from this, growing at an average annual rate of 10.7% since 2007 to ¥31,200 in 2015.

As the expansion of capital investment in China has relaxed, the pace of GDP growth has fallen. It has run below 7% in the last two years (2015 and 2016) for the first time since China's accession to the World Trade Organization. But this was anticipated; China transformed its economy toward encouraging growth in domestic demand in order to exploit the rising incomes of its population. A problem seems to be, however, that China seems to be promoting a transition to full-blown US-style consumerism. Despite the rush toward such consumerism, residential energy use continues to lag overall energy use in China; households' share of energy use has declined from 14.3% in 1992 to 11.0% by 2014. This means that China's energy conservation efforts and low carbon policies have largely focused on industrial establishments. Given its energy security concerns, global warming pressures, and internal environmental concerns, China undoubtedly should be more cautious and alter its policy course to include households so that the society as a whole focuses on a model with low carbon consumption.

Policies that can enable or ameliorate energy security, energy conservation, air pollution, and global warming concerns are grounded in energy use. As discussed at the outset, China has drastically slowed its energy use. If it could more fully decouple its emissions production from its economic growth, however, global GHG goals could be within reach. This is because other developing nations might be inclined to follow in China's footsteps (Jotzo and Teng, 2014).

In this paper, we explored the long-term trends of household $CO_2$ emission and related driving forces of changing household indirect $CO_2$ emission. We do so using a multiplicative structural decomposition to explore what is changing among Chinese households. Is it population rises, heightened urbanization, changes in preferences, or simply increased spending potential that is enabling the rise in household $CO_2$ emission? As China's households move up the consumption ladder, our results indicate that household-based $CO_2$ emission likely will continue to rise for some time. Growth prospects look especially high for rural China where energy use lags heavily. Based on our results, we also offer some valuable policy suggestions for China to achieve its peak carbon emission target around 2030 from a household perspective.

## Research approach

Household energy consumption contains household direct energy use and indirect energy use. Households use energy directly for heating, lighting, transportation, and other purposes, and indirectly through purchased goods (e.g. food, cloth, etc.) and services (e.g. insurance, public transport, ect.).[1] In this regard, total household $CO_2$ emissions ($F$) in this paper refer to the sum of direct $CO_2$ emissions ($F^d$) and indirect $CO_2$ emissions ($F^i$) associated with energy used directly and indirectly by households.

Households' $CO_2$ emissions change over time for a variety of reasons. Structural decomposition analysis (SDA) is commonly used to understand the underlying driving forces of change in energy use and $CO_2$ emissions. As it uses IOTs, SDA can account both the supply-and-demand side effects, as well as distinguishing between direct and indirect effects through the supply chain (Feng et al., 2012; Miller and Blair, 2009).

Many researchers have used SDA to examine $CO_2$ trends in China. Peters et al. (2007) and Guan et al. (2009), for example, found trend effects on $CO_2$ emissions from technology improvement, economic structure change, urbanization, and lifestyles changes for the 1992–2002 and 2002–2005 periods. Both sets of authors found that final demand was a key driving factor. Follow-up research by Minx et al. (2011) found that capital investment was the dominant emissions driver from 2005 to 2007. Focusing on energy use, Zhang and Lahr (2014) found that capital investment and exports contributed most to the change in energy use from 2002 to 2007 and that China's production had shifted toward more energy-intensive industries. Zhang et al. (2016) used SDA and found that lifestyle changes appear to have led to the use of more energy by households both directly and indirectly. The rising demand for more life convenience, therefore, seems likely to drive Chinese households to become more energy-intensive in the future.

Following Zhang et al. (2016), we use SDA in this chapter to explore changes in $CO_2$ emissions that can be tracked to household final uses rather than in energy used indirectly by households. $CO_2$ emissions that stem from household spending can be expressed mathematically as

$$F^i = \mathbf{f}'(\mathbf{I} - \mathbf{A})^{-1}\mathbf{h} = \mathbf{f}'\mathbf{Lh} \qquad (7.1)$$

Let $n$ be the number of industries, the other definitions are as follows: $F^i$ is the $CO_2$ emissions embodied in goods and services that are consumed by households

(Scalar); $\mathbf{f}$ the vector with $f_k$ as the $CO_2$ emissions per unit of output for industry $k$ ($n \times n$ matrix); $\mathbf{L}$ the Leontief-inverse matrix $\mathbf{L} \equiv (\mathbf{I} - \mathbf{A})^{-1}$, which is a matrix of total input requirements ($n \times n$ matrix); $\mathbf{I}$ the identity matrix ($n \times n$ matrix); $\mathbf{A}$ is a $n \times n$ matrix that shows the intersectoral direct requirements of each sector's production; $\mathbf{h}$ is household consumption of production by industry ($n \times 1$ vector).

Since China has experience rapid urbanization during the past three decades, we adopted Zhang et al. (2016)'s way to decompose household spending $\mathbf{h}$ into $\mathbf{h} = \mathbf{H}_p.\mathbf{p}_s$ to show the differences of urban and rural household spending. $\mathbf{H}_p$ denotes per capita sectoral expenditures by urban and rural households ($n \times 2$ matrix) and $\mathbf{p}_s$ is the two-element vector representing the population of rural and urban households. We further decompose $\mathbf{H}_p$ and $\mathbf{p}_s$ into structure and volume components with and $\mathbf{p}_s = p.\mathbf{u}$. $\mathbf{H}_s$ is household consumption preference by urban and rural households ($n \times 2$ matrix), and $\hat{y}$ is a $2 \times 2$ diagonal matrix that shows per capita household expenditure of urban and rural households. The p denotes total population ($2 \times 1$ vector) and $\mathbf{u}$ is the urban and rural shares of total population ($2 \times 1$ vector).

We could decompose household indirect $CO_2$ emissions into six partial factors which are related to changes in population levels ($\Delta p$), urbanization ($\Delta \mathbf{u}$), emission intensity ($\Delta \mathbf{f}$), interindustry input mix ($\Delta \mathbf{L}$), household consumption preference ($\Delta \mathbf{H}_s$), and per capita household consumption level ($\Delta \hat{y}$)$^2$ :

$$\frac{F_1^i}{F_0^i} = \frac{\mathbf{f}_1' \mathbf{L}_1 \mathbf{h}_1}{\mathbf{f}_0' \mathbf{L}_0 \mathbf{h}_0} = (2a) \times (2b) \times (2c) \times (2d) \times (2e) \times (2f) \tag{7.2}$$

$$= \frac{\mathbf{f}_1' \mathbf{L}_1 \mathbf{h}_1}{\mathbf{f}_0' \mathbf{L}_1 \mathbf{h}_1} \tag{7.2a}$$

$$\times \frac{\mathbf{f}_0' \mathbf{L}_1 \mathbf{h}_1}{\mathbf{f}_0' \mathbf{L}_0 \mathbf{h}_1} \tag{7.2b}$$

$$\times \frac{\mathbf{f}_0' \mathbf{L}_0 (\mathbf{H}_{s1} \hat{y}_1)(p_1 \mathbf{u}_1)}{\mathbf{f}_0' \mathbf{L}_0 (\mathbf{H}_{s0} \hat{y}_1)(p_1 \mathbf{u}_1)} \tag{7.2c}$$

$$\times \frac{\mathbf{f}_0' \mathbf{L}_0 (\mathbf{H}_{s0} \hat{y}_1)(p_1 \mathbf{u}_1)}{\mathbf{f}_0' \mathbf{L}_0 (\mathbf{H}_{s0} \hat{y}_0)(p_1 \mathbf{u}_1)} \tag{7.2d}$$

$$\times \frac{\mathbf{f}_0' \mathbf{L}_0 (\mathbf{H}_{s0} \hat{y}_0)(p_1 \mathbf{u}_1)}{\mathbf{f}_0' \mathbf{L}_0 (\mathbf{H}_{s0} \hat{y}_0)(p_0 \mathbf{u}_1)} \tag{7.2e}$$

$$\times \frac{\mathbf{f}_0' \mathbf{L}_0 (\mathbf{H}_{s0} \hat{y}_0)(p_0 \mathbf{u}_1)}{\mathbf{f}_0' \mathbf{L}_0 (\mathbf{H}_{s0} \hat{y}_0)(p_0 \mathbf{u}_0)}, \tag{7.2f}$$

where $\Delta \mathbf{f}$ (Equation 7.2a) represents the effects of changes in $CO_2$ emissions per unit of gross output by industry; $\Delta \mathbf{L}$ (Equation 7.2b) represents the effects of changes in sub-industrial structure; $\Delta \mathbf{H}_s$ (Equation 7.2c) represents the effects of changes in household consumption preferences; $\Delta \hat{y}$ (Equation 7.2d) indicates the effects of changes in per capita household consumption level; $\Delta p$ (Equation 7.2e) shows the effects of changes in total population; and $\Delta u$ (Equation 7.2f) indicates the effects of changes in China's urbanization level.

The household energy and $CO_2$ emission data were built on two main sources: China's Energy Statistical Yearbooks and national IOT. The $CO_2$ emissions from the combustion of fuels were calculated using the IPCC reference approach (IPCC, 1996). China's national input-output tables are used to calculate indirect $CO_2$ emissions for urban and rural households. Here we use the IOTs for 1992 (119 sectors), 1997 (124 sectors), 2002 (122 sectors), 2007 (135 sectors), and recently released 2012 (139 sectors) from National Bureau of Statistics of China (NBS). To maintain consistency in this study, we aggregate all IOTs to 85 industrial sectors. Also, all tables are adjusted to the 2012 constant prices to make them comparable. The energy data were taken from China's Energy Statistical Yearbook (NBS, 1998, 2009, 2014a). The 1992 energy data has 36 industrial sectors, the 2012 data has 46 industrial sectors, and the energy data for other corresponding years contains 44 industrial sectors. Similar to Peters et al. (2007) and Zhang et al. (2016), the energy data was mapped to 85 economic sectors used in the IOTs through a coordinate matrix. The demographic data of urban and rural population is from the China Statistical Yearbook (NBS, 2014b).

## Residential $CO_2$ emissions

### *Residential direct $CO_2$ emissions*

From 1992 to 2002, household direct $CO_2$ emissions decreased from 295 million metric tons (MMT) to 209 MMT. Then it rose gradually at an average annual rate of 5.6% to 360 MMT of $CO_2$ in 2012. Meanwhile household indirect $CO_2$ increased at an average annual rate of 5.3% from 881 MMT in 1992 to 2490 MMT in 2012 (see Figure 7.1). In 2012, Chinese households' $CO_2$ emissions in aggregate was split by about 13:87 between direct and indirect emissions. Interestingly, from 1992 to 2012, aggregate direct $CO_2$ emissions rose 25% for rural households and 18% for urban households. Meanwhile, over the same period, aggregated indirect $CO_2$ emission increased only 25% for total rural households but 341% for total urban households. These changes were largely caused by the rapid urbanization and residential fuel substitution in China. Indeed, between 1992 and 2012, the share of urban population in China had rose from 27.5% to 52.6%, with its total urban population increased 121%, while its total rural population decreased 24%.

Household energy consumption per capita has risen in both rural and urban China (see Figure 7.2). The fuel mix of both urban and rural households changed quite a bit from 1992 to 2012. The rising wealth, improving transportation, and expanding electrical grid enabled rural residents to purchase more commercial energy resources such as coal, gas, and electricity (Wang and Feng, 2001). Urban households experienced a parallel transition. Their relatively higher wealth and more central locations enabled them to spend much larger shares of their consumption on commercial energy (Pachauri and Jiang, 2008). Direct use of coal

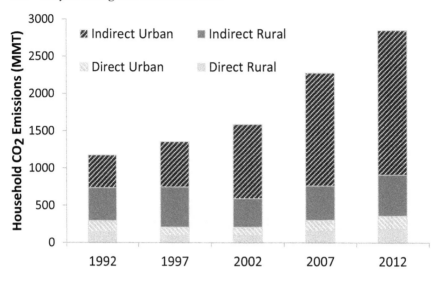

*Figure 7.1* Resident's direct and indirect $CO_2$ emissions

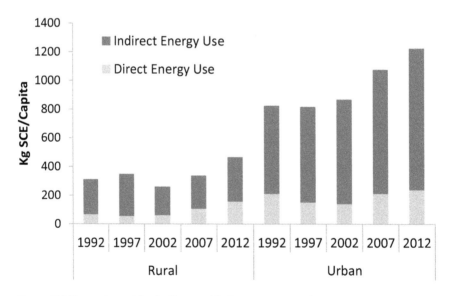

*Figure 7.2* Per capita resident's direct and indirect energy requirements

by households fell steadily; residents moved to units with central heating and switched to electricity for cooking and water heating. Coal's share decreased from 83.8% in 1992 to 23.9% by 2012. Within 20 years, direct coal use per capita by urban households dropped precipitously from 163 kg to 21 kg, while it edged up slightly for rural households from 63 kg to 79 kg. The decreasing direct use of coal in homes significantly improved indoor air quality. With increased income, the type of energy resources used directly by households became more diversified: electricity, municipally provided heating, liquefied petroleum gas (LPG), and natural gas became more widely used. Electricity's share rose most rapidly from 6.2% in 1992 to 27.9% in 2012. From 1992 to 2012, electricity usage per capita rose from 112 to 500 kWh for urban residents and from 33 to 414 kWh for rural residents.

Compared to their rural counterparts, China's urban residents use greater shares of alternative commercial fuels such as natural gas, heat, and LPG. Urban residents nearly fully replaced coal through the use of electricity, gasoline, natural gas, and LPG. In this regard, rural households have more work ahead. Direct coal use per capita by rural households kept rising from 2002 to 2012. In some rural areas that have limited access to electricity, coal continues to replace some non-commercial energy sources, such as firewood, straw, and other biomasses, as important energy sources for cooking and heating. While the rural-urban gap in direct household energy use shrank, by 2012 a typical urban resident still used 51% more direct energy than did a typical rural resident. The direct energy used by urban residents rose rapidly from 2002 to 2012, and the growth showed no sign of relenting (see Figure 7.2). But rural residents showed an even greater proportional change in their demand for direct energy use, especially for alternative commercial energy beside coal. Hence rises in per capita residential direct energy use should be expected in both urban and rural areas of China in the future.

Due to fuel substitution in residential direct energy use, per capita direct $CO_2$ emissions of urban residents decreased from 466 kg in 1992 to 201 kg in 2002, but rose to 264 kg by 2012. Natural gas consumption per capita by urban residents rose at an average annual rate of 16% from 2002 to 2012. Indeed, the contribution of natural gas to all direct $CO_2$ emission rose from 10% in 2002 to 33% in 2012 for urban households (see Table 7.1). Trends in direct $CO_2$ emission per capita in rural areas were generally similar, but attained urban levels (268 kg) by 2012. The contribution of coal to direct $CO_2$ emissions by rural households decreased but only to 78% by 2012.

*Table 7.1* Contribution of different fuels to residential direct $CO_2$ emissions

|      |       | Coal | Gasoline | Kerosene | Diesel Oil | LNG | Natural Gas |
|------|-------|------|----------|----------|------------|-----|-------------|
| 1992 | Rural | 98%  | 0%       | 2%       | 0%         | 0%  | 0%          |
|      | Urban | 91%  | 0%       | 0%       | 0%         | 5%  | 3%          |
| 1997 | Rural | 95%  | 1%       | 2%       | 1%         | 2%  | 0%          |
|      | Urban | 66%  | 5%       | 0%       | 3%         | 22% | 5%          |
| 2002 | Rural | 93%  | 1%       | 1%       | 2%         | 3%  | 0%          |
|      | Urban | 52%  | 6%       | 0%       | 5%         | 26% | 10%         |
| 2007 | Rural | 84%  | 5%       | 0%       | 3%         | 8%  | 0%          |
|      | Urban | 37%  | 10%      | 0%       | 8%         | 25% | 19%         |
| 2012 | Rural | 78%  | 9%       | 0%       | 5%         | 7%  | 0%          |
|      | Urban | 17%  | 18%      | 0%       | 11%        | 20% | 33%         |

Increases in the ownership of private vehicles continue to play an ever-important role in residential direct $CO_2$ emissions. Over the decade ending in 2012, their contribution rose from 11% to 29% for urban households and rose from 3% to 14% for rural households. As more residents, both urban and rural, use more natural gas as well as motor vehicles, there is little reason to believe that direct $CO_2$ emissions produced by households will do anything but rise.

### *Residential indirect $CO_2$ emissions*

$CO_2$ emissions embodied in goods and services consumed by a typical rural resident have also experienced major transformations. From 1992 to 1997, per capita indirect $CO_2$ emissions in rural areas rose at an average annual rate of 4.2% to 638 kg. Subsequently, it decreased at an average annual rate of 5.2% to 490 kg in 2002. It then rose through 2012 at an average annual rate of 5.8% to 860 kg. From 1997 to 2002, per capita rural household consumption only rose 5.0%, while the average energy requirement per unit of output had decreased by 33.4%. Energy efficiency gains, fuel substitution in production processes, changes in the rural households' consumption preferences, and relative stagnant levels of rural household consumption all contributed to the annual 5.2% drop in per capita indirect $CO_2$ emissions of rural households from 1997 to 2002.

For urban households, per capita indirect $CO_2$ emissions rose relatively steadily from 1992 to 2012, at an average annual rate of 3.5% to 2,722 kg. The gap in indirect $CO_2$ emissions per capita between urban and rural households expanded over the first 15 years of that period – a typical urban resident emitted 163% more indirect $CO_2$ through goods and services than his or her rural counterparts in 1992 and 305% more by 2007. But the gap closed to 217% by 2012.

Households emitted more $CO_2$ indirectly than directly over the study period. Indeed, the contribution of indirect $CO_2$ emissions of urban household rose from 75% in 1992 to 91% in 2002 and then held fairly steady through 2012. Due to rural fuel shortages, the share of indirect $CO_2$ emitted by rural households rose from 75% in 1992 to 83% in 1997; it then slowly declined to prior levels by 2012. As the supplies of rural energy resources became more abundant, the direct $CO_2$ emitted by rural residents rose more rapidly than did the indirect $CO_2$ emissions.

Households accounted for 51% of all $CO_2$ emissions in China in 1992, but just 31% in 2012. China's economy is now turning back to households for economic growth. Thus, it is clear that China must start to focus more on households when identifying $CO_2$ emission-reduction options. In this vein, diagnosing the driving forces of trends for household indirect $CO_2$ emission is important as well.

## The contribution of drivers to household $CO_2$ emissions

### *Overview of the driving forces of household indirect $CO_2$ emissions*

Table 7.2 shows the overall average Fisher index as well as for each SDA component. Based on the figures in that table, changes in household consumption per

*Table 7.2* Average annual changing rates of driving forces of household indirect $CO_2$ emissions

|  | $\Delta f$ | $\Delta L$ | $\Delta H_s$ | $\Delta \hat{y}$ | $\Delta u$ | $\Delta p$ | *Total* |
|---|---|---|---|---|---|---|---|
| 1992–1997 | −2.8% | −1.1% | −0.3% | 7.6% | 1.0% | 1.1% | 5.4% |
| 1997–2002 | −6.8% | 0.7% | 0.6% | 6.7% | 1.8% | 0.8% | 3.8% |
| 2002–2007 | −9.1% | 7.1% | 1.3% | 5.7% | 1.8% | 0.6% | 7.5% |
| 2007–2012 | −1.6% | −2.9% | −0.8% | 7.9% | 1.5% | 0.5% | 4.7% |

capita ($\Delta \hat{y}$) and changes in emission efficiency ($\Delta f$) most affected the growth of household indirect $CO_2$ emissions from 1992 to 2012. Changes in the level of per capita consumption ($\Delta \hat{y}$), dominated the growth in $CO_2$ emissions – effectively causing them to rise at an average annual rate of 7.6% from 1992 to 1997. It remained high and dominant through all four study sub-periods. Emission efficiency improvements ($\Delta f$) tended to counteract influences of increments in per capita consumption. In fact, emission efficiency improvements more than offset the effects of household consumption per capita from 1997 to 2007. After 2007, emission efficiency gains nearly disappeared (edged downward to just 1.6% annually).

Changes in household preferences ($\Delta H_s$) tended to effect little change in household indirect $CO_2$ emissions, enabling annualized changes in $CO_2$ emissions on the order of just −0.8% to 1.3%. Annualized changes in $CO_2$ emissions attributable to interindustry input mix ($\Delta L$) – akin to technology change – only became sizeable after 2002 when it surprising caused emissions to grow to 7.1% through 2007; this component's effects switched signs, reducing emissions by an average annual rate of 2.9% thereafter.

During the study period, demographic factors always tended to cause household indirect $CO_2$ emissions to grow in China. However, their contributions to the change in $CO_2$ emissions have tended to be comparatively small. And, except for the first of the five-year subperiods, urbanization effects ($\Delta u$) dominated population growth effects ($\Delta p$). This domination is likely due to China's enforcement of its one-child policy; the effects of population growth have decreased gradually from 1.1% annually in the 1992–1997 period to 0.5% in the 2007–2012 period.

By focusing on the recent periods, we now further explore the contributions of household consumption preferences, household consumption levels, and demographic changes in more detail.

### *Household consumption preferences*

From 1992 to 2012, per capita annual spending rose significantly for both urban and rural households. The share of spending on core necessities – food and clothing – by all households, decreased from around 67% in 1992 to about 44% in 2012. Meanwhile, the share of household expenditures on health care, transportation, and communication services increased from 1992 to 2012. Chinese households clearly pursued a more comfortable style of living that depends on a developed service sector.

The nature of lifestyle changes affected households' indirect $CO_2$ emissions. Households shifted their consumption preferences ($\mathbf{\Delta H_s}$) in a manner that helped to reduce their indirect $CO_2$ emissions from 1992 to 1997 (see Table 7.2). Shifts towards spending on services partly explain these reductions. However, changes in household consumption preferences thereafter and through 2007 caused household indirect $CO_2$ emissions to rise.

A key element, from 2002 to 2007, was households' rising use of production from the Utilities sector, which accounted for 63% of the rise in indirect $CO_2$ emissions per capita in rural areas and 54% for urban areas (see Table 7.3). Not

*Table 7.3* Per capita household indirect $CO_2$ emissions in China from 2002 to 2012

| Sector | Urban | | | | | Rural | | | | |
|---|---|---|---|---|---|---|---|---|---|---|
| | 2002 | 2007 | 2012 | 02–07 | 07–12 | 2002 | 2007 | 2012 | 02–07 | 07–12 |
| Agriculture | 43 | 55 | 61 | 12 | 6 | 20 | 25 | 30 | 5 | 6 |
| Mining | 56 | 58 | 84 | 2 | 27 | 15 | 15 | 25 | 0 | 10 |
| Food & Tobacco products | 58 | 91 | 91 | 33 | −0.4 | 19 | 28 | 38 | 8 | 10 |
| Textile Products | 24 | 25 | 22 | 1 | −3 | 5 | 6 | 6 | 1 | 1 |
| Sawmill, Paper, Printing & Recreation Goods | 28 | 31 | 27 | 3 | −4 | 7 | 7 | 8 | 1 | 1 |
| Petro-, Chemical & Non-metal Mineral Products | 265 | 332 | 329 | 68 | −3.3 | 71 | 86 | 106 | 15 | 20 |
| Metal Smelting, Pressing & Metal Products | 136 | 195 | 198 | 58 | 4 | 33 | 44 | 54 | 11 | 10 |
| Machinery & Transportation Equipment | 15 | 16 | 13 | 2 | −3 | 4 | 4 | 3 | 0 | −1 |
| Electric & Electronic Products | 7 | 6 | 4 | −1 | −2 | 1 | 1 | 1 | 0 | 0 |
| Other Manufacturing | 6 | 3 | 2 | −4 | −1 | 1 | 1 | 1 | −1 | 0 |
| Utilities | 1127 | 1403 | 1538 | 276 | 135 | 260 | 358 | 487 | 98 | 129 |
| Construction | 2 | 3 | 1 | 1 | −1 | 1 | 0 | 0 | 0 | 0 |
| Transportation & Wholesale | 88 | 109 | 141 | 21 | 33 | 22 | 29 | 41 | 7 | 13 |
| Postal, Information & Software Services | 46 | 63 | 87 | 17 | 24 | 10 | 14 | 24 | 5 | 10 |
| Finance, Insurance & Real Estate | 21 | 29 | 38 | 8 | 8 | 9 | 8 | 11 | −1 | 2 |
| Commercial, Catering & Hotel | 32 | 44 | 48 | 12 | 4 | 7 | 12 | 13 | 5 | 2 |
| Education, Health, Sports & Recreation | 15 | 17 | 16 | 2 | −1 | 3 | 4 | 5 | 1 | 1 |
| Other Service | 14 | 19 | 21 | 5 | 1 | 3 | 4 | 5 | 1 | 1 |
| Total | 1983 | 2498 | 2722 | 515 | 224 | 490 | 645 | 860 | 155 | 214 |

surprisingly, during this same period, per capita electricity consumption rose 80% to 394 kWh for urban households and 172% 234 kWh for rural households. Thus the rising use of electricity explains much of rapid rise in indirect $CO_2$ emissions for all households. Outside of the Utilities sector, much of increase in indirect household emissions was due to rises in the consumption of services by energy-intensive Transportation and Wholesale sector, which accounted for 15% and 6% of indirect $CO_2$ emissions for rural and urban households, respectively. This rising indirect $CO_2$ emissions of the Transportation and Wholesale Service sector reflects China's ever-improving market accessibility and the increasing sensitivity of its consumer market to prices and product variety.

In the 2002–2007 period, Petroleum, Chemical, and Non-metal Mineral Products accounted for 13% of the rise in per capita indirect $CO_2$ emissions for urban residents and 9% for rural residents. Per capita household indirect $CO_2$ emissions of products from this sector rose 68 kg for urban residents and 15 kg for urban residents. A large part of this increment was undoubtedly caused by the rising use of privately owned vehicles especially in urban China. Metal Smelting, Pressing, and Metal Products accounted for 11% of the rise in per capita indirect $CO_2$ emissions of urban residents and 7% for rural residents. Households' rising consumption of living space and ownership of home appliances explains much of such indirect $CO_2$ emissions (Zhang et al., 2016).

The Food and Tobacco Products sector accounted for 6% of increment of per capita indirect $CO_2$ emissions of urban residents and 5% of rural residents. This increment likely reflects the increasing demand for processed food, particularly meat, in both urban and rural China. From 2002 to 2007, households have been increasingly shifting their consumption toward more energy- and carbon-intensive goods and services.

Fortunately, changes in household consumption preferences ($\Delta H_s$) helped reduce household indirect $CO_2$ emissions from 2007 to 2012. For urban households, per capita indirect $CO_2$ emissions actually decreased 3.3 kg from the Petroleum, Chemical & Non-metal Mineral Products sector. Also, per capita household indirect $CO_2$ emissions of products from Metal Smelting, Pressing, and Metal Products rose only 4 kg for urban residents. Per capita households indirect $CO_2$ emissions from Postal, Information, and Software Services sector increased 24 kg for urban residents and 10 kg for their rural counterparts. Rural households' indirect $CO_2$ emissions per capita from the Food and Tobacco Products sector increased 37% to 38 kg in 2012. This rise accounted for 5% of the rise in indirect $CO_2$ emissions by rural households. Meanwhile, urban households' indirect $CO_2$ emissions via Food and Tobacco Products sector actually decreased 0.4 kg from 2007 to 2012. From 2007 to 2012, urban households have been gradually shifting their consumption pattern toward low carbon goods and services.

### *Household consumption level*

With rapid economic growth, households' incomes have increased steadily in both urban and rural China. Average per capita income rose at an average annual rate of 8.3% from 4,989 Yuan in 1992 to 24,565 Yuan in 2012 in urban areas but just 6.5% annually from 2,261 Yuan to 7,917 Yuan in rural areas (constant 2012 prices). Needless to say, large urban and rural disparities in income per capita persist across China. Rapid income growth has enabled significant lifestyle changes that have led households to become increasingly responsible for China's $CO_2$ emissions.

Chinese households have tended to adopt more energy-intensive and carbon-intensive lifestyles (Golley and Meng, 2012). According to Zhang et al. (2016), Chinese households have increased their living spaces, electric appliance ownership, demands for space heating and cooling, and personal mobility. Each of these elements alone would lead any household anywhere to be responsible for more $CO_2$ emissions.

Better housing conditions have been responsible for higher indirect household $CO_2$ emissions through the enhanced use of products of the Metal Smelting, Pressing, and Metal Products and Petroleum, Chemical, and Non-metal Mineral Products sectors in the home construction process. Improved personal mobility has tended to increase $CO_2$ emissions directly via the use of vehicles that burn petrol and indirectly through the supply chain required to produce the vehicles, the construction of transportation infrastructures, and so on. As their incomes rise and residences enlarge, Chinese households have been buying more home appliances. The spreading use of home appliances has lifted households' $CO_2$ emissions indirectly both at utilities through the direct use of electricity and through appliance production.

As incomes in China continue to increase, more and more households will climb the consumption ladder. And as long as they have aspirations for an easier life – one with improved housing conditions, personal mobility, indoor climate control, and time-saving devices – Chinese households will consume in a more carbon-intensive manner; just how carbon intensive it will be remains unclear.

### Demographic changes

Since 1992 and through 2012, China's population rose 0.7% annually to reach a total of 1.35 billion inhabitants. The number of households grew even faster – 1.8% annually and now at a count of 433.1 million. The difference in these two changes is explained by a reduced average size of China's households, which declined by nearly a whole person to 3.02 people per household over the 20 years ending in 2012. Still, rapid urbanization appears to be a main motivation for this change over the past two decades; the urban share of China's population, which was 27.5% in 1992, increased to 52.6% by 2012. According to China's New Urbanization Plan (2014–2020), the share of urban population in China is expected to rise to 60% in 2020. This plan foresees 100 million moving to China's cities by 2020.

Over the last few years, China has relaxed its one-child policy to counter the problems created by it in which the count of China's elderly was poised to become substantially larger than that of the working population that would be available to support it. In November 2013, China adjusted its family planning policy to allow couples to have a second child if one spouse was an only child. In October 2015, China further loosened its fertility policy to allow all couples to have two kids (China Daily, 2015). The policy change has brought a "second-child baby boom" to China. It is set to bring an extra 15 million newborns within five years (People's Daily, 2016).

The aforementioned prospective demographic changes are likely to manifest in household consumption levels and patterns through several different pathways. First, small households consume more energy and resources per capita. China's shift to smaller households poses serious challenges to energy conservation and $CO_2$ emissions (Liu and Diamond, 2005). Second, with rapid urbanization, the geographical expansion of large cities and newly formed urban zones dramatically increased the demand for buildings and transportation infrastructure (Fernandez, 2007). Meanwhile, due to the huge urban-rural gap per capita in $CO_2$ household emissions, urbanization should in the foreseeable future continue to significantly enhance the total household $CO_2$ emissions, both directly and indirectly. Third, the universal second-child policy will not only bolster population growth but also spur new spending on health care, clothing, educational goods and services, and related items. In summary, the combined demographic trends of ever-smaller household sizes, increasing urbanization, and a planned baby boom will continue to cause household $CO_2$ emissions to surge in the long run.

## Conclusions

Chinese households' $CO_2$ emissions have risen 142% from 1,176 MMT in 1992 to 2,850 MMT in 2012. The rural-urban gap in $CO_2$ emissions between urban and rural households has risen too, so that in 2012, household $CO_2$ emissions per capita were 1,128 kg for rural households and 2,986 kg for urban households. Households have been increasingly shifted their consumption towards more energy- and carbon-intensive goods, like Primary Iron and Steel Manufacturing. From 1997 to 2007, the main factors increasing such emissions were income levels, consumption preferences, and interindustry input mix. Further increases in demand for living space, electric appliance ownership, heating and cooling, and personal mobility will cause China's residential sector to become more emissions-intensive.

The lifestyle changes mentioned above could amplify $CO_2$ emissions even further by inducing changes in China's production structure. Fortunately, both changes in interindustry input mix and household consumption preferences have helped reduce household indirect $CO_2$ emissions from 2007 to 2012. Moreover, urban households have been gradually shifting their consumption pattern toward low carbon goods and services. Generally speaking, emission efficiency gains have largely offset the effects of household consumption rises, but this was not the case during the most recent sub-period studied here – 2007 to 2012.

China's household energy consumption is lower than the Western standards, but its potential for growth looms large. As their incomes rise, Chinese households tend to consume more, as was mentioned earlier. China's newly formed urban middle class has been emulating energy-addicted Western lifestyle with the purchase of cars, bigger homes, and evermore labor-saving appliances. At the same time, rapid urbanization is inducing smaller household sizes, narrowing the urban-rural income gap, and providing large sources of domestic demand and services. Since rural households have been producing fewer $CO_2$ emissions, their potential producing more of emissions per capita is particularly high if they continue a desire to emulate their urban counterparts. With income-induced lifestyle change, increasing urbanization, and the pending "second-child baby boom", household-based $CO_2$ emissions could well rise for many years to come. In this vein, a focus on household-based $CO_2$ emissions is paramount in any policy developments or further research on carbon emissions in China.

China is now encouraging private consumption to boost its economy. Given this and the trends promising rises in household-based emissions per capita, it is clear that guiding Chinese residents' lifestyles toward low carbon consumption must be part of a strategy used by China to achieve its 2030 peak carbon emission target. A low-carbon future depends on what we do today. The long-run lock-in effect of infrastructure binds future households' choices through the sets of alternatives that China makes available now, such as greener buildings, more public transit, and supporting renewable energy technologies (e.g., the generation of electricity through wind, solar, geothermal, and hydropower). Thus the Chinese government must take an active, central role in promoting green consumption by implementing regulations, such as stricter building codes and higher energy efficiency standards as well as coordinate cross-sector policies that may have potential environmental impacts on household decisions. Corporations and enterprises also should adopt low-carbon responsibility by managing emissions through their supply chains as well as by facilitating low-carbon consumption through labeling such as via a green-product certification system. In all, China needs to shift to a low carbon economy that will help counter climate change and at the same time promote economic and social progress.

## Acknowledgement

This research was supported by the National Science Foundation of China (Grant No. 71403118), and the Clean Development Mechanism Project of China's National Development and Reform Commission (Grant No. 2013056).

## Notes

1 Here, direct energy use only refers to commercial energy. Non-commercial energy sources such as firewood, straw and biogas are also important energy sources for rural residents. In 2007, the average non-commercial energy use per capita for rural residents was 357 kg SCE. Thus rural households consumed far more direct energy when non-commercial energy is considered.
2 Earlier we only showed one of two possible polar decompositions. Like many other studies, we examine both polar decompositions in the end using Fisher indices – the geometric means of the polar decompositions – to analyze results as suggested by Dietzenbacher et al. (2000).

# References

China Daily (Producer). (2015). *Two-child policy is a turning point for China*. Retrieved December 31, 2016, from www.chinadaily.com.cn/china/2015-10/30/content_22329186.html

Dietzenbacher, E., Hoen, A. R., and Los, B. (2000). Labor productivity in Western Europe 1975–1985: An intercountry, interindustry analysis. *Journal of Regional Science*, *40*(3), 425–452.

Enerdata. (2016). *Global energy statistical yearbook 2016*, available online in May 2017 at https://yearbook.enerdata.net/.

Feng, K., Siu, Y. L., Guan, D., and Hubacek, K. (2012). Analyzing drivers of regional carbon dioxide emissions for China. *Journal of Industrial Ecology*, *16*(4), 600–611.

Fernandez, J. E. (2007). Resource consumption of new urban construction in China. *Journal of Industrial Ecology*, *11*(2), 99–115.

Golley, J., and Meng, X. (2012). Income inequality and carbon dioxide emissions: The case of Chinese urban households. *Energy Economics*, *34*(6), 1864–1872.

Green, F., and Stern, N. (2017). China's changing economy: implications for its carbon dioxide emissions. *Climate Policy*, 17(4), 423–442.

Guan, D., Peters, G. P., Weber, C. L., and Hubacek, K. (2009). Journey to world top emitter: An analysis of the driving forces of China's recent $CO_2$ emissions surge. *Geophysical Research Letters*, *36*(4).

Hubacek, K., Feng, K., and Chen, B. (2011). Changing lifestyles towards a low carbon economy: An IPAT analysis for China. *Energies*, *5*(1), 22–31.

IPCC. (1996). *IPCC guidelines for national greenhouse gas inventories*. Geneva, Switzerland: Technical Report. Intergovernmental Panel on Climate Change.

Jotzo, F., and Teng, F. (2014). China's climate and energy policy. In L. Song, R. Garnaut & C. Fang (Eds.), *Deepening reform for China's long-term growth and development* (pp. 207–228). Canberra, Australia: Australian National University Press.

Liu, J., and Diamond, J. (2005). China's environment in a globalizing world. *Nature*, *435*(7046), 1179–1186.

Miller, R. E., and Blair, P. D. (2009). *Input-output analysis: Foundations and extensions* (2nd ed.). Cambridge: Cambridge University Press.

Minx, J. C., Baiocchi, G., Peters, G. P., Weber, C. L., Guan, D., and Hubacek, K. (2011). A "carbonizing dragon": China's fast growing $CO_2$ emissions revisited. *Environmental Science & Technology*, *45*(21), 9144–9153.

NBS. (1998). *1991–1996 China energy statistical yearbook*. Beijing, China: National Bureau of Statistics of China.

NBS. (2009). *2009 China energy statistical yearbook*. Beijing, China: National Bureau of Statistics of China.

NBS. (2014a). *2014 China energy statistical yearbook*. Beijing, China: National Bureau of Statistics of China.

NBS. (2014b). *2014 China statistical yearbook*. Beijing, China: National Bureau of Statistics of China.

Pachauri, S., and Jiang, L. (2008). The household energy transition in India and China. *Energy Policy*, *36*(11), 4022–4035.

People's Daily (Producer). (2016). *Two-child policy creates baby boom in China*. Retrieved December 31, 2016, from http://en.people.cn/n3/2016/0803/c90882-9094691.html

Peters, G. P., Weber, C. L., Guan, D., and Hubacek, K. (2007). China's growing $CO_2$ emissions a race between increasing consumption and efficiency gains. Environmental Science & Technology, *41*(17), 5939–5944.

Wang, X., and Feng, Z. (2001). Rural household energy consumption with the economic development in China: stages and characteristic indices. *Energy Policy*, *29*(15), 1391–1397.

The World Bank. (2016a). *GNI per capita, atlas method (current US$)*. Retrieved December 31, 2016, from http://data.worldbank.org/indicator/NY.GNP.PCAP.CD?end=2015& locations=CN&start=1962&view=chart

The World Bank. (2016b). *Household final consumption expenditure (% of GDP)*. Retrieved December 31, 2016, from http://data.worldbank.org/indicator/NE.CON.PETC.ZS

Xinhua News (Producer). (2015). *Enhanced actions on climate change: China's intended nationally determined contributions*. Retrieved December 31, 2016, from http://news. xinhuanet.com/english/china/2015-06/30/c_134369837.htm

Zhang, H., and Lahr, M. L. (2014). Can the carbonizing dragon be domesticated? Insights from a decomposition of energy consumption and intensity in China, 1987–2007. *Economic Systems Research*, *26*(2), 119–140.

Zhang, H., Lahr, M. L., and Bi, J. (2016). Challenges of green consumption in China: a household energy use perspective. *Economic Systems Research*, *28*(2), 183–201.

# 8 The road to Paris with energy-efficiency strategies and GHG emissions-reduction targets

## The case of Spain

*Rosa Duarte, Julio Sánchez Chóliz*
*and Cristina Sarasa*

### Introduction

In December 2015, over 120 countries, various non-governmental organizations, and many corporate leaders reached the so-called Paris Accords (PA or COP21) within the United Nations Framework Convention on Climate Change (FCCC). The PA seeks to strengthen the global response to the threat of climate change in order to achieve sustainable development with zero emissions by 2100 and simultaneously to advance poverty eradication and equity, globally. The PA has recently been accepted and ratified by more than 55 parties to the convention, including the European Union (EU).

The EU also signed on to the Kyoto first commitment period (2008–2011), pledging to reduce its emissions by 6% compared to 1990 levels. The second commitment period of Kyoto (2013–2020) covered the period between 2013 and the start of a new global agreement, and is therefore valid until the new PA. The EU countries (together with Iceland) agreed to jointly meet a 20% reduction target compared to 1990, in line with the EU's own targets.

The EU climate strategy aims to achieve an economy-wide GHG reduction target of at least 20% by 2020 compared to 1990, 40% by 2030, and 80% by 2050 (EU, 2016b). As the EU's emissions for 2005 are slightly lower than those of 1990, we use emissions in 2005 as the reference point.

Moreover, in 2020, the emissions trading system (ETS) will cover around 45% of EU GHG emissions, mainly emissions from the power, industry, and aviation sectors. The EU wants these types of emissions to be 21% lower than in 2005 in all countries. For the remaining sectors, not covered by ETS and accounting for around 55% of the total EU emissions, the targets differ according to national wealth. Both measures globally represent an approximate 20% cut below 1990 levels by 2020. For Spain, the overall requirement is 10% above 2005 levels (see Figure 8.A.1 in the Appendix). Additionally, by 2020, the EU aims to obtain 20% of its energy from renewable sources and to improve energy efficiency by 20%. More specifically, the EU as a whole aims for a share of renewables of around 10% in the transport sector.

Regarding the situation in 2030, the target of a 40% reduction in emissions is planned to be achieved with reductions of 43% of the emissions of sectors with ETSs and with reductions of 30% in the remaining sectors, for which it will be necessary to establish individual binding targets. Regarding the share of renewables, the target for 2030 is to achieve from this source at least 27% of the energy consumed in the EU. Additionally, in relation to improving efficiency, the European Council has planned an energy saving target of 27%, with a potential revision up to 30%. The additional annual investment required to implement these targets is estimated at € 38 billion for the EU as a whole over the period 2011–2030, representing approximately 0.26% of the EU's overall added value in 2015 (Eurostat, 2016). The objective is to achieve a reduction of 80% by 2050, after a 60% decline by 2040. This 80% reduction aims to be achieved as a reduction in domestic (own) emissions, thus avoiding any recourse to international credits.

In this context, what can be said specifically about Spain, a country with important external energy dependence of about 80% compared to 55% in the EU. In Spain, in line with the EU strategies, two governmental plans for energy diversification and savings have been defined, one for the period 2004–2010 and the other for 2011–2020 (IDAE, 2016a, 2016b), which we can call PER 2005–2010 and PER 2011–2020.

The current PER, covering the period 2011–2020 was approved by the government on 11 November 2011, in accordance with Directive 2009/28 / EC of the European Parliament and of the European Council, dated 23 April 2009 (EU, 2009). The European standards set for Spain the objective that renewable sources will account for at least 20% of final energy consumption in 2020 – the same target as for the EU average – together with a minimum contribution of 10% of renewable energy sources in transport, objectives which were incorporated in the PER 2011–2020. According to forecasts, production of renewable electricity by 2020 should exceed 38% of total national production. PER 2011–2020 analyzes the technical aspects of the study of the evolution of energy transport facilities in general, the study of the management of the electrical system, and makes a set of proposals for action for the integration of renewable energies and improved distribution. In terms of generation, the objective is to prioritize the use of electrical energy from renewable energy sources and suggests the need for a stable and predictable economic framework that encourages generation from such resources, while ensuring that associated investments will obtain reasonable rates of return.

The PER 2011–2020 divides the necessary investments into three main areas: electric, thermal, and biofuels. The planned investments and the corresponding support (additional costs of administration and the private sector) are included in Table 8.1.

As shown in the table, an additional investment is predicted during the decade of more than 62 billion euros, of which 55 billion correspond to electricity generation facilities and more than 6 billion to thermal installations. The additional support from the Administration is 1.259 billion and from the private sector around 23 billion. This means that the investments and costs attributable to the Plan exceed 87 billion euros and that we can assume an annual cost of less than

Table 8.1 PER 2011–2010, investment and support forecast

| (Thousand euros) Investment | 2011 | 2012 | 2013 | 2014 | 2015 | 2016 | 2017 | 2018 | 2019 | 2020 | Total 2011–2020 |
|---|---|---|---|---|---|---|---|---|---|---|---|
| Electrical area | 6,993 | 7,117 | 4,734 | 4,043 | 4,320 | 4,663 | 4,938 | 5,559 | 6,377 | 6,998 | 55,743 |
| Thermal area | 353 | 362 | 420 | 451 | 676 | 746 | 724 | 794 | 843 | 911 | 6,279 |
| Biofuels | 0 | 0 | 0 | 0 | 45 | 300 | 0 | 30 | 300 | 100 | 775 |
| **Total investment** | **7,346** | **7,479** | **5,153** | **4,494** | **5,041** | **5,709** | **5,662** | **6,383** | **7,520** | **8,009** | **62,797** |
| Cost for the Public Administration | | | | | | | | | | | |
| Public investment aids | 24 | 64 | 81 | 95 | 107 | 123 | 131 | 139 | 136 | 137 | 1,037 |
| Financing | 4 | 7 | 10 | 12 | 14 | 17 | 19 | 21 | 24 | 26 | 155 |
| Other policies (information, etc.) | 2 | 14 | 7 | 7 | 6 | 6 | 6 | 6 | 6 | 6 | 67 |
| **Subtotal Public Adm** | | **85** | **98** | **114** | **128** | **146** | **156** | **166** | **166** | **169** | **1,259** |
| Cost for the private sector | | | | | | | | | | | |
| Renewable electricity premiums (base scenario) | 489 | 1,325 | 1,954 | 2,283 | 2,502 | 2,671 | 2,790 | 2,923 | 3,078 | 3,218 | 23,235 |
| Incentives to renewable heat | — | 2 | 8 | 13 | 18 | 23 | 27 | 31 | 34 | 36 | 191 |
| **Subtotal private sector** | **489** | **1,327** | **1,962** | **2,296** | **2,520** | **2,694** | **2,817** | **2,954** | **3,112** | **3,254** | **23,426** |
| **Total, costs (base scenario)** | **520** | **1,413** | **2,060** | **2,410** | **2,648** | **2,841** | **2,973** | **3,120** | **3,278** | **3,423** | **24,686** |

Source: IDAE (2016b), page 570

9 billion euros, or approximately 0.7% of the expected average Spanish GDP (about 1300 billion euros). We will assume, therefore, that non-investment spending will be about 25 billion, approximately 0.2% of GDP, leaving an additional 0.5% for investment.

## Methodology

This work presents the development of a multi-sector, dynamic Computable General Equilibrium (CGE) model to represent the Spanish economy in 2010. The work is based on previous energy-related CGE models. Specifically, the production and consumption structure follows Duarte, Rebahi, et al. (2014); the dynamic path is included as in Duarte, Sánchez-Chóliz, et al. (2014), and different specifications on the use of private cars by consumers follows the work of Figus et al. (2016).

Our work uses a recursive dynamic CGE model to evaluate the long-term economic and environmental impacts up to 2020, 2030, 2040, and 2050.

The input-output table consists of 34 economic activities, two production factors (labour and capital), and other accounts, such as Households, Companies, Savings/Investment, Government, and a Foreign sector. The latter consists of two other accounts: transactions carried out with the rest of the European Union (EU), and with the rest of the world (ROW). The special interest in our study is focused on the energy sector, which is disaggregated into four energy accounts: coal, petroleum, gas, and electricity.

We explain here the nesting and relationships among energy sectors, with the rest of the sectors in production and consumption.

Figure 8.1 represents the structure of the production sectors. Total output is obtained through a combination of a value-added-energy, aggregate-transport composite and all other intermediate inputs according to a Leontief function (fixed technical coefficients). The value-added-energy, aggregate-transport composite is a multi-level constant elasticity of substitution (CES) production function, combining an aggregate of energy and transport services, capital, and labor. On the right side, travel by air and sea includes an additional nest as it is more difficult to substitute between them because they are not used for short-distance transport. On the left side, the structure of the energy aggregate follows the GTAP-E model (Burniaux and Truong, 2002). Demand for energy is a CES composite of electricity and a fossil fuels aggregate, which is itself a CES composite of coal and oil-gas that represents an additional bundle to substitute between oil and biofuel.

Concerning consumption, Figure 8.2 presents consumer preferences defined by a three-stage nested CES utility function. In the case of the transport services aggregate, consumers choose the mean of transport following a Leontief function between land, air, and sea, as well as other transports, on the assumption that this decision depends on distance travelled rather than relative prices.

Concerning factor markets, the labour and capital factors are considered to be mobile across sectors. The model also includes a wage curve to consider unemployment. The elasticity parameters are selected on the basis of a review of the literature on this topic.

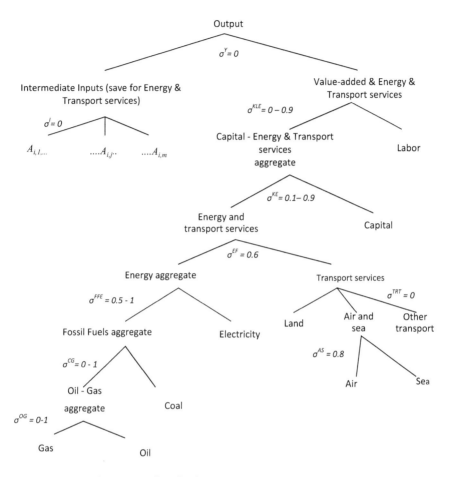

*Figure 8.1* Nested structure of production

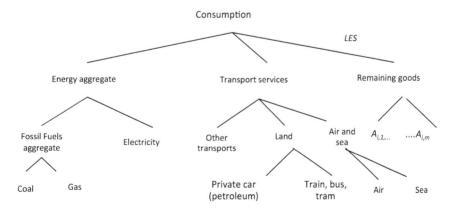

*Figure 8.2* Household consumption nesting structure

The earlier model is calibrated for the Spanish economy of 2010 and dynamically extended for the period 2010–2050. The values of the main parameters of the dynamic model are obtained from actual average data for Spain for a period of ten years 2005–2015 (INE, 2005–2015). Specifically, the annual interest rate is 4.22% and the growth rate is 0.77%. The relationship between capital and investment in the steady state is obtained from the calibration of the model using the information of the Spanish input-output table (IOT). A detailed description of this dynamic can be found in Duarte, Sánchez-Chóliz, et al. (2014).

The attribution of emissions to final demand is obtained using input-output models (see also Turner et al., 2012 and Duarte, Rebahi, et al., 2014). In this regard, the emissions estimated in the CGE model take into account both household direct emissions, $E^{DH}$, and emissions from production activities, $E^{PA}$.

$$E = E^{DH} + E^{PA} \tag{8.1}$$

$E^{DH}$ emissions are obtained as the product of a vector $\mathbf{i}$ of emissions per unit of each type ("Coal", "Refined oil", and "Gas") of energy by household consumption vector $\mathbf{c}$. $E^{PA}$ emissions are calculated using the input-output model (Sánchez-Chóliz et al., 2007).

$$E^{PA} = \mathbf{d}' \, (\mathbf{I\text{-}A})^{-1}\mathbf{s}, \tag{8.2}$$

where $\mathbf{d}$ is a vector of productive emissions intensities (Kt of $CO_2$eq per monetary unit of output), $(\mathbf{I\text{-}A})^{-1}$ is the Leontief inverse matrix, and $\mathbf{s}$ is the vector of final demand.

We consider greenhouse gas (GHG) emissions expressed in kilotons of equivalent carbon dioxide (Kt of $CO_2$eq), with information obtained from the emissions satellite accounts provided by the Spanish National Statistics Institute (INE, 2010).

## Future scenario for the Spanish economy

### *Baseline scenario: balance path and description for 2010*

The baseline scenario, used to evaluate the impacts of our scenarios described in the following section, is calibrated by assuming an annual interest rate of 4.22% and a growth rate of 0.77% (INE, 2005–2015). The balance path from 2020 to 2050 represents the expected evolution if no environmental policies are implemented.

Direct and indirect emissions for the baseline scenario, both the base year and the evolution of emissions of the balance path, are presented in Table 8.2. We assume that the unit vector of emissions (Kt of $CO_2$eq per monetary unit of output) does not vary.

As we can observe, economic activities in 2010 account for 79.11% of GHG emissions, and emissions from production activities associated with households

*Table 8.2* Spanish GHG emissions in the baseline scenario (2010, 2020, 2030, 2040, and 2050)

|  | 2010 | | 2020 | 2030 | 2040 | 2050 |
|---|---|---|---|---|---|---|
|  | GHG (Kt) | % | GHG (Kt) | GHG (Kt) | GHG (Kt) | GHG (Kt) |
| Household direct emissions (1) | 73,351 | 20.89 | 79,198 | 85,512 | 92,330 | 99,690 |
| Emissions from production activities (2) | 277,720 | 79.11 | 300,028 | 323,947 | 349,773 | 378,942 |
| *Households* | 126,893 | *36.14* | 133,328 | 143,957 | 155,434 | 167,826 |
| *Export* | 87,089 | *24.81* | 92,865 | 100,268 | 108,262 | 116,893 |
| *Government* | 27,971 | *7.97* | 29,576 | 31,934 | 34,480 | 37,229 |
| *NPISH* | 797 | *0.23* | 834 | 901 | 973 | 1,050 |
| *Investment* | 34,971 | *9.96* | 43,424 | 46,886 | 50,624 | 55,944 |
| **Total emissions (1 + 2)** | **351,070** | **100.00** | **379,226** | **409,459** | **442,103** | **478,632** |
| **% change to 2005 emissions** | −19.05 | | −13.47 | −6.57 | 0.88 | 9.21 |

Source: Own elaboration

are the most significant; 126,893 Kt of $CO_2$eq, followed by emissions associated with exports that represent 24.81% of GHG emissions. Additionally, household direct emissions represent 20.89% of GHG emissions, which is lower than indirect emissions but still significant. In sum, in a first analysis, we can see that emissions associated with household activities are significant.

Specifically, the sectoral structure of direct emissions is presented in Table 8.3 for the base year 2010. Emissions from "Electricity" represent the most significant account, followed by the "Agriculture and Livestock" sector and "Land transport services". Their shares are, respectively, 13.28%, 11.57%, and 10.10% of total GHG emissions. Note that emissions associated with transport services are larger if we include sea, air, and other transport services. Then, "Refined petroleum products" represent around 4.47% of GHG emissions.

Table 8.4 presents the structure of indirect emissions associated with production activities in 2010, showing that GHG emissions associated with household consumption are mainly due to the "Services", "Industry", and "Energy" sectors, while "Industry" represents a significantly larger share of emissions attributable to exports. Then emissions associated with government and NPISH are explained by the "Services" sector (mainly education and health), and those associated with investment arise primarily from the "Construction" sector.

Regarding the emissions in 2005, based on data from EU (2016a), and assuming the growth and interest rates previously established, there are reductions in total emissions in 2020 and 2030. However, without changes in the current path, increases in emissions could be observed from 2040 that goes against the "Paris Accords".

Table 8.3 Structure of direct atmospheric emissions in Spain in 2010

| Sectors | GHG (Kt) | % | Sectors | GHG (Kt) | % | Sectors | GHG (Kt) | % |
|---|---|---|---|---|---|---|---|---|
| Agriculture and livestock | 40,604 | 11.57 | Construction materials | 34,035 | 9.69 | Hotels and restaurants | 1,848 | 0.53 |
| Forestry | 67 | 0.02 | Metal products and machinery | 13,256 | 3.78 | Communication services | 678 | 0.19 |
| Aquaculture | 2,772 | 0.79 | Other metal products | 2,168 | 0.62 | Credit and Insurance | 445 | 0.13 |
| Coal | 5,099 | 1.45 | Machinery | 720 | 0.20 | Real estate | 93 | 0.03 |
| Refined petroleum products | 15,696 | 4.47 | Manufacture of motor vehicles | 1,585 | 0.45 | Public administration | 4,258 | 1.21 |
| Electricity | 46,639 | 13.28 | Transport equipment | 364 | 0.10 | Education | 1,265 | 0.36 |
| Gas | 13,230 | 3.77 | Furniture | 477 | 0.14 | Health care | 1,424 | 0.41 |
| Water | 13,915 | 3.96 | Construction | 1,608 | 0.46 | Other services | 888 | 0.25 |
| Agri-food industry, beverages and tobacco | 6,289 | 1.79 | Commercial services | 6,515 | 1.86 | Households | 73,351 | 20.89 |
| Textile products | 726 | 0.21 | Land transport services | 35,469 | 10.10 | | | |
| Wood and cork | 805 | 0.23 | Sea transport services | 3,387 | 0.96 | | | |
| Paper, publishing and printing | 3,270 | 0.93 | Air transport services | 4,875 | 1.39 | | | |
| Chemical products | 12,222 | 3.48 | Other transport services | 1,029 | 0.29 | **TOTAL** | **351,070** | **100.00** |

Source: Own elaboration

Table 8.4 Structure of indirect atmospheric emissions in Spain in 2010

| | Households | | Exports | | Government | | NPISH | | Investment | |
|---|---|---|---|---|---|---|---|---|---|---|
| | GHG (Kt) | % | GHG (Kt) | % | GHG (Kt) | % | GHG (Kt) | % | GHG (Kt) | % |
| Agriculture | 10,124 | 7.98 | 9,315 | 10.70 | 102 | 0.36 | 0 | 0.00 | 1,084 | 2.80 |
| Energy | 27,808 | 21.91 | 6,777 | 7.78 | 1 | 0.00 | 0 | 0.00 | 223 | 0.58 |
| Industry | 35,218 | 27.75 | 53,879 | 61.87 | 5,608 | 20.05 | 0 | 0.00 | 8,654 | 22.38 |
| Construction | 1,267 | 1.00 | 251 | 0.29 | 313 | 1.12 | 0 | 0.00 | 23,324 | 60.31 |
| Services | 41,106 | 32.39 | 5,992 | 6.88 | 19,332 | 69.12 | 797 | 100.00 | 4,978 | 12.87 |
| Transport and communications | 11,369 | 8.96 | 10,874 | 12.49 | 2,614 | 9.35 | 0 | 0.00 | 411 | 1.06 |
| TOTAL | 126,893 | 100 | 87,089 | 100 | 27,971 | 100 | 797 | 100 | 38,673 | 100 |

*Simulated scenarios*

Our simulated scenarios are based on criteria from the Paris Agreement and the EU climate strategies and targets, considering Spain specifically. We focus on energy production, energy use, and direct and indirect emissions in all scenarios, showing the results as percentage changes compared to the baseline path, and to 2005 emissions in all scenarios. We simulate the improvement in all cases as a logistic evolution to capture the gradual adaptation of the populace to policy targets. This allows us to consider a period of acceleration in the transformation towards a low-carbon society that goes from approximately 1920 to 1945 (the prior years of adaptation) and the later years of assimilation toward the 2100 goal of zero emissions.

We design the following three scenarios:

- **Scenario 1** includes the improvements in the use of energy produced by the current technologies; in other words, the reduction of the unit direct coefficient of emissions from productive activities and from households. This improvement does not involve a change in technology, but does require a reduction in energy wastage and emissions. It addresses measures such as the use of better insulation in production processes and in homes, improvements in electrical distribution networks, and the fixing of temperature caps in heating and cooling. Recycling processes are also involved. The reduction of transportation of goods, via the substitution more local goods is also assumed. Specifically, we model a logistic evolution that attains the 20% improvement by 2050.
- **Scenario 2** simulates technological improvements in the use of energy, both in production and households, implying a better use of technology. For instance, the replacement of obsolete or low-efficiency devices by appliances labeled Class A or higher, the use of electric cars, and improvements in electrical distribution networks. Following the Paris Agreement and the proposals from the EU, we consider that the agricultural sectors improve by 10% by 2050, the industry and transport sectors improve by 30% by 2050, and the remaining sectors improve by 40% y 2050. The improvement in energy sectors by households is also 30% by 2050. We again consider that the coefficients of emissions per unit of output are not fixed, as the coefficients of energy use change and the sectoral ratios of "emissions/energy used" are fixed. This involves something new, compared with prior work in the literature.
- **Scenario 3** includes both Scenarios 1 and 2, simultaneously.

The cost of improvement follows the PER for the period 2011–2020, involving an annual spending of 0.2% of total production.[1] Additionally, annual investment by sectors in technology is 0.5% of total production. For simplicity, these payments are considered as fixed coefficients. The 0.2% of expenditure is obtained as an indirect tax on production, depending on the emissions by sector and is included in Scenario 1. Then, the improvement in Scenario 2 is funded by an indirect tax to collect 0.5% of total production and depends on the energy use by sectors. Scenario 3 includes both taxes.

Finally, we consider that the total reduction towards zero emissions should be achieved by renewable energies, which will be addressed in future works.

## Results

The following tables present the impacts of previous scenarios, defined based on reductions in energy wastage and on gradual technological improvements in the use of energy. We present the results as percentage changes in the values of the baseline path, covering the period 2010–2050.

Reductions in energy wastage are addressed through a logistic reduction on coefficients of emissions in Scenario 1. Table 8.5 shows that total emissions could fall by more than 40% by 2050, compared to a scenario without changes, which means a reduction of 35.20% relative to emissions in 2005. This allows us to achieve (or at least to advance significantly towards) the objectives proposed in the Paris Agreement and in EU climate strategies. As expected, the use of energy is not reduced significantly because the cuts in emissions do not arise from changes in energy efficiencies, but from reductions in coefficients of emissions associated with waste. In any case, Table 8.6 shows that reductions in industrial energy use are greater than reductions in household energy use due to the limiting effect of taxes.

Scenario 2 simulates improvements in energy efficiency in production and in households, in line with the guidelines proposed in the Paris Agreement, which leads to a reduction in the use of energy of more than 20% in households, and more than 10% in industry by 2050. Thus, total energy use could be reduced by around 15% by 2050, with significant reductions in the consumption of oil, coal, and electricity. These reductions in the use of energy imply cuts in the coefficients of emissions that finally suppose a reduction in total emissions of more than 10% by 2050 compared to a baseline without technological improvements and a reduction of 1.31% compared to emissions in 2005. Indeed, falls in direct household emissions are around 20%, but emissions from production activities are lower. We should note that the reduction in this scenarios are lower than the improvements in energy efficiency due to the rebound effect produced by lower energy costs that increase real income associated with higher efficiencies, leading to an increase in the use of other goods and services.

Finally, both strategies, simultaneously applied in Scenario 3, imply a larger reduction in total emissions by 2050 that could reach almost 50% in total emissions compared to the baseline without improvements and a reduction of 42.88% in total emissions compared to emissions in 2005. This finding entails a large reduction in emissions in line with the EU proposals. This reduction could be even larger in household direct emissions.

Additionally, the total use of energy is reduced by 15.14% in coal, 17.25% in oil, 14.69% in electricity, and 11.50% in gas.

Table 8.5 Percentage change in direct and indirect emissions

| | Scenario 1 | | | | Scenario 2 | | | | Scenario 3 | | | |
|---|---|---|---|---|---|---|---|---|---|---|---|---|
| | 2020 | 2030 | 2040 | 2050 | 2020 | 2030 | 2040 | 2050 | 2020 | 2030 | 2040 | 2050 |
| Household direct emissions (1) | −7.46 | −27.29 | −36.23 | −41.13 | 6.55 | −15.82 | −18.18 | −18.07 | −14.40 | −39.64 | −48.59 | −52.50 |
| Emissions from production activities (2) | −7.57 | −25.65 | −33.30 | −41.33 | 0.36 | −7.48 | −8.49 | −8.60 | −11.41 | −33.31 | −41.19 | −47.13 |
| Households | −7.49 | −25.87 | −33.74 | −41.06 | 1.11 | −8.55 | −9.96 | −9.79 | −11.22 | −34.12 | −42.22 | −47.77 |
| Export | −7.81 | −25.41 | −32.71 | −41.31 | −0.99 | −7.05 | −7.78 | −7.54 | −12.07 | −33.07 | −40.64 | −46.68 |
| Government | −7.37 | −26.02 | −34.08 | −40.88 | 1.14 | −6.22 | −7.31 | −7.41 | −10.29 | −32.25 | −40.42 | −46.07 |
| NPISH | −7.70 | −26.04 | −33.89 | −41.19 | 0.82 | −5.85 | −6.17 | −5.80 | −11.72 | −32.31 | −40.07 | −45.51 |
| Investment | −7.43 | −25.25 | −32.68 | −42.46 | 0.45 | −6.03 | −6.37 | −8.12 | −11.33 | −32.10 | −39.73 | −46.86 |
| **Total emissions (1+2)** | **−7.54** | **−25.99** | **−33.91** | **−41.29** | **1.66** | **−9.22** | **−10.51** | **−10.58** | **−12.04** | **−34.64** | **−42.73** | **−48.25** |
| **% change to 2005 emissions** | **−19.15** | **−30.13** | **−32.63** | **−35.20** | **−11.11** | **−14.29** | **−8.78** | **−1.31** | **−23.08** | **−38.29** | **−41.62** | **−42.88** |

Source: Own elaboration

Table 8.6 Percentage change in the use of energy

| | | Scenario 1 | | | | Scenario 2 | | | | Scenario 3 | | | |
|---|---|---|---|---|---|---|---|---|---|---|---|---|---|
| | | 2020 | 2030 | 2040 | 2050 | 2020 | 2030 | 2040 | 2050 | 2020 | 2030 | 2040 | 2050 |
| Household energy use | Coal | −0.33 | −0.42 | −0.52 | −0.62 | −1.05 | −18.27 | −21.92 | −21.75 | −1.41 | −18.59 | −22.29 | −22.18 |
| | Oil | −0.30 | −0.39 | −0.49 | −0.59 | −1.31 | −17.79 | −21.28 | −21.09 | −1.63 | −18.09 | −21.63 | −21.50 |
| | Electricity | −0.31 | −0.40 | −0.50 | −0.60 | −1.07 | −18.35 | −22.02 | −21.84 | −1.40 | −18.66 | −22.37 | −22.26 |
| | Gas | −0.31 | −0.40 | −0.50 | −0.60 | −1.07 | −18.35 | −22.02 | −21.84 | −1.40 | −18.66 | −22.37 | −22.26 |
| Industry energy use | Coal | −1.17 | −1.26 | −1.34 | −1.43 | −4.59 | −12.33 | −14.21 | −14.06 | −5.69 | −13.32 | −15.23 | −15.14 |
| | Oil | −1.20 | −1.27 | −1.35 | −1.43 | −4.37 | −11.78 | −13.78 | −13.68 | −5.51 | −12.66 | −14.69 | −14.64 |
| | Electricity | −2.02 | −2.11 | −2.19 | −2.27 | −5.02 | −9.42 | −10.75 | −10.67 | −7.00 | −11.39 | −12.74 | −12.72 |
| | Gas | −0.63 | −0.71 | −0.80 | −0.89 | −1.15 | −6.78 | −8.59 | −8.57 | −1.76 | −7.40 | −9.26 | −9.31 |
| **Total energy use** | **Coal** | **−1.17** | **−1.25** | **−1.34** | **−1.43** | **−4.58** | **−12.34** | **−14.22** | **−14.07** | **−5.69** | **−13.33** | **−15.24** | **−15.14** |
| | **Oil** | **−0.85** | **−0.94** | **−1.02** | **−1.11** | **−3.21** | **−14.07** | **−16.63** | **−16.50** | **−4.04** | **−14.73** | **−17.33** | **−17.25** |
| | **Electricity** | **−1.67** | **−1.75** | **−1.84** | **−1.93** | **−4.20** | **−11.27** | **−13.08** | **−12.98** | **−5.84** | **−12.89** | **−14.73** | **−14.69** |
| | **Gas** | **−0.57** | **−0.66** | **−0.75** | **−0.84** | **−1.13** | **−8.73** | **−10.85** | **−10.81** | **−1.70** | **−9.30** | **−11.48** | **−11.50** |

Source: Own elaboration

These results achieve the objective of reducing emissions considerably, although larger efforts to facilitate efficiency improvements, to promote the reduction of waste, and to study and supervise the rebound effect in other goods are required.

Table 8.7 shows the results in energy production by sectors, for all scenarios. As expected, the largest reduction in the use of energy obtained in Scenario 2 leads to more significant falls in the energy production of electricity, coal, oil, and gas due to improved technology. The reduction of energy waste leads to smaller cuts in energy production.

When we observe the impacts of these measures on the economy, Table 8.8 presents a summary of the main issues, percentage changes in relation to the baseline scenario. The payment of the cost of prior strategies involves slight reductions in total private consumption induced by price hikes, and a decline in disposable income after increasing taxes. However, the reduction in income through lower energy costs in Scenario 2 leads to an increase in the expense of other goods and services (rebound effect) that could drive increases in total consumption by 2050, in line with increases in total production driven by improvements in the use of one of the main inputs (energy), broadly in line with total exports rising, while total imports are reduced. Indeed, unemployment is reduced from 2040.

*Table 8.7* Percentage change in sectoral energy production

| | Scenario 1 | | | |
| | 2020 | 2030 | 2040 | 2050 |
|---|---|---|---|---|
| Electricity production | −1.68 | −1.77 | −1.85 | −1.94 |
| Coal production | −0.75 | −0.84 | −0.93 | −1.02 |
| Oil production | −1.58 | −1.67 | −1.75 | −1.84 |
| Gas production | −0.57 | −0.66 | −0.75 | −0.84 |
| | Scenario 2 | | | |
| | 2020 | 2030 | 2040 | 2050 |
| Electricity production | −4.24 | −11.31 | −13.12 | −13.02 |
| Coal production | −3.66 | −11.78 | −13.66 | −13.49 |
| Oil production | −7.40 | −17.86 | −20.33 | −20.20 |
| Gas production | −1.13 | −8.73 | −10.85 | −10.81 |
| | Scenario 3 | | | |
| | 2020 | 2030 | 2040 | 2050 |
| Electricity production | −5.89 | −12.94 | −14.79 | −14.75 |
| Coal production | −4.33 | −12.54 | −14.44 | −14.33 |
| Oil production | −8.88 | −19.13 | −21.61 | −21.54 |
| Gas production | −1.70 | −9.30 | −11.48 | −11.50 |

Source: Own elaboration

*Table 8.8* Macroeconomic results (% change)

| | Scenario 1 | | | |
|---|---|---|---|---|
| | *2020* | *2030* | *2040* | *2050* |
| Total production | −0.34 | −0.42 | −0.50 | −0.58 |
| Total exports | −0.36 | −0.44 | −0.52 | −0.61 |
| Total imports | −0.46 | −0.54 | −0.63 | −0.71 |
| Total private consumption | −0.31 | −0.40 | −0.50 | −0.60 |
| Unemployment | 1.24 | 1.48 | 1.74 | 1.99 |
| | Scenario 2 | | | |
| | *2020* | *2030* | *2040* | *2050* |
| Total production | −0.98 | −0.65 | −0.18 | 0.24 |
| Total exports | −1.28 | −0.87 | −0.38 | 0.03 |
| Total imports | −1.54 | −2.35 | −2.31 | −1.95 |
| Total private consumption | −0.94 | 0.30 | 1.06 | 1.59 |
| Unemployment | 3.79 | 0.68 | −1.34 | −2.72 |
| | Scenario 3 | | | |
| | *2020* | *2030* | *2040* | *2050* |
| Total production | −1.33 | −1.07 | −0.66 | −0.31 |
| Total exports | −1.64 | −1.35 | −0.93 | −0.59 |
| Total imports | −2.01 | −2.82 | −2.85 | −2.56 |
| Total private consumption | −1.28 | −0.08 | 0.61 | 1.05 |
| Unemployment | 5.09 | 2.15 | 0.32 | −0.84 |

Source: Own elaboration

## Conclusions

This paper presents a first attempt to evaluate alternative proposals of the Paris Agreement by 2050. We design a dynamic CGE model with a high level of detail on energy and transport services structures, for the period of 2010–2050, in which the Spanish economy advances to zero emissions by 2100. Our simulations assess alternative policy options in two lines: improvements in the use of energy through reductions in energy waste and emissions, which are simulated via coefficients of emissions abatement, and efficiency improvements in the use of energy through the replacement of obsolete or low-efficiency devices, both in production and consumption functions. In both scenarios, improvements are modeled using technological progress as a logistic evolution to capture the gradual adaptation of citizens and firms to policy targets by 2050. We include an approximation of the payment of estimated costs of the PA via taxes on emissions-intensive and/or energy-intensive products. Certain conclusions can be derived from this study.

First, the reduction of emission coefficients for fixed technologies (associated with a lower energy vintage in households and production activities) is an efficient way to achieve a large emissions abatement, in line with the proposals of the Paris Agreement and the goal of zero emissions by 2100. Specifically, more than 40% of total emissions could be reduced, compared with a baseline scenario without policies and more than 35% compared to emissions in 2005.

Second, efficiency improvements in the use of energy allow for a considerable reduction in the total use of energy (coal, oil, electricity, and gas) with more substantial cuts in household energy use than in industrial energy use, and then we can considerably reduce the necessary emissions associated with production. Moreover, the total energy production is also reduced, showing an improved use of energy inputs in production as total production rises by 2050. This result means that output could be produced by using less energy and attaining similar economic results in income or private consumption. However, this reduction in the energy bill implies increases in income that lead to an increase in the use of other goods and services. This rebound effect could involve important declines in the rate of improvements initially achieved through energy efficiency. This result notes the possible existence of a trade-off between efficiency improvements to reduce the use of energy and consequently positive impacts in disposable income that encourage emissions. In any case, our findings show that impacts on total output are not significant and therefore, alternative technologies for a more efficient use of energy can be implemented and be consistent with economic growth.

Finally, both strategies together allow for the achievement of the double objective of reducing emissions and reducing the use of total energy in the economy, thus reinforcing both processes with the reductions proposed by the Paris Agreement.

Our simulations suggest that, by 2050, the emissions reductions could be 48.25%, compared to the expected evolution if nothing is done – reductions which are undoubtedly very important to progress in the battle against climate change. Moreover, these figures, when compared to 2005 levels, represent reductions of 42.88%, which are far from zero emissions, but are nevertheless an important first step. Moreover, the use of renewable energies, non-emitting energies, such as nuclear, and other alternatives, such as carbon sequestration (not analyzed in this chapter) will undoubtedly produce important reductions in the future.

However, our results also indicate that large efforts are required to achieve the objective of zero emissions by 2100. Our strategies present the road towards these objectives, reflecting the potential benefits along with the possible drawbacks. Advances in this field will lead us to extend this work to include renewable resources in future work that should be promoted to counteract potential increases in emissions.

## Acknowledgments

The authors would like to express their gratitude for funding received from the Spanish Ministry of Science and Innovation by Projects ECO2013–41353-P and ECO2016–74940-P, and from the Aragonese Government and the *European* Regional Development Fund by Consolidated Research Group S10 in 2014, 2015, and 2016.

# Appendix

*Table 8.A.1* Targets for the EU-15 countries under "burden-sharing" (2008–2012)

| EU-15 | −8% | Bulgaria | −8% |
|---|---|---|---|
| Austria | −13% | Croatia | −5% |
| Belgium | −7.5% | Czech Republic | −8% |
| Denmark | −21% | Estonia | −8% |
| Finland | 0% | Hungary | −6% |
| France | 0% | Latvia | −8% |
| Germany | −21% | Lithuania | −8% |
| Greece | +25% | Poland | −6% |
| Ireland | +13% | Romania | −8% |
| Italy | −6.5% | Slovakia | −8% |
| Luxembourg | −28% | Slovenia | −8% |
| Netherlands | −6% | | |
| Portugal | +27% | Cyprus | N/A |
| Spain | +15% | Malta | N/A |
| Sweden | +4% | | |
| United Kingdom | −12.5% | | |

Source: EU. (2016a). Annual European Union greenhouse gas inventory 199020132014 and inventory report 2016. Executive summary. Brussels, Belgium.: European Commission.

*Table 8.A.2* Overview of Member States' contributions to EU GHG emissions excluding LULUCF from 1990 to 2013 in $CO_2$-equivalent (million tonnes)

| Member State | 1990 | 1995 | 2000 | 2005 | 2010 | 2011 | 2012 | 2013 |
|---|---|---|---|---|---|---|---|---|
| Austria | 79 | 79 | 80 | 92 | 85 | 83 | 80 | 80 |
| Belgium | 147 | 154 | 149 | 145 | 133 | 123 | 119 | 119 |
| Bulgaria | 109 | 75 | 60 | 64 | 61 | 66 | 61 | 56 |
| Croatia | 35 | 25 | 27 | 31 | 28 | 28 | 26 | 24 |
| Cyprus | 6 | 7 | 8 | 10 | 10 | 10 | 9 | 8 |
| Czech Republic | 193 | 153 | 146 | 144 | 136 | 135 | 131 | 127 |
| Denmark | 69 | 77 | 70 | 65 | 62 | 57 | 53 | 55 |
| Estonia | 40 | 20 | 17 | 18 | 20 | 20 | 19 | 22 |
| Finland | 71 | 72 | 70 | 69 | 76 | 68 | 62 | 63 |
| France | 549 | 548 | 554 | 555 | 516 | 489 | 490 | 490 |
| Germany | 1,248 | 1,120 | 1,044 | 993 | 943 | 923 | 928 | 951 |

*Table 8.A.2* (Continued)

| Member State | 1990 | 1995 | 2000 | 2005 | 2010 | 2011 | 2012 | 2013 |
|---|---|---|---|---|---|---|---|---|
| Greece | 105 | 111 | 128 | 136 | 119 | 116 | 113 | 105 |
| Hungary | 94 | | 74 | 76 | 65 | 64 | 60 | 57 |
| Ireland | 57 | 60 | 69 | 71 | 63 | 59 | 60 | 59 |
| Italy | 521 | 533 | 554 | 578 | 506 | 494 | 469 | 437 |
| Latvia | 26 | 13 | 10 | 11 | 12 | 11 | 11 | 11 |
| Lithuania | 48 | 22 | 20 | 23 | 21 | 21 | 21 | 20 |
| Luxembourg | 13 | 10 | 10 | 13 | 12 | 12 | 12 | 11 |
| Malta | 2 | 2 | 3 | 3 | 3 | 3 | 3 | 3 |
| Netherlands | 219 | 231 | 219 | 213 | 214 | 200 | 196 | 196 |
| Poland | 474 | 445 | 393 | 398 | 408 | 405 | 399 | 395 |
| Portugal | 60 | 71 | 84 | 88 | 70 | 69 | 67 | 65 |
| Romania | 253 | 184 | 141 | 147 | 118 | 123 | 121 | 111 |
| Slovakia | 76 | 55 | 50 | 52 | 47 | 46 | 44 | 44 |
| Slovenia | 19 | 19 | 19 | 20 | 19 | 19 | 19 | 18 |
| Spain | 291 | 331 | 390 | 441 | 357 | 355 | 349 | 322 |
| Sweden | 72 | 74 | 69 | 67 | 65 | 61 | 57 | 56 |
| United Kingdom | 804 | 755 | 720 | 698 | 616 | 570 | 586 | 572 |
| EU-28 | 5, 680 | 5, 322 | 5, 177 | 5, 224 | 4, 786 | 4, 630 | 4, 563 | 4, 477 |

Source: European Commission (2016b)

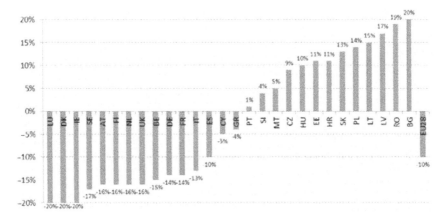

*Figure 8.A.1* Member State GHG emissions limits in 2020 compared to 2005 levels

Source: European Commission (2016a)

# Note

1  We calculate these percentages on total production rather than GDP, based on a first cautious approach.

# References

Burniaux, J.-M., and Truong, T. P. (2002). *GTAP-E: an energy-environmental version of the GTAP model*. GTAP Technical Papers, 18.

Duarte, R., Rebahi, S., Sánchez-Chóliz, J., and Sarasa, C. (2014). Household's behaviour and environmental emissions in a regional economy. *Economic Systems Research*, 26(4), 410–430.

Duarte, R., Sánchez-Chóliz, J., and Sarasa, C. (2014). *Could a crowd of small actions make a significant change to reduce emissions? A dynamic CGE analysis for Spain*. Paper presented at the VI Congress of the Spanish-Portuguese Association of Resource and Environmental Economics, Girona, Spain.

EU. (2009). Directive 2009/28/EC of the European Parliament and of the Council of 23 April 2009 on the promotion of the use of energy from renewable sources and amending and subsequently repealing Directives 2001/77/EC and 2003/30/EC. *Official Journal of the European Union* (Vol. 5). European Parliament.

EU. (2016a). Annual European Union greenhouse gas inventory 199020132014 and inventory report 2016. Executive summary. Brussels, Belgium: European Commission.

EU. (2016b). *Climate strategies and targets*. Brussels, Belgium: European Commission.

Eurostat. (2016). *GDP at current market prices, 2005 and 2013–2015*. Brussels, Belgium: European Commision.

Figus, G., Turner, K., and McGregor, P. (2016). *Can the rebound effect reduce fuel poverty?* Glasgow, UK: University of Strathclyde.

IDAE. (2016a). *Renewable energy plan 2005–2010*. Madrid, Spain: Institute for the Diversification and Saving of Energy.

IDAE. (2016b). *Renewable energy plan 2011–2020*. Madrid, Spain: Institute for the Diversification and Saving of Energy.

INE. (2005–2015). *Remissions accounts to the atmosphere*. Madrid, Spain: Instituto Nacional de Estadística.

INE. (2010). *Emissions accounts to the atmosphere*. Madrid, Spain: Instituto Nacional de Estadística.

Sánchez-Chóliz, J., Duarte, R., and Mainar, A. (2007). Environmental impact of household activity in Spain. *Ecological Economics*, 62(2), 308–318.

Turner, K., Munday, M., McGregor, P., and Swales, K. (2012). How responsible is a region for its carbon emissions? An empirical general equilibrium analysis. *Ecological Economics*, 76, 70–78.

# Part III

# Key drivers in carbon emissions and improvements in energy efficiency

# 9 Global drivers of change in GHG emissions from a consumption perspective

## Carbon footprint accounting in a post-Paris world

*Soeren Lindner, José-Manuel Rueda-Cantuche and Richard Wood*

## Introduction

The Conference of Parties (COP 21) held in Paris in 2016 re-iterated the scientific evidence that global temperature increase must not exceed 2˚C by 2050 and that, therefore, international and national climate policies need to aim towards partial or even full decarbonization of energy systems, industries and sectors. In order to allow decarbonization to happen efficiently, fast traditional policies based on accounting greenhouse gas (GHG) emissions from a production perspective ought to be supplemented with a consumption-based approach. This outcome sends a clear signal to the LCA community that carbon footprint studies have relevance and potentially strong impacts on climate policymakers who try to formulate the right carbon policies in an interwoven, globalized economy. However, to formulate good consumption-based policies along international supply chains and for governments to implement them successfully requires, first and foremost, an analysis of the driving forces of carbon footprint growth.

Often it is postulated that efficiency improvements are not significant enough to reach mitigation targets when analyzing the impacts of a rapidly developing world. In order to inform policy derivation on tackling the drivers of changes in emissions, it is then necessary to isolate the impacts along the supply chain of aspects such as technology change, efficiency improvements, changing consumer habits, rising levels of affluence and population growth. Further, the electricity sector bears the highest potential to reduce carbon emissions globally, with studies showing that a full decarbonization of the electricity sector is possible if the right policies are set in place that allow initiation of fuel-switch and change to non-fossil-fuel-based technologies (Knobloch and Mercure, 2016). The question then arises as to what factors specifically act on the carbon footprint related to fossil fuel combustion emissions and do they differ from those driving the footprint of non-fossil-fuel combustion emissions? Understanding the global relationship between forces on the consumption side acting on the producer of goods and services, who themselves rely on energy inputs with various fuel mixes, is key to sustainable mitigation policy that covers the entire supply chain.

Today, we live in a world in which economic production process and supply chains are international and global trade of goods and services from production sites in one country to final consumers in another is very common. In this globalized network of production and consumption linkages, an active debate remains over the question of which side should be held accountable for reducing the associated GHG emissions, the producer or the consumer? The Kyoto Protocol (1997) and its follow-up agreements envisage a production-based accounting system. Production-based accounts differ substantially from consumption-based accounts, where goods associated with emissions are ultimately consumed. Over time, the discussion of production- versus consumption-based accounting took on many facets; among them sprung up questions of how to appropriately account for consumption-based emissions along global supply chains and which data and models to use to trace emissions – a topic that has been addressed in previous work and is summarized in Wiedmann (2009).

One constant in the debate outlined earlier is the role of international trade in respect to carbon leakage (Peters and Hertwich, 2008). The shifting of $CO_2$ emissions from developed to developing countries has been well documented in the literature and is a problem because emerging economies, under original Kyoto agreements, do not have a legal obligation to reduce these emissions. Lately, scholars have been estimating the contribution of GHG emissions from international trade compared to domestic emissions. Estimates indicate that nowadays international export-based emissions make up 30% of global emissions (Andrew et al., 2013; Caldeira and Davis, 2011; Peters and Hertwich, 2008; Peters et al., 2011). For example, Peters et al. (2011) find that 23% of global $CO_2$ emissions, or 6.2 gigatonnes $CO_2$, were traded internationally – primarily as exports from China and other emerging markets to consumers in developed countries. In European countries, more than 30% of consumption-based emissions were imported, with net imports to many Europeans countries actually exceeding 4 tons of $CO_2$ per person in 2004. Contrast these numbers with Chinese export emissions, which reach 30% of total emissions produced in China (Liu et al., 2016). Finally, a consumption-based inventory of the United Kingdom found that growing consumption in the country increased embodied emissions in imports faster than those in domestic production. Consequently, the United Kingdom's total carbon footprint increased 12% between 1992 and 2004, whereas its production based emissions inventory decreased by only 5% (Wiedmann et al., 2010). A recent UK study recommended that consumption-based inventories be constructed as a complement to current territorial emissions inventories (Barrett et al., 2013).

Beyond the mere quantification of GHG emissions embodied in international trade, there is the question of which factors drive the growth of emissions. Answering such broad questions requires an understanding of changes in international global trade structures, final demand structures (consumption), production technologies and emissions factors. Few studies have carried out a decomposition of global embodied carbon pathways, although such an exercise is critical for a full understanding of production and consumption-based emissions. To support policy based on a consumption-based accounting perspective, it is foremost important to understand the drivers of global emissions and the role of international trade.

We focus on two critical areas in this study: 1) the internationalization of GHG supply chains and 2) the role of emission factors and fuel mixes in the internationalization of GHG supply chains. We briefly cover the motivation of each area.

### *Internationalization of GHG emissions*

In the light of effects of rapid globalization and escalating international trade on environmental impacts at the national level, research has recently narrowed its focus of evaluating the role of consumption in driving GHG emissions and the potential for consumer-based changes in behaviour in order to reduce such emissions. Several scholars have pointed towards the growing influence of international trade on national emission trends, in particular the growing regional disparity between western developed countries and global producer havens such as China and India (Peters et al., 2011; Wiedmann et al., 2010). Most developed countries have increased their consumption-based emissions more than territorial emissions. A number of studies have quantified the emissions embodied in global trade. Davis and Caldeira (2010) found that between 1990 and 2008, emissions from production of traded goods and services have increased from 4.3 Gt $CO_2$ to 7.8 Gt $CO_2$.

Consumption includes final domestic consumption, end-use organizational consumption and consumption involved in intermediate goods and supply chains. For example, we know that behaviour, lifestyle and culture have a considerable influence on energy use and associated emissions, with a high mitigation potential in some sectors, in particular when complementing technological and structural change (Edenhofer et al., 2014). European policymakers have sent a signal that evaluating consumer behaviour is important: for example, the Roadmap for moving to a competitive low carbon economy in 2050 and the Transport White Paper both acknowledge that behavioural changes may be needed to reach the emissions targets and that the targets may be reached at lower costs if the adoption of more sustainable consumption patterns and lifestyles are achieved.

Next to quantifying the impacts of consumer behaviour on emissions through – for example, trade – it is essential to identify the forces that have caused such changes over time. For China, it was found that increase of emissions by household consumption in Chinese mega cities was partially offset by an improvement in technology (efficiency improvements) in some key manufacturing sectors (Guan et al., 2008). Therefore, when evaluating drivers of emissions in Europe, such undertaken must be guided by questions such as "how does change over time in production structure towards green growth, a service sector oriented- and knowledge-based economy within a single European market affect emissions" and "how does Europe's change in international trade over time affect emissions embodied in trade?"

In order to quantify drivers of emissions change and evaluate the impact of consumer behavior we apply structural decomposition analysis (SDA) within a global multi-regional input-output framework (MRIO). A MRIO allows for tracing all emissions that are associated with final products back to the country that generated emissions and therefore provides much more accurate estimates than bilateral trade models or single region models. We use a MRIO model called EXIOBASE, which has a highly disaggregated

### Fuel combustion emissions versus emissions from non-fuel combustion processes

With carbon emissions related to fuel combustion still making up 70% of total anthropogenic emissions globally in 2015 (IEA, 2016), the potential to decarbonize this sector and therefore to play the major contributing role towards the path of reaching global mitigation targets is obvious. Studies have pointed out that full decarbonization of the energy sector is possible by 2050 (Knobloch and Mercure, 2016), primarily by substituting the fossil-fuel based energy technology fleet with renewable and low-carbon options. In other words, technological change at the level of electricity generation is a mandatory step towards achieving the ambitious targets set out in the Paris Agreement. The importance for input-output-based LCA type studies of a disaggregated electricity sector with a high resolution, reflecting technological detail as much as possible, has been pointed out (Lindner et al., 2012; Lindner, Legault, et al., 2013). For one, adding bottom-up technological detail at the power plant level to top down MRIO LCA models allows for the investigation of the effect of technological substitution on $CO_2$ emissions over time much better than aggregated models because individual plant technologies are obviously represented. Also, adding more detail to one sector reduces uncertainty of the environmental impact to be measured (Lenzen, 2011). Adding detailed bottom-up technologies at the power plant level can reduce uncertainty of $CO_2$ footprint estimates significantly. For countries, such as China which act as the production haven for goods and services exported globally it is particularly important to have represented as much technological detail as possible so that emissions embodied in trade are estimated with as much accuracy as possible (Lindner, Liu, et al., 2013).

Emission factors determine the amount of carbon oxidized per unit of fuel consumed, which largely reflect the quality of the fuel. For example, brown coal has generally lower emission factors then the higher quality black coal, in other words more amount of brown coal is needed to generate the same amount of energy as with black coal. As such, one can also understand emission factors as reflecting the efficiency of primary fuels that are being converted to secondary fuels such as electricity. Liu et al. (2015) recently showed for China that advanced sampling techniques for fuel quality alters energy data results and different emission factors. They concluded that related carbon emissions which are derived from annually published energy data in China could be in fact be over-estimated up to 15%. In top-down LCA models, the emission factors for a specific fuel, such as coal, are usually aggregated by general fuel type in the environmental accounting matrix. A more disaggregated version with detailed emissions factor by specific fuel qualities (i.e. brown coal, black coal) allows for a more accurate estimation of emissions. Disaggregation, therefore, adds value to LCA-type models by giving more trust and certainty to policymakers who use model results to form consumption-based policies.

The efforts undertaken in this study to disaggregate by fuel type and electricity generation technology is done to analyze how driving factors of carbon footprint growth affect types of fuels differently. Different regions and countries use a different fuel mixes and electricity generation technologies that enter production processes, resulting in country-specific GHG emissions per unit of production. The main goal of distinguishing between country-specific fuel mixes and emission factors in this study is to see whether there are different factors driving emissions from fossil fuel combustion versus emissions related to non-fossil fuel combustion. Changes in energy technologies in a country are better reflected over the time frame of the study. For example, changes in trade patterns over time, or a change in production structure, could mean that a country is producing a different set of goods and products that have different energy input requirements.

## Literature review

### *Structural decomposition analysis*

In order to understand historical changes in economic, environmental, employment, or other indicators it is useful to assess the driving forces or determinants that underlie these changes. This is typically done with index analysis, a technique in which aggregate factors are broken down into individual contributors. Broadly, decomposition studies can be broken down into two main schools, those utilizing index decomposition analyses (IDA) and those using structural decomposition analysis (SDA). The details of each decomposition methods and advantages and disadvantages are discussed in detail in Ang (2004). For input-output analysis (IOA), SDA has been shown to be superior (Su and Ang, 2012).

This paragraph explains structural decomposition by adapting mathematical notation in the typical form used for describing input output algebra. According to Rose and Chen (1991), SDA can be defined as "analysis of economic change by means of a set of comparative static changes in key parameters in an input-output table". If one asks the question, for example, which factors among economic growth, trade, population change and material intensity drive change in total output over time, then SDA can give the answer. Using this technique in effect means decomposing parts of the fundamental Leontief equation and calculating the effect each part has on an economic change. The basic Leontief equation is briefly reviewed next.

If we have a matrix $\mathbf{Z}$, row wise extrapolation shows which industries a single industry sells to, and reading down a column reveals whom a single industry buys from. A single element, within z, is akin to any given economic transaction from the ith sector to the jth industry or sector. Hence it follows logically that the total output $(x_i)$ of a particular sector is

$$x_i = z_{i1} + z_{i2} + \ldots + z_{ij} + y_i, \qquad (9.1)$$

where $y_i$ defines final demand for a product produced by the particular sector. Dividing each element, $z_{ij}$, along row i by output $x_i$ allows replacement of each element in $Z$ can be with a technical coefficient:

$$a_{ij} = \frac{z_{ij}}{x_j}. \tag{9.2}$$

In the matrix expression, $A = Z\hat{x}^{-1}$.
Substituting for (9.2) in equation (9.1) forms

$$x_i = a_{i1}x_1 + a_{i2}x + \ldots + a_{ij}x_i + y_i, \tag{9.3}$$

which becomes

$$x = Ax + y. \tag{9.4}$$

Solving for Y gives the well-known Leontief equation:

$$x = (I - A)^{-1} y, \tag{9.5}$$

where $x$ and $y$ are vectors of total output and final demand, respectively; I is the identity matrix; and A is the technical coefficient matrix, which shows the inter-industry requirements. $(I - A)^{-1}$ is known as the Leontief inverse (further identified as $L$). It indicates the inter-industry requirements of the *ith* sector to deliver a unit of output to final demand. Since the 1960s, the IO framework has been extended to account for increases in the pollution associated with industrial production due to a change in final demand (Miller and Blair, 2009).

Now, consider total output $X$ calculated in two different years, $t_1$ and $t_2$. The change in output can be expressed as

$$\Delta x = L_1 y_1 - L_0 y_0. \tag{9.6}$$

Equation 9.6 can be rewritten in its decomposed form:

$$\Delta x = \Delta L y_1 + L_0 \Delta y, \tag{9.7}$$
$$\Delta x = \Delta L y_0 + L_1 \Delta y. \tag{9.8}$$

To calculate the influence each term has on the change in output, the suggestion is to take the mean of the two first terms and the mean of the two second. Thus, the effect of a change in the Leontief matrix, $L$ on total output $x$ is $(\Delta L y_1 + \Delta L y_2)/2$. And similarly, the effect of a change in final demand $y$ on total output $X$ is $(L_0 \Delta y + L_1 \Delta y)/2$.

The Leontief equation can be expressed as the product of more than two terms. For example, if final demand is represented as the product of total final demand

$(\mathbf{t}_y)$ and the proportions of final demand spend by region of origin and type of product $(\mathbf{p}_y)$, then $\mathbf{x} = \mathbf{Lt}_y\mathbf{p}_y$. Expressing output as the product of three terms yields six decomposition equations describing change in output:

$$\Delta\mathbf{x} = \Delta\mathbf{Lt}_{y1}\mathbf{p}_{y1} + L_0\Delta\mathbf{t}_y\,\mathbf{p}_{y1} + L_0\mathbf{t}_{y0}\Delta\mathbf{p}_y, \tag{9.9}$$

$$\Delta\mathbf{x} = \Delta\mathbf{Lt}_{y1}\mathbf{p}_{y1} + L_0\Delta\mathbf{t}_y\,\mathbf{p}_{y0} + L_0\mathbf{t}_{y1}\Delta\mathbf{p}_y, \tag{9.10}$$

$$\Delta\mathbf{x} = \Delta\mathbf{Lt}_{y0}\mathbf{p}_{y1} + L_1\Delta\mathbf{t}_y\,\mathbf{p}_{y1} + L_0\mathbf{t}_{y0}\Delta\mathbf{p}_y, \tag{9.11}$$

$$\Delta\mathbf{x} = \Delta\mathbf{Lt}_{y0}\mathbf{p}_{y0} + L_1\Delta\mathbf{t}_y\,\mathbf{p}_{y1} + L_1\mathbf{t}_{y0}\Delta\mathbf{p}_y, \tag{9.12}$$

$$\Delta\mathbf{x} = \Delta\mathbf{Lt}_{y1}\mathbf{p}_{y0} + L_0\Delta\mathbf{t}_y\,\mathbf{p}_{y0} + L_1\mathbf{t}_{y1}\Delta\mathbf{p}_y, \tag{9.13}$$

$$\Delta\mathbf{x} = \Delta\mathbf{Lt}_{y0}\mathbf{p}_{y0} + L_1\Delta\mathbf{t}_y\,\mathbf{p}_{y0} + L_1\mathbf{t}_{y1}\Delta\mathbf{p}_y. \tag{9.14}$$

Again, the influence of the first term (change in Leontief matrix) can be calculated as the mean of the six first terms in the six decompositions. However, Dietzenbacher and Los (1998) note that the maximum, minimums and standard deviations of each term can also be considered. It follows that 4 terms yield 24 or 4! Decomposition forms and the general case "n" terms yield n! decomposition forms. Rose and Casler (1996) state that the decompositions should have the properties of being "(1) mutually exclusive and (2) completely exhaustive" (Rose and Casler, 1996, p. 34). Determining the 120 individual and exclusive decompositions for a five-term problem seems complex. But fortunately, Dietzenbacher and Los (1998) present a general case for determining each of the n decomposition equations and it is reproduced in its entirety next.

Take the equation

$$\mathbf{y} = \mathbf{x}_1\mathbf{x}_2\ldots\mathbf{x}_n. \tag{9.15}$$

The additive decomposition of $\Delta\mathbf{y}$ can be formed by starting with the $t = 1$ terms to the right and ending with the $t = 0$ terms at the left:

$$\Delta\mathbf{y} = (\Delta\mathbf{x}_1)\mathbf{x}_2(1)\mathbf{x}_3(1)\ldots\mathbf{x}_{n-1}(1)\mathbf{x}_n(1) + \mathbf{x}_1(0)(\Delta\mathbf{x}_2)\mathbf{x}_3(1)\ldots\mathbf{x}_{n-1}(1)$$
$$\mathbf{x}_n(1) + \ldots + + \mathbf{x}_1(0)\mathbf{x}_2(0)\mathbf{x}_3(0)\ldots(\Delta\mathbf{x}_{n-1})\mathbf{x}_n(1) + \mathbf{x}_1(0)\mathbf{x}_2(0)$$
$$\mathbf{x}_3(0)\ldots\mathbf{x}_{n-1}(0)(\Delta\mathbf{x}_n). \tag{9.16}$$

This is the format of equation (9.15). Starting from the other end, in the format of equation (9.16) gives

$$\Delta\mathbf{y} = (\Delta\mathbf{x}_1)\mathbf{x}_2(0)\mathbf{x}_3(0)\ldots\mathbf{x}_{n-1}(0)\mathbf{x}_n(0) + \mathbf{x}_1(1)(\Delta\mathbf{x}_2)\mathbf{x}_3(0)\ldots\mathbf{x}_{n-1}(0)$$
$$\mathbf{x}_n(0) + \ldots + + \mathbf{x}_1(1)\mathbf{x}_2(1)\mathbf{x}_3(1)\ldots(\Delta\mathbf{x}_{n-1})\mathbf{x}_n(0) + \mathbf{x}_1(1)\mathbf{x}_2(1)$$
$$\mathbf{x}_3(1)\ldots\mathbf{x}_{n-1}(1)(\Delta\mathbf{x}_n). \tag{9.17}$$

## 2.2. Application of structural decomposition analysis to MRIO databases

Recently global multi-region input-output (MRIO) databases and models have gained importance for being used to measure GHG emissions from a consumption perspective (as opposed to territorial production-based accounting). Environmentally extended MRIO modelling allows tracing emissions of industrial sectors, regions and countries along the entire supply chain. Interested readers may consult Wiedmann (2009) and Barrett et al. (2013) who provide detailed reviews on the method and applications of MRIO and consumption-based accounting.

The leading global MRIO databases used today, such as EORA, WIOD, EXIOBASE and GTAP, are well documented in the literature: a summary and comparison of the databases are given in Moran and Wood (2014). Also, Owen et al. (2014) provide an analytical comparison on drivers of uncertainty between leading MRIO models. Current research focuses on understanding why the leading global databases give different results on $CO_2$ emissions output (production and consumption) and on the extent to which these differences could act as a limitation in climate policymaking. Owen et al. (2014) applied SDA, comparing results of different MRIO databases with each other. The goal in their study was to trace down the sources causing differences in results between the leading global MRIO databases. Thus, instead of using SDA to understand the drivers of change over time, the drivers of the variation in emissions calculated by a pair of different MRIO databases for the same year are considered in this study. The technique allowed them to separate the influence of different parameters on the results, enabling investigation of how source data, system structure, technical coefficients and final demand contribute to variations in consumption-based emissions of countries as calculated by different MRIO databases. Although useful insights can be gained from this analysis, SDA alone cannot determine the exact cause of database variation.

Liu et al. (2016) use the LMDI-1 index decomposition on a modified Global Trade Analysis Project (GTAP) database. They split China into 30 regions and nest this domestic MRIO into the GTAP model. By decomposing key factors contributing to the imbalance of emissions embodied in China's international trade they manage to quantify the underlying factors driving these emissions. They find that primary factor for the large quantities of net emissions embodied in Chinese exports are due to their reliance on coal energy and the very high-energy intensity of exporting industries, which are concentrated in a small number of less-developed provinces. They conclude that domestic climate policy ought to focus and target specifically these concentrated key polluting sectors in provinces such as Shandong and Jiangsu, as this could reduce greatly emissions embodied in international trade.

In 2014, Xu and Dietzenbacher conducted a similar study, although focusing on global international trade. They conducted a structural decomposition analysis on emissions embodied in trade (EET) (Xu and Dietzenbacher, 2014). By using the Global World Input Output Database (WIOD) they were the first to ever conduct a SDA on a multi-regional input output database. Previously, SDA had only been applied to single region models for a group of countries, or through bilateral trade analysis (Alcantara and Duarte, 2004; Xu and Dietzenbacher, 2014). Now, with a MRIO database, structural changes of EET can be analyzed – i.e. how and why EET changed in countries between given time frames. They find first that the level of emissions embodied in trade has increased at a much faster rate than total emissions from production. In almost all countries, emissions embodied in exports and imports have increased, indicating the relative increase of importance of global trade as a contributor to emissions in comparison to domestic ones. Furthermore, they find that EET growth is primarily due to changes in final demand levels, complemented by substantial changes in trade structures. A steady reduction in emission intensities somewhat counters the increase through final demand, but does not completely compensate the growth. Technological change has relatively small effects on emissions embodied in trade. Results show that emerging economies such as China and India play an increasingly important role in the trade of emissions. SDA made it possible to break down potential driving forces of the geographical separation between generation of emissions and consumption.

Another decomposition study applied to a full MRIO is that of Zhang and Lahr (2014). They use a seven-region model for China to perform a regional analysis on the drivers of energy consumption in China in the period between 1987 and 2007. Regional energy use is analyzed from both production and final demand side. The production side allows an analysis of changes in energy use efficiency, production structure, role of imported inputs and inter-regional trade of intermediate goods. On the final demand side, the impact of changes in the final demand level, impact of interregional trade of final goods and services and final demand structure such as capital investment, export and household energy consumption of each region is analyzed. Zhang and Lahr (2014) use a multiplicative SDA framework to decompose the changes in energy consumption into its determinants. For the final demand, they denote to changes of capital investment for commodity produced in a region, and the export of commodities produced in such region. Based on Dietzenbacher et al. (2000), they decompose into effect of changes in energy per unit of output, effect of changes in production structure (L) and changes in final demand (f). Final demand is further decomposed into intermediate trade coefficients that show input shares of each region in aggregated inputs by industry by region. Similarly, Xu and Dietzenbacher (2014) find that final demand change outpaced efficiency improvements and drove up energy use in all regions. From 2002 to 2007, changes in production structure enhanced energy consumption in most regions because more energy-intensive goods for capital investment and export were produced. They recommend that implementing regional-specific policies be designed to promote production structure change and reduce energy demand in China.

## Methods

In this section, we outline the form of decomposition taken in this work. We start with the relationship

$$Q = \mathbf{cSLu}^k y^k p^k, \tag{9.18}$$

where Q is the total consumption-based footprint on country k; c is the characterization of stressors (in aggregated/normalized impacts, such as global warming potential, or total energy use); S is the stressor matrix (for example, tons of $CO_2$ or $CH_4$, directly emitted from each of the IO sectors); L is the Leontief matrix, showing total output of each sector per unit of final demand; u is the product mix of final consumption (in percentage of total consumption) for country k; y is the affluence, in total monetary consumption per capita; and p is the countries' population.

We can further diagonalize cS and/or u to keep resolution of source (cS) or destination of products (u):

$$Q = \widehat{cS} Lu^{\hat{k}} y^k p^k. \tag{9.19}$$

Analyzing change via discrete time intervals, we represent the decomposition as

$$\Delta Q = \Delta(\underline{cS})^* Lu^{\hat{k}} y^{\hat{k}} p^{\hat{k}} + \underline{cS} \Delta Lu^{\hat{k}} y^{\hat{k}} p^{\hat{k}} + \underline{cSL} \Delta u^{\hat{k}} y^{\hat{k}} p^{\hat{k}}$$
$$+ \underline{cSL} u^{\hat{k}} \Delta y^{\hat{k}} p^{\hat{k}} + \underline{cSL} u^{\hat{k}} y^{\hat{k}} \Delta p^{\hat{k}}. \tag{9.20}$$

All terms with a delta represent the difference between year 1 and year 2, and all terms without a delta take the value along the time period dependent on the index chosen

Further, L can be decomposed into (Equation 10, Hoekstra and v.d. Bergh, 2003):

$$\Delta \mathbf{L} = \mathbf{L}_0 \Delta \mathbf{A} \mathbf{L}_1 \tag{9.21}$$

Hence

$$\Delta Q = \Delta(\underline{cS})^* Lu^{\hat{k}} y^{\hat{k}} p^{\hat{k}} + \underline{cS} L_0 \Delta A L_1 u^{\hat{k}} y^{\hat{k}} p^{\hat{k}} + \underline{cSL} \Delta u^{\hat{k}} y^{\hat{k}} p^{\hat{k}}$$
$$+ \underline{cSL} u^{\hat{k}} \Delta y^{\hat{k}} p^{\hat{k}} + \underline{cSL} u^{\hat{k}} y^{\hat{k}} \Delta p^{\hat{k}}. \tag{9.22}$$

To see the effects of the globalization of supply chains in the changes of emissions embodied in trade, we can further decompose the technical coefficient matrix (A) into product technology, or production structure (H) and trade effects (T), and Xu and Dietzenbacher (2014) provide a detailed explanation of this method, which makes use of the Hadamard product. Similarly, the final demand mix u can be decomposed in the same fashion. The final decomposition of seven different drivers is summarized in equation (9.23) as well as Table 9.1. Note that for the GHG analysis, we decomposed the emissions intensities into fuel combustion emissions and non-fuel combustion emissions. As opposed to other literature (e.g. Wood (2009)), the mix of emissions as structural effects, and hence as terms in the decomposition, we disaggregate the variables and decompose them side by side.

$$\Delta Q = \Delta(cS)^* Lu^{\hat{k}} y^{\hat{k}} p^{\hat{k}} + cSL_0 \Delta H \otimes TL_1 u^{\hat{k}} y^{\hat{k}} p^{\hat{k}}$$
$$+ cSLH \otimes \Delta TLu^{\hat{k}} y^{\hat{k}} p^{\hat{k}} + cSL\Delta y_t \otimes y_H y^{\hat{k}} p^{\hat{k}}$$
$$+ cSLy_t \otimes y_H y^{\hat{k}} p^{\hat{k}} + cSLu^{\hat{k}} \Delta(y^{\hat{k}} p^{\hat{k}}). \tag{9.23}$$

*Table 9.1* Definitions of variables

| Variable | Description | Dimension |
|---|---|---|
| q | Total impact | Scalar |
| c | Characterization of stressors | Number of stressors |
| s | Stressor matrix | Number of stressors x number of IO sectors |
| L | Leontief matrix | Number of IO sectors x number of IO sectors |
| u | Product mix matrix (product demand/GDP) | Number of IO sectors |
| $y$ | Affluence = GDP/capita | Scalar |
| $p$ | Population | Scalar |
| Q | Total impact | Number of IO sectors x number of IO sectors |
| $\mathbf{u}_{curr}$ | Product mix matrix of current consumption (product demand hhd +gov/GDP) | Number of IO sectors |
| $\mathbf{u}_{cap}$ | Product mix matrix of capital (GFCF + Stocks)/GDP | Number of IO sectors |
| A | Coefficient matrix | Number of IO sectors x number of IO sectors |
| T | Technology matrix | Number of IO sectors x number of IO sectors |
| H | Trade matrix | Number of IO sectors x number of IO sectors |

### MRIO database

We use a MRIO database called EXIOBASE, which has a highly disaggregated sector classification (augmenting environmentally sensitive sectors such as energy and agriculture), and a fully trade-linked SUT system.

EXIOBASE is an environmentally extended MRIO database that was created for use in analysis relevant to EU policy. It provides harmonized economic and environmental accounts on regional detail for 28 EU member states as well as 16 non-EU countries. Each country is represented by 163 industries and 200 product sectors as well as 9 subcategories of value added and 7 categories of final demand. In addition, the database contains environmental extensions consisting of 172 water extensions, 189 energy products, 222 used and non-used extractions, 13 types of land, 14 categories of labor accounts, 26 combustion air emissions, 14 non-combustion air emissions and releases of N and P to water. The 16 non-EU countries included in EXIOBASE were selected on the basis of contribution to global GDP, trade with the EU, and the amount of pollution embodied in trade. Together, the 16 selected rest of the world (RoW) countries cover 92% of non-EU global GDP and over 80% of trade with the EU (Tukker et al., 2009). Trade with and economic activity of all other RoW countries is modelled as 'true rest of the world', divided in five different continents, to make the inter-industry portion of the model a closed system. EXIOBASE has its major strength in providing more sector detail compared to any other MRIO database, which in most cases only distinguish a small number of environmentally sensitive sectors.

**Results**

Here we present the results for the decomposition of GHG emissions. For all results, the SDA was performed for each pair of years using yearly deflated monetary IOTs to perform the analysis. In this section, we present regional and temporal aggregation of the results in order to summarize the results. The aggregation over a period of time was done by summing the yearly changes, thus maintaining the dynamics for each year. Correspondingly, the regional aggregation was obtained by summing yearly changes for each country.

The figures in this section display the contribution of seven different factors to total footprint growth. As explained in the methods, the factors used here are as follows:

- Stressors intensity (S), which represents the GHG emissions of each sector divided by its monetary output. A change in S reflects changes in productivity within each industry.
- Trade in supply chain (T), which represents the origin of inputs in the supply chain. A change in T can show the migration of resource extraction or manufacturing stages to other countries, a change in the amount of production that takes place domestically and a change in trade partners.
- Production structure (H), which represents the economic structure of the domestic industry – that is, the changes in the amount and composition of inputs to production.
- Trade to final demand (YT), which shows the change in direct imports to final consumers.
- Final demand structure (YH), which represents the product mix consumed in final demand. This factor shows how much of total expenditure is being spent in different products – for example, how much of household consumption is being spent on transportation compared to the amount spent on food.
- Affluence (y), measured in total expenditure per capita.
- Population (P).

*Results on greenhouse gas emissions*

Figure 9.1 shows absolute changes in total GHG footprint between 1995 and 2009.

Changes in absolute GHG emissions are dominant in China, India, Middle East, the United States and Mexico. Diamonds mark total changes in footprints, while bars show the contribution of different variables to the footprint growth. It can be noted that changes in emission intensity and changes in the production structure and affluence, measured in total consumption per capita, dominate as drivers for the changes.

The large footprint difference for some countries – and large changes in different factors – makes it difficult to perceive the trend among different countries. For that reason, the contribution of each factor is further represented in Figure 9.2, but this time in relative terms. In it, percentages correspond to changes relative to

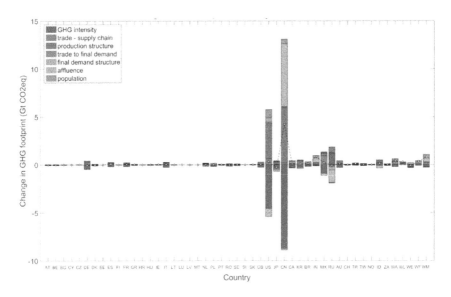

*Figure 9.1* Absolute change in greenhouse gas footprints between 1995 and 2009, in Gt
   $CO_2$-eq

Note: Diamonds mark the change in footprints. Columns represent the contribution of each factor to
the change.

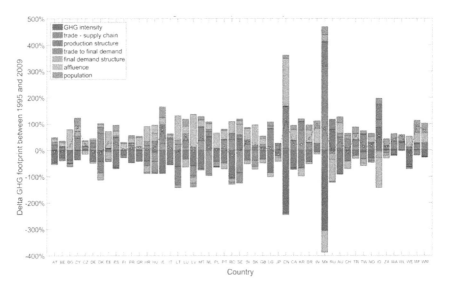

*Figure 9.2* Relative change in greenhouse gas footprints between 1995 and 2009, in Gg
   $CO_2$-eq

Note: Diamonds mark the change in footprints. Columns represent the contribution of each factor to
the change.

1995 footprints. In this figure, 100% growth in GHG footprints means a doubling of the total footprint between 1995 and 2009.

Figure 9.2 shows the pattern observed previously is common for most countries – with affluence and efficiency improvements growing in large, and often in opposite, directions. For some countries, the growth in consumption per capita outweighs the reduction in GHG emission intensity, resulting in a rise of emissions despite of higher emission productivity.

The changes in the global supply chains – in the technology matrix – are also relevant. Here these changes are divided in two different factors: the production structure (H), which indicates the changes in inputs to different industries in each country and trade in the supply chain (T), which represents the origin for these inputs. It can be noted that, for some countries such as China (CN), the United States (US) and Taiwan (TW), the production structure plays a major role in GHG emissions growth. In other countries, such as Mexico (MX), Korea (KR) and Denmark (DK), the change in the origin of inputs becomes a more important driver for changes in GHG footprints.

The period covered in Figures 9.1 and 9.2 corresponds to very different periods with different dynamics that deserve further detailing. Figure 9.3 presents a break down in four different periods, showing the years that led to the financial crisis and the post-crisis period, up to 2009, for three different regions. The regional break-down was chosen due to the different dynamics that drive the footprint growth and economic activity: China reflects a producing region, which experienced significant economic growth in the past decade, and the European Union and the OECD countries, which reflect two regions of high affluence and consumption.

We can see a common pattern for all regions in the period, with different dynamics behind these patterns. From 1995 to 1999, the detailed regions presented a small increase in emissions (relative to 1995). In all regions, the GHG intensity of output decreased considerably from 1995 to 2007, and this situation reverted in the period post-2007. The period before the financial crisis experiences a more significant increase in GHG footprints for China and for the EU, but a relatively constant footprint growth for the OECD as a whole. After 2007, the developed economies experienced a decrease in their footprints, led mainly due to lower consumption per capita, while in China, emissions kept rising, but at a slower pace. The main driver for emissions growth in China post-2007 was the growth in affluence.

The factors that influenced the most, however, vary between the regions. In China, the production structure and affluence greatly influenced the emissions growth until 2007, reflecting a period of high economic growth and industrialization. For the EU, affluence was the main driver for emissions growth, and together with the production structure, it contributed to the growth of emissions before 2007, and to the decrease in the footprints in the last period. The structure of the economy, both the production and trade partners, was the main driver for the emissions growth in the OECD in the late 1990s. Emissions grew at a constant pace from 1995 top 2007, decreasing after the financial crisis mainly due to the decrease in consumption per capita.

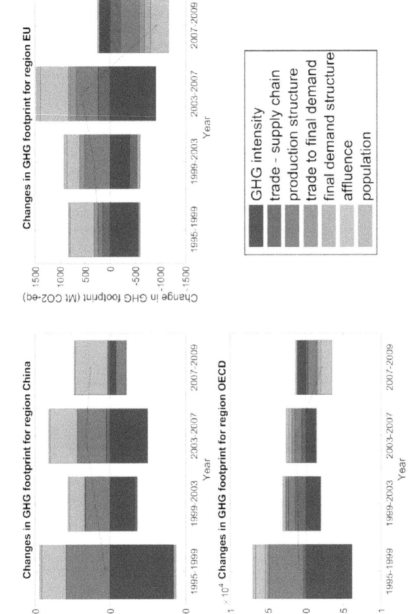

*Figure 9.3* Total changes in greenhouse gas footprints per four-year period for three regions: China, EU and OECD

There are important changes in the decomposition of GHG footprints from combustion and non-combustion processes, as can be seen in Figure 9.4. Overall, most changes in GHG footprints come from combustion processes. For non-combustion processes, affluence no longer becomes the main driver. We can also note that the non-combustion emissions present a much smaller growth than combustion emissions during the entire period for all regions, in absolute (total emissions) and relative terms (compared to 1995 emissions).

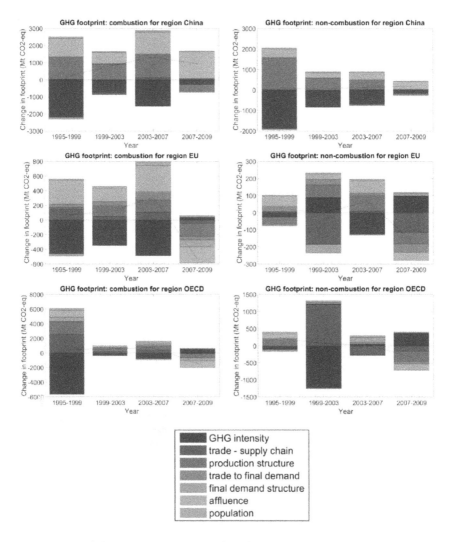

*Figure 9.4*  Total changes in combustion (left) and non-combustion (right) greenhouse gas footprints

## Conclusions

The changes in emissions in global supply chains is an important subject of study. To understand how GHG emissions have evolved in the past, we have to look at the drivers for these changes. The work looked at changes in emissions efficiency, the changes due to trade related effects (both for intermediate producers and final consumers), the changes due to technology effects (both for intermediate producers and final consumers) and the change due to affluence and population.

Trade is an important driver for global GHG emissions growth, but it is not as important as growth in affluence and overall industry efficiency. This is only true, however, when looking at global emissions growth. When taking into account regional shifts in GHG emissions footprints over time, the displacement of industries from developed economies in the European Union and the OECD, and the increase in imports to final demand contributes to emissions growth, mainly from combustion. For non-combustion emissions, changes in trade partners seem to decrease GHG footprints.

Different dynamics act on the footprint growth over time and in different regions. GHG emissions and energy consumption are mainly driven by the increase of consumption per capita in developing economies, such as China, and in the European Union. This growth in affluence reduces (or even reverts) gains in carbon and energy efficiency. We see that trade is an important driver for carbon footprints change in developed economies.

This work implies that a) efficiency effects have been historically most successful, and should be continued where possible until limits are reached, and b) policy must tackle the strong growth of affluence effects if it is going to reduce emissions, as the large growth in consumption per capita counteracts gains in efficiency. Changes in consumption patterns – that is, changes in the mix of products consumed, haven't shown a significant effect in the changes of energy or GHG footprints so far. While trade could allocate production to more efficient countries to reduce resource use and pollution, historically, the effect of trade has been to increase energy and combustion GHG footprints in developed economies.

Consumption-based emission accounting has been increasingly applied in a policy context within the EU, mainly as a tool to provide better understanding of emissions embodied in trade. However, although consumption-based emissions inventories reveal embedded emissions and supply chain linkages that production-based inventories do not, they should not be considered as the single solution for climate policy, only provide additional information that has application to climate policy. Different emission inventories, such as territorial, production and consumption based, have different system boundaries which will place focus on alternative mitigation strategies. The different emissions inventories, therefore, contain *complementary* information and thus consumption-based emission inventories should be considered together with others. Such recommendation is in line with outcomes of the Paris Agreement, which calls for a policy combination of production and consumption. In terms of policy analysis, consumption-based emissions have been used to explore trade policy and how changing consumption patterns could contribute to a reduction in global emissions. A good example of how EU governments have applied consumption-based emissions can be found in the United Kingdom. The Committee on Climate change in the United Kingdom produced a report for the UK government that explored emission in the future and researched the issue of competitiveness linked to imports and embodied emissions. Other European countries shall follow and take stock of their consumption-based emissions and how their trade linkages with other countries impact their emissions household.

## References

Alcantara, V., and Duarte, R. (2004). Comparison of energy intensities in European Union countries: Results of a structural decomposition analysis. *Energy Policy, 32*(2), 177–189.

Andrew, R. M., Davis, S. J., and Peters, G. P. (2013). Climate policy and dependence on traded carbon. *Environmental Research Letters, 8*(3), 034011.

Ang, B. W. (2004). Decomposition analysis for policymaking in energy: Which is the preferred method? *Energy Policy, 32*(9), 1131–1139.

Barrett, J., Peters, G., Wiedmann, T., Scott, K., Lenzen, M., Roelich, K., and Le Quéré, C. (2013). Consumption-based GHG emission accounting: A UK case study. *Climate Policy, 13*(4), 451–470.

Caldeira, K., and Davis, S. J. (2011). Accounting for carbon dioxide emissions: A matter of time. *Proceedings of the National Academy of Sciences, 108*(21), 8533–8534.

Davis, S. J., and Caldeira, K. (2010). Consumption-based accounting of $CO_2$ emissions. *Proceedings of the National Academy of Sciences, 107*(12), 5687–5692.

Dietzenbacher, E., Hoen, A. R., and Los, B. (2000). Labor productivity in Western Europe 1975–1985: an intercountry, interindustry analysis. *Journal of Regional Science, 40*(3), 425–452.

Dietzenbacher, E., and Los, B. (1998). Structural decomposition techniques: Sense and sensitivity. *Economic Systems Research, 10*(4), 307–324.

Edenhofer, O., Pichs-Madruga, R., Sokona, Y., Kadner, S., Minx, J. C., Brunner, S., . . . Blanco, G. (2014). Technical summary: Contribution of working group III to the fifth assessment report of the IPCC. In I. P. O. C. Change (Ed.), *Climate change 2014: Mitigation of climate change*. Cambridge, UK and New York: Cambridge University Press.

Guan, D., Hubacek, K., Weber, C. L., Peters, G. P., and Reiner, D. M. (2008). The drivers of Chinese CO 2 emissions from 1980 to 2030. *Global Environmental Change, 18*(4), 626–634.

Hoekstra, R., and Van den Bergh, J. C. (2003). Comparing structural decomposition analysis and index. *Energy Economics, 25*(1), 39–64.

IEA. (2016). *International energy outlook*. Paris, France: IEA.

Knobloch, F., and Mercure, J.-F. (2016). The behavioural aspect of green technology investments: a general positive model in the context of heterogeneous agents. *Environmental Innovation and Societal Transitions, 21*, 39–55.

Lenzen, M. (2011). Aggregation versus disaggregation in input – output analysis of the environment. *Economic Systems Research, 23*(1), 73–89.

Lindner, S., Legault, J., and Guan, D. (2012). Disaggregating input – output models with incomplete information. *Economic Systems Research, 24*(4), 329–347.

Lindner, S., Legault, J., and Guan, D. (2013). Disaggregating the electricity sector of China's input – output table for improved environmental life-cycle assessment. *Economic Systems Research*, *25*(3), 300–320.

Lindner, S., Liu, Z., Guan, D., Geng, Y., and Li, X. (2013). CO 2 emissions from China's power sector at the provincial level: Consumption versus production perspectives. *Renewable and Sustainable Energy Reviews*, *19*, 164–172.

Liu, Z., Guan, D., Wei, W., Davis, S. J., Ciais, P., Bai, J., . . . Marland, G. (2015). Reduced carbon emission estimates from fossil fuel combustion and cement production in China. *Nature*, *524*(7565), 335–338.

Liu, Z., Davis, S. J., Feng, K., Hubacek, K., Liang, S., Anadon, L. D., . . . Guan, D. (2016). Targeted opportunities to address the climate-trade dilemma in China. *Nature Climate Change*, *6*(2), 201–206.

Miller, R. E., and Blair, P. D. (2009). *Input-output analysis: Foundations and extensions* (2nd ed.). Cambridge: Cambridge University Press.

Moran, D., and Wood, R. (2014). Convergence between the Eora, WIOD, EXIOBASE, and OpenEU's consumption-based carbon accounts. *Economic Systems Research*, *26*(3), 245–261.

Owen, A., Steen-Olsen, K., Barrett, J., Wiedmann, T., and Lenzen, M. (2014). A structural decomposition approach to comparing MRIO databases. *Economic Systems Research*, *26*(3), 262–283.

Peters, G. P., and Hertwich, E. G. (2008). CO$_2$ embodied in international trade with implications for global climate policy. Environ. Sci. Technol., 2008, 42 (5), pp 1401–1407

Peters, G. P., Minx, J. C., Weber, C. L., and Edenhofer, O. (2011). Growth in emission transfers via international trade from 1990 to 2008. *Proceedings of the National Academy of Sciences*, *108*(21), 8903–8908.

Rose, A., and Casler, S. (1996). Input – output structural decomposition analysis: A critical appraisal. *Economic Systems Research*, *8*(1), 33–62.

Rose, A., and Chen, C.-Y. (1991). Sources of change in energy use in the US economy, 1972–1982: A structural decomposition analysis. *Resources and Energy*, *13*(1), 1–21.

Su, B., and Ang, B. (2012). Structural decomposition analysis applied to energy and emissions: some methodological developments. *Energy Economics*, *34*(1), 177–188.

Tukker, A., Poliakov, E., Heijungs, R., Hawkins, T., Neuwahl, F., Rueda-Cantuche, J. M., . . . Bouwmeester, M. (2009). Towards a global multi-regional environmentally extended input – output database. *Ecological Economics*, *68*(7), 1928–1937.

Wiedmann, T. (2009). A review of recent multi-region input – output models used for consumption-based emission and resource accounting. *Ecological Economics*, *69*(2), 211–222.

Wiedmann, T., Wood, R., Minx, J. C., Lenzen, M., Guan, D., and Harris, R. (2010). A carbon footprint time series of the UK – results from a multi-region input – output model. *Economic Systems Research*, *22*(1), 19–42.

Wood, R. (2009). Structural decomposition analysis of Australia's greenhouse gas emissions. *Energy Policy*, *37*(11), 4943–4948.

Xu, Y., and Dietzenbacher, E. (2014). A structural decomposition analysis of the emissions embodied in trade. *Ecological Economics*, *101*, 10–20.

Zhang, H., and Lahr, M. L. (2014). China's energy consumption change from 1987 to 2007: A multi-regional structural decomposition analysis. *Energy Policy*, *67*, 682–693.

# 10 South America's global value chains and $CO_2$ emissions embodied in trade

## An input-output approach

*José Durán Lima and Santacruz Banacloche*

## Introduction

The Paris Agreement on Climate Change came into force on 4 November 2016. Through a series of voluntary proposals by the signatory countries of the agreement, called Intended Nationally Determined Contributions (INDCs), the parties propose to reduce greenhouse gases (GHG) emissions. In that sense, most Latin American countries have also contributed with their INDCs (UN, 2015).

Latin America is a vast region in natural resources, which doesn't emit a large amount of greenhouse gases, but has been damaged by the increase in these gases in the atmosphere (Coronado et al., 2014). The rise in global temperature brings a reduction of soil water, loss of biodiversity, and a decrease of yields in crop production, among other factors that would also change the geographical location of natural ecosystems (FAO, 2008). The current situation indicates that inevitable and irreversible effects of climate change will impact on Latin America and Caribbean countries (Zevallos et al., 2015), not only on production and trade but also on the food and water security where agriculture and food production related exports are relevant and hydroelectric, the most representative source of renewable energy, is directly dependent on rainfalls (Balza et al., 2016).

Latin America and the Caribbean have proved to be a GHG net consumer (Tukker et al., 2014). In this context, studying international trade from an environmental perspective is a relevant issue since almost 30% of global emissions are related to exports (Kanemoto et al., 2014). Emissions embodied in goods and services from carbon-intensive countries are relevant in South America as a deficit trade region in manufactured goods (ECLAC, 2015). Recent projects have been developed to create a South American Input-Output Matrix (ECLAC and IPEA, 2016) to facilitate the measurement of global value chains (GVC). Unfortunately, Environmental Extended Input-Output Approaches in the region are scarce due to data unavailability.

The main goal of this chapter is to show where South America is placed both in the GVC and as a $CO_2$ emissions producer to assess the region capabilities in mitigation and adaptation policies. As an example, a case study of Colombia as an importer/exporter in terms of $CO_2$ emissions is presented. In sections 10.2 and 10.3, data sources and the methodology used are provided. Section 10.4 highlights the main results on South America's GVC and environmentally sensitive indus-tries, as well as an example of emissions balances in Colombia from a production and consumption-based perspective. This chapter concludes with a final discussion about the role of South America in the world and the challenges of decarbonization.

## Data sources

To analyze the linkages between value chain analysis and the environmental impact generated by $CO_2$ emissions, the following data sources are used:

- Total $CO_2$ emission by country from World Bank (The World Bank, 2016), International Energy Agency (IEA, 2008, 2015b).
- IEA-OECD (IEA, 2008, 2015a), GTAP (Badri and Walmsley, 2008) and EORA (Lenzen et al., 2013) sectoral data on $CO_2$ emissions.
- Trade data from COMTRADE database (UN, 2016) (SITC Rev. 1).
- Trade in Value Added Database from OECD and WTO (OECDStat, 2015).
- South American Input-Output Matrix and Mexico (ECLAC and IPEA, 2016).
- EE-SUT data (Environmental Extended Supply-Use Tables) from DANE (Departamento de Administración Nacional de Estadística), the Colombian National Statistics Institute.

$CO_2$ emissions information and its sectoral structure to every country in the world (Badri and Walmsley, 2008; IEA, 2015a; Lenzen et al., 2012; The World Bank, 2016) will allow us to identify the region and the world situation, depend-ing on the relative share of emissions. Similar analyses have already been dis-cussed (Balza et al., 2016; Frohmann et al., 2012).

An industry-level trade database (SITC Rev.1) provides the vision of the emis-sions content on trade and its intensity, determining the higher or lower environ-mental sensitivity and the trade balance associated with the products exported by the sub-region countries.

From the information in the TiVA database (OECDStat, 2015), some results on the level of forward and backward linkages for some countries in the region and in South America are presented. On the other hand, the South American matrix will serve as the main basis for the analysis of value chains and productive links based on the intraregional trade of intermediate inputs. Finally, combining the sectoral $CO_2$ emission vector for the case of Colombia and the National IOT resulting from the South American Matrix, both Trade Emissions Balance (TEB) and Responsibility Emissions Balance (REB) have been calculated (Serrano and Dietzenbacher, 2010).

By obtaining data from the Regional South American Input-Output Table (ECLAC and ILO, 2016), GVC in the region have been assessed. This is a pow-erful public database co-funded by the Economic Commission for Latin Amer-ica and the Caribbean (ECLAC, UN) and the Instituto de Pesquisa Econômica Aplicada (IPEA, Brazil). The South American Input-Output Table consists of a 10-region matrix and 40 sectors for the year 2005 and 2011. It also provides national matrices where a Single Regional Input Output Analysis environmentally extended has been created (Miller and Blair, 2009).

The case study chosen is Colombia because of two main reasons: 1) Colombia is one of the largest South American economies after Brazil and Argentina and 2) data availability: Colombia's Statistics Institute is one of the most developed in the region and provides an Environmental Satellite Accounts based on its National Input-Output Tables (called NAMEA in the literature). Consistent Environmental Extended Input-Output Analyses in South America are scarce. Brazil and Mexico are countries included in multiregional input-output databases such as the World Input-Output Database (WIOD), facilitating the analysis and implications of mitigation policies as INDCs proposed by the parties of the Paris Agreement. Unfortunately, environmental data disaggregated by sectors has not been assembled in South America yet. Therefore, Colombia stands as a new example within South America.

## Methodologies

The present work is addressed by combining four complementary methodologies:

- analysis of national and sub-regional forward and backward linkages from Rasmussen-Hirschman index;
- determination of the proportion of trade with greater environmental sensitivity;
- calculation of similarity indices to compare emissions reported by DANE with other alternative bases; and
- responsibility and Trade Emissions Balances Analysis using Input-Output Tables.

The first two methodologies are used to determine the level of domestic and intraregional chaining in South America. The last two methodologies link the economic activity with the environmental impact.

The classification of environmentally sensitive industries (ESI) developed by Low and Yeats (1992) is based on the criterion of increased spending on the reduction and control of the contamination per unit of production. To determine more precisely which industries fall within this criterion, they used the following condition: only those industries that incurred expenses of this type greater than 1% of the total sales were considered (as a reference, they used US data from 1988). The identification of the ESI was done using the SITC on its three-digit group level. It could thereby determine that 40 industries met the condition and could be aggregated into five sectors of ESI or dirty sectors: those of "iron and steel", those of "non-ferrous base metals", those of "industrial chemicals", those of "pulp and paper" and those of "non-metallic minerals". These industries are in capital-intensive sectors with high intensity of energy and land use. This classification gathers elements associated with its production, such as the intensity of use of natural resources, skilled labor, product development, use of production factors and technical level (Durán Lima et al., 2016).

The similarity index (SI) is calculated as the aggregation of the minimum participation of each product group in the total exports of each country or region to a market of homogeneous destination, which can be a sub-region or the world.

$$SI = \sum_{k=1}^{n} Min\left[\frac{x_i^k}{x_i}, \frac{x_j^k}{x_j}\right],$$

(10.1)

where $x_i^k$ are country i's exports of product k, $x_j^k$ are country j's exports, $x_i$ and $x_j$ are the total exports of the two countries and $n$ is the number of products. Note that the calculation can also be performed from the view of the imports of the destination market. The result of the index ranges from 0 to 1. If the two countries have totally different emission structures, the SI will take a value of 0, which is an indicator for the absence of similarity.

Finally, to calculate the emissions balances, a correlation between the 61 sector environmental vector ($CO_2$) of the National Colombian Input-Output Table and the 40 sector South American matrix has been carried out to work with the South American table form and store the $CO_2$ emissions vector for future Environmental Satellite Accounts in South America. When creating an emissions multiplier, it is supposed that other countries use the same technology as Colombia does, due to de introduction of their production into the Colombian model via imports (domestic technology assumption).

First, both Producer's Responsibility (PR) and Consumer's Responsibility (CR) have been calculated (expressions 10.2 and 10.3), to assess the $CO_2$ production and the carbon footprint in Colombia (Hoekstra and Wiedmann, 2014):

$$PR = \hat{e}\left(I - A^d\right)^{-1} y^d = P^d\left(y^r + y^x\right),$$

(10.2)

where $\hat{e}$ is the $CO_2$ emissions coefficient, $\left(I - A^d\right)^{-1}$ is the Leontief Inverse (for total domestic output requirements) and $y^d$ the final domestic demand is split in inner demand $y^r$ and final exports $y^x$.

$$CR = \left[\hat{e}\left(I - A^d\right)^{-1} y^r\right] + \left[\hat{e}\left(I - A^t\right)^{-1}\left[A^m\left(I - A^d\right)^{-1} y^r + y^m\right]\right]$$
$$= \left[P^d y^r + P^t\left[A^m\left(I - A^d\right)^{-1} y^r\right] + P^t y^m\right],$$

(10.3)

where $\hat{e}\left(I - A^t\right)^{-1}$ is emissions embodied in total output requirements, both imported and domestic, needed in production; $A^m\left(I - A^d\right)^{-1} y^r$ is the foreign content in final demand for domestically produced products; and $y^m$ is final imports.

The REB is the difference between the PR and the CR (expression 10.4). As an accounting identity, TEB and REB provide the same result:

$$REB = PR - CR.$$

(10.4)

On one hand, emissions embodied in trade have also been calculated (expression 10.5 and 10.6) to assess the TEB, which is defined as the difference between emissions embodied in exports ($E^x$) minus emissions embodied in imports ($E^m$) (expression 10.7):

$$E^x = \hat{e}\left(I - A^d\right)^{-1} y^x + \hat{e}\left(I - A^t\right)^{-1}\left[A^m\left(I - A^d\right)^{-1} y^x\right]$$
$$= P^d y^x + P^t\left[A^m\left(I - A^d\right)^{-1} y^x\right]. \tag{10.5}$$

In expression 5, the first component is emissions embodied in domestic requirements needed to satisfy foreign final demand; the second component is total emissions embodied in foreign content in foreign final demand for domestically produced goods and services.

$$E^m = \hat{e}\left(I - A^t\right)^{-1}\left[A^m\left(I - A^d\right)^{-1} y^d + y^m\right]$$
$$= P^t\left[A^m\left(I - A^d\right)^{-1} y^d + y^m\right]. \tag{10.6}$$

For expression 10.6, the first component is emissions embodied in foreign content in final demand for domestically produced products; the second component is emissions embodied in final imports. As an accounting identity, REB is equal to TEB.

$$TEB = E^x - E^m \tag{10.7}$$

## Main results

### *Latin America in the worldwide $CO_2$ emissions context*[1]

Carbon dioxide ($CO_2$) stands out as the most important GHG in terms of climate change. About 80% of $CO_2$ emissions come from energy, which rest over fossil fuels (IEA, 2015b). Global $CO_2$ emissions increased at an annual rate of 2.5% between 1960 and 2014, going from 9,400 million tons up to 36,100 (see Figure 10.1). The biggest increases have been in the last five years, with China's increase in emissions being particularly explosive, which has positioned itself as a major player in the world economy since its entry into the WTO. In this way, in 2014, China was the country with the highest emissions in the world (28%). In the case of Latin America, there is an increase in the share of global emissions, which slightly exceeds 5%.

In Latin America, South America represents 64% of total emissions in the period 2012–2014. Inside the sub-region, Brazil highlights as the major $CO_2$ emitter, with 41% of South American $CO_2$ emissions, followed by Argentina (17%) and Venezuela (17%). Despite being the third largest South American economy with a share of 9% of the regional GDP in this period, Colombia emits 7% of regional $CO_2$ (see Figure 10.2). Due to the low impact of South America in $CO_2$ global emissions, the need for the region to develop its economy and fight against poverty and the "adjustment gap" created because of not having adequately adapted

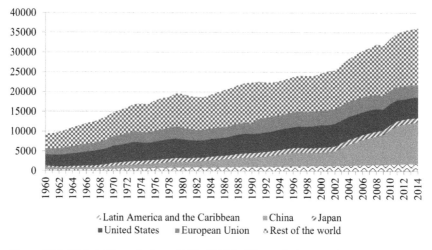

*Figure 10.1* Global CO$_2$ emissions, 1960–2014 (millions of gigagrams)

Source: Own elaboration on the basis of World Bank database.

## LATIN AMERICA AND THE CARIBBEAN

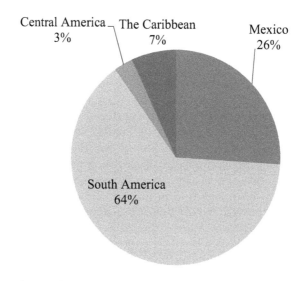

*Figure 10.2* Latin America and the Caribbean, subregions and countries, CO$_2$ emissions, 2012–2014 (in percentages)

*Figure 10.2.A* Latin American and the Caribbean

Source: Own elaboration on the basis of World Bank database and IEA

**SOUTH AMERICA**

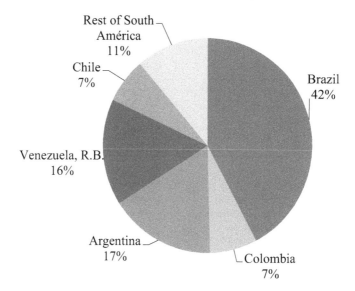

*Figure 10.2.B*  South America

Source: Own elaboration on the basis of World Bank database and IEA

to today's climate risks (Zevallos et al., 2015), mitigation policies seem in some countries not to be a priority.

At the sector level, emissions from fossil fuel combustion are concentrated in a few sectors. The transport sector accounts for more than a third of the emissions (37%), followed by electricity and gas (21%) and mining (energy) (6.3%) (see Table 10.1). Using the EORA database (Lenzen et al., 2013), the results showed that the first two sectors mentioned above represented the highest incidence in South American emissions (37% and 16%, respectively). In all previous cases, there is a direct link with the productive structure of the countries of the region and their energy requirements in the production process, which includes the emissions from the extraction process, and the transport of inputs between different locations inwards and between the countries in South America. Among the primary agro-export sectors, $CO_2$ emissions represent 4.6%, with a higher intensity in agriculture, Land Use, Land-Use Change and Forestry (LULUCF) excluded (3.4%).

In terms of manufacturing sectors, the region has a higher intensity of emissions in two clusters: the petrochemical and the metal mechanical. In the first case, rubber and plastic (including other chemicals), as well as coke, refined petroleum and nuclear fuel are responsible for about 10% of emissions. On the other side, the production of minerals and metals (metallic and non-metallic) and its related products account for 11% of the total. In this sense, EORA shows similar results (22.8%).

The use of fossil fuels is the main factor of $CO_2$ generation, needed in industrial production, transportation, electricity, and agriculture. Although the LULUCF

*Table 10.1* South America, $CO_2$ emissions, 2004 and 2011 (in gigagrams)

| Sectors | 2004 | 2011 | 2004 | 2011 |
|---|---|---|---|---|
| Agriculture and forestry | 13,713 | 20,789 | 3.3 | 3.4 |
| Hunting and fishing | 5,283 | 7,483 | 1.3 | 1.2 |
| Mining and quarrying (energy) | 16,063 | 38,318 | 3.9 | 6.3 |
| Mining and quarrying (non-energy) | 7,202 | 13,748 | 1.7 | 2.3 |
| Meat and meat products | 1,829 | 2,856 | 0.4 | 0.5 |
| Wheat products and pasta | 170 | 355 | 0 | 0.1 |
| Sugar and confectionery | 921 | 1,047 | 0.2 | 0.2 |
| Other processed food | 3,888 | 6,845 | 0.9 | 1.1 |
| Beverages and tobacco | 1,051 | 1,773 | 0.3 | 0.3 |
| Textiles | 2,027 | 2,070 | 0.5 | 0.3 |
| Apparel | 437 | 787 | 0.1 | 0.1 |
| Footwear | 344 | 374 | 0.1 | 0.1 |
| Wood and products of wood and cork | 6,560 | 8,447 | 1.6 | 1.4 |
| Coke, refined petroleum and nuclear fuel | 30,437 | 25,114 | 7.4 | 4.1 |
| Rubber and plastics products | 33,516 | 30,660 | 8.1 | 5 |
| Other non-metallic mineral products | 18,388 | 31,990 | 4.4 | 5.2 |
| Iron and steel | 22,527 | 24,107 | 5.4 | 3.9 |
| Non ferrous metals | 9,294 | 11,778 | 2.2 | 1.9 |
| Fabricated metal products | 1,544 | 2,095 | 0.4 | 0.3 |
| Machinery and equipment n.e.c. | 1,660 | 2,015 | 0.4 | 0.3 |
| Office, accounting and computing machinery | 342 | 906 | 0.1 | 0.1 |
| Motor vehicles, trailers and semi-trailers | 238 | 607 | 0.1 | 0.1 |
| Other transport equipment | 164 | 245 | 0 | 0 |
| Manufacturing n.e.c.: recycling (including furniture) | 1,766 | 2,809 | 0.4 | 0.5 |
| Electricity and gas | 65,509 | 128,539 | 15.8 | 21.1 |
| Construction | 2,138 | 2,868 | 0.5 | 0.5 |
| Transportation | 154,452 | 226,422 | 37.3 | 37.1 |
| Post and telecommunication | 437 | 373 | 0.1 | 0.1 |
| Finance and insurance | 332 | 297 | 0.1 | 0 |
| Business services of all kinds | 1,754 | 2,861 | 0.4 | 0.5 |
| Other services | 10,021 | 12,019 | 2.4 | 2 |
| **Total** | **414,007** | **610,596** | **100** | **100** |

Note: Sector-reported emissions are rather scarce in national statistics due to the absence of substantial results in Environmental Satellite Accounts. The sectoral distribution analyzed in Table 10.1 is based on estimates made by academics linked to the GTAP Purdue University, which is based on the IEA energy database, built based on the energy balances of each country in the world.

Source: Own elaboration on the basis of World Bank database

represented in 2005 is 12% of GHG global emissions, in Latin America and the Caribbean, that percentage was 46%. In fact, 61% of Brazilian GHG emissions in that year came from LULUCF (Frohmann et al., 2012).

## Global value chains in South America and environmentally sensitive industries

The available evidence on the role of the Latin American and Caribbean countries in Global Value Chains (GVC) shows that they participate less than countries in other regions (Durán Lima and Zaclicever, 2013; ECLAC, 2014a, 2014b, 2016; Hernández et al., 2014). Taken all together, the region's participation in GSCs, calculated by a participation index expressed in percentages of gross exports from six countries of Latin America (Argentina, Brazil, Chile, Colombia, Costa Rica and Mexico) between 2000 and 2011, is low compared with that of Asia and other regions and countries of the world, especially if Mexico is excluded (see Table 10.2).

A disaggregated analysis of participation in GSCs by the contribution of intraregional trade showed the proportion of intraregional linkages to be very low in Latin America (9% of both backward and forward links), certainly compared with other regions of the world. In South-East Asia, for example, participation is from four to six times as great (40% in backward linkages and 58% in forward linkages; see Figure 10.3). Case studies based on industry- and firm-level research by country reveal that the region's role in GSCs is quite heterogeneous. The different countries in the region participate in a wide range of GSCs, from agriculture to mining, manufacturing and services, with varying results. Costa Rica and Mexico are the most entwined countries in the North American value chain led by the

*Table 10.2* Selected regions and countries: backward and forward participation in global supply chains, 2000 and 2011 (percentages of total gross exports)

| Country or region | Year | Backward participation[a] | Forward participation[b] | Global value chains participation index |
|---|---|---|---|---|
| Latin America | 2000 | 24.8 | 14.1 | 38.9 |
| (6 countries)[c] | 2011 | 20.1 | 21 | 41.2 |
| South America | 2000 | 12.5 | 18.8 | 31.3 |
| (4 countries)[d] | 2011 | 13 | 24.7 | 37.7 |
| Mexico | 2000 | 34.3 | 10.4 | 44.8 |
| | 2011 | 31.7 | 15.1 | 46.8 |
| Asia | 2000 | 24.4 | 20.2 | 44.6 |
| | 2011 | 28.6 | 22.5 | 51.1 |
| China | 2000 | 25 | 21.3 | 46.3 |
| | 2011 | 30.4 | 21.1 | 51.5 |
| United States | 2000 | 37.2 | 10.8 | 47.9 |
| | 2011 | 32.1 | 15.6 | 47.7 |
| European Union | 2000 | 12.5 | 24.4 | 37 |
| | 2011 | 15 | 24.9 | 39.8 |
| World | 2000 | 22 | 21 | 43.1 |
| | 2011 | 25.4 | 23.3 | 48.8 |

Notes: a  Foreign value added as a share of gross exports. This "upstream" measure indicates backward participation.
b  Value added in the country as a share of other countries' exports. This "downstream" measure indicates forward participation.
c  Argentina, Brazil, Chile, Colombia, Costa Rica and Mexico.
d  Argentina, Brazil, Chile and Colombia.

Source: Economic Commission for Latin America and the Caribbean (ECLAC) and International Labour Organization (ILO) on the basis of information from the Organization for Economic Cooperation and Development (OECD)/World Trade Organization (WTO), Trade in Value Added Database (TIVA) [online] www.oecd.org/sti/ind/measuringtradeinvalue-addedanoecd-wtojointinitiative.htm

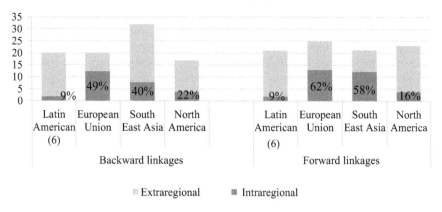

*Figure 10.3* Selected regions and countries: decomposition of the global value chains participation index, 2011 (percentages of total gross exports)

Note: Latin American countries: Argentina, Brazil, Chile, Colombia, Costa Rica and Mexico.

Source: Authors, on the basis of J. López, "Trade Policy Implications of Global Value Chains", presentation at the Asia-Pacific Economic Cooperation (APEC) Public Private Dialogue on Regional and Global Value Chains in Latin America and the Caribbean, Lima, 2016 [online] www. cepal.org/sites/default/files/events/files/3_javier_lopez.pdf.

United States. The greatest participation by Mexican firms is in the automotive, electronics, medical equipment and telecommunications sectors.

The available evidence seems to show that there are intraregional systems of shared production chains in a limited group of sectors between countries forming part of the same integration mechanism, be this the Southern Common Market (MERCOSUR), the Andean Community or the Central American Common Market. Particularly noteworthy are the cases of Argentina, Brazil and Uruguay in MERCOSUR; Ecuador, Colombia and Peru in the Andean Community; Costa Rica, Guatemala and Honduras in the Central American Common Market; and bilateral trade relations between Mexico and Brazil and among the members of the Pacific Alliance. This evidence highlights the lack of relevance in Latin American value chains and becomes a clue about the impact of $CO_2$ emissions embodied in trade.

Different ECLAC studies have concluded that the greatest linkages where heavy industries are concerned are in the chemical and petrochemical, metallurgy and automotive and vehicle parts sectors, and it has been noted that there is great potential in some light industries, such as food, drinks and tobacco; paper and cardboard; textiles and apparel; and pharmaceuticals (Durán Lima et al., 2016). These types of industries have proved to be environmentally sensitive. Several factors help to explain the differences in participation between the region's countries, with one being natural resource endowments. The wealth of natural resources in many countries of South America such as Chile and Peru has contributed to the development of supply chains based on these (in export agriculture and mining, for instance), while holding back the development of other chains.

By using the ESI index, among South American countries, most environmentally sensitive industries are metals and metal products, followed by petroleum and mining, chemicals and pharmaceutical products and wood and paper products (see Figure 10.4). Countries mainly import environmentally sensitive products

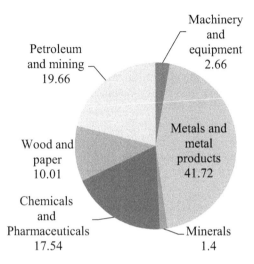

*Figure 10.4 (A and B)* South America, environmentally sensitive industries in international trade, 2015 (in percentages)

*Figure 10.4.A* Exports: 17.6

Source: Own elaboration on the basis of COMTRADE database

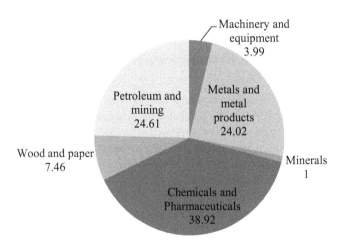

*Figure 10.4.B* Imports: 23.5

Source: Own elaboration on the basis of COMTRADE database

from three industries: chemicals and pharmaceuticals, petroleum and mining and metals and metal products. ESI exports account for the 17.6% of total South American countries' exports to the world, and ESI imports account for the 23.5% of total South American countries' imports to the world.

Table 10.3 shows how despite the trade balance surplus in the region, in 2015, ESI trade balance is negative; imports intensive in capital, energy and land use tend to be larger than exports and create more impact in the environment, according to other researches of the region (Ray, 2016). Chile is the exception, mainly due to copper-related exports. Latin America stands out as the largest copper ore producer in the world, driven by Chilean production. In 2007, Latin America produced 38% of this copper ore, but the copper footprint was 6% of its final consumption (Tukker et al., 2014).

*Table 10.3* South America, ESI trade balance, 2015 (in percentages and million dollars)

| Countries | ESI exports | ESI imports | ESI Trade balance | Trade balance |
| --- | --- | --- | --- | --- |
| Argentina | 8.5 | 20.9 | −7,879 | −5,238 |
| Bolivia (Plurinational State of) | 6.6 | 30 | −2,391 | −1,725 |
| Brazil | 18.2 | 25.6 | −9,440 | 17,352 |
| Chile | 39.5 | 19.8 | 12,229 | −478 |
| Colombia | 10.6 | 26.6 | −10,673 | −19,436 |
| Ecuador | 4.5 | 25.1 | −4,559 | −3,738 |
| Paraguay | 1.8 | 32.6 | −3,209 | −1,968 |
| Peru | 21 | 23.2 | −3,055 | −10,515 |
| Uruguay | 6.5 | 18.5 | −1,261 | −1,874 |
| Venezuela | 14.2 | 18 | 4,388 | 43,010 |
| **South America** | **17.6** | **23.5** | **−25,848** | **15,390** |

Source: Own elaboration on the basis of COMTRADE database

## Estimates of participation in national and regional supply chains in South America

Given a lack of databases for analyzing the participation of all the region's countries in GSCs, what will now be presented are indices of forward and backward linkages for 2005 calculated from information in the national IOTs available for ten countries in South America (Figure 10.5) with sectoral spillover capacities in each country. The aggregate spillover resulting from intra-South American trade ties are considered. Backward linkages are a basis for measuring a sector's potential direct spillover effects on other sectors linked to it by its demand for intermediate consumption goods, driving activity in these sectors. A typical example of this type of linkage is production in the automotive sector, which activates countless other sectors.

Forward linkages, meanwhile, measure a sector's ability to drive other sectors by its supply capacity – i.e. through sales of products that in turn are intermediate

———Backward linkages    ········ Forward linkages

*Figure 10.5* South America (ten countries): domestic forward and backward sectoral linkages, 2005 (percentages)

Source: Own elaboration on the basis of information from the input-output matrices of the countries
of South America for 2005

inputs for other industries. Taking the South American countries together, 19 sectors with mainly forward linkages were identified and just 11 with mainly backward linkages. The conclusion from analyzing domestic linkages is that there are
more forward linkages and very few backward linkages.

Almost half of the sectors in the countries of South America have more forward
than backward linkages. Specifically, these are sectors that supply intermediate
inputs needed for other sectors to produce. Predominant among these sectors are
farming and stockbreeding, minerals, wood and paper, basic chemicals, rubber
and plastic, non-metallic minerals and mineral and steel products, in the case of
goods, and electricity, transportation, telecommunications, finance and business
services, in the case of services.

As for backward linkages, the sectors driving these are rather few in number.
Chief among them are the agriculture and forestry sector, sectors producing other
food products and drinks and the vehicle production, construction, transportation
and other services sectors, which require intermediate inputs from different sectors. To obtain a rough measure of the potential spillover effects deriving from the
forward or backward linkages of the intersectoral purchases and sales of the other
South American trading partners, the linkage indicators were recalculated, but
this time only for sectors without linkages, to check whether this had the effect of

increasing the level of linkage. In this way, it was found that only a small number of sectors were driven by the greater South American subregion.[2]

It is estimated that the links thus created by intraregional trade participation are still confined to just a handful of sectors, being concentrated in well-defined and limited relationships in a set of sectors within groups of countries, such as the intra-industry relationships (with potential for development) arising from trade between Colombia, Ecuador and Peru in the case of the Andean community, in sectors such as milling and pastas, textiles and refined oil and coke; between Argentina, Brazil and Uruguay in the case of MERCOSUR in sectors such as iron and steel, metal products, machinery and equipment and electrical machinery an appliances sectors, plus the electricity and financial sectors, and between Chile, Colombia and Peru in the non-energy mining sector, the textile sector and the other services sector, all of which are South American countries in the Pacific Alliance (Durán Lima and Cracau, 2016; Rosales, 2014). In all the cases, purchases of intermediate inputs are the drivers that foster the value chains.

### *Colombia and the emissions balances*

This section presents an analysis of emission balances that considers the emission database presented by DANE. Although other sources that also include a disaggregation of $CO_2$ emissions for Colombia are available, it was decided to choose the national source since it captures the specific emissions of the sugar and confectionery sector more accurately, which is underestimated in the GTAP database, EORA and IEA (See Figure 10.6).

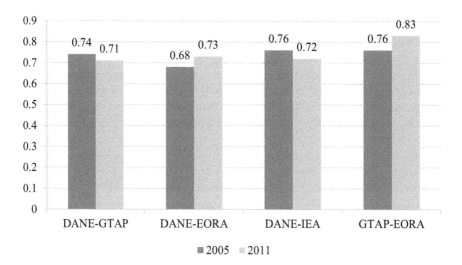

*Figure 10.6* Colombia: similarity indices according different databases, 2005 and 2011

Source: Authors' elaboration based on DANE, GTAP, IEA and EORA emission databases

In Latin America and the Caribbean, there are two clearly distinguishable groups of countries: those in the process of accession to the OECD and those still focused on improving living standards. Colombia is part of the first group of countries, demonstrating its commitment to further strengthening public policies and economic performance, looking to improve competitiveness and meeting the environmental standards required by the OECD (Zevallos et al., 2015). Colombia has proved to be one of the Latin American countries that less GHG emissions per capita generate (1.4 $CO_2$eq metric tons), below countries such as Brazil (2.3), Chile (4.2), Mexico (4.3) or Argentina (4.7). Latin American and Caribbean average is over 2.9% in $CO_2$eq metric tons per capita (Frohmann et al., 2012). In fact, despite the increase of $CO_2$ emissions, the share of total $CO_2$ emissions in the region has fallen from 5.2% in 1995 to 4.1% in 2005 and 4.4% in 2011. In this sense, the Kyoto Protocol and lately by Paris Agreement goals to achieve emission reductions in GHG are seen from the perspective of the PR or territorial responsibility. In the PR, it is assumed that $CO_2$ emissions responsibility falls on the goods and services producer country, independent of where goods and services are consumed (inwards or outwards). In this case, Colombia should take care of its domestic production (final domestic demand) – that is, everything the country produces to final domestic consumption, public expenditure and investment within the country, plus exports. Intermediate and final imports do not account for the PR, leaving international trade aside.

Under the CR, Colombia should respond to the emissions embodied in goods and services consumed, independent of where they have been produced. In this sense, emissions embodied in the inward final demand, emissions embodied in intermediate and final imports required in Colombia to produce are accounted. CR matches the concept of carbon footprint, the most significant component within the ecological footprint, which consists of a group of sub-footprints that measure the appropriation of natural resources or *land footprint* and the generation of residual or *energy footprint* (Hoekstra and Wiedmann, 2014). Every footprint is a useful indicator of human pressure in the environment. Although criteria to measure the "capacity" burdened or assimilated by the land is ambiguous, the "ecological budget" is being more depleted, turning into an ecological deficit that doesn't respect future generations.

Thanks to this measure, embodied emissions in trade or *virtual carbon in trade* can be assessed. A column reading shows that other services, transportation and construction are the main consumers of $CO_2$ emissions. A row reading displays Transportation and Sugar as the most polluting driving sectors. These two sectors are not only the main producers but also relevant consumers of $CO_2$ emissions in the Colombian economy.

Figure 10.7 establishes a comparison of PR and CR in 2005 and 2011. In this sense, the main producers of emissions are Transportation (26.6% of total emissions produced), Sugar (17.2%) and Electricity (11.6%). Other services (23.5%), Construction (14.6%) and Transportation (14.5%) stand out as main consumers of $CO_2$ emissions. In 2011, the main producers of emissions are still Transportation (28.5% of total emissions produced), Other Services (13.5%) and Sugar (12.8%).

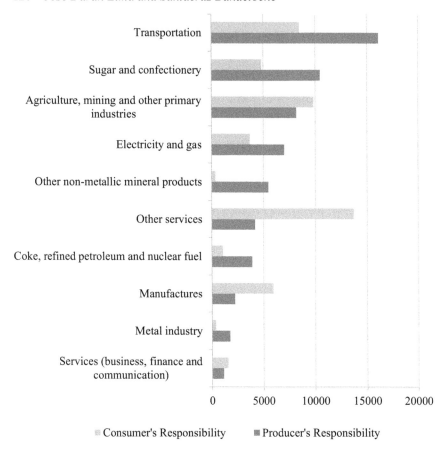

*Figure 10.7 (A and B)* Colombia: producer and consumer's responsibility in 2005 and 2011 (emissions in Gg CO₂)

*Figure 10.7.A* Colombia: producer and consumer's responsibility in 2005 and 2011 (emissions in Gg CO₂)

Source: Own elaboration on the basis of the South American Input-Output Table and DANE

As consumers of emissions, it highlights other services (26.8%), and Transportation (15%) and Construction (14.1%) stand out. By comparing 2005 and 2011, we see that both years have the same productive structure of $CO_2$ emissions from a sectoral view. However, emissions concentration rises from 78.2% to 79.8% as an increase of the share in sectors such as Transportation, Other Services, Petroleum and Construction. On the other hand, Sugar and Confectionery, Electricity and Non-metallic Minerals Shares decrease. Except for other services, most polluting sectors have become more efficient so that in 2011 they emitted less $CO_2$ per million. Thus the concentration increased because of a rise on production to satisfy final demand.

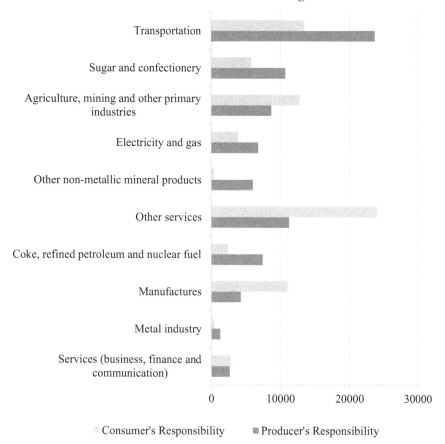

*Figure 10.7.B* Colombia: producer and consumer's responsibility in 2011 (emissions in Gg CO$_2$)

Source: Own elaboration on the basis of the South American Input-Output Table and DANE

It is interesting to stop in the Sugar and Confectionery sector, since it is one of the most polluting Colombian industries. In 2005, over 92.45% of energy products used (measured in terajoules) came from the sugar cane bagasse as a fuel; in 2011, the share was of 94.45%. Using rudimentary techniques and low technology intensive capital damages the production efficiency.

Depending on international trade, PR will be higher or lower than CR. In the Colombian case, TEB in 2005 was positive, which means that PR was higher than CR. Emissions embodied in exports exceeded in 2.366,8 CO$_2$ Gg the emissions embodied in imports (see Figure 10.8). These emissions contrast with the commercial balance that measures the net balance of exports and imports. In 2005, the commercial balance was negative in $709.12 million. Despite importing more than exporting, emissions embodied in trade suggest that the problem comes

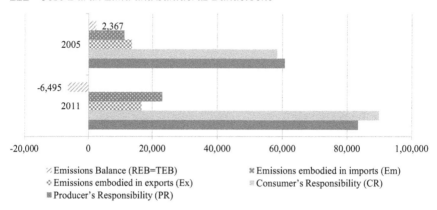

*Figure 10.8* Colombia: trade emissions balance (emissions in Gg CO$_2$)

Source: Own elaboration based on the South American Input-Output Table and DANE

from carbon-intensive industries and energy efficiency disadvantages. In 2011, the Colombian case is the opposite, with a negative TEB of 6.495 CO$_2$ Gg that comes from the rise of emissions embodied in imports and a commercial balance surplus. In this sense, despite the fact that Colombia exports more goods and services than imports, embodied emissions in imports are larger than in exports. This may be explained by the increase of imports from carbon-intensive countries such as China (Peters et al., 2011), which is a net exporter of GHG emissions to Latin America and the Caribbean (Ray, 2016). Besides, comparing 2005 and 2011, almost every sector in Colombia improves its CO$_2$ emissions intensity, except for basic chemical products, rubber and plastic products, communication equipment and medical, precision and optical instruments.

Figure 10.8 shows the growth of the Colombian carbon footprint, mainly driven by emissions embodied in imports. Trade patterns in Colombia have changed from 2005 to 2011. In 2005, the United States of America was the main exporter to Colombia (28.5%), followed by Mexico (8.3%), China (7.6%) and Brazil (6.5%). In 2011, the USA's share decreased (25%) and China became the second largest exporter (15%), followed by Mexico (11%), and has proved to be the largest CO$_2$ emitter in the world (Peters et al., 2011).

The rise in production and total exports was higher than the PR and emissions embodied in exports. This is explained by a more efficient production: in 2005, Colombian GDP emitted 0.24 CO$_2$ Gg per million. In 2011, every million produced 0.14 CO$_2$ Gg. In terms of sectors, the main emission-producing sectors of the Colombian economy have increased their production efficiency, becoming sectors that are more environmentally friendly, except for the other services sector. For every million dollars produced, the transportation sector has gone from generating 1.19 Gg of CO$_2$ in 2005 to emitting 0.79 Gg in 2011. The electricity and gas sector has reduced its emissions from 0.9 Gg of CO$_2$ per million to 0.41 Gg. The most polluting sector per million produced is Sugar and Confectionery, which has seen its ratio descending from 5.93 Gg of CO$_2$ to 3.02 Gg.

Looking at the energy mix data provided by the International Energy Agency (IEA, 2015b), in 2005, 57.3% of total primary energy consumption came from fossil fuels, decreasing to the 56.2% in 2011. Colombia changed its energy mix, consuming slightly less carbon-intensive energies. Besides, $CO_2$/GDP ratio decreased, with a more efficient production in 2011. Thus the increase in PR is explained mainly by economic growth. As a $CO_2$ consumer, it highlights the relevance of emissions embodied in imports.

TEB and REB results just provide net measurement of international trade impact on emissions, without the chance to establish a multiregional scenario where countries are disaggregated. This is a disadvantage because, although in 2011, Colombia became a benefited country of carbon leakages, with current calculations, it is impossible to precisely measure which countries bear that burden and their share of embodied emissions in trade.

## Discussion

It has been determined that Latin America and the Caribbean, especially South America, have a pattern of international insertion linked to a production pattern that emits strong emissions in traditional sectors such as transportation, electricity and gas, energy mining. When it comes to manufacturing, there are high emissions in the chemical and petrochemical sectors, rubber and plastics, metal ores, iron and steel and related products. Of these, the chemical and petrochemical sector, as well as wood and paper, appear with a high environmental sensitivity.

Among all the countries of the region, only Chile and Venezuela, R. B. showed an export pattern of higher incidence of emissions included in their exports than those originated in their imports, which are explained by the cases of copper and oil – the main export products in each case. It is striking that Colombia has a high trade deficit in environmentally sensitive products that accounts for slightly more than half of the country's trade deficit in 2015. The results of the PR and CR estimated with the national IOT conclude with similar results.

Decarbonization is a great challenge in Latin America and the Caribbean. South America is not an exception. Besides, the region faces other challenges in terms of economic growth and development, poverty and inequality reductions, investment in infrastructures and other issues that might be considered as priorities. Depending on the countries, trying to combine efforts to fight against economic, social and environmental issues is not feasible in the short term. In fact, adaptation policies that respond to the consequences of the current environmental situation in Latin America and the Caribbean are at least as important as mitigation strategies. This is reflected in INDCs presented by Latin American countries, whose mitigation commitments vary widely depending on the format and weight of reductions. For example, Chile's commitment consists of emissions reductions per GDP unit. Another mitigation effort, proposed by countries such as Argentina, Colombia, Ecuador, Paraguay or Peru, consists of estimating how the emissions would be by 2030 if the current trend of emissions continued – *business-as-usual* (BAU) emission forecast – and then establishing a target of reduction from this forecast. As the main polluting country,

Brazil is committed to reduce its emissions to 37% of the 2005 baseline. Mexico, the second main polluting country, is intended to reduce its emissions to 25% in regard to the BAU forecast in 2030. Besides, almost every South American country has presented conditioned commitments, attending to funding from developed countries.

One of the most important challenges in Latin America and the Caribbean is to reduce its dependency on fossil fuels, whose demand is expected to increase due to economic growth. Thus mitigation policies are focused on fostering the use of renewable energies and fighting against deforestation (especially in Brazil).

In the case of Colombia, the country has demonstrated improvement in its performance in meeting the environmental standards required by the OECD. Turning the energy matrix into a cleaner one, less dependent on fossil fuels; diminishing carbon-intensive countries exports dependence and strengthening more efficient trade patterns; and resorting to adaptation and mitigation policies, as well as instruments of international cooperation such as Clean Development Mechanisms, are essential to reaching the 20% reduction established as the mitigation commitment in the Paris Agreement. Thus Transportation, Sugar and Confectionery are the most polluting sectors in their production processes. It would be a paradox to produce ethanol as a biofuel that is less polluting than fossil fuels by emitting this large amount of $CO_2$. Modernizing the sugar sector as a mitigation policy would contribute to reducing $CO_2$ emissions in order to achieve the national commitment of 20% reduction of GHG emissions.

Last but not least, the present research developed for Colombia shows the potential of Environmental Satellite Accounts and the opportunity to manage public policies from national sectoral emission structures. In the absence of official information in several countries in the region, the estimated information of sectoral emissions by international projects such as GTAP, WIOD, EXIOBASE or EORA can provide insights into the state of regional or national participation. However, further efforts to validate the reliability and consistency of such databases for the region are needed in order to carry out new studies that will deepen the effects of the decarbonization in Latin America and the Caribbean.

## Notes

1 Because GTAP has a higher level of disaggregation than EORA, this section presents sectoral analyses based on information from the GTAP database. Calculation of similarity indexes between both sources of information was obtained in an index of 0.7, which shows a high degree of similarity.
2 Particular sectors and linkages are showed in (ECLAC/ILO, 2016).

Disclaimer: the opinions expressed in this article are those of the authors and do not necessarily reflect the views of ECLAC

## References

Badri, N. G., and Walmsley, T. L. (2008). *Global trade, assistance, and production: The GTAP 7 data base*. Center for Global Trade Analysis, Purdue University.
Balza, L., Espinasa, R., and Serebrisky, T. (2016). *Lights on? Energy needs in Latin America and the Caribbean to 2040*. Inter-American Development Bank, Washington, USA.

Coronado, H., Jaime, H., and Gamba, P. (2014). *Crecimiento bajo en carbono: políticas en Bolivia (Estado Plurinacional de), Colombia, Nicaragua y el Perú*. Santiago de Chile, Chile: ECLAC, United Nations.

DANE. (2016). *Sistema Estadístico Nacional*. Bogota, Colombia: Departamento Administrativo Nacional de Estadística. Retrieved from www.dane.gov.co.

Durán Lima, J. E., Alvarez, M., and Cracau, D. (2016). *Manual on foreign trade and trade policy: Basics, classifi cations and indicators of trade patterns and trade dynamics*. Santiago de Chile, ECLAC. United Nations.

Durán Lima, J. E., and Cracau, D. (2016). *The Pacific Alliance and its economic impact on regional trade and investment: Evaluation and perspectives*. Santiago de Chile, ECLAC. United Nations.

Durán Lima, J. E., and Zaclicever, D. (2013). *América Latina y el Caribe en las cadenas internacionales de valor*. Santiago de Chile, ECLAC. United Nations.

ECLAC. (2014a). *Comercio internacional y desarrollo inclusivo: construyendo sinergias (LC/G.2562)*. Santiago de Chile, Chile: United Nations.

ECLAC. (2014b). *Panorama de la Inserción Internacional de América Latina y el Caribe, 2014. Integración regional y cadenas de valor en un escenario externo desafi ante (LC/G.2625-P)*. Santiago de Chile, Chile: United Nations.

ECLAC. (2015). *Panorama de la Inserción Internacional de América Latina y el Caribe: La crisis del comercio regional: diagnóstico y perspectivas*. Santiago de Chile, Chile: United Nations.

ECLAC. (2016). *Latin America and the Caribbean in the world economy: The region amid the tensions of globalization*. Santiago de Chile, Chile: United Nations.

ECLAC, and ILO. (2016). *Mejoras recientes y brechas persistentes en el empleo rural Coyuntura Laboral en América Latina y el Caribe*. Santiago de Chile, Chile: United Nations, ILO.

ECLAC, and IPEA. (2016). *La matriz de insumo-producto de América del Sur: principales supuestos y consideraciones metodológicas*. Santiago de Chile, Chile: United Nations.

FAO. (2008). *Climate change and food security: A framework document*. Rome, Italy: Food and Agriculture Organization.

Frohmann, A., Mulder, N., Olmos, X., and Herreros, S. (2012). *Huella de carbono y exportaciones de alimentos: Guía práctica*. Santiago de Chile, Chile: ECLAC, United Nations.

Hernández, R., Martínez Piva, J. M., and Mulder, N. (2014). Global value chains and world trade: Prospects and challenges for Latin America. Santiago de Chile, ECLAC. United Nations.

Hoekstra, A. Y., and Wiedmann, T. O. (2014). Humanity's unsustainable environmental footprint. *Science*, *344*(6188), 1114–1117.

IEA. (2008). *World energy outlook 2008*. Paris, France: IEA, OECD.

IEA. (2015a). *$CO_2$ emissions from fuel combustion*. Paris, France: IEA.

IEA. (2015b). *$CO_2$ emissions from fuel combustion, highlights*. Paris, France: IEA, OECD.

Kanemoto, K., Moran, D., Lenzen, M., and Geschke, A. (2014). International trade undermines national emission reduction targets: New evidence from air pollution. *Global Environmental Change*, *24*, 52–59.

Lenzen, M., Kanemoto, K., Moran, D., and Geschke, A. (2012). Mapping the structure of the world economy. *Environmental Science & Technology*, *46*(15), 8374–8381.

Lenzen, M., Moran, D., Kanemoto, K., and Geschke, A. (2013). Building Eora: A global multi-region input – output database at high country and sector resolution. *Economic Systems Research*, *25*(1), 20–49.

Low, P., and Yeats, A. (1992). Do "dirty" industries migrate? In P. Low (Ed.), *International trade and the environment* (pp. 89–103). Washington, DC: The World Bank.

Miller, R. E., and Blair, P. D. (2009). *Input-output analysis: Foundations and extensions* (2nd ed.). Cambridge: Cambridge University Press.

OECDStat. (2015). *Trade in Value Added (TiVA)*. OECD, WTO. Paris, France.

Peters, G. P., Minx, J. C., Weber, C. L., and Edenhofer, O. (2011). Growth in emission transfers via international trade from 1990 to 2008. *Proceedings of the National Academy of Sciences, 108*(21), 8903–8908.

Ray, R. (2016). The Panda's Pawprint: The environmental impact of the China-led re-primarization in Latin America and the Caribbean. *GEGI Working Paper*. Boston, MA: Boston University.

Rosales, V. (2014). La Alianza del Pacífico y el MERCOSUR: hacia la convergencia en la diversidad. Santiago de Chile, Chile: ECLAC, United Nations.

Serrano, M., and Dietzenbacher, E. (2010). Responsibility and trade emission balances: An evaluation of approaches. *Ecological Economics, 69*(11), 2224–2232.

Tukker, A., Bulavskaya, T., Giljum, S., de Koning, A., Lutter, S., Simas, M., Stadler, K., Wood, R. (2014). *The global resource footprint of nations: Carbon, water, land and materials embodied in trade and final consumption calculated with EXIOBASE 2.1* (p. 8). Leiden/Delft/Vienna/Trondheim.

UN. (2015). *Adoption of the Paris Agreement. /CP/2015/L.9*. United Nations Framework Convention on Climate Change.

UN. (2016). *COMTRADE database UN statistics division*. New York: UN.

The World Bank. (2016). *Databank*. Washington, DC: The World Bank.

Zevallos, P., Castro, R., Aldana, R., and Apaclla, K. (2015). *Monitoreando la descarbonización y la resiliencia en la Región de América Latina y el Caribe*. IDDRI Working paper. Paris, France.

# 11 Structural analysis of the top-five most GHG emitting economies

*Pablo Ruiz-Nápoles, Javier Castañeda-León and Eduardo Moreno-Reyes*

To Dr. José Sarukhán Kermez, Tyler Prize for Environmental Achivement, 2017, Emeritus Professor at National Autonomous University of Mexico (UNAM), former Rector of UNAM.

## Introduction

On December 12, 2015, the United Nations Framework Convention on Climate Change (UNFCC) – made up of 196 country members – adopted the Paris Agreement text (UNFCCC, 2015). The main purpose of the agreement is to prevent the increase in the planet's temperature below 2°C, with respect to the pre-industrial-age level and keep on working to limit this rise to 1.5°C. The idea is that by the end of this century, the planet's temperature should not be higher than 1.5°C, with respect to the pre-Industrial Revolution level. The difference with respect to the Kyoto 1997 Protocol is that by 2020, all parties that signed the agreement have the obligation of explaining, each one of them, what measures are they implementing to actually reduce greenhouse gase (GHG) emissions.

Based on previously produced works on this matter with the same approach (Ruiz-Nápoles, 2011, 2012, 2013; Ruiz-Nápoles and Puchet-Anyul, 2014), we are analyzing the top-five economies that produced 50% of GHG global emissions in 2011, which are China, the United States, India, Russia and Japan.

We are building and developing an Environmental Input-Output (EIO) model of each one of these economies for the purpose of analyzing the effects of a change in technology in some of the key sectors in each economy, identified as both strategic and high GHG emitters. The period in which this impact analysis is carried out goes from 2011 to 2030. The main idea is to find out to what extent the use of more efficient technologies in key economic sectors makes the reduction of GHG emissions possible under a scenario of GDP growth predicted by the OECD for these countries.

The work is divided into seven sections, including this introduction. In the second section, we discuss climate change and its relation to economic activities. In the third, we present EIO-type models. In the fourth section, we present our EIO model and show the five countries committed to GHG reductions for 2030 under the Paris Agreement. In the fifth section, we study the economic structure of the selected countries, their key and higher GHG emitting sectors. And, in the sixth section, we use the IO model for estimating the five countries' GHG emissions in the long run, first in a business-as-usual (BAU) scenario and then with the introduction of technological changes in selected sectors of the five countries for estimating their GHG long-run emissions. These trends are presented along with those trends consistent with the targeted GHG emissions committed under the agreement for each country. The final section includes a summary and conclusions.

It must be said from the beginning that, although most of the information we are using here may be called hard data since it comes from official sources and has been subject to verification, the resulting forecasted data and the simulations only indicate tendencies subject to assumptions and not real values, as in any other model interpreting the economic reality.

## Anthropogenic climate change and mitigation policies

Anthropogenic climate change is defined as "a change of climate which is attributed directly or indirectly to human activity that alters the composition of the global atmosphere and which is in addition to natural climate variability observed over comparable time periods" (IPCC, 2007, Annex II). It is in part the result of the atmospheric concentrations of GHG. They are those gaseous constituents of the atmosphere, both natural and anthropogenic, that absorb and emit radiation at specific wavelengths within the spectrum of thermal infrared radiation emitted by Earth's surface, the atmosphere itself and by clouds. This property causes the greenhouse effect. Water vapor ($H_2O$), carbon dioxide ($CO_2$), nitrous oxide ($N_2O$), methane ($CH_4$) and ozone ($O_3$) are the primary GHG in Earth's atmosphere. Besides $CO_2$, $N_2O$ and $CH_4$, the Kyoto Protocol deals with the GHG sulphur hexafluoride ($SF_6$), hydro-fluorocarbons (HFCs) and per-fluorocarbons (PFCs), (IPCC, 2007, Annex II). GHG are primarily produced by the combustion of fossil fuels, agriculture, land-use changes and production of materials such as cement, as well as the burning of waste.

Climate change consists of a gradual increase in the planet's temperature, rise in sea levels and changes in rainfall patterns, as well as in the frequency, magnitude and intensity of extreme weather events such as droughts and floods. Although this tendency has been scientifically verified, there is still some degree of uncertainty about the magnitude and velocity of these changes at a regional scale. However, based on the current state of knowledge, it is possible to identify some of the cause-effect chain relations between GHG sources, GHG emissions, global warming and its climatic consequences.

This has allowed some analysts to foresee various future scenarios for the economy, based on which we can assess, from an economic perspective, the possible consequences of climate change and the alternative options for adaptation and mitigation policies, in order to face the problem.

Mitigation has been defined as

> the technological change and substitution that reduce resource inputs and emissions per unit of output. Although several social, economic and technological policies would produce an emission reduction, with respect to Climate

Change, mitigation means implementing policies to reduce greenhouse gas emissions and enhance sinks.

(IPCC, 2011b, Annex I)

However, as some expert has pointed out, it is not only emissions intensity reduction (i.e. GHG emissions per unit of output) but also absolute emissions reduction which is important in mitigation.

Mitigation policies are aimed at the reduction of fossils fuels consumption and substitution towards low-carbon sources (and the capture and storage of carbon from emissions); therefore, the factors that cause it must be dealt with. These factors are mainly population dynamics, urbanization, production and consumption increases; energy efficiency and technology innovation tendencies; and the economic structure in each country. All these factors are related to economic activity: production, trading, consumption and investment.

In order to design a mitigation scenario, it is necessary to identify those economic sectors of production, or industries, which directly or indirectly generate GHG emissions becoming, therefore, the sectors that call for special attention; these are key sectors for mitigation. This can be seen as a supply-side view, though, since there is also a demand side of the problem which is related to consumption, investment and exporting, and could also be subject to mitigation policy actions.

In turn, the costs of mitigation measures depend on various local circumstances – for example, in the case of production, the specific form of economic growth and the introduction of technology developments in the production process aimed to reduce GHG emissions. Besides, climate change mitigation impacts are unevenly distributed among sectors and depend on the direct or indirect use of fossil fuels combustion of each and every sector of the economy. In short, the economic costs of climate change mitigation depend fundamentally on both the energy-use intensities of economic sectors and industries, and the absolute value of their corresponding GHG emissions. (IPCC, 2001)These two are associated with the technological characteristics of their respective processes of production.

Economic models of different types deal with various aspects of climate change mitigation policies, or with the same aspects, but using different approaches and inbuilt assumptions (macroeconomic models, econometric models, general equilibrium models, etc.).

The present study is in principle concerned only with those models within the input-output or structural analysis tradition, which can be defined as mezzo-economic models – that is to say, they are not macro- or micro-economic models. They deal with sectoral economic magnitudes.

We are building and developing an EIO model applied to five economies for the purpose of analyzing the effects of a change in technology in some of the key sectors of the economy identified as both strategic and high GHG emitters. The period in which this impact analysis is studied goes from 2011 to 2030. The main idea is to find out to what extent the use of more efficient technologies in key economic sectors makes the reduction of GHG emissions possible.

*Policy instruments and economic models*

In order to induce the use of technology that reduces GHG emissions by the producers (switching from a conventional technology to an abatement one), every
government has a variety of instruments and measures to apply: market-based
programs, regulatory measures, voluntary agreements, scientific research and
development (R&D) and infrastructural measures. IPCC maintains the idea that
there is no single best instrument or measure to apply but rather a combination
of measures adapted to national, regional and local conditions will be required
(IPCC, 1996). The same position is favored by the OECD in its studies.

Whatever the extent of market-oriented policies carried out between 1988
and 2005, they did very little in solving the GHG emissions problem called climate change. Nicholas Stern pointed out in his review, in 2006 after 18 years of
the IPCC foundation (IPCC, 2011a), that climate change was "the greatest and
widest-ranging market failure ever seen" (Stern, 2006, 2007). Of course, he had
not witnessed the so called sub-prime financial crisis of 2008, initiated in the
United States and extended to rest of the world, which was also a market failure.
Stern (2006, 2007) also called for a "major change" (as opposed to a marginal
one) in GHG reductions, which, as all major changes in the economy must, in our
opinion, must be led by the state in each country's case.

The need for state intervention arises also from the existence of market imperfections in each and every economy in the world. It is not surprising that the OECD
emphasizes that putting a price on GHG emissions through price mechanisms has
the limitation that "they do not address the full range of market imperfections that
prevent emissions to be cut at least cost, such as information problems" (Duval,
2008 p. 31).

The OECD finds also that empirical analysis indicates that the most important
determinant of innovation in the area of renewable energy technologies is general
innovative capacity. According to Furman, *et al.* (2002 p. 899),

> National innovative capacity is the ability of a country to produce and com-
> mercialize a flow of innovative technology over the long term. National inno-
> vative capacity depends on the strength of a nation's common innovation
> infrastructure, the environment for innovation in a nation's industrial clus-
> ters, and the strength of linkages between these two.

However, the OECD study says in the case of energy "public policy makes a
difference. Public R&D expenditures on renewable energies induce innovation,
as do targeted measures such as renewable energy certificates and feed-in tariffs"
(Haščič, *et al.*, 2010 p. 44).

## Applied environmental input-output models

Since Leontief's works on pollution, cleaning up issues (Leontief, 1970, 1973),
there have been various IO models and analytical devices developed from them.

Some advances appear in input-output textbooks, for instance Miller and Blair (2009) and Ten Raa (2006); others have been IO models or analytical instruments applied to particular cases of sectors and/or regions or countries – for example, Duchin and Lange (1992, 1994), Idenburg and Wilting (1998), Kratena and Schleicher (1999), Idenburg and Wilting (2000)), Lenzen et al. (2004) Wilting et al. (2004), Kelly (2006), Munksgaard et al. (2005)and Brink and Idenburg (2007).

From a theoretical approach to the pollution cleaning model, there have also been some developments; the most mentioned in the literature are Steenge (1978), Lowe (1979), Qayum (1991), Arrous (1994), Lager (1998) and Luptacik and Böhm (1999).

Leontief's model, which may be called standard EIO, is usually described as

$$
\begin{bmatrix} I - A_{11} & -A_{12} \\ -\alpha A_{21} & I - \alpha A_{22} \end{bmatrix} \begin{bmatrix} x_1 \\ x_2 \end{bmatrix} = \begin{bmatrix} y \\ 0 \end{bmatrix},
\tag{11.1}
$$

where $A_{11}$ = square matrix of conventional input-output coefficients; $A_{12}$ = coefficient matrix of economic inputs per unit level of abatement activities; $A_{21}$ = matrix showing environmental pollution per unit of production by the conventional sectors; $A_{22}$ = matrix showing pollution generated as a by-product of abatement activities; $x_1$ = vector of production levels of the conventional sectors; $x_2$ = levels of abatement activities; y = vector of final demand for conventional goods; $\alpha$ = diagonal matrix with the percentage of the pollution which has to be eliminated.

All of the aforementioned authors found that this model is characterized by a number of assumptions in the way it is formulated that causes limitations of various types when it comes to being applied for policy evaluation with respect to air pollution (Steenge, 1978, p. 482; Lowe, 1979, p. 112; Qayum, 1991, p. 428; Arrous, 1994, p. 106; Lager, 1998, p. 205; Luptacik and Böhm, 1999, p. 265; Brink and Idenburg, 2007, p. 3).

Leontief's system as represented by equation (11.1) has become an important framework for addressing economy-environment relationships. The approach is, however, characterized by a number of assumptions that cause some problems with the implementation of the model for environmental policy analysis. These have been pointed out and dealt with in several studies. We mention three of them that are relevant for the analysis of environmental policies with respect to GHG emissions.

In the first place, pollution is supposed to be eliminated once it is released into the environment (surface water, atmosphere, etc.). Although this might be the case for certain types of pollution (such as waste), in the case of most gaseous substances (such as GHG and air pollutants), once they are released into the atmosphere, it is hardly possible to eliminate them (Lager, 1998). Instead, pollution has to be reduced at the source through the use of less polluting alternative production technologies. This can be achieved through the substitution of conventional production technology by less polluting production technologies or else by applying add-on abatement technologies to conventional production technologies. This has two important implications: (i) abatement activities (and their cost and effect) are directly related to the pollution at the various specific sources and (ii) different substitution and add-on technologies will be available for each of the various sources, which implies that the cost of reduction and the reduction potentials are sector specific.

Secondly, in the standard EIO model, it is assumed that the degree of abatement – i.e. the proportions of pollutants eliminated, represented by α in (11.1) – are exogenous to the model. Moreover, the proportional emission reduction is the same for each sector. With abatement taking place once pollutants are released into the environment, this might be right, because the abatement costs for a unit of pollution are the same, regardless of the source of pollution. The approach implies that the cost of abatement is spread over the sectors according to their relative contribution to total pollution. In the context of sector-specific abatement, this will not result in an efficient use of scarce resources to reduce environmental pollution. In fact, it reflects the instrument of environmental policy called command and control, prescribing the same abatement technology for each sector.

Taking these limitations into account, the authors reformulated the model in a suitable way to solve the problems found for the analytical purposes they had in mind.

### *Pollution abatement and technological change models*

There is in the economic literature a limited number of references regarding applied IO models specifically related to climate change, mitigation technologies and impacts on evaluation at a national level. We narrow our criterion for selection to those coincidental with the purpose of our study – i.e. the analysis of the introduction of new technologies for GHG emissions reduction on the economy as a whole; there are two outstanding works worth mentioning, both EIO models applied to the Dutch economy: a dynamic input-output model called *Dimitri* (Idenburg and Wilting, 2000, 2004; Wilting et al., 2004) and an optimization of pollution-abatement technologies model (Brink and Idenburg, 2007).

In *Dimitri*, a crucial aspect for the dynamics and the introduction of new technologies are the variables and equations regarding: investment by sector, capital goods capacity (existing, expected and planned) by sector, depreciation rates by sector and the matrix of capital coefficients. The installed technology is a mix of technologies implemented in previous periods. As a result of depreciation and new investments, the installed technology in all sectors changes every period. After installing new technologies, the technological matrix depicts the new installed mix of technologies. The model estimates the technological matrices for each period. In the price side of this model, the costs are compiled from the operational costs, the return of capital and a revaluation of the capital stock. Sectoral prices are accounted for by the model, prices on labor and other value-added categories are external (Idenburg and Wilting, 1998, 2000, 2004; Wilting et al., 2004).

The cost-effective, pollution-abatement technologies model, developed by Brink and Idenburg (2007), is not dynamic, and it is built with the purpose of studying the effects of the application of the best GHG abatement technology per sector, choosing one among various (at least two) alternatives. The selection is based on a total cost analysis implemented in an optimization IO model. The technologies considered for election are all add-on technologies – that is, they do not imply a change in the product or in the production process. The model is to be applied to a permit scheme which works under free-market rules. That is to say, the authors privilege in their model an environmental policy of GHG reduction through a permit market system.

In the building and development of an EIO model for these five selected countries, we have a different objective from the studies mentioned earlier and some others somehow related. The EIO model we are applying to the five selected countries will show how GHG emissions reducing technologies applied in key sectors of the economy will reduce overall emissions through their direct and indirect effects in the economy. The model will assume the application of a set of abatement technologies in the strategic-pollutant sector and will estimate first its effectiveness in terms of GHG emissions reduction.

An alternative scenario will be the BAU – i.e. no technical change – tendency of the economic structure and GHG emissions, taking as external data the GDP projections for 2030 from the OECD (OECDStat, 2016)

## The model and the selected countries

### *Environmental input-output model*

We now present the EIO model for estimation of GHG emissions produced in the economy as the result of the interaction of all the sectors in the economy.

First, following Miller and Blair's (2009) notation, we start with the formal IO model in money terms for any economy:

$$\mathbf{x}_t = \mathbf{Z}_t\,\mathbf{i} + \mathbf{f}_t, \tag{11.2}$$

where $\mathbf{x}_t$ = gross output vector in time $t$, $\mathbf{Z}_t$ = IOM in time $t$, $\mathbf{i}$ = summation vector and $\mathbf{f}$ = final demand vector, with all vectors of order $n$ and the matrix of order $n \times n$.

With the introduction of $\mathbf{A}$, the technical coefficient matrix, equation (11.2), can be written as

$$\mathbf{x}_t = \mathbf{A}_t\,\mathbf{x}_t + \mathbf{f}_t. \tag{11.3}$$

Thus we arrive to the usual solution for the model:

$$\mathbf{x}_t = (\mathbf{I} - \mathbf{A}_t)^{-1}\,\mathbf{f}_t. \tag{11.4}$$

This is the standard demand-driven model to which we introduce emissions by sector to gross output ratio as $e_i = g_i x_i$, where $e_i$ is the total emissions by sector in GHG units and $x_i$ is the gross product by sector in monetary units.

Thus the equation for the vector of emissions per unit of output is

$$\hat{\mathbf{e}} = \hat{\mathbf{g}}\,\hat{\mathbf{x}}^{-1}, \tag{11.5}$$

where $\hat{e}$ = diagonal matrix of coefficients of sector GHG emissions per unit of gross output in GHG $CO_2$ equiv. units, $\hat{g}$ is the diagonal matrix of emissions by sector in GHG units and $\hat{x}^{-1}$ = diagonal matrix of gross output by sector.

We now introduce the equation of GHG pollution by-products:

$$x^p_t = \hat{e}\, x_t, \tag{11.6}$$

where $x^p_t$ = vector of pollution levels measured in GHG units and $\hat{e}$ = diagonal matrix of GHG emissions per unit of output $x$.

By combining (11.4) and (11.6), we get

$$x^p_t = \hat{e}\,(I - A_t)^{-1} f_t. \tag{11.7}$$

To make this model operational for our purposes, we now define the variables and its sources, which are the same for the five selected countries:

> $Z$ = IOM (total transactions), $x$ = gross output, $f$ = final demand vector, $t = 2011$ and $n = 35$, for each of the five selected countries, reported by the World Input-Output Database (WIOD).
>
> > (Dietzenbacher et al., 2013)
>
> $A_t$ = Technical coefficient matrix, where $t = 2011$ and the order $n = 35$. This matrix was calculated for each country using data from WIOD.
>
> > (Timmer et al., 2015)
>
> $B_t$ = Allocation coefficient matrix, where $t = 2011$ and the order $n = 35$. This matrix was calculated for each country using data from WIOD.
>
> > (Timmer et al., 2015)
>
> $g$ = Vector of GHG emissions by sector for each of the five selected countries estimated with data both from the WIOD
>
> > (Timmer et al., 2015).
>
> These emissions are measured in gigagrams of $CO_2$ equivalent (see the note on GHG emissions in the Appendix in this chapter).

For the matrices and vectors related as well as GHG emissions, we use the 35 industrial sectors classification, also from WIOD, as described in Table 11.1.

### Main GHG emitting countries

For selecting the countries for this study, we consider the data provided by the World Bank. Table 11.2 shows the top-five GHG emitter countries, which together represent almost half of world GHG total emissions. The selected countries were China, the United States, India, Russia and Japan. They are all important countries

*Table 11.1* Thirty-five sectors of the WIOD 2011 matrix

| No. | Sector Name |
|---|---|
| 1 | Agriculture, Hunting, Forestry and Fishing |
| 2 | Mining and Quarrying |
| 3 | Food, Beverages and Tobacco |
| 4 | Textiles and Textile Products |
| 5 | Leather, Leather and Footwear |
| 6 | Wood and Products of Wood and Cork |
| 7 | Pulp, Paper, Paper, Printing and Publishing |
| 8 | Coke, Refined Petroleum and Nuclear Fuel |
| 9 | Chemicals and Chemical Products |
| 10 | Rubber and Plastics |
| 11 | Other Non-Metallic Mineral |
| 12 | Basic Metals and Fabricated Metal |
| 13 | Machinery, Nec |
| 14 | Electrical and Optical Equipment |
| 15 | Transport Equipment |
| 16 | Manufacturing, Nec; Recycling |
| 17 | Electricity, Gas and Water Supply |
| 18 | Construction |
| 19 | Sale, Maintenance and Repair of Motor Vehicles |
| 20 | Wholesale Trade and Commission Trade |
| 21 | Retail Trade, Repair of Household Goods |
| 22 | Hotels and Restaurants |
| 23 | Inland Transport |
| 24 | Water Transport |
| 25 | Air Transport |
| 26 | Other Supporting and Auxiliary Transport Activities |
| 27 | Post and Telecommunications |
| 28 | Financial Intermediation |
| 29 | Real Estate Activities |
| 30 | Renting of M&Eq and Other Business Activities |
| 31 | Public Admin and Defence; Compulsory Social Security |
| 32 | Education |
| 33 | Health and Social Work |
| 34 | Other Community, Social and Personal Services |
| 35 | Private Households with Employed Persons |

Source: World Input-Output Database (WIOD)

regarding production and trade; four of them are highly populated, and the first two are considered the engines for the world's economic growth. In short, these are the countries in which a set of GHG emissions mitigation policies is urgently required, and they can make a change in the world emissions tendencies.

These five countries all signed and ratified the Paris Agreement of December 2015, so they committed themselves to reduce the level of GHG emissions by 2030 in a determined amount, starting in a given year. The summary of these reductions goals is shown in Table 11.3, and the details of the original sources are in the Appendix in this chapter.

*Table 11.2* Greenhouse gas emissions in 2011

*Top-Five Countries*

| No. | Country | GHG Emissions | Share of World |
|-----|---------|---------------|----------------|
| | | Gg CO$_2$ Equiv. | Total Emissions |
| 1 | China | 12,064,260 | 23.18% |
| 2 | United States | 6,571,654 | 12.63% |
| 3 | India | 2,828,846 | 5.43% |
| 4 | Russia | 2,777,724 | 5.34% |
| 5 | Japan | 1,396,767 | 2.68% |
| | Total | 25,639,251 | 49.26% |

Source: World Bank, World Development Indicators (2017)

*Table 11.3* Committed reductions of GHG emissions by the five selected countries

| Starting year | China | US | India | Russia | Japan |
|---------------|-------|-----|-------|--------|-------|
| | 2014 | 2005 | 2021 | 2020 | 2020 |
| GHG emissions CO$_2$eq | 13,161,340 | 5,580,711 | 4,671,709 | 2,806,603 | 1,194,079 |
| Goal year | 2030 | 2025 | 2030 | 2030 | 2030 |
| Min GHG reduction | 5,414,375 | 4,129,726 | 6,233,604 | 1,838,283 | 829,808 |
| Max GHG reduction | 5,250,303 | 4,018,112 | 6,141,254 | 1,715,732 | 829,808 |
| Base year | 2005 | 2005 | 2005 | 1990 | 2013 |
| GHG emissions CO$_2$eq | 6,382,873 | 5,580,711 | 1,805,184 | 2,451,045 | 1,121,362 |

Note: Intended Nationally Determined Contribution (INDC)

Source: UNFCCC and World Resources Institute (CAIT Climate Data Explorer)

## Strategic and high GHG emitting sectors

In the first part of this section, we use various IO techniques to identify those industries of the economy that may be called strategic from a structural point of view. In the second, we measure GHG emissions by industry and identify those considered as high emitters both in relative and absolute terms. We apply these techniques to the five selected countries.

We are using the IOMs for these selected economies reported by the WIOD for 2011 (Timmer et al., 2015). The type of matrix we are using is the total requirements matrix (that including imported inputs). For GHG emissions, we are using those consistent with the matrices also reported by WIOD (Timmer et al., 2015).

### *Strategic or key economic sectors*

In IOA, sectors or industries are labelled as strategic or key due to their effects on others, either through demand or through supply.

In particular, the relation between one sector or industry and the rest is called *linkage*; there are *forward linkages*, those related to supply, and *backward linkages*, those related to demand. We first need to find out the existence of linkages between industries and, in each case, its relative importance. So those industries that have many linkages with others, and those linkages are very strong, will transmit backwardly or forwardly economic effects to others. These industries or sector are then called *strategic* or *key*. The reason they are called this is that the increase or decrease in their production may cause a demand pull and/or a supply push of variations to other industries with effects on overall gross production, input consumption and/or labor employment.

We make use of some basic indicators that allow us to evaluate the relative importance of all industries and classify them according to their capacity to transmit economic impulses through the system that represents the IOM.

Dietzenbacher (1992), following the pioneer works of Rasmussen (1956), Chenery and Watanabe (1958) and Cella (1984), in measuring backward and forward linkages within structural analysis, developed a methodology based on eigen-values associated with the IOM to formulate most adequate measures.

The equation for forward linkages is

$$U_j = nz / (\mathbf{i}'z) \text{ with } \mathbf{B_z} = \lambda_z, \tag{11.8}$$

and the equation for backward linkages is

$$U_i = nq' / (q'\mathbf{i}) \text{ with } q'\mathbf{A} = \lambda q', \tag{11.9}$$

where $U_j$ = Dietzenbacher F.L. Index, $U_i$ = Dietzenbacher B.L. Index, $n$ = number of sectors in the matrix, $\mathbf{A}$ = technical coefficient matrix, $\mathbf{B}$ = allocation coefficient matrix, $\mathbf{i}$ = summation vector, $z$ = right-hand side eigenvector of matrix $\mathbf{B}$, $q$ = left-hand side eigenvector of matrix $\mathbf{A}$, (') = transposition and $\lambda$ = dominant eigenvalue of respective matrix.

We applied this methodology to estimate forward and backward linkages in the five selected countries and to determine the value of these indexes, which are the key sectors of these economies. The results are shown in Table 11.4. The values of these indicators, which are shadowed in the table, are the ones which are greater than one, meaning they are the most important.

In Table 11.5, we present the key sectors according to Dietzenbacher Index, which were both common to two or more countries and suitable to modify their production processes in order to reduce GHG emissions.

### 5.2. Main sectors emitting GHG

We take the GHG emissions in $CO_2$ equivalent for each sector of the 35 in the IOM from the same source, WIOD, which matches roughly the World Bank data in the total for 2011. The GHG emissions are expressed in gigagrams of carbon dioxide equivalent (Gg $CO_2$eq) that result from summing up the emissions of

Table 11.4 Key sectors of the five selected countries

| No. | Sector Name | China | | US | | India | | Russia | | Japan | |
|---|---|---|---|---|---|---|---|---|---|---|---|
| | | B.L. | F.L. | B.L. | F.L. | B.L. | F.L. | B.L. | F.L. | B.L. | F.L. |
| 1 | Agriculture, Hunting, Forestry and Fishing | 0.50 | 0.84 | 1.55 | 1.10 | 0.29 | 1.08 | 0.97 | 1.62 | 0.83 | 0.45 |
| 3 | Food, Beverages and Tobacco | 0.79 | 1.20 | 2.25 | 3.28 | 1.02 | 1.62 | 1.28 | 2.18 | 0.90 | 1.53 |
| 4 | Textiles and Textile Products | 1.45 | 1.84 | 1.60 | 0.19 | 1.61 | 1.93 | 1.04 | 0.12 | 1.01 | 0.17 |
| 8 | Coke, Refined Petroleum and Nuclear Fuel | 1.13 | 0.57 | 1.26 | 1.45 | 1.00 | 1.47 | 0.97 | 2.38 | 2.05 | 1.58 |
| 9 | Chemicals and Chemical Products | 1.36 | 2.13 | 1.57 | 1.74 | 1.47 | 1.54 | 1.26 | 0.99 | 1.61 | 1.97 |
| 10 | Rubber and Plastics | 1.60 | 1.09 | 1.62 | 0.51 | 1.82 | 0.68 | 1.51 | 0.45 | 1.66 | 1.01 |
| 12 | Basic Metals and Fabricated Metal | 1.45 | 3.74 | 1.64 | 1.45 | 1.86 | 4.10 | 1.29 | 2.33 | 1.97 | 4.44 |
| 13 | Machinery, | 1.61 | 2.14 | 1.30 | 0.76 | 1.83 | 1.42 | 1.55 | 1.08 | 1.38 | 1.27 |
| 14 | Electrical and Optical Equipment | 1.95 | 5.49 | 0.62 | 0.58 | 1.77 | 1.34 | 1.42 | 0.71 | 1.40 | 2.23 |
| 15 | Transport Equipment | 1.83 | 2.01 | 2.23 | 2.35 | 1.88 | 2.03 | 2.88 | 2.75 | 2.38 | 4.45 |
| 16 | Manufacturing; Recycling | 1.11 | 0.18 | 1.15 | 0.29 | 2.75 | 2.30 | 1.36 | 0.27 | 1.43 | 0.22 |
| 17 | Electricity, Gas and Water Supply | 1.23 | 1.15 | 0.47 | 0.27 | 1.31 | 1.08 | 1.15 | 2.23 | 1.30 | 1.48 |
| 18 | Construction | 1.40 | 3.96 | 0.97 | 1.72 | 1.42 | 5.74 | 1.11 | 2.64 | 1.06 | 2.68 |
| 22 | Hotels and Restaurants | 0.72 | 0.40 | 1.03 | 1.51 | 0.82 | 0.55 | 0.85 | 0.29 | 0.67 | 0.82 |
| 23 | Inland Transport | 0.76 | 0.41 | 0.94 | 0.61 | 1.26 | 3.48 | 1.01 | 1.64 | 0.62 | 0.55 |

FL = Forward Linkage Dietzenbacher Index
BL = Backward Linkage Dietzenbacher Index

Source: Elaborated with data from WIOD

*Table 11.5* Nine key sectors in the five selected countries

| No. | Sector Name | Countries |
|---|---|---|
| 8 | Coke, Refined Petroleum and Nuclear Fuel | 2 |
| 9 | Chemicals and Chemical Products | 4 |
| 12 | Basic Metals and Fabricated Metal | 5 |
| 13 | Machinery, | 4 |
| 14 | Electrical and Optical Equipment | 4 |
| 15 | Transport Equipment | 4 |
| 17 | Electricity, Gas and Water Supply | 3 |
| 18 | Construction | 3 |
| 23 | Inland Transport | 2 |

Source: Elaborated with data from WIOD

three gases: carbon dioxide ($CO_2$), methane ($CH_2$) and nitrous oxide ($N_2O$) that together are represent in most countries and in the average 98% of total GHG emissions. We are considering, as the sources do, only GHG emissions generated in production and distribution of goods and services, and no other emissions generated in consumption.

The GHG emissions by sector for the five selected countries in 2011 are shown in Table 11.6.

*Sector output multipliers*

The impacts of demand on gross output are usually measured by the so-called output multipliers. They measure the impact of sector or total demand on gross output by sector. These output multipliers are derived directly from matrix **A** – the technical coefficient matrix. The formula for output multipliers using Miller and Blair (2009 pp. 245–246) terminology is as follows:

Let $\mathbf{L} = (\mathbf{I} - \mathbf{A})^{-1}$ so, $\mathbf{L} = [l_{ij}]$

$$m\,(o)_j = \sum_{i=1}^{n} l_{ij}. \tag{11.10}$$

*Emissions multipliers*

In order to establish the highest GHG emitter sectors in an IO model such as the one we built for these five economies, there are three possible indicators: (a) total emissions by sector, vector **g**; (b) coefficients of emissions per unit of output, by sector, vector **ê**; and (c) a total GHG emissions multiplier by sector, which we can derive from matrix $(\mathbf{I} - \mathbf{\Psi})^{-1}$ – an inverse of matrices of emissions by emissions measured in GHG units per unit of output. In fact, to get this indicator (c), we have to first calculate (a) and (b). This matrix is analogous to the Leontief inverse matrix $(\mathbf{I} - \mathbf{A})^{-1}$. Like **A**, $\mathbf{\Psi}$ gives us the direct and indirect (GHG emissions) requirements to satisfy a unit of final demand expressed in GHG units. Following

*Table 11.6* GHG emissions by sector in the five selected countries in 2011

*Gigagrams CO$_2$Eq*

| Sector | China | US | India | Russia | Japan |
|---|---|---|---|---|---|
| Agriculture, Hunting, Forestry and Fishing | 1,556,266 | 479,704 | 782,219 | 184,631 | 42,343 |
| Mining and Quarrying | 1,064,495 | 373,984 | 187,831 | 244,111 | 24,515 |
| Food, Beverages and Tobacco | 91,827 | 62,721 | 81,760 | 5,730 | 13,389 |
| Textiles and Textile Products | 64,130 | 9,147 | 12,575 | 568 | 2,312 |
| Leather, Leather and Footwear | 4,587 | 160 | 424 | 97 | 150 |
| Wood and Products of Wood and Cork | 15,683 | 15,070 | 14,147 | 2,017 | 1,923 |
| Pulp, Paper, Paper, Printing and Publishing | 67,430 | 63,513 | 10,495 | 1,823 | 13,433 |
| Coke, Refined Petroleum and Nuclear Fuel | 133,597 | 191,913 | 56,830 | 75,197 | 30,503 |
| Chemicals and Chemical Products | 395,503 | 156,351 | 68,977 | 70,013 | 58,302 |
| Rubber and Plastics | 30,261 | 5,467 | 3,883 | 693 | 3,039 |
| Other Non-Metallic Mineral | 919,931 | 112,403 | 105,200 | 80,344 | 65,635 |
| Basic Metals and Fabricated Metal | 813,545 | 104,222 | 145,240 | 199,977 | 121,640 |
| Machinery, Nec | 50,492 | 16,924 | 6,804 | 2,757 | 2,932 |
| Electrical and Optical Equipment | 24,601 | 11,247 | 4,794 | 1,185 | 6,274 |
| Transport Equipment | 32,866 | 20,827 | 13,184 | 2,814 | 6,791 |
| Manufacturing, Recycling | 7,315 | 3,890 | 1,158 | 536 | 2,541 |
| Electricity, Gas and Water Supply | 4,306,429 | 2,115,370 | 962,936 | 929,101 | 355,125 |
| Construction | 92,477 | 43,593 | 14,518 | 8,642 | 29,053 |
| Sale, Maintenance and Repair of Motor Vehicles | 213 | 6,104 | 511 | 1,208 | 1,734 |
| Wholesale Trade and Commission Trade | 10,628 | 32,366 | 1,156 | 6,764 | 14,864 |
| Retail Trade, Repair of Household Goods | 9,490 | 81,298 | 5,065 | 4,429 | 16,747 |
| Hotels and Restaurants | 28,010 | 64,421 | 24,065 | 2,336 | 12,557 |
| Inland Transport | 130,472 | 243,980 | 40,788 | 209,003 | 36,400 |
| Water Transport | 129,880 | 58,528 | 7,129 | 4,187 | 87,019 |
| Air Transport | 101,203 | 161,304 | 3,494 | 27,311 | 22,169 |
| Other Supporting Activities | 40,053 | 57,935 | 4,100 | 5,643 | 1,798 |
| Post and Telecommunications | 7,534 | 32,334 | 2,675 | 2,261 | 3,147 |
| Financial Intermediation | 4,211 | 31,663 | 773 | 1,820 | 3,873 |
| Real Estate Activities | 5,288 | 10,040 | 362 | 6,391 | 3,521 |
| Renting of M&Eq and Other activities | 33,740 | 107,314 | 5,015 | 2,966 | 18,079 |
| Public Admin and Defence; Social Security | 34,274 | 262,024 | 1,032 | 6,168 | 23,288 |
| Education | 24,898 | 15,902 | 1,765 | 4,731 | 6,165 |
| Health and Social Work | 30,074 | 90,408 | 1,209 | 4,071 | 13,424 |
| Other Community, Social and Personal Services | 314,476 | 205,398 | 145,618 | 98,929 | 43,922 |
| Private Households with Employed Persons | 0 | 0 | 0 | 0 | 0 |
| Total | 10,575,876 | 5,247,526 | 2,717,729 | 2,198,454 | 1,088,609 |

Source: WIOD and World Bank

the methodology suggested by King et al. (2012) based on Hewings (1985) for the employment model, we calculate this matrix (see the Appendix) from equation (11.5) and using equations (11.2) to (11.7).

We obtained

$$\left(\mathbf{I} - \hat{\mathbf{e}}\mathbf{Z}\hat{\mathbf{g}}^{-1}\right)^{-1}\hat{\mathbf{e}}\mathbf{f} = \mathbf{g}, \tag{11.11}$$

which is equal to

$$\left(\mathbf{I} - \mathbf{\Psi}\right)^{-1}\hat{\mathbf{e}}\mathbf{f} = \mathbf{e}, \tag{11.12}$$

where: $\mathbf{\Psi}$ = emissions by emissions coefficient matrix.

It is possible to show that the matrix emissions by emissions $\left(\mathbf{I} - \mathbf{\Psi}\right)^{-1}$ is a similar matrix to the inverse Leontief matrix $\left(\mathbf{I} - \mathbf{A}\right)^{-1}$. So if we treat $\left(\mathbf{I} - \mathbf{\Psi}\right)^{-1}$ as we do $\left(\mathbf{I} - \mathbf{A}\right)^{-1}$, we can define

$$\mathbf{D} = \left(\mathbf{I} - \mathbf{\Psi}\right)^{-1} = [d_{ij}]. \tag{11.13}$$

Then we can estimate GHG emissions multipliers with the formula

$$m\,(e)_j = \sum_{i=1}^{n} d_{ij}. \tag{11.14}$$

Each one of the emission multipliers gives us the total emissions per unit of gross output in a given sector produced by gross output. So it measures all the direct and indirect effects generated in the whole economy and produced by a unit of gross output in one sector in terms of GHG emissions.

Thus we estimated these multipliers for the selected countries in the 35 sectors of production that reported the WIOD in 2011. These multipliers are shown in Table 11.7 and Figure 11.1.

*Table 11.7* GHG emission multipliers by sector of the five selected countries 2011

| No. | Sector | China | US | India | Russia | Japan |
|---|---|---|---|---|---|---|
| 1 | Agriculture, Hunting, Forestry and Fishing | 1.958 | 1.749 | 2.570 | 2.161 | 0.527 |
| 2 | Mining and Quarrying | 2.983 | 1.045 | 3.772 | 1.679 | 1.163 |
| 3 | Food, Beverages and Tobacco | 1.401 | 0.904 | 2.086 | 1.104 | 0.343 |
| 4 | Textiles and Textile Products | 1.297 | 0.605 | 1.517 | 0.916 | 0.311 |
| 5 | Leather, Leather and Footwear | 1.125 | 0.400 | 1.182 | 0.924 | 0.271 |
| 6 | Wood and Products of Wood and Cork | 1.412 | 0.874 | 2.419 | 1.160 | 0.407 |
| 7 | Pulp, Paper, Paper, Printing and Publishing | 1.489 | 0.485 | 1.869 | 1.088 | 0.316 |
| 8 | Coke, Refined Petroleum and Nuclear Fuel | 1.939 | 0.878 | 1.689 | 1.664 | 0.630 |
| 9 | Chemicals and Chemical Products | 2.124 | 0.748 | 1.963 | 2.642 | 0.581 |
| 10 | Rubber and Plastics | 1.607 | 0.498 | 1.688 | 1.408 | 0.411 |
| 11 | Other Non-Metallic Mineral | 3.527 | 1.821 | 4.409 | 3.603 | 1.234 |
| 12 | Basic Metals and Fabricated Metal | 2.210 | 0.709 | 2.693 | 2.719 | 0.680 |
| 13 | Machinery, | 1.374 | 0.353 | 1.341 | 1.302 | 0.309 |
| 14 | Electrical and Optical Equipment | 1.180 | 0.200 | 1.217 | 1.262 | 0.322 |

*(Continued)*

*Table 11.7* (Continued)

| No. | Sector | China | US | India | Russia | Japan |
|-----|--------|-------|-----|-------|--------|-------|
| 15 | Transport Equipment | 1.167 | 0.433 | 1.491 | 0.968 | 0.330 |
| 16 | Manufacturing, Recycling | 1.099 | 0.319 | 0.989 | 1.316 | 0.391 |
| 17 | Electricity, Gas and Water Supply | 9.560 | 6.371 | 14.929 | 6.841 | 1.410 |
| 18 | Construction | 1.678 | 0.344 | 1.382 | 1.055 | 0.323 |
| 19 | Sale, Maintenance and Repair of Motor Vehicles | 0.000 | 0.172 | 0.150 | 0.472 | 0.242 |
| 20 | Wholesale Trade and Commission Trade, | 0.506 | 0.139 | 0.125 | 0.602 | 0.099 |
| 21 | Retail Trade, Except of Motor Vehicles | 0.547 | 0.185 | 0.142 | 0.475 | 0.150 |
| 22 | Hotels and Restaurants | 1.117 | 0.378 | 1.570 | 1.067 | 0.253 |
| 23 | Inland Transport | 1.087 | 0.894 | 1.156 | 2.394 | 0.293 |
| 24 | Water Transport | 1.618 | 1.942 | 2.193 | 2.304 | 1.882 |
| 25 | Air Transport | 2.651 | 1.359 | 1.304 | 2.822 | 0.820 |
| 26 | Other Supporting and Auxiliary Activities | 1.082 | 0.454 | 1.420 | 1.011 | 0.159 |
| 27 | Post and Telecommunications | 0.563 | 0.210 | 0.766 | 0.589 | 0.101 |
| 28 | Financial Intermediation | 0.316 | 0.091 | 0.245 | 0.466 | 0.079 |
| 29 | Real Estate Activities | 0.214 | 0.076 | 0.103 | 0.800 | 0.034 |
| 30 | Renting of M&Eq and Other Business Activities | 0.847 | 0.134 | 0.365 | 0.457 | 0.133 |
| 31 | Public Admin and Defence; Social Security | 0.718 | 0.273 | 0.009 | 0.782 | 0.164 |
| 32 | Education | 0.785 | 0.339 | 0.137 | 0.628 | 0.086 |
| 33 | Health and Social Work | 1.239 | 0.182 | 0.522 | 0.691 | 0.201 |
| 34 | Other Community, Social and Personal Services | 1.631 | 0.351 | 3.279 | 3.535 | 0.226 |
| 35 | Private Households with Employed Persons | 0.000 | 0.000 | 0.240 | 0.000 | 0.000 |

Source: Elaborated with data from WIOD and the World Bank

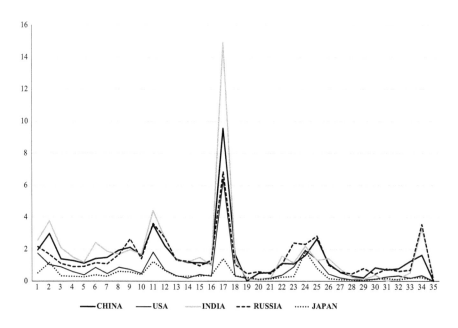

*Figure11.1* Emissions multipliers by sector 2011

Source: Estimated with data from WIOD

*Table 11.8* High GHG emitting sectors in 2011

| No. | Sector | Countries |
|---|---|---|
| 2 | Mining and Quarrying | 3 |
| 8 | Coke, Refined Petroleum and Nuclear Fuel | 3 |
| 9 | Chemicals and Chemical Products | 3 |
| 11 | Other Non-metallic Mineral | 4 |
| 12 | Basic Metals and Fabricated Metal | 3 |
| 17 | Electricity, Gas and Water Supply | 5 |
| 23 | Inland Transport | 3 |
| 24 | Water Transport | 5 |
| 25 | Air Transport | 2 |

Source: Elaborated with data from WIOD

With the information in Table 11.7, we elaborated a short list of high emitting sectors for all five countries in 2011, which is shown in Table 11.8.

If we compare Table 11.8 with Table 11.5, we find that the intersection of the two sets is made up of five sectors – those shadowed in Table 11.8 – and from that group, we established the subgroup of four sectors in which we propose to make a technological change in the five economies under study. These are (8) Coke, Refined Petroleum and Nuclear Fuel; (12) Basic Metals and Fabricated Metal; (17) Electricity, Gas and Water Supply and (23) Inland Transport. In this selection, we left out of consideration sector (9) Chemicals and Chemical Products because this sector includes a great variety of products which involve quite different techniques of production. We carried out a detailed analysis of these four sectors which is included in the Appendix of this chapter.

## Projected tendencies for GHG emissions of the five selected countries

### GHG emissions projected to 2030 with no technical change (BAU)

We use the model specified in equations (11.2) to (11.7) for estimating the GHG emissions of each of the five selected countries from 2011 to 2030 under the BAU scenario. Equation (11.7) will give us the estimations in which the independent variable is the final demand vector **f**, which is measured in money terms: to be precise, in US dollars.

Thus we recall equation (11.7) as $\mathbf{x}^p_t = \hat{\mathbf{e}} \, (\mathbf{I} - \mathbf{A}_t)^{-1} \mathbf{f}_t$.

### Assumptions about GDP growth

Variable **f** in equation (11.7) should be forecasted first, so we estimated **f** for the years from 2012 to 2030, taking the rates of growth of GDP for each country estimated and forecasted by OECD for those years. The rates are shown in Table 11.9.

*Table 11.9* Real GDP annual growth rates 2008–2030 (top-five countries)

| Year | China | US | India | Russia | Japan |
|------|-------|------|-------|--------|-------|
| 2008 | 9.6% | −0.3% | 6.1% | 5.2% | −1.0% |
| 2009 | 9.2% | −2.8% | 5.2% | −7.8% | −5.5% |
| 2010 | 10.4% | 2.5% | 11.1% | 4.5% | 4.7% |
| 2011 | 9.3% | 1.8% | 7.8% | 4.3% | −0.5% |
| 2012 | 7.7% | 2.8% | 4.9% | 3.4% | 1.4% |
| 2013 | 7.7% | 1.9% | 4.5% | 1.3% | 1.5% |
| 2014 | 7.4% | 2.8% | 4.9% | 0.5% | 1.2% |
| 2015 | 7.3% | 3.5% | 5.9% | 1.8% | 1.2% |
| 2016 | 6.7% | 3.3% | 6.1% | 3.9% | 0.7% |
| 2017 | 6.2% | 3.0% | 6.0% | 3.9% | 0.6% |
| 2018 | 5.8% | 2.8% | 5.9% | 3.6% | 0.8% |
| 2019 | 5.4% | 2.6% | 5.9% | 3.3% | 0.9% |
| 2020 | 5.1% | 2.6% | 5.9% | 3.1% | 1.0% |
| 2021 | 4.9% | 2.5% | 5.9% | 2.9% | 1.0% |
| 2022 | 4.6% | 2.5% | 5.9% | 2.9% | 1.1% |
| 2023 | 4.4% | 2.4% | 5.9% | 2.8% | 1.1% |
| 2024 | 4.2% | 2.4% | 5.9% | 2.8% | 1.2% |
| 2025 | 4.0% | 2.4% | 5.9% | 2.8% | 1.2% |
| 2026 | 3.9% | 2.4% | 5.9% | 2.8% | 1.3% |
| 2027 | 3.7% | 2.4% | 5.8% | 2.7% | 1.3% |
| 2028 | 3.6% | 2.4% | 5.8% | 2.7% | 1.3% |
| 2029 | 3.5% | 2.3% | 5.7% | 2.6% | 1.3% |
| 2030 | 3.5% | 2.3% | 5.6% | 2.6% | 1.4% |

Source: Organization for Economic Cooperation and Development (OECD)

The line between the 2015 and 2016 values means that those above the line are actual values and those below are forecasted ones.

With data from Table 11.9, we draw the graphs in Figure 11.2, showing the forecasted trends of GDP growth by OECD for the period of 2015–2030. We can observe that what is expected from these countries is a moderate rate of economic growth, which is below 5% a year, except for India, with the lowest by 2030 being Japan.

These data make up the scenario on which we are calculating GHG emissions trends for the period 2011–2030. The important aspect of this estimation is that we are assuming that not one of these five countries is making a technological change in this period so as to reduce the level of GHG emissions on the side of production and distribution of goods and services. In other words, what is called BAU with respect to changes in the technology are aimed at reducing the use of fossil fuels.

### Results of the BAU model

The results of our model estimation of GHG emissions for the five selected countries are shown in Table 11.10 and Figure 11.3. They indicate that the selected

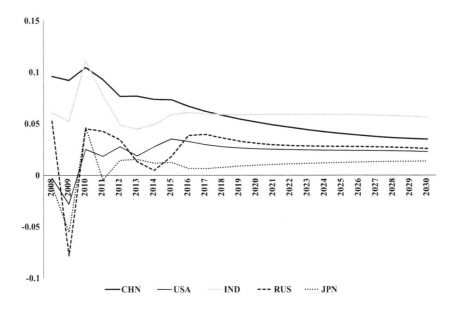

*Figure 11.2* GDP growth of five selected countries 2008–2030 (annual rates of variation)

Source: Elaborated with data from OECD

*Table 11.10* Estimated total GHG emissions of the five selected countries (BAU scenario)

| Year | China | US | India | Russia | Japan |
|------|-------|-----|-------|--------|-------|
| 2011 | 10,575,876 | 5,247,526 | 2,717,729 | 2,198,454 | 1,088,609 |
| 2012 | 11,385,201 | 5,393,370 | 2,850,429 | 2,273,982 | 1,104,361 |
| 2013 | 12,258,581 | 5,494,670 | 2,978,033 | 2,303,969 | 1,121,362 |
| 2014 | 13,161,340 | 5,646,045 | 3,124,425 | 2,314,854 | 1,134,421 |
| 2015 | 14,125,851 | 5,844,986 | 3,307,780 | 2,356,769 | 1,148,545 |
| 2016 | 15,070,829 | 6,036,512 | 3,508,615 | 2,447,625 | 1,156,066 |
| 2017 | 16,005,874 | 6,215,568 | 3,717,652 | 2,544,206 | 1,163,468 |
| 2018 | 16,933,496 | 6,387,297 | 3,936,576 | 2,635,992 | 1,172,301 |
| 2019 | 17,855,556 | 6,555,933 | 4,167,504 | 2,722,793 | 1,182,597 |
| 2020 | 18,773,232 | 6,724,076 | 4,412,134 | 2,806,603 | 1,194,079 |
| 2021 | 19,687,023 | 6,893,130 | 4,671,709 | 2,889,292 | 1,206,498 |
| 2022 | 20,597,050 | 7,063,806 | 4,947,108 | 2,972,191 | 1,219,708 |
| 2023 | 21,503,476 | 7,236,502 | 5,238,977 | 3,056,160 | 1,233,645 |
| 2024 | 22,406,769 | 7,411,512 | 5,547,804 | 3,141,709 | 1,248,281 |
| 2025 | 23,308,008 | 7,589,113 | 5,873,958 | 3,229,082 | 1,263,596 |
| 2026 | 24,209,245 | 7,769,649 | 6,217,729 | 3,318,310 | 1,279,576 |
| 2027 | 25,113,612 | 7,953,497 | 6,579,321 | 3,409,213 | 1,296,197 |
| 2028 | 26,024,986 | 8,140,780 | 6,958,782 | 3,501,365 | 1,313,392 |
| 2029 | 26,947,814 | 8,330,223 | 7,356,007 | 3,594,099 | 1,331,048 |
| 2030 | 27,887,117 | 8,520,096 | 7,770,808 | 3,686,551 | 1,349,035 |

Source: Elaborated with data estimated by the model

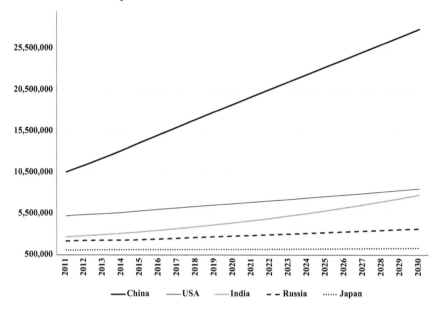

*Figure 11.3* Estimated GHG emissions by country 2011–2030 (Gigagrams $CO_2$eq)
Source: Elaborated with data from WIOD

five countries together will increase their GHG emissions in 2030, almost double what they were in 2011, but not all at the same rate. China shows the most striking results, since the forecasted level in GHG emissions for 2030 is about three times that of 2011, and in the same period, China is said to reduce its rate of growth from 9.3% in 2011 to 3.5% in 2030. Another quite interesting case is India, which will increase its GHG emissions by 2.8 times by 2030 from what it was in 2011. In this case, India is assumed to be growing at a rate between 5% and 6% in the period of 2015–2030, the highest rate of this group (see Table 11.9). The United States will keep its position as second in the most GHG emitting countries group. All this is a simulation given the assumption that there is no technological change in any of these five economies.

## Projections of GHG emissions with technical change

### The model and its assumptions

We are now simulating a technological change in four sectors of the five economies under study to discover what their GHG emissions trend would be were these changes adopted. The four sectors are those we chose in the previous section: (8) Coke, Refined Petroleum and Nuclear Fuel; (12) Basic Metals and Fabricated Metal; (17) Electricity, Gas and Water Supply; and (23) Inland Transport.

We selected from the same database (WIOD) the countries where these sectors were the less GHG emitting and take the input vectors from their respective matrices and introduced them in the matrices of the five selected countries. Then we ran the model. For this purpose, we now use the following equation:

$$\mathbf{x}^p_{\ t} = \hat{\mathbf{e}}^+ \, (\mathbf{I} - \mathbf{A}^+_{\ t})^{-1} \mathbf{f}_{t}, \tag{11.15}$$

where $\mathbf{A}^+_{\ t}$ = matrix modified with different inputs vectors for four sectors, $\mathbf{f}_t$ = final demand projected for each country as shown in Table 11.9 and $\hat{\mathbf{e}}^+$ = emissions vector in which some coefficients are substituted for the corresponding to the new four sectors introduced.

The column vectors of any **A** matrix can be interpreted as technologies of particular industries or sectors in the respective economies that are a technical combination of inputs to produce a given product or a set of them which are close substitutes.

To select each matrix vector to produce a technological change, we chose the sector with the lowest GHG emission multiplier from the whole database of WIOD. It is implied that this vector corresponds to a country that is utilizing the technology producing that low level of GHG emissions. The names of sectors and the countries' IOMs from which they were taken are shown in Table 11.11.

*Projections results and comparisons by country*

With the results of all the projections to 2030, GHG emissions goals, GHG emissions under the BAU scenario and GHG emissions with technical change, we will now to analyze these GHG emissions trends country by country. In the following figures, the line that represents the technical change scenario trend falls down in a straight one-year pattern and then starts growing again. It is a very strong downswing due to the fact that we are not assuming a period of adaptation of the new technologies to each economy of various years, only one. In the end, it has no consequences. What matters is the year 2030 in which we are assuming all new technologies should be well adapted.

*Table 11.11* Selected sectors with the lowest GHG emissions multipliers

| Sector | No. | Country |
| --- | --- | --- |
| Coke, Refined Petroleum and Nuclear Fuel | 8 | Denmark |
| Basic Metals and Fabricated Metal | 12 | Denmark |
| Electricity, Gas and Water Supply | 17 | France |
| Inland Transport | 23 | Sweden |

Source: WIOD

*Table 11.12* Estimated Total GHG emissions of China GHG (Gg $CO_2$eq)

| Year | BAU | INDC | WTCH |
|------|------|------|------|
| 2011 | 10,575,876 | | |
| 2012 | 11,385,201 | | |
| 2013 | 12,258,581 | | |
| 2014 | 13,161,340 | 13,161,340 | |
| 2015 | 14,125,851 | 12,450,610 | |
| 2016 | 15,070,829 | 11,778,260 | |
| 2017 | 16,005,874 | 11,142,218 | 16,005,874 |
| 2018 | 16,933,496 | 10,540,523 | 7,417,287 |
| 2019 | 17,855,556 | 9,971,321 | 7,821,171 |
| 2020 | 18,773,232 | 9,432,856 | 8,223,136 |
| 2021 | 19,687,023 | 8,923,469 | 8,623,399 |
| 2022 | 20,597,050 | 8,441,590 | 9,022,013 |
| 2023 | 21,503,476 | 7,985,732 | 9,419,050 |
| 2024 | 22,406,769 | 7,554,492 | 9,814,715 |
| 2025 | 23,308,008 | 7,146,539 | 10,209,479 |
| 2026 | 24,209,245 | 6,760,617 | 10,604,243 |
| 2027 | 25,113,612 | 6,395,534 | 11,000,378 |
| 2028 | 26,024,986 | 6,050,167 | 11,399,582 |
| 2029 | 26,947,814 | 5,723,449 | 11,803,804 |
| 2030 | 27,887,117 | 5,414,375 | 12,215,241 |

Notes: BAU: Business as usual (no technological change)

INDC: Intended National Determined Contribution

WTCH: Modified trend with technological change

Source: Elaborated with data estimated by the model

CHINA

The results for China are shown in Table 11.12 and Figure 11.4. China has committed itself to accomplishing a very strong reduction of its GHG emissions by 2030, almost half of the estimated level of 2011, starting in 2014. In our model, we estimate that China will increase this level around 164% in the same period in our BAU scenario. Thus its goal is 80% below the estimated BAU level, which means doing nothing. Now our alternative scenario – that is, to change the technology in four selected sectors of the economy, would produce a forecasted level for 2030 that is not below the 2011 level; in fact, it is higher by 15%, but below the BAU forecasting by 56%. In short, China will do better if they can accomplish the GHG emissions goal. The question is, what is the mitigation policy necessary to obtain the desired results?

THE UNITED STATES

The United States results appear in Table 11.13 and Figure 11.5. In this case, the committed GGH emissions goal by 2030 is also below the 2011 level, but by 21%. With respect to the forecasted level in the BAU scenario, the goal level is below by 51%. In this case, our forecasted level with technical change is below the BAU

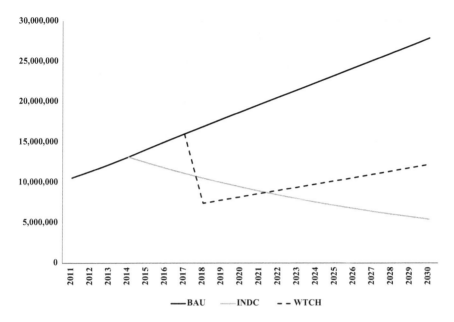

*Figure 11.4* Estimated total GHG emissions of China (Gigagrams CO₂eq)

Note: Elaborated with data from our model and from WIOD

*Table 11.13* Estimated total GHG emissions of the United States GHG (Gg CO₂eq)

| Year | BAU | INDC | WTCH |
|------|-----|------|------|
| 2011 | 5,247,526 | 5,098,695 | |
| 2012 | 5,393,370 | 5,022,508 | |
| 2013 | 5,494,670 | 4,947,459 | |
| 2014 | 5,646,045 | 4,873,532 | |
| 2015 | 5,844,986 | 4,800,709 | |
| 2016 | 6,036,512 | 4,728,974 | |
| 2017 | 6,215,568 | 4,658,312 | 6,215,568 |
| 2018 | 6,387,297 | 4,588,705 | 3,498,141 |
| 2019 | 6,555,933 | 4,520,138 | 3,590,498 |
| 2020 | 6,724,076 | 4,452,596 | 3,682,585 |
| 2021 | 6,893,130 | 4,386,063 | 3,775,171 |
| 2022 | 7,063,806 | 4,320,525 | 3,868,646 |
| 2023 | 7,236,502 | 4,255,965 | 3,963,226 |
| 2024 | 7,411,512 | 4,192,370 | 4,059,074 |
| 2025 | 7,589,113 | 4,129,726 | 4,156,341 |
| 2026 | 7,769,649 | 4,129,726 | 4,255,215 |
| 2027 | 7,953,497 | 4,129,726 | 4,355,904 |
| 2028 | 8,140,780 | 4,129,726 | 4,458,473 |
| 2029 | 8,330,223 | 4,129,726 | 4,562,226 |
| 2030 | 8,520,096 | 4,129,726 | 4,666,214 |

Notes: BAU: Business as usual (no technological change)

INDC: Intended National Determined Contribution

WTCH: Modified trend with technological change

Source: Elaborated with data estimated by the model

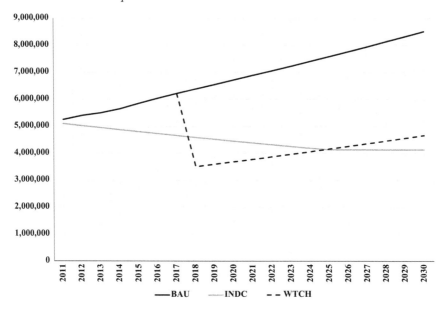

*Figure 11.5* Estimated total GHG emissions of the United States (Gigagrams CO$_2$eq)
Source: Elaborated with data from our model and from WIOD

level 45%, which is close to the goal level. This might mean that mitigation policies applied may be somehow similar to the ones we are suggesting.

INDIA

India is the only country in this group that has not made a commitment to reducing
its absolute level of GHG emissions for 2030, but only the coefficient of emissions per unit of output, so the forecasted GHG emissions goal in absolute terms
will be in 2030 129% above the one reported in 2011. And it is only 20% below
the forecasted BAU level. The level of GHG emissions forecasted by our model
under the scenario of technical change for 2030 is almost 44% of the level in the
BAU scenario. This is shown in Table 11.14 and Figure 11.6. This suggests that
if India follows this type of mitigation policy, it will be able to reduce, in fact, its
absolute level of GHG emissions by 2030.

RUSSIA

Russia's forecasted levels of GHG emissions, under the alternative scenarios and
the committed goals, for 2030 are shown in Table 11.15 and Figure 11.7. This case
is similar to that of the USA, but not in the level, of course. The goal for Russia
means to reduce by 2030 the level of GHG emissions in absolute terms 16% with
respect to the level reported in 2011. This would a level 51% below our forecast
under the BAU scenario. The forecasted level with technical change is 30% below

*Table 11.14*  Estimated total GHG emissions of India GHG (Gg CO₂eq)

| Year | BAU | INDC | WTCH |
|------|-----|------|------|
| 2011 | 2,717,729 | | |
| 2012 | 2,850,429 | | |
| 2013 | 2,978,033 | | |
| 2014 | 3,124,425 | | |
| 2015 | 3,307,780 | | |
| 2016 | 3,508,615 | | |
| 2017 | 3,717,652 | | |
| 2018 | 3,936,576 | | |
| 2019 | 4,167,504 | | |
| 2020 | 4,412,134 | | 4,412,134 |
| 2021 | 4,671,709 | 4,671,709 | 2,623,279 |
| 2022 | 4,947,108 | 4,823,852 | 2,777,921 |
| 2023 | 5,238,977 | 4,980,949 | 2,941,813 |
| 2024 | 5,547,804 | 5,143,163 | 3,115,227 |
| 2025 | 5,873,958 | 5,310,659 | 3,298,370 |
| 2026 | 6,217,729 | 5,483,610 | 3,491,407 |
| 2027 | 6,579,321 | 5,662,194 | 3,694,449 |
| 2028 | 6,958,782 | 5,846,593 | 3,907,526 |
| 2029 | 7,356,007 | 6,036,998 | 4,130,577 |
| 2030 | 7,770,808 | 6,233,604 | 4,363,498 |

Notes: BAU: Business as usual (no technological change)

INDC: Intended National Determined Contribution

WTCH: Modified trend with technological change

Source: Elaborated with data estimated by the model

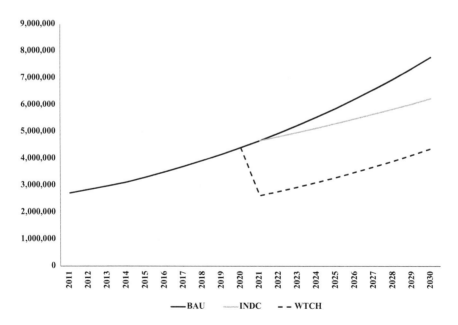

*Figure 11.6*  Estimated Total GHG Emissions of India (Gigagrams CO₂eq)

Source: Elaborated with data from our model and from WIOD

*Table 11.15* Estimated total GHG emissions of Russia GHG (Gg $CO_2$eq)

| Year | BAU | INDC | WTCH |
|------|-----|------|------|
| 2011 | 2,198,454 | | |
| 2012 | 2,273,982 | | |
| 2013 | 2,303,969 | | |
| 2014 | 2,314,854 | | |
| 2015 | 2,356,769 | | |
| 2016 | 2,447,625 | | |
| 2017 | 2,544,206 | | |
| 2018 | 2,635,992 | | |
| 2019 | 2,722,793 | | 2,722,793 |
| 2020 | 2,806,603 | 2,806,603 | 1,174,125 |
| 2021 | 2,889,292 | 2,690,321 | 1,208,718 |
| 2022 | 2,972,191 | 2,578,857 | 1,243,398 |
| 2023 | 3,056,160 | 2,472,011 | 1,278,526 |
| 2024 | 3,141,709 | 2,369,592 | 1,314,315 |
| 2025 | 3,229,082 | 2,271,416 | 1,350,867 |
| 2026 | 3,318,310 | 2,177,308 | 1,388,195 |
| 2027 | 3,409,213 | 2,087,098 | 1,426,224 |
| 2028 | 3,501,365 | 2,000,627 | 1,464,775 |
| 2029 | 3,594,099 | 1,917,738 | 1,503,570 |
| 2030 | 3,686,551 | 1,838,283 | 1,542,247 |

Notes: BAU: Business as usual (no technological change)

INDC: Intended National Determined Contribution

WTCH: Modified trend with technological change

Source: Elaborated with data estimated by the model

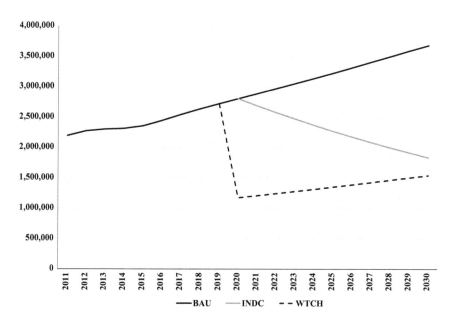

*Figure 11.7* Estimated total GHG emissions of Russia (gigagrams $CO_2$eq)

Source: Elaborated with data from our model and from WIOD

*Table 11.16* Estimated total GHG emissions of Japan GHG (Gg CO$_2$eq)

| Year | BAU | INDC | WTCH |
|---|---|---|---|
| 2011 | 1,088,609 | | |
| 2012 | 1,104,361 | | |
| 2013 | 1,121,362 | | |
| 2014 | 1,134,421 | | |
| 2015 | 1,148,545 | | |
| 2016 | 1,156,066 | | |
| 2017 | 1,163,468 | | |
| 2018 | 1,172,301 | | |
| 2019 | 1,182,597 | | |
| 2020 | 1,194,079 | 1,194,079 | 1,194,079 |
| 2021 | 1,206,498 | 1,151,403 | 730,869 |
| 2022 | 1,219,708 | 1,110,253 | 738,871 |
| 2023 | 1,233,645 | 1,070,573 | 747,314 |
| 2024 | 1,248,281 | 1,032,312 | 756,180 |
| 2025 | 1,263,596 | 995,418 | 765,458 |
| 2026 | 1,279,576 | 959,842 | 775,138 |
| 2027 | 1,296,197 | 925,538 | 785,207 |
| 2028 | 1,313,392 | 892,460 | 795,623 |
| 2029 | 1,331,048 | 860,564 | 806,319 |
| 2030 | 1,349,035 | 829,808 | 817,215 |

Notes: BAU: Business as usual (no technological change)

INDC: Intended National Determined Contribution

WTCH: Modified trend with technological change

Source: Elaborated with data estimated by the model

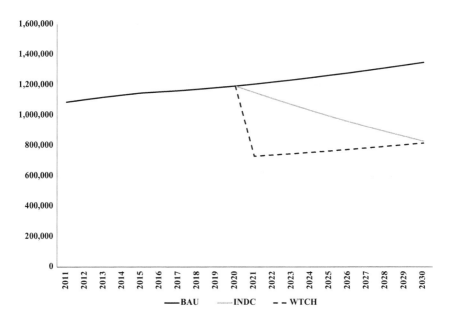

*Figure 11.8* Estimated total GHG emissions of Japan (gigagrams CO$_2$eq)

Source: Elaborated with data from our model and from WIOD

that of 2011 and 58% below the BAU forecasted level for 2030. So it seems that they too are following a mitigation policy similar to the one we are suggesting.

JAPAN

The Japan forecasted levels of GHG emissions are shown in Table 11.16 and Figure 11.8. It is one country that expects a very low level of growth in the following years to 2030, so its forecasted level, under the BAU scenario, is only 24% higher than the level reported in 2011. The committed goal is to reduce that level of 2011 in 24% and the level forecasted by our model under technical change coincides with the countries goal level, meaning that both levels are around 39% below the BAU forecasted level of GHG emissions. So in this case, it seems they are actually following a mitigation policy similar to the one suggested here – that is, a technical change in a few sectors.

## Summary and conclusions

We have studied the economies of five countries which were regarded as the most GHG emitting countries in 2011 according to the data from the World Bank. These countries signed the Paris Agreement on Climate Change in December of 2015, produced by the United Nations, and participated in the Conference of the Parties of the UNFCCC in which the parties established their goals for GHG emissions reduction called INDC.

The importance of these countries is that their GHG emissions represented in 2011 around half of all GHG emissions in the world, according to the various international sources. This means that what they do, or do not do, to reduce the GHG emissions surely has an impact on anthropogenic climate change.

Thus the purpose of studying these five countries has concentrated on analyzing the trends their GHG emissions will follow from 2011 to 2030. In order to accomplish this objective, we have used some techniques derived from structural analysis or IOA. We use all IO data from the WIOD, including GHG emissions by sector.

These IO techniques allowed us to determine which sectors of the five economies can be considered key sectors in the sense that they have the stronger linkages to the rest of them in the economy under study. We determined those sectors for the five economies and chose those that were common to all five. Also, we could establish through these techniques what sectors were the higher GHG emitters in each of the economies under study, and we also selected those high emitting sectors that were common to all five.

Based on previous studies, we built an EIO model, with the purpose of forecasting GHG emissions of each of the five economies under two alternative scenarios. Since the IO model is a demand-driven one, we use the concept and values of final demand as the independent variable. We obtained the reported values of final demand from 2012 to 2014, and we applied the growth rates forecasted by the OECD for GDP to the final demand for 2015 to 2030. One of the scenarios was the so-called BAU, which means doing nothing to reduce GHG emissions. The other scenario utilized the same independent variable with the same values, but a different IOM – one that was modified to incorporate a technological change in four selected sectors which were identified both as key sectors and high GHG emitters. This was done taking the technical vectors from other economies and introducing them in our five economies. That is, we *simulated* a technical change in our five economies.

The comparison of the three trends of GHG emissions by country can be summarize as follows:

• Three countries, the USA, Russia and Japan established clear and feasible goals for 2030, and their target trends suggest they will be (or maybe already are) applying mitigation policies that consist of technological changes in sectors that are key or high emitting sectors, or both, such as the ones we chose for the study.
• China is a special case, because it has been identified as the highest GHG emitter country. Its committed goals for 2030 are very low as compared to the other four countries, relatively speaking. Our simulated forecasting of GHG emissions reduction through technical change is above the level they are committed to reach. The question is then, what is the adequate mitigation policy to get these results?
• The other case is India, which is not committed to reducing the absolute GHG emissions level, so in order to actually reduce this level of emissions for 2030, they should apply a technological change such as the one we are suggested here and in the sectors chosen.

Using this model with technical change to forecast gross output, we predict an increases in gross output without additional GHG emissions, which proves that the sectors chosen in the countries from which we took them are not only less

*Table 11.17* World forecasted GHG emissions 2011–2030 Gigagrams $CO_2$eq

| Countries | 2011 | | 2030 | | |
| --- | --- | --- | --- | --- | --- |
| | World Bank | WIOD | INDC | BAU | WTCH |
| CHINA | 12,064,260 | 10,575,876 | 5,414,375 | 27,887,117 | 12,215,241 |
| USA | 6,571,654 | 5,247,526 | 4,129,726 | 8,520,096 | 4,666,214 |
| INDIA | 2,828,846 | 2,717,729 | 6,233,604 | 7,770,808 | 4,363,498 |
| RUSSIA | 2,777,724 | 2,198,454 | 1,838,283 | 3,686,551 | 1,542,247 |
| JAPAN | 1,396,767 | 1,088,609 | 829,808 | 1,349,035 | 817,215 |
| Subtotal | 25,639,251 | 21,828,194 | 18,445,796 | 49,213,606 | 23,604,414 |
| Rest of the World | 26,410,600 | 22,484,888 | 19,000,732 | 50,694,181 | 24,314,545 |
| WORLD Total | 52,049,851 | 44,313,082 | 37,446,528 | 99,907,788 | 47,918,959 |
| *Stern Review* | 50,000,000 | | | 62,000,000 | |

Notes: WIOD = World Input-Output Database

INDC = Intended National Determined Contribution

BAU = Business as usual trend

WTCH = With technological change trend

GHG emitters but also more productive than the existing ones in the five countries in the study. Although this is not shown in this already long chapter.

We include a final table, Table 11.17, which shows the overall results and allows us to make comparisons between countries. The comparisons we made in the previous section of this chapter are shown in this table. To conclude, we must pay attention to the comparison of the figures, those from different sources and from our model, with those produced by Stern (2007, p. 173). According to this comparison, we were, in 2011, already above Stern's projected BAU trend line, and if we do nothing, we will in 2030 be generating close to 100,000,000 Gg of GHG emissions, well above Stern's figure, which was 62,000,000 Gg of GHG emissions, roughly.

## Acknowledgments

The authors express their gratitude to Martín Puchet Anyul, professor in the Graduate Studies Program in Economics at UNAM, for his valuable advisory in building the EIO model, also to Víctor Hernández, undergraduate student in economics at UNAM, for his assistantship in running the model in Mathematica. Of course, all errors and opinions are solely the responsibility of the authors.

# Appendix

## Methodological notes

### *Note on GHG emissions*

GHG emissions data we used for the five countries under study to analyze and forecast their trends were the GHG emissions vector by sector from the WIOD Environmental Accounts (www.wiod.org/database/eas13). They are consistent with the WIOD IOA for the same countries.

However, these vectors by sector (35) are estimated by WIOD separately for the three main GHG. Thus there are three emissions vectors: carbon dioxide ($CO_2$), nitrous oxide ($N_2O$) and methane ($CH_4$), with information available up to 2009. In order to get one single vector of total GHG emissions, we had to sum up the three vectors in common $CO_2$ equivalent units, utilizing conversion factors for the three gases provided by the Intergovernmental Panel on Climate Change (IPCC, 2000).

Now in order to estimate the GHG emission vector for 2011, we used a different source, the World Bank, which estimates the same group of gases and the same unit measure $CO_2$ equivalent.

We then compared the annual information we get from these two sources for the period of 1995–2009, checking that the differences were very small, and the total followed the same trend in that period.

Now, since we were analyzing GHG emissions generated in production and not in consumption, we took the proportion of intermediate uses to total uses from WIOD data and applied it to the World Bank data for 2011. And we distributed the GHG emissions by sector according to the WIOD proportions for 2009. The same process is carried out for each of the five countries under study.

## Note on intended national determined contributions INDC

In accordance with the Paris Agreement (UNFCCC, 2015), each signing country is assumed to make public its IINDC – that is, its committed goals of GHG emissions reduction for 2030. The source that is following these INDC is the World Resources Institute (2016) in its CAIT Paris Contributions Map.

We found for our selected countries the respective websites for INDC:

## China:

http://www4.unfccc.int/submissions/INDC/Published%20Documents/China/
1/China's%20INDC%20-%20on%2030%20June%202015.pdf
www.unfccc.int

## USA:

http://www4.unfccc.int/submissions/INDC/Published%20Documents/
United%20States%20of%20America/1/U.S.%20Cover%20Note%20
INDC%20and%20Accompanying%20Information.pdf

## India:

http://www4.unfccc.int/submissions/INDC/Published%20Documents/India/1/
INDIA%20INDC%20TO%20UNFCCC.pdf
www.unfccc.int

## Russia:

http://www4.unfccc.int/submissions/INDC/Published%20Documents/Rus-
sia/1/Russian%20Submission%20INDC_eng_rev1.doc
Russian Submission INDC_eng_rev1.doc – Climate change
www.unfccc.int

## Japan:

http://www4.unfccc.int/submissions/INDC/Published%20Documents/
Japan/1/20150717_Japan's%20INDC.pdf
www.unfccc.int

## Note on the emissions by emissions matrix

We can obtain matrix $(I - \Psi)^{-1}$, following Hewings (1985) and King et al. (2012), for the analysis of employment. We start from equations (11.2) and (11.5) in the model:

$$x = Zi + f,$$ (11.A.1)
$$\hat{e} = \hat{g}\,\hat{x}^{-1}.$$ (11.A.2)

We multiply both sides of equation (11.A.1) by $\hat{g}\,\hat{x}^{-1}$, so we get

$$\hat{g}\,\hat{x}^{-1}x = \hat{g}\,\hat{x}^{-1}Zi + \hat{g}\,\hat{x}^{-1}f.$$ (11.A.3)

Table 11.A.1 Measures of central tendency of the GHG emissions in four sectors of the five selected countries Gigagrams $CO_2$eq and relative values

| | No. of Obs. | Mean value | Sta. Dev. | Max value | Sector 8 | Mean > or < | Sector 12 | Mean > or < | Sector 17 | Mean > or < | Sector 23 | Mean > or < |
|---|---|---|---|---|---|---|---|---|---|---|---|---|
| **China** | | | | | | | | | | | | |
| Total Emissions | 35 | 302,168 | 781,549 | 4,306,430 | 133,597 | ∨ | 813,545 | ∧ | 4,306,429 | ∧ | 130,472 | ∧ |
| Emissions coeff. | 35 | 0.47 | 1.08 | 6.06 | 0.35 | ∨ | 0.42 | ∨ | 6.06 | ∧ | 0.32 | ∨ |
| Emissions multi. | 35 | 1.54 | 1.60 | 9.56 | 1.94 | ∧ | 2.21 | ∧ | 9.56 | ∧ | 1.09 | ∧ |
| **US** | | | | | | | | | | | | |
| Total Emissions | 35 | 149,929 | 359,369 | 2,115,370 | 191,913 | ∧ | 104,222 | ∨ | 2,115,370 | ∧ | 243,980 | ∧ |
| Emissions coeff. | 35 | 0.43 | 1.07 | 6.16 | 0.28 | ∨ | 0.20 | ∨ | 6.16 | ∧ | 0.63 | ∨ |
| Emissions mult. | 35 | 0.74 | 1.10 | 6.37 | 0.88 | ∧ | 0.71 | ∨ | 6.37 | ∧ | 0.89 | ∧ |
| **India** | | | | | | | | | | | | |
| Total Emissions | 35 | 77,649 | 205,421 | 962,936 | 56,830 | ∨ | 145,240 | ∧ | 962,936 | ∧ | 40,788 | ∧ |
| Emissions coeff. | 35 | 0.84 | 2.03 | 11.38 | 0.38 | ∨ | 0.64 | ∨ | 11.38 | ∧ | 0.14 | ∨ |
| Emissions multi. | 35 | 1.80 | 2.53 | 14.93 | 1.69 | ∨ | 2.69 | ∧ | 14.93 | ∧ | 1.16 | ∧ |
| **Russia** | | | | | | | | | | | | |
| Total Emissions | 35 | 62,813 | 165,425 | 929,101 | 75,197 | ∧ | 199,977 | ∧ | 929,101 | ∧ | 209,003 | ∧ |
| Emissions coeff. | 35 | 0.58 | 1.09 | 5.56 | 0.36 | ∨ | 1.29 | ∧ | 5.56 | ∧ | 1.49 | ∧ |
| Emissions multi. | 35 | 1.51 | 1.29 | 6.84 | 1.66 | ∧ | 2.72 | ∧ | 6.84 | ∧ | 2.39 | ∧ |
| **Japan** | | | | | | | | | | | | |
| Total Emissions | 35 | 31,103 | 62,429 | 355,125 | 30,503 | ∨ | 121,640 | ∧ | 355,125 | ∧ | 36,400 | ∧ |
| Emissions coeff. | 35 | 0.16 | 0.28 | 1.07 | 0.14 | ∨ | 0.19 | ∧ | 1.07 | ∧ | 0.14 | ∨ |
| Emissions multi. | 35 | 0.42 | 0.42 | 1.88 | 0.63 | ∧ | 0.68 | ∧ | 1.41 | ∧ | 0.29 | ∨ |

Sector 8 Coke, Refined Petroleum and Nuclear Fuel
Sector 12 Basic Metals and Fabricated Metal
Sector 17 Electricity, Gas and Water Supply
Sector 23 Inland Transport

Source: Elaborated with Data from WIOD

We now substitute $\mathbf{i}$, the summation column vector with $\hat{\mathbf{g}}^{-1}\mathbf{g}$ in equation (11.A.3), and solving for $\mathbf{g}$ we get

$$\hat{\mathbf{g}}\,\hat{\mathbf{x}}^{-1}\mathbf{Z}\,\hat{\mathbf{g}}^{-1}\mathbf{g}+\hat{\mathbf{g}}\,\hat{\mathbf{x}}^{-1}\mathbf{f}=\mathbf{g}. \tag{11.A.4}$$

It follows that

$$\hat{\mathbf{g}}\,\hat{\mathbf{x}}^{-1}\mathbf{f}=\mathbf{g}-\hat{\mathbf{g}}\,\hat{\mathbf{x}}^{-1}\mathbf{Z}\,\hat{\mathbf{g}}^{-1}\mathbf{g}, \tag{11.A.5}$$

$$\hat{\mathbf{g}}\,\hat{\mathbf{x}}^{-1}\mathbf{f}=\left(\mathbf{I}-\hat{\mathbf{g}}\,\hat{\mathbf{x}}^{-1}\,\mathbf{Z}\hat{\mathbf{g}}^{-1}\right)\mathbf{g}. \tag{11.A.6}$$

Now, substituting $\hat{\mathbf{e}}$ for $\hat{\mathbf{g}}\,\hat{\mathbf{x}}^{-1}$ in (11.A.6) we get,

$$\left(\mathbf{I}-\hat{\mathbf{e}}\mathbf{Z}\hat{\mathbf{g}}^{-1}\right)^{-1}\hat{\mathbf{e}}\mathbf{f}=\mathbf{g}, \tag{11.A.6}$$

$$\left(\mathbf{I}-\mathbf{\Psi}\right)^{-1}\hat{\mathbf{e}}\mathbf{f}=\mathbf{g}, \tag{11.A.7}$$

where $\mathbf{\Psi}=\hat{\mathbf{e}}\mathbf{Z}\hat{\mathbf{g}}^{-1}$ a matrix of GHG emissions by GHG emissions,

### Note on high GHG emissions calculations

Following the model for emissions multipliers shown in the previous note, we calculated the three indicators mentioned for four sectors in the five selected countries. To determine whether these sectors were high GHG emitting ones to be included in our final set of selected sectors, we estimated their measures of central tendency, which results are shown in Table 11.A.1.

### References

Arrous, J. (1994). The Leontief pollution model: a systematic formulation. *Economic Systems Research*, 6(1), 105–104.
Brink, C., and Idenburg, A. (2007). *Cost-effective pollution-abatement in an input-output model*. Paper presented at the 16th International Input-Output Conference, July, Istanbul, Turkey.
Cella, G. (1984). The input-output measurement of interindustry linkages. *Oxford Bulletin of Economics and Statistics*, 46(1), 73–84.
Chenery, H. B., and Watanabe, T. (1958). An International comparisons of the structure of production. *Econometrica: Journal of the Econometric Society*, no. 26 487–521.
Dietzenbacher, E. (1992). The measurement of interindustry linkages: Key sectors in the Netherlands. *Economic Modelling*, 9(4), 419–437.
Dietzenbacher, E., Los, B., Stehrer, R., Timmer, M., and De Vries, G. (2013). The construction of world input – output tables in the WIOD project. *Economic Systems Research*, 25(1), 71–98.
Duchin, F., and Lange, G.-M. (1992). Technological choices and prices, and their implications for the US economy, 1963–2000. *Economic Systems Research*, 4(1), 53–76.
Duchin, F., and Lange, G.-M. (1994). *The future of the environment: Ecological economics and technological change*. Oxford: Oxford University Press.
Duval, R. (2008). A taxonomy of instruments to reduce greenhouse gas emissions and their interactions. *OECD Economic Department Working Papers* (636), 0_1.

Furman, J. L., Porter, M. E., and Stern, S. (2002). The determinants of national innovative capacity. *Research policy*, *31*(6), 899–933.

Haščič, I., Johnstone, N., Watson, F., and Kaminker, C. (2010). *Climate policy and technological innovation and transfer*. OECD Working Papers. Paris: OECD.

Hewings, G. (1985). *Regional input-output analysis*. Regional Research Institute, West Virginia University. Beverly Hills: SAGE Publications

Idenburg, A., and Wilting, H. (1998, 18–22 May). *Technological choices and the eco-efficiency of the economy: A dynamic input-output approach*. Paper presented at the Twelfth International Conference on Input-Output Techniques, New York.

Idenburg, A., and Wilting, H. (2000, 21–25 August). *DIMITRI: A dynamic input-output model to study the impacts of technology related innovations*. Paper presented at the XIII International Conference on Input-Output Techniques, University of Macerata, Italy.

Idenburg, A., and Wilting, H. (2004). DIMITRI: A model for the study of policy issues in relation to the economy, technology, and the environment. In J. C. van den Bergh and M. Janssen (Eds.), *Economics of industrial ecology* Materials Structural Change and Spatial Scales, MIT Press: Cambridge MA (pp. 223–254).

IPCC. (1996). Technologies, policies and measures for mitigating climate change: Technical Paper for IPCC working group 2. Geneva, Switzerland: Intergovernmental Panel on Climate Change WMO, UNEP.

IPCC. (2000). *Special report emissions scenarios. IPCC Working Group III*. Geneva, Switzerland: Intergovernmental Panel on Climate Change WMO, UNEP.

IPCC. (2001). Ch. 7: Costing methodologies. In B. Metz, O. Davidson, R. Stewart and J. Pan (eds.) *Climate change 2001: Mitigation* (pp. 451–498). Cambridge University Press: Cambridge, UK: Intergovernmental Panel on Climate Change.

IPCC. (2007). Climate Change 2007 Synthesis Report Contribution of Working Groups I, II and III to the Fourth Assessment Report of The Intergovernmental Panel on Climate Change. Core Writing Team, Pachauri R.K., and Reisinger A. Geneva, Switzerland, p. 104.

IPCC. (2011a). *Intergovernmental panel on climate change*. Retrieved from www.ipcc.ch/organization/organization_history.shtml

IPCC. (2011b). *Special report on renewable energy sources and climate change mitigation*. Cambridge, UK and New York: Intergovernmental Panel on Climate Change WMO, UNEP.

Kelly, J. A. (2006). *An overview of the RAINS model*. Environmental Protection Agency. Ireland.

King, A., Parra, J. C., and Pino, O. (2012). National economy 2008: A look from the perspective of the linkages for employment matrix size 111*111. *European Scientific Journal*, *8*(19), 118.

Kratena, K., and Schleicher, S. (1999). Impact of carbon dioxide emissions reduction on the Austrian economy. *Economic Systems Research*, *11*(3), 245–261.

Lager, C. (1998). Prices of Goods' and "Bads": An application of the Ricardian theory of differential rent. *Economic Systems Research*, *10*(3), 203–223.

Lenzen, M., Pade, L.-L., and Munksgaard, J. (2004). $CO_2$ multipliers in multi-region input-output models. *Economic Systems Research*, *16*(4), 391–412.

Leontief, W. (1970). Environmental repercussions and the economic structure: An input-output approach. *The Review of Economics and Statistics*, 53(2), 262–271.

Leontief, W. (1973). National income, economic structure, and environmental externalities. In E. Moss (ed.) *The Measurement of Economic and Social Performance* Studies in Income and Wealth vol. 38, New York: National Bureau of Economic Research (pp. 565–576).

Lowe, P. D. (1979). Pricing problems in an input-output approach to environment protection. *The Review of Economics and Statistics*, vol. LXI, no.1 pp. 110–117.

Luptacik, M., and Böhm, B. (1999). A consistent formulation of the Leontief pollution model. *Economic Systems Research, 11*(3), 263–276.

Miller, R. E., and Blair, P. D. (2009). *Input-output analysis: Foundations and extensions* (2nd ed.). Cambridge: Cambridge University Press.

Munksgaard, J., Wier, M., Lenzen, M., and Dey, C. (2005). Using input-output analysis to measure the environmental pressure of consumption at different spatial levels. *Journal of Industrial Ecology, 9*(1–2), 169–185.

OECDStat. (2016). *GDP long-term forecast (indicator)* (Publication no. 10.1787/d927bc18-en). Paris: OECD.

Qayum, A. (1991). A reformulation of the Leontief pollution model. *Economic Systems Research, 3*(4), 428–430.

Rasmussen, P. N. (1957). *Studies in Inter-sectoral Relations* (Vol. 15). E. Harck.Amsterdam: North Holland.

Ruiz-Nápoles, P. (2011). *Greenhouse gas emissions in Mexico, relative costs estimations and policy implications*. Paper presented at the 19th International Input-Output Conference, Alexandria VA.

Ruiz-Nápoles, P. (2012). *Low carbon development strategy for Mexico: An input – output analysis* (pp. 69). United Nations Environment Program (UNEP) French Agency for Development (AFD). Mexico City: Secretary of Environment and Natural Resources of Mexico.

Ruiz-Nápoles, P. (2013). *Crecimiento bajo en carbono y adopción de tecnologías para la mitigación: Los casos de la Argentina y el Brasil*. Santiago de Chile, Chile: División de Desarrollo Sostenible y Asentamientos Humanos. CEPAL, Unidad de Cambio Climático.

Ruiz-Nápoles, P., and Puchet-Anyul, M. (2014). *Choice of techniques for minimizing Greenhouse-gas emissions: an Input-Output exercise for the Mexican economy*. Paper presented at the 22nd IIOA Conference, Lisbon, Portugal.

Steenge, A. E. (1978). Environmental repercussions and the economic structure: Further comments. *The Review of Economics and Statistics*, vol. 60 no. 3, 482–486.

Stern, N. H. (2006). Stern review on the economics of climate change. London, UK: HM Treasury.

Stern, N. H. (2007). *The economics of climate change: The Stern review*. Cambridge: Cambridge University Press.

Ten Raa, T. (2006). *The economics of input-output analysis*. Cambridge: Cambridge University Press.

Timmer, M. P., Dietzenbacher, E., Los, B., Stehrer, R., and de Vries, G. J. (2015). An illustrated user guide to the world iInput – output database: The case of global automotive production. *Review of International Economics, 23*(3), 575–605.

UNFCCC. (2015). *Paris agreement*. United Nations Framework Convention on Climate Change. http://unfccc.int/paris_agreement/items/9485.php

Wilting, H. C., Faber, A., and Idenburg, A. M. (2004). *Exploring technology scenarios with an input-output model*. Paper presented at the International Conference on "Input-Output and General Equilibrium: Data, Modelling and Policy Analysis". September 2–4 2004 Brussels, Belgium.

The World Bank 2017. *World GHG emissions*. Retrieved from http://data.worldbank.org/indicator/EN.ATM.GHGT.KT.CE

The World Bank 2017. World development indicators. Retrieved from http://data.world bank.org/

World Resources Institute. (2016). *CAIT contributions map*. World Resources Institute Retrieved from http://cait.wri.org/indc/

# 12 Life-cycle environmental and natural resource implications of energy efficiency technologies

*Sangwon Suh, Edgar Hertwich, Stefanie Hellweg and Alissa Kendall*

## Introduction

According to the International Energy Agency (IEA), energy efficiency improvement since 1990 avoided over 10 billion metric tonnes of $CO_2$ emissions (IEA, 2015), which amount to about 20% of current annual greenhouse gas (GHG) emissions at the global scale. Improvement in energy efficiency of production was also identified as the largest source of GHG emission reductions in the 5th Assessment Report of the Intergovernmental Panel for Climate Change (IPCC, 2014) (Edenhofer et al., 2014; Chapter 5).

As such, many views energy efficiency as a truly benign source of energy. Lovins (2005), for example, states, "Increasing energy end-use efficiency [. . .] is generally the largest, least expensive, most benign, most quickly deployable, least visible, least understood, and most neglected way to provide energy services." On the other hand, it is also well understood that energy efficiency reduces the costs of energy services, thereby growing demand and economic production, and potentially negating its benefits (Saunders, 1992). Despite the presence of such 'rebound effects', literature generally finds favorable net effect of energy efficiency improvement with regard to GHG emission mitigation (Barker et al., 2007; Bentzen, 2004; Greening et al., 2000; Sorrell, 2007).

Energy efficiency improvement is often achieved by deploying new energy efficient infrastructure, equipment, or technology, which has implications for net life-cycle environmental and natural resource impacts. Moreover, among the existing life-cycle assessment (LCA) studies on energy efficiency, few cover more than GHG emissions (Bribián et al., 2011; Hawkins et al., 2013; Kneifel, 2010; Tähkämö et al., 2012). Comparisons between different efficiency technologies based on existing studies is further hampered by the variations in the underlying system boundary and data sources among studies.

The recent publications of the aforementioned special issue aims at advancing our understanding of life-cycle environmental and natural resource implications of energy efficiency technologies. Contributions to the special issue cover a range of technologies – for both production and consumption of energy – including lighting, building energy management, co-generation, copper smelting, industrial symbiosis, and transportation and logistics. It also addresses a number of key questions in understanding the impact of energy efficiency technologies such as rebound effect and discrepancy between design and operation. Some of the publications in the special issue utilize the same pool of underlying data for life-cycle inventory (LCI) and a common methodological platform (Gibon et al., 2015) for an easier comparison between them.

What follows is a brief overview of these publications to the aforementioned special issue divided into four groups: (1) built environment, (2) industrial technologies, (3) transportation, and (4) unintended consequences.

## Built environment

Heating and cooling is the major driver of energy use in buildings. Building energy management systems (BEMS) allow a more dynamic and tighter control of heating and cooling in response to its demand through the use of various technologies including sensor networks, demand predictions, and information and communication technologies. As BEMS requires additional investment in – e.g. sensor networks and control equipment – it remains a question as to whether the benefits of the system as a whole outweigh the costs in terms of the environmental and natural resource impacts. Beucker et al. (2015) analyze the life-cycle environmental and natural resource benefits and costs of BEMS. The authors find that the amount of GHG emissions avoided by BEMS would be about 40 times greater than the emissions from producing the system. Global potential for GHG emission savings and environmental co-benefits of BEMS are found to be substantial when deployed widely. This study also shows that the GHG mitigation potential of BEMS through saving electricity diminishes in the next decades as underlying electricity is decarbonized under the 2°C scenario, whereas mitigation achieved through saving natural gas remains virtually unchanged.

Another approach to reduce building energy use for heating and cooling is to improve building envelopes. Pomponi et al. (2015) evaluate the life-cycle environmental impacts of double skin façade (DSF) using a detailed bill of materials and a building energy simulation tool combined with location-specific data. The results show that DSF reduces operational energy use, while adding additional impacts due to the materials needed for DSF. In particular, the study highlights the impacts embodied in the 'Structure & Clamp' and 'Glass' used for DSF. Overall, the study concludes that DSF provides a net GHG savings with potential environmental co-benefits.

Cubi et al. (2015) compare three roofing options: white roof, green roof, and photovoltaic (PV) roof. Previous studies on these roofing options are based on the conditions of low-latitude (i.e. warmer) countries. This study, on the other hand, focuses on high-latitude locations in Canada. The results show that PV roofs provide the most significant benefits, while white roofs applied to the three Canadian cities considered in this study increase the overall life-cycle environmental impacts due to increased heating demand. Green roofs are shown to provide net benefits in most impact categories considered, although smaller than those of PV roofs.

Another important energy use in buildings, beside heating and cooling, is artificial lighting. Bergesen et al. (2015) examine the potential for light emitting diode (LED) technologies in reducing GHG emissions and their life-cycle environmental and natural resource implications. The study incorporates the grid mix differences between eight global regions and technology roadmap scenarios for 2030 and 2050. The results show that LED technologies' potential to mitigate GHG emissions and their environmental co-benefits are significant in all regions. As some LED technologies require exotic metals, however, the results show that the LEDs increase metal resource consumption in the midterm, which is subsequently offset by material efficiency improvements in the long term.

## Industrial technologies

The second group of papers deals with industrial technologies. Kikuchi, Kanematsu, Ugo, et al. (2015) present an analysis of a potential industrial symbiosis centered on a regional cogeneration power plant utilizing local biomass resources on a remote island in Japan with a stand-alone energy system. The industrial symbiosis achieves energy efficiency by improving the utilization of a sugar mill cogeneration plant and by converting underutilized biomass residuals from a sugar mill (bagasse) along with wood residues from mills and forest thinning. The study concludes that implementing industrial symbiosis strategies and using local resources can provide up to 16% more of the island's electricity demand than is currently met. The different qualities of energy in supply and demand (e.g. characterized by temperature of generated heat), as well as the spatial and temporal matching of supply and demand, are important factors in determining total fossil energy savings.

In a companion paper, Kikuchi, Kanematsu, Sato, et al. (2015) present an energy cascading study for Japan and assess the future environmental impacts of distributed energy systems. They examined the possibilities for increased energy efficiency in industry through the use of distributed co-generation (heat and power) and multi-generation (heat, power, and steam) technologies. Qualities of energy supply and demand were collected for industrial sectors in Japan. Currently, most industrial processes operate at low temperatures between 50 and 100°C, illustrating the potential of substituting single-generation technologies (boilers or power generators) with multi-generation technologies and highlighting opportunities for industrial (trans-sector) symbiosis. The role of co-generation is examined in future scenarios up to the year 2050, using LCA for the evaluation. The future grid mix proved to be a sensitive parameter for the performance of cogeneration technologies.

The paper by Kulczycka et al. (2015) also deals with the future evolution of technology performance, but in the sector of the metal industry, focusing on copper smelting technologies. LCA was used to assess the environmental impacts of shaft and flash furnace-based smelting technologies. Future changes in these technologies as well as the background system were considered within a scenario analysis. The results refer to a functional unit of 1 tonne of refined Cu. The results show that the flash-furnace technology outperforms the shaft furnace in terms of environmental impacts. For example, reductions of GHG emissions of between 29 and 56% are simulated, for 2010 and 2015, respectively, by only switching to the flash-furnace technology. Further environmental improvement can be achieved by changes in the electricity mix. Overall, improvements are projected to be larger in the coming decades, flattening out in the future.

## Transportation

The third group of papers focuses on transportation and logistics. Nahlik et al. (2015) analyze life-cycle impacts of freight transportation in California and the potential for reducing them under the constraints imposed by the existing configuration of transportation infrastructure and modal preference that limits intermodal substitution. Previous LCA studies tend to compare different modes of freight transportation using ton-km as the functional unit, while in reality, substitution between them is severely limited by various constraints such as infrastructure and market configurations. The authors show that heavy-duty trucks are responsible for the majority of the direct GHG emissions from freight movement within California and compare a number of options to reduce them. Based on the comparison and a scenario analysis, the authors show that improvement in energy efficiency of freight movement through increased hybrid or liquid natural gas (LNG) trucks alone is unlikely to accomplish the GHG emission reduction goal set by the California Air Resources Board and a rapid penetration of what the authors call, 'zero emission vehicles (ZEVs)' would be needed.

Taptich et al. (2015) analyzed the life-cycle GHG emissions of fuel efficiency improvement, demand switching between modes, and large-scale electrification of fleets for both freight and passenger transportation technologies of 2010. The study then extends the analysis to 2030 and 2050 using IEA's Blue Map scenario and distinguishes eight global regions. Results show significant regional differences in environmental impacts among the options analyzed. They find as much as 90% GHG emission reduction potential through fuel efficiency improvement in passenger transportation, but find much smaller gains from freight. They also emphasize that no single strategy will serve all regions. For example, vehicle electrification generally results in GHG emission reductions in OECD countries, while in non-OECD countries, electrification may increase emissions due to carbon-intensive electricity. The study finds larger GHG emission reduction potential in non-OECD countries due to their relatively low fuel efficiency standards.

## Unintended consequences

Freeman et al. (2015) address the rebound effect using a novel approach through employing a systems dynamics model rather than using a more common econometric or equilibrium approach. The focus of their research is the GHG emissions of private cars in the United Kingdom. Their model allows them to explore relationships between different variables that can, potentially, explain past developments. They can also be used to explore future developments and simulate the effect of policies. Their modeling indicates that the structural rebound largely offsets the emissions gains to be expected from efficiency gains alone. Assessing the European Union's policy target of reducing GHG emissions by 40% by 2030, the paper finds that all considered strategies need to be employed to achieve this target and that efficiency gains by themselves will not suffice, given rebound effects.

## Future research needs

In this issue, we gathered assessments of the environmental implications of energy efficiency improvements in buildings, transport, metal refining, and combined heat and power production. The coverage of technology options, while broad, is both selective and not comprehensive. Reviewing the literature, there are many options for efficiency and demand-side reductions that have not yet been assessed from a life-cycle point of view, calling for additional research in this direction.

Although the analyses presented in these articles incorporate a large amount of quantitative information, data availability and quality, especially those from developing and least-developed countries, remain a challenge. It is also notable that quantitative uncertainty analysis beyond sensitivity analysis is beyond the scope of the studies presented in this chapter.

One of the biggest challenges in understanding the efficacy of efficiency technologies is the al dimension. Inherent behavioral indeterminacy and our limited understanding of human decision-making processes are, in our opinion, the key elements missing in some of the optimistic views on efficiency technologies. Decisions have to be made based on imperfect knowledge and limited foresight, and under dynamic market conditions. More fundamentally, it is a human condition to make mistakes and suboptimal choices, which may create a path-dependency in technology choice. In these circumstances, understanding whether, to what extent, and how rapidly a certain technology will be adopted by the society becomes a challenging yet crucial question in assessing its life-cycle environmental and natural resource costs and benefits.

Another area of research need is the understanding of innovation. Innovations are, by definition, hard to predict. At the same time, our ability to understand the outcomes of promoting an energy efficiency technology depends on our ability to understand how rapidly the technology will evolve relative to competing technologies. The current state of practice is to assume a fixed efficiency improvement, say, 1.5%/annum. Due to the exponential nature of such parameters, the results are often highly sensitive to such assumptions.

## Discussion

Overall, the picture of energy efficiency technologies painted by the recent literature reviewed in this chapter is somewhat complex. The benefits of efficiency technologies are clear: they reduce GHG emissions and allow co-benefits from a life-cycle point of view (Bergesen et al., 2015; Beucker et al., 2015; Kikuchi, Kanematsu, Sato, et al., 2015; Kikuchi, Kanematsu, Ugo, et al., 2015; Kulczycka et al., 2015; Pomponi et al., 2015). However, the magnitude – and in a few cases even the sign – of such effects vary widely among the technologies and regions considered due to the climatic conditions (Cubi et al., 2015), transportation infrastructure (Nahlik et al., 2015), and energy systems that they are embedded in (Taptich et al., 2015). As a result, in some cases, such as electrification of passenger cars in the regions with carbon-intensive electricity (Taptich et al., 2015), efficiency technologies may even increase overall GHG emissions. A few studies also indicate a trade-off especially between environmental and resource objectives (Bergesen et al., 2015). Although the overall amount of additional resource needs for implementing efficiency technologies may be small, some elements may raise concerns given the scarcity and heterogeneity of supply. Moreover, it is a sobering observation that, although the potential reduction in GHG emissions and other environmental impacts through efficiency technologies can be substantial, efficiency technologies alone will not be able to meet the GHG emission targets considered in this chapter (Freeman et al., 2015; Taptich et al., 2015), thus calling for a concerted action involving multiple instruments to cope with climate change.

## Acknowledgement

This chapter was reproduced with minor modification from its original published form as an editorial for the *Journal of Industrial Ecology* for the special issue that the authors co-edited (*Suh et al., 2016*; DOI: 10.1111/jiec.12435).

## Notes

1  www.unep.org/resourcepanel/
2  Available free online at http://onlinelibrary.wiley.com/doi/10.1111/jiec.2016.20.issue-2/ issuetoc.

## References

Barker, T., Ekins, P., and Foxon, T. (2007). The macro-economic rebound effect and the UK economy. *Energy Policy*, *35*(10), 4935–4946.
Bentzen, J. (2004). Estimating the rebound effect in US manufacturing energy consumption. *Energy Economics*, *26*(1), 123–134.
Bergesen, J. D., Tähkämö, L., Gibon, T., and Suh, S. (2015). Potential long-term global environmental implications of efficient light-source technologies. *Journal of Industrial Ecology*. 20(2), 263–275.
Beucker, S., Bergesen, J. D., and Gibon, T. (2015). Building energy management systems: Global potentials and environmental implications of deployment. *Journal of Industrial Ecology*. 20(2), 223–233.

Bribián, I. Z., Capilla, A. V., and Usón, A. A. (2011). Life cycle assessment of building materials: Comparative analysis of energy and environmental impacts and evaluation of the eco-efficiency improvement potential. *Building and Environment*, *46*(5), 1133–1140.

Cubi, E., Zibin, N. F., Thompson, S. J., and Bergerson, J. (2015). Sustainability of rooftop technologies in cold climates: Comparative life cycle assessment of white roofs, green roofs, and photovoltaic panels. *Journal of Industrial Ecology*. 20(2), 249–262.

Edenhofer, O., Pichs-Madruga, R., Sokona, Y., Farahani, E., Kadner, S., Seyboth, K., . . . Eickemeier, P. (2014). *Climate change 2014: Mitigation of climate change*. Contribution of Working Group III to the Fifth Assessment Report of the Intergovernmental Panel on Climate Change (pp. 511–597). New York, Cambridge University Press.

Freeman, R., Yearworth, M., and Preist, C. (2015). Revisiting Jevons' paradox with system dynamics: Systemic causes and potential cures. *Journal of Industrial Ecology*. 20(2), 349–353.

Gibon, T., Wood, R., Arvesen, A., Bergesen, J. D., Suh, S., and Hertwich, E. G. (2015). A methodology for integrated, multiregional life cycle assessment scenarios under large-scale technological change. *Environmental Science & Technology*, *49*(18), 11218–11226.

Greening, L. A., Greene, D. L., and Difiglio, C. (2000). Energy efficiency and consumption – the rebound effect – a survey. *Energy Policy*, *28*(6), 389–401.

Hawkins, T. R., Singh, B., Majeau-Bettez, G., and Strømman, A. H. (2013). Comparative environmental life cycle assessment of conventional and electric vehicles. *Journal of Industrial Ecology*, *17*(1), 53–64.

IEA. (2015). *Energy efficiency market report 2015*. Paris, France: IEA.

IPCC. (2014). Summary for policymakers. In *Climate change 2014: Mitigation of climate change*. Contribution of Working Group III to the Fifth Assessment Report of the Intergovernmental Panel on Climate Change. Intergovernmental Panel on Climate Change. New York, Cambridge University Press.

Kikuchi, Y., Kanematsu, Y., Sato, R., and Nakagaki, T. (2015). Distributed cogeneration of power and heat within an energy management strategy for mitigating fossil fuel consumption. *Journal of Industrial Ecology*, 20(2), 289–303.

Kikuchi, Y., Kanematsu, Y., Ugo, M., Hamada, Y., and Okubo, T. (2015). Industrial symbiosis centered on a regional cogeneration power plant utilizing available local resources: A case study of Tanegashima. *Journal of Industrial Ecology*, 20(2), 276–288.

Kneifel, J. (2010). Life-cycle carbon and cost analysis of energy efficiency measures in new commercial buildings. *Energy and Buildings*, *42*(3), 333–340.

Kulczycka, J., Lelek, Ł., Lewandowska, A., Wirth, H., and Bergesen, J. D. (2015). Environmental impacts of energy-efficient Pyrometallurgical Copper smelting technologies: The consequences of technological changes from 2010 to 2050. *Journal of Industrial Ecology*, 20(2), 304–316.

Lovins, A. (2005). *Energy end-use efficiency*. Snowmass, CO: Rocky Mountain Institute.

Nahlik, M. J., Kaehr, A. T., Chester, M. V., Horvath, A., and Taptich, M. N. (2015). Goods movement life cycle assessment for greenhouse gas reduction goals. *Journal of Industrial Ecology*. 20(2), 317–328.

Pomponi, F., Piroozfar, P. A., and Farr, E. R. (2015). An investigation into GHG and non-GHG impacts of double skin Façades in office refurbishments. *Journal of Industrial Ecology*, 20(2), 234–248.

Saunders, H. D. (1992). The Khazzoom-Brookes postulate and neoclassical growth. *The Energy Journal*, 13(4), 131–148.

Sorrell, S. (2007). *The rebound effect: An assessment of the evidence for economy-wide energy savings from improved energy efficiency*. London: UK Energy Research Centre.

Suh, S., Hertwich, E., Hellweg, S., and Kendall, A. (2016). Life cycle environmental and natural resource implications of energy efficiency technologies. *Journal of Industrial Ecology, 20*(2), 218–222.

Tähkämö, L., Puolakka, M., Halonen, L., and Zissis, G. (2012). Comparison of life cycle assessments of LED light sources. *Journal of Light & Visual Environment, 36*(2), 44–54.

Taptich, M. N., Horvath, A., and Chester, M. V. (2015). Worldwide greenhouse gas reduction potentials in transportation by 2050. *Journal of Industrial Ecology*.20(20), 329–340.

# Part IV
# Policy tools

# 13 Carbon leakage risk criteria for improving INDC effectiveness

*Guadalupe Arce, Luis Antonio López,*
*María Ángeles Cadarso and Nuria Gómez*

## Introduction

The fight against climate change requires global action and the dissemination of effective international cooperation mechanisms (IEA, 2008; IPCC, 2007a). The Paris Agreement of 2015 constitutes a milestone in the fight against climate change as a multilateral agreement for 197 countries, both developed and emerging ones. These countries have introduced a national emission reduction plan based on quantities predefined in the agreement (intended nationally determined contributions, INDCs) for 2020 that can be updated every five years to avoid an increase in global average temperatures and to limit them to 1.5°C. However, once INDCs are announced, signatory countries, unilaterally or through agreements with other countries, are responsible for employing mitigation policies that allow them to reach such objectives. Achieving the more restrictive goals agreed upon in Paris requires the use of targeted and articulated measures that at the moment are not very well defined (Peters, 2016). In addition to the great expectations placed on carbon dioxide removal (CDR) technologies, reservations about their actual effectiveness have solicited caution and the need to continue to rely on carbon reduction policies as main instruments (Clarke, 2014; Fuss et al., 2014; Peters, 2016). In this regard, INDCs are an appropriate step forward that must be adequately implemented. Of the potential measures that could be considered for implementing INDCs, we focus on an improved version of the EU Emissions Trading System (EU ETS), which has proven effective for carbon curbing.

Reliance on individual national targets without a proper policy coordination between countries leads to the existence of carbon leakages via international trade since some countries could meet their commitments through such leakages. As more developed regions have access to technologies, economic capacities and cleaner sector structures, they can set more ambitious emissions reduction commitments than emerging and developing countries and can thereby encourage such leakages. With respect to these environmental terms, companies affected by increased production costs could transfer – either fully or partially – their emission-intensive activities or energy uses to countries with weaker environmental regulations that are less efficient in environmental terms (the so-called *pollution havens*) (Copeland and Taylor, 2004). In turn, developed countries can mitigate their domestic $CO_2$ emissions while shirking their responsibilities as producers. However, this is a "fake benefit", as such countries increase their carbon footprint as long as their imports from developing countries that are less efficient in environmental terms increase both directly and indirectly (Kanemoto et al., 2014; Skelton, 2013; Steen-Olsen et al., 2012).

Unilateral climate change policy makes it essential to study the impacts that such policies may have on the competitiveness of firms, sectors and countries (IEA, 2005). In this context, the European Union Emissions Trading Scheme (EU-ETS) is a key European instrument for achieving INDCs. In addition, it is one of the few mitigation policies that expressly considers in its design the threat of carbon leakages and the potential to significantly harm the competitiveness of EU industries: the main arguments presented by industry lobbies against the imposition of more stringent environmental policies and against the establishment of a full auctioning system (Monjon and Quirion, 2011). Therefore, the aim of this study is to assess whether Directive 2003/87/EC and subsequent amendment 2009/29/EC, which regulates the EU-ETS, allow for the adequate identification of sectors at risk of carbon leakages, thus preventing carbon leakages through international trade and serving as an effective tool keeping European Union (EU) on the path to the 1.5°C target.

Previous to the current implementation period of the EU-ETS (2013–2020), most emission allowances have been allocated to firms without cost (at least 95% during the first period, at least 90% in the second and at least 80% in the third). Under Directive 2009/29/EC, changes intended to increase EU-ETS efficiency (e.g. by increasing auctioned allowances) apply from 2013. Sectors not deemed at significant risk of carbon leakage received 80% of their benchmarked allocation for free in 2013, and this will decline to 30% in 2020 as a prelude to the application of the auction system to all allowances, which will be established in 2027. However, Directive 2009/29/EC provides exemptions for sectors or subsectors that are exposed to a "significant risk of carbon leakage". These sectors and subsectors will continue to receive all of their emissions allowances for free from 2013 to 2020 unless their carbon leakage exposure status changes. The Directive identifies industries that are vulnerable to carbon leakage depending on direct and/or indirect additional costs resulting from its application (criterion 1 of the Directive) and/or on the intensity of trade with third-party countries (criterion 2 of the Directive).[1] Therefore, it is essential to properly identify sectors actually subjected to a significant risk of carbon leakage and in which environmental costs are a key factor affecting firm location decisions (Carević, 2015; Demailly and Quirion, 2006; Peters and Hertwich, 2008; J. Reinaud, 2008b; Van Asselt and Brewer, 2010). Studies such as Kettner et al. (2008), Clò (2010), Sato et al. (2015), and Juergens et al. (2013), which seek to improve this identification, claim that EU-ETS operation must be improved because it is not possible to solve competitiveness problems in practice through the introduction of the ETS, and the EU-ETS also does not create sufficient incentives to reduce emissions.

The EU trade intensity criterion does not consider the emissions embodied in trade when identifying industries at risk of carbon leakage, nor does it recognize that the intensity of virtual carbon is different in developed and emerging economies; such calculations are presented in the carbon leakage literature (Peters and Hertwich, 2008). In addition, the trade intensity value serves as an inadequate basis for carbon leakage assessment, as it cannot measure the ability to pass through carbon costs (Sato et al., 2015). Thus, the Directive may be excluding industries at risk of carbon leakage because imports are produced in heavily polluting countries, although they are not important in relative monetary terms and as a result fail to reduce the EU carbon footprint, which could increase with the increase in such imports. Conversely, the Directive may be including other industries that do not present a real risk of carbon leakage, as imports come from less-polluting countries, and these industries may obtain windfall profits through free allocation (Martin et al., 2014).

The methodology proposed involves the use of an environmentally extended bilateral input-output model (BTIO, see Peters (2008)) to identify EU industries at direct risk of carbon leakage. We identify industries at a direct risk of carbon leakage (DRCL) by taking into account direct emissions linked to production in each sector and at total risk of carbon leakage (TRCL) when considering the total (both direct and indirect) amount of domestic carbon embodied. We identify sectors at risk of carbon leakage using these two criteria and compare them to sectors identified in the EU-ETS under the trade intensity criterion. We use data from the World Input-Output Database (WIOD), which provides an input-output framework combined with environmental accounts, thus allowing us to properly evaluate carbon leakage potentials depending on the virtual carbon content of international trade.

This chapter is organized as follows. Section 2 describes the methodology and databases used. Section 3 presents the main results of the study, and section 4 presents a discussion and conclusions.

## Methodological proposal

Carbon leakage is defined in the literature as a reduction in carbon dioxide emissions in countries that have signed agreements to reduce emissions that is over-compensated by an increase in emissions in countries that employ no mechanisms of emissions control (IPCC, 2007b). Peters and Hertwich (2008) distinguish between two types of carbon leakage: "strong carbon leakage," whereby production is moved from a country subjected to emissions reduction agreements to another with less-stringent environmental legislation, and "weak carbon leakage", which is calculated by taking into account $CO_2$ embodied in imports into countries imposing stricter environmental regulations from countries that have not signed an emissions reduction agreement. However, Jakob and Marschinski (2013), in reference to the EU, and L.-A. López et al. (2014), in reference to Spain, state that these measures of carbon leakage are not sufficient for evaluating the impact of climate policies on trade, as carbon leakage levels may increase not simply when the production of carbon-intensive goods has been offshored to more emission-intensive countries but simply when domestic exporters begin to use cleaner technologies.

The Directive 2009/29/EC considers whether a sector or subsector is exposed to significant carbon leakage risks according to two criteria. The first one requires a trade intensity level of higher than 10%, defined as the degree of openness in an industry in relation to surrounding regions, together with a substantial increase in production costs (higher than 5%) resulting from additional costs from implementing the Directive. The second criterion requires that there is a significant risk of carbon leakage by exclusively considering trade intensity (TI) (whenever it exceeds 30%). We focus on the latter criterion.

Trade intensity refers to the degree of openness in an industry relative to surrounding regions. The EU, according to Directive 2009/29/EC, calculates this as the ratio between the total value of exports to third-party countries to the value of imports from third-party countries divided by market size, as is shown in expression (13.1):

$$TI_i^r = \frac{x_i^r + \sum_{s=1}^n m_i^{rs}}{y_i^{rr} + \sum_{s=1}^n m_i^{rs}} \quad \forall r \text{ and } s \neq r, \tag{13.1}$$

where $TI_i^r$ refers to the trade intensity or trade openness of a region $r$ (in our case, the EU) for products fabricated by sector $i$, $x_i^r$ denotes exports from region $r$ of sector $i$, $y_i^{rr}$ refers to region $r$ domestic demand of sector $i$ and $\sum_{s=1}^n m_i^{rs}$ denotes total imports into sector $i$ in $n$ regions in which the EU trades. Finally, if we add the TI measure for all sectors, we have an index that reflects the risk of carbon leakage in the region. This applies for this measure and for the others defined below.

An isolated TI measure does not account for carbon leakage or virtual carbon embodied in trade flows; therefore, it lacks environmental efficiency (Clò, 2010). It is possible that for some EU sectors, a high TI does not involve high levels of virtual carbon or vice versa. As a result, the Directive may be failing to control carbon leakage by increasing polluting imports from sectors not considered at risk according to TI, thus reducing EU carbon producer responsibility at the expense of increasing the EU carbon footprint. As our proposal implies considering environmental efficiency, we combined the trade intensity measure proposed by the EU with carbon emissions content information. We define two measures for assessing risks of carbon leakage in sectors while taking into account virtual carbon embodied in trade. One might rightfully say that the TI indicator of the Directive is measured when the market's size is large enough to support carbon leakage, whereas a proper indicator should show whether the potential environmental harm is significant enough to result in carbon leakage.

Specifically, we use an emissions coefficient that differs for each region and sector such that we take into account the different $CO_2$ emissions intensity levels of each region for every sector. We use a BTIO model instead of a multiregional input-output approach (MRIO), as we are interested in considering complete information on virtual carbon related to trade flows[2] between each pair of regions.

The BTIO model provides emissions embodied in exports owing to the exporter country, and so it allows one to isolate the contributions of the last country to the global value chain. However, because intermediate imports and exports are endogenous, the MRIO model includes emissions embodied in exports from any inputs used in the production processes of the exported commodity; thus, only a part of the emissions corresponds to the exporter country, whereas the majority corresponds to industries and countries in its supply chain. Several papers have indicated that MRIO is the most appropriate tool for researching the related consumption-based accounting or carbon footprints and for the trade analysis of greenhouse gases (GHG) (Kanemoto et al., 2012; Peters et al., 2012; Wiedmann and Barrett, 2013). A MRIO is not more complete than a BTIO, but the two allocate global emissions differently. However, a MRIO makes it more difficult to allocate specific responsibility for emissions and hence represents a loss of transparency (Atkinson et al., 2011; Peters, 2008). Moreover, a BTIO is useful for associating virtual carbon flows with bilateral trade flows, which may indicate that the BTIO model is superior for the analysis of trade and climate policies among different regions whenever an agreement affects their jurisdictions (Peters, 2008; Zhang, 2012).[3] The fact that the INDCs set by signatories of the Paris Agreement are not sufficient to achieve the target of 2°C reinforces the need for further and broader mitigation actions and to explore potential bilateral agreements (e.g. President Obama's plan between the USA and China and free-trade agreements with the EU) (UNEP, 2016). This underscores the necessity for further regional/bilateral studies that can guide such agreements.

Two are the proposed measures. First, we consider direct emissions made by sector $i$ in each of the regions and define the "direct risk of carbon leakage" (DRCL) as follows:

$$DRCL_i^r = \frac{f_i^r x_i^r + \sum_{s=1}^{n} f_i^s m_i^{rs}}{f_i^r y_i^{rr} + \sum_{s=1}^{n} f_i^r m_i^{rs}} \quad \forall r \text{ and } s \neq r, \tag{13.2}$$

where $\left( f_i^r = \dfrac{F_i^r}{q_i^r} \right)$ is the region $r$ emission coefficient of each sector $I$ or emissions per unit produced calculated as emissions generated by each sector ($F_i^r$) when producing ($q_i^r$) and $f_i^s$ is the same coefficient for region $s$ (the rest of the regions). Direct domestic emissions by sector are obtained by summing up the rows of the emissions matrices of equation (13.2), and they are equal independent of the model used (BTIO or MRIO).

DRCL considers only direct domestic emissions incorporated into the productive processes of industries that trade in relation to domestic emissions associated with EU sector production. This measure matches the producer's responsibility or territory criterion used in the Kyoto Protocol for allocating emissions to countries. In those sectors that are at a direct risk of carbon leakage, aggressive home-country environmental legislation may incentivize the offshoring of production. This phenomenon has been referred to as the pollution-haven effect as proposed by Copeland and Taylor (2004) and as confirmed by Levinson and Taylor (2008) and Wagner and Timmins (2009). It is similar to weak and strong carbon leakage definitions provided by Peters and Hertwich (2008), although these authors consider total, direct and indirect emissions embodied in trade, and the direct measure that we propose does not consider indirect emissions.

Moreover, risks of carbon leakage are not only present due to the environmental efficiency of production processes but also due to the environmental impact of production processes of inputs used directly and indirectly. Considering total emissions, both direct and indirect, of a BTIO, the TRCL[4] criterion is

$$TRCL_i^r = \frac{\varepsilon_i^r x_i^r + \sum_{s=1}^{n} \varepsilon_i^s m_i^{rs}}{\varepsilon_i^r y_i^{rr} + \sum_{s=1}^{n} \varepsilon_i^s m_i^{rs}} \forall r \text{ and } s \neq r,$$  (13.3)

where $\varepsilon_i^r$ is the emissions multiplier, calculated as $\varepsilon_i^r = \hat{f}^r \left(I - A^{rr}\right)^{-1} i'$, that quantifies the direct and indirect emissions per unit of final demand (Atkinson et al., 2011; Kanemoto et al., 2012; Peters, 2008). In addition, $\hat{f}^r$ is a diagonal matrix, $i'$ is a column vector of zeros except for a one in the $i$th position in sector $i$ $A^{rr}$ and is the domestic technical coefficients matrix. As we are using a BTIO, we only include virtual carbon embodied in trade and emissions directly and indirectly embodied in inputs coming from within the country and exclude the contributions of global value chains.

TRCL includes the total, direct and indirect domestic emissions/virtual carbon embodied in EU sector production and in the traded goods of each sector (consistent with IPCC (2007b) and Peters and Hertwich (2008)). The incorporation of indirect emissions is important if we aim to reduce the environmental impacts of trade, as linkage effects are responsible for an increase of virtual carbon in relation to developed country imports versus those of emerging countries (L.-A. López et al., 2014). A complete measure that includes (domestic) indirect emissions linked to international trade has also been used by Jakob et al. (2013), though it is not commonly used in related literature that only considers electricity emissions (C. Böhringer et al., 2012; Steininger et al., 2014).

We used WIOD, specifically the "WIOT_Regs" for 2009, which provides information on trade and production together with environmental information and total $CO_2$ data for seven regions, with a disaggregation of 35 industries (Timmer et al., 2015). We consider all EU countries as a single region in addition to the Euro-zone and non-Euro EU to obtain information on six regions (EU, NAFTA, China, East Asia, BRIIAT and RoW)[5] and 35 industries.

## Results

As stated earlier, in attending to item 16 of Article 10 *bis* of Directive 2009/29/EC, the EU concludes that a sector or subsector is exposed to a significant risk of carbon leakage when the intensity of trade with third-party countries (TI from expression 1) exceeds 30%. Considering this, the sectors presenting a significant risk of carbon leakage are Mining and Quarrying (63%), Electrical and Optical Equipment (48%), Leather and Footwear (46%), Textiles and Textile Products (44%), Chemical (41%), Machinery (39%) and Transport Equipment (32%).[6] Trade intensity growth is explained by the increasing external openness of the European economy and by the intensification of international production fragmentation (Cadarso et al., 2010).

Figure 13.1 illustrates the trade intensity of each sector based on exports and imports and by country of origin. This distinction is relevant in relation to carbon leakages. First, policy implications are different when the risk of carbon leakage results from exports or imports, and when these imports come from developed or developing countries. When this is not taken into account, the TI criterion is limited in identifying exposure to international markets. Martin et al. (2014), for instance, propose considering sectors at risk of carbon leakage as only those presenting high levels of trade intensity and as those in less developed countries. Second, for industries whose main markets fall outside of domestic environmental policies, even when establishing border adjustments, the cost disadvantage is increased vis-á-vis competitors from abroad in foreign markets (Christoph Böhringer et al., 2015).

For six out of seven of the industries at risk of carbon leakage, the importance of exports based on the EU criterion of carbon leakage is significant. However, for Mining and Quarrying, the EU's risk of carbon leakage is attributed to imports of raw materials not found in the EU and mainly from RoW. The share of exports is particularly strong in high-technology industries (high value-added and significant

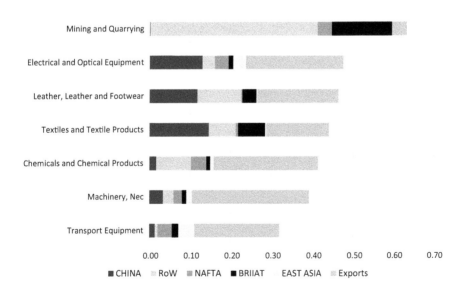

*Figure 13.1* Sectors at risk of carbon leakage according to the EU criterion of trade intensity (TI > 30%), 2009

product differentiation) related to Machinery, Transport Equipment, Chemicals and Electrical and Optical Equipment (e.g. computers), in which exports explain more than 73%, 65%, 62% and 50% of overall risks of carbon leakage, respectively. These figures reveal the strong capacities for European industries to satisfy domestic demand and to export to other regions of the world. However, in the two low-technology manufacturing sectors identified, Textile Products and Leather and Footwear, the weight of exports can explain only 35% and 43% of the risk of carbon leakage. These industries have allocated the offshoring process to low-wage countries because they offer unskilled labour, and when relocation is complete, goods enter the economy as final goods (Cadarso et al., 2010; Feenstra and Hanson, 1996). As a result, the Textiles, Leather and Footwear industries, to which Electrical and Optical Equipment must be added, show the most significant largest imports from China, respectively, accounting for 15%, 12% and 13% of trade intensity levels.

Nevertheless, the TI index only accounts for trade by measuring risks of carbon leakage. The indicator is not sufficient because it does not measure carbon leakage itself or virtual carbon in trade flows. The TI measure implicitly assumes that the likelihood of carbon leakage increases with the size of the commodity market. It has also been shown that companies most affected by climate legislation and more susceptible to carbon leakage are carbon-intensive industries (Martin et al., 2014). Therefore, TI cannot answer the following question: How much virtual carbon is involved in such traded commodities? While some carbon-intensive industries do not trade intensively with other countries, and for this reason are not considered at risk of carbon leakage according to TI, their imports can be significant contributors to the EU carbon footprint. Moreover, the situation may change over time when costs of production increase (Sato et al., 2015), causing carbon leakage to potentially occur. Our objective is to measure risks of carbon leakage by considering the carbon content of such trade through the proposed DRCL and TRCL measures.

Figure 13.2 shows sectors (at the NACE 2 level) that for 2009 were at risk of carbon leakage according to our criteria and compares the results with the TI index. Broadly, two features of the figure should be commented on. First, the number of sectors at risk of carbon leakage increases alongside direct and total virtual carbon in the measure (DRCL and TRCL, respectively) rather than the intensity of trade alone. Second, sectors show similar ordering for all of the criteria but with increasing exception in the order set by the TI index: four exceptions in the DRCL and eight in the TRCL. This means that differences are more remarkable when we use total carbon embodied in trade, TRCL, rather than the other two measures. More precisely, we comment on results obtained from the measures proposed.

### *Sectors at risk of carbon leakage according to the DRCL measure.*

When we take into account the direct emissions of each sector, the new approach does not allow us to exclude any sector at risk of carbon leakage previously

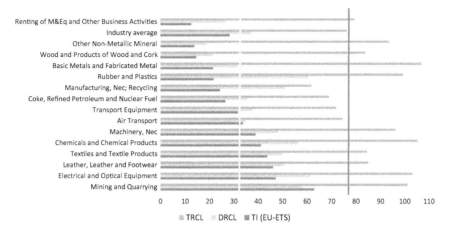

*Figure 13.2*  Sectors at risk of carbon leakage according to TI (TI > 30%), DRCL (DRCL > 30%) and TRCL (TRCL > industry average = 76.46%), 2009 (%)

Note: The first vertical line shows the 30% threshold and the second line shows the industry average of the TRCL threshold

identified by EU legislation. In addition, we can identify four new sectors at risk of carbon leakage (Figures 13.3 and 13.4). Two of these, Rubber and Plastics (60%) and Basic Metals and Fabricated Metals (32%), produce homogeneous intermediate inputs and are also intensive sectors of direct emissions; therefore, it is easy for both to cause carbon leakage (J. Reinaud, 2008a). It must be noted that the energy processing industry (Coke, Refined Petroleum and Nuclear Fuel (36%) and Manufacturing, Nec and Recycling (51%)), which is intensive in processes of international fragmentation of production, produces materials that enter the EU as final goods.

Considering the carbon content of trade increases risk in sectors such as the Rubber and Plastics and Manufacturing sectors to maximum levels. However, they were not found to be at risk when using the TI measure of the Directive. In these cases, imports in monetary value were not relevant enough, but their carbon embodiment shows that importing these products (mainly from RoW, see Figure 13.3) can have a strong impact on the carbon footprint of the EU. The positive difference between DRCL and TI shows that these sectors exhibit a higher share of direct emissions in trade than their share of trade measured in monetary terms: This occurs for all of the sectors considered with the exception of the Mining and Quarrying industry, which reaches high trade and emissions intensity levels. Due to the lower emissions intensity of EU industries, the incorporation of direct emissions results in a decline in the share of total exports from the EU according to the DRCL measure and in an increase in the importance of EU imports relative to that found using the TI measure (Figures 13.2 and 13.3).

A trade structure can determine the success or failure of an environmental policy. New trading patterns whereby countries import large proportions of virtual

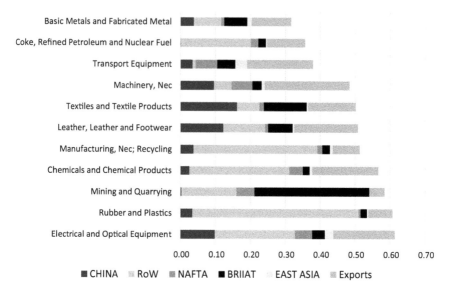

*Figure 13.3* Sectors at risk of carbon leakage according to the DRCL criterion (DRCL > 30%), 2009 (%).

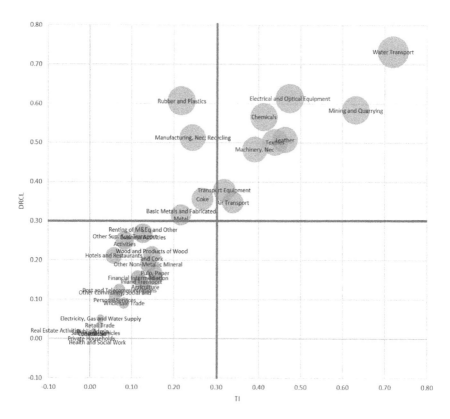

*Figure 13.4* Comparison of sectors at risk of carbon leakage following the TI and DRCL measures

carbon from emerging countries must be considered in addition to trade intensity levels and the origins and carbon intensity of imports. In Figure 13.3, we highlight the importance of direct emissions embodied in imports from the RoW for almost all sectors (Textiles, Leather and Footwear; Electrical and Optical Equipment from China and from BRIIAT in Textiles and Basic and Fabricated metals). In fact, at an international scale, non-energy intensive manufactured products versus energy intensive products dominate net transfers of $CO_2$ emissions from non-Annex-B to Annex-B countries (Peters et al., 2011). Including these as industries with carbon leakage risks is convenient when the aim is to reduce the carbon footprint of the EU economy.

### 3.2. *Total risk of carbon leakage (TRCL) by sector*

The TRCL measure results in more differences in relation to the other criteria. These differences are explained by the fact that the TRCL index changes the position of a sector relative to TI and DTCL. Rather than considering a sector as a producer, TRCL considers a sector as a consumer of inputs required directly and indirectly for sector production. Within the context of a BTIO model, it implies that TRCL accounts for domestic indirect emissions as well. As is shown in Figure 13.1 (and Table 13.A.1 in the annex), figures of TRCL are much larger than those of TI and DRCL because through the calculation of total domestic virtual carbon, we allocate to the producing sector total emissions embodied in domestic inputs directly and indirectly used to produce a good. This makes it necessary to change the threshold to consider a sector at risk of carbon leakage. We choose as a threshold the industry average of total carbon content (76.46%). Thus a sector is at risk of carbon leakage when its TRCL value is higher than the average (Figure 13.2).

In terms of environmental policies, this measure shows that the negative impact of international trade on the environment is dependent on the relevance of indirect virtual carbon in goods traded, thus highlighting the need to take it into account if we wish to reduce its impact (L. A. López et al., 2013). The TRCL measure is useful in assessing domestic indirect carbon leakage,[7] which is associated with the impact of EU-ETS legislation in terms of increasing sector costs as electricity costs, among others, that are transmitted to final prices (J. Reinaud, 2008a) and which are subject to the Directive.

According to the TRCL (Figure 13.5), four sectors previously at risk of carbon leakage are no longer at risk: Air Transport; Transport Equipment; Coke, Refined Petroleum and Nuclear Fuel; and Manufacturing, Nec. and Recycling. The first two were found to present risks of carbon leakage according to TI and the last two were added according to the DRCL. This means that these sectors have directly polluting production processes, but the production processes of the inputs that they use are not as polluting as those of other industrial sectors. By contrast, two new industries are at risk of carbon leakage, as they use comparatively more inputs, directly or indirectly, with polluting production processes: Wood and Wood products and Cork and Other Non-Metallic Minerals and the

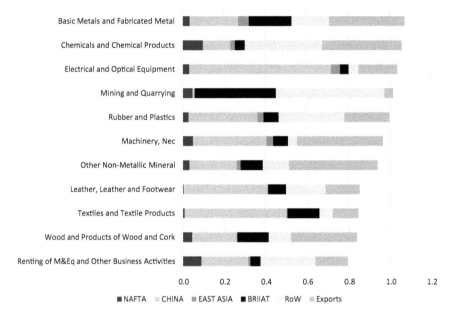

*Figure 13.5* Sectors at risk of carbon leakage according to the TRCL criterion (TRCL >
76.46%, industry average), 2009 (%).

Note: This figure does not show the water transport sector, which presents the highest TRCL values
(3,850, due to exports 3,315).

service sector (M&Eq Renting and Other Business Activities). This is also shown
in Figure 13.6. The absence of carbon content measurements under the TI criterion implies excluding sectors in quadrant B and including some of quadrants C
and D. Differences in risks of carbon leakage marked by the two criteria may be
behind concerns regarding the excess free allocation of allowances in the EU-ETS
(Sato et al., 2015). This result was also found by Martin et al. (2014) from a firm-
level dataset of interviews with managers in six European countries.

By distinguishing between imports and exports, and by considering the origins
of imports, Figure 13.5 shows the growing significance of carbon emissions from
China in almost all sectors at risk of carbon leakage when indirect emissions are
considered. This can be attributed to emissions of the highly polluting electricity
sector, which under the TRCL measure are redistributed to the sector that uses
electricity inputs. As a result, a Chinese emissions market would relax carbon
leakage risks in these sectors. In addition, being export or import intensive could
have different implications for sector carbon leakage risks (Martin et al., 2014).
Sectors show very different patterns regarding import and export emissions content. On the one hand, the more export oriented a sector is, the more likely that
sector will experience a cost disadvantage. On the other hand, the carbon content
of imports should be relevant in cases of domestic full auctioning with border tax

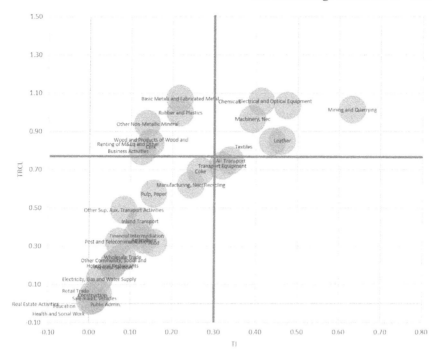

*Figure 13.6* Comparison of sectors at risk of carbon leakage following the TI and TRCL
measures

adjustments for imports, which in combination is said to offer added advantages
in terms of mitigation (Sato et al., 2015).

The downside of the TRCL measure relates to the fact that it holds industries
responsible for polluting inputs that they acquire along their global value chain,
partly because they lack information about their own chains (O'Rourke, 2014)
but also because this could raise concerns regarding their viability (as is shown by
Christoph Böhringer et al. (2015) for Switzerland and by Cadarso et al. (2012) for
Spain for contexts of shared responsibility).

## Conclusions

Our analysis identifies industries at risk of carbon leakage based on the carbon
content of trade as a necessary first step to addressing the problem of which anti-
leakage measure is more efficient: a border adjustment tax or a free allocation of
allowances (C. Böhringer et al., 2012; Monjon and Quirion, 2011). In addition,
three elements will force the EU to evaluate other mitigation policies that are not
solely based on the producer responsibility principle. First, under current legislation, the share of virtual carbon embodied in the imports of developed countries has continued to grow (Peters et al., 2012), both among emerging countries

and developing countries (Arce et al., 2016). Second, developed countries are committed to ensuring unilateral mitigation and more ambitious policies (Barrett et al., 2013). Finally, the existing INDCs are not sufficient to meet the target of limiting the temperature increase to 2°C, as outlined by the Paris Agreement.

Of the improvements needed to make the EU-ETS a better tool, we focus on the number of free allowances and on their allocation. The number of free allowances must be carefully calculated so that the resulting price for allowances after inter-firm negotiations occur is in line with an adequate globally uniform carbon price. Although the globally uniform carbon price is a profusely studied theoretical concept, discussing it can lead to an adequate resulting price for the EU-ETS. Whether the EU-ETS is exportable and how it should be applied under different geographical scenarios are central questions that must be addressed. We consider the ETS to be a sound and realistic policy alternative to a uniform carbon price.

The proposed TRCL criterion would be appropriate as a tool for the assessment of competitiveness loses that a full auctioning of allowances would cause in European products relative to imported ones. This can be concluded because the TRCL measures the increase in the relative costs of domestic production due to emissions allowances in terms of direct carbon content and total embodied virtual carbon (direct and indirect).

Once industries at risk of carbon leakage are identified, the next step involves assessing the allocation of allowances following a consumption-based principle rather than the producer-based one used in the Directive: a full auctioning of allowances to emissions linked to the share of production directed to domestic final demand plus emissions embodied in imports and free allocation to virtual carbon embodied in exports. Unilateral policies combined with border carbon adjustments and export rebates appear to be some of most efficient ways to reduce leakages, which indicates the advantage of following a policy more similar to consumption-based accounting. Jakob et al. (2013), Sakai and Barrett (2016) and Steininger et al. (2014) evaluate the effectiveness of the use of a consumption-based criterion to establish a border tax adjustment through a unilateral climate policy. They reach different conclusions regarding the reduction of carbon leakages via the proposed measure, with the first and second coming to negative conclusions and with the third coming to a positive conclusion. As a result, more analyses based on a broader range of allocation emissions alternatives must be conducted.

### Acknowledgement

We gratefully acknowledge the support of the Ministry of Economy, Industry and Competitiveness (project ECO2016–78939-R) and the regional government "Junta de Comunidades de Castilla-La Mancha" (project PPII-2014–006-P). Guadalupe Arce also thanks the Spanish Ministry of Education, Culture and Sports through the National FPU Program (grant ref. FPU 13/05869).

# Notes

1 Specifically, it considers that a sector or subsector is at significant risk of carbon leakage if the sum of direct and indirect additional costs from the application of the Directive 2009/29/EC production cost increases by more than 5% and when trade intensity exceeds 10%; thus, both criteria are considered. However, only one is sufficient when the sum of direct and indirect additional costs from the application of the Directive increases by at least 30% or when the trade intensity among third-party non-community countries exceeds 30%; in such cases, the EU will also consider a sector or subsector to be at a significant risk of carbon leakage.
2 The BRIO model provides emissions embodied in exports owed to the exporter country. However, the MRIO model includes emissions embodied in exports from inputs used in production processes of the exported commodity; thus, only part of the emissions corresponds to the exporter country, whereas the majority corresponds to industries and countries that supply these inputs.
3 For example, under the EU-ETS, benchmarking is established based on technologies used in regions signed to the agreement (similar a BTIO) while gradually assigning emissions rights depending on the risks of carbon leakage to other regions. In this sense, the agreement encourages technological changes within the regions and at the same time penalizes other global value chains.
4 The TRCL result in expression (13.3) is a number, but we can obtain a matrix that replaces the final demand vector (in our case exports and imports) with a diagonal matrix and multiply it by a matrix of the emissions multiplier rather than by a vector, and we can use f as a diagonal matrix. This matrix result presents in columns the same result that we have in (13.3), and in rows, it provides only direct emissions from the sector embodied in trade; therefore, the result would be the same as expression (13.2).
5 Euro-zone: Austria, Belgium, Cyprus, Estonia, Finland, France, Germany, Greece, Ireland, Italy, Luxembourg, Malta, the Netherlands, Portugal, Slovakia, Slovenia and Spain. Non-Euro EU: Bulgaria, the Czech Republic Denmark, Hungary, Latvia, Lithuania, Poland, Romania, Sweden and the United Kingdom. NAFTA: Canada, Mexico and the USA. East Asia: Japan, Korea and Taiwan. BRIIAT: Australia, Brazil, India, Indonesia, Russia and Turkey.
6 Water and Air Transport are the only service sectors at risk of carbon leakage according to the directive criterion. However, these services are particular in that it is necessary to transport commodities through international trade, although this is concentrated at the global level to a few countries, and this excludes its consideration as a sector at risk of carbon leakage.
7 The proposed measure is superior to that proposed under the 2009/29/EC Directive in that we consider direct electricity costs and indirect costs associated with all inputs consumed by export industries (broadening the criterion to scope 3 of the GHG Protocol).

# References

Arce, G., López, L. A., and Guan, D. (2016). Carbon emissions embodied in international trade: The post-China era. *Applied Energy*, 184, 1063–1072. doi: http://dx.doi.org/10.1016/j.apenergy.2016.05.084

Atkinson, G., Hamilton, K., Ruta, G., and Van Der Mensbrugghe, D. (2011). Trade in "virtual carbon": Empirical results and implications for policy. *Global Environmental Change*, 21(2), 563–574. doi: http://dx.doi.org/10.1016/j.gloenvcha.2010.11.009

Barrett, J., Peters, G. P., Wiedmann, T., Scott, K., Lenzen, M., Roelich, K., and Le Quéré, C. (2013). Consumption-based GHG emission accounting: A UK case study. *Climate Policy*, 13(4), 451–470.

Böhringer, C., André, M., and Schneider, J. (2015). Carbon tariffs revisited. *Journal of the Association of Environmental and Resource Economists, 2*(4), 629–672. doi: 10.1086/683607

Böhringer, C., Carbone, J., and Rutherford, T. (2012). Unilateral climate policy design: Efficiency and equity implications of alternative instruments to reduce carbon leakage. *Energy Economics, 34*, 208–217.

Cadarso, M. A., Gómez, N., López, L. A., and Tobarra, M. A. (2010). $CO_2$ emissions of international freight transport and offshoring: Measurement and allocation. *Ecological Economics, 69*, 1682–1694.

Cadarso, M. A., Gómez, N., López, L. A., and Tobarra, M. A. (2012). International trade and shared environmental responsibility by sector: An application to the Spanish economy. *Ecological Economics, 83*, 221–235.

Carević, M. (2015). Carbon leakage in the EU in the light of the Paris climate agreement. *Croatian Yearbook of European Law and Policy, 11*, 47–71.

Clarke, L. E. A. (2014). *Climate change 2014: Mitigation of climate change* (O. E. A. Edenhofer, Ed.). Cambridge: Cambridge University Press.

Clò, S. (2010). Grandfathering, auctioning and carbon Leakage: Assessing the inconsistencies of the new ETS Directive. *Energy Policy, 38*, 2420–2430.

Copeland, B., and Taylor, M. S. (2004). Trade, growth and the environment. *Journal of Economic Literature, 42*(1), 7–71.

Demailly, D., and Quirion, P. (2006). $CO_2$ abatement, competitiveness and leakage in the European cement industry under the EU-ETS: Grandfathering versus output-based allocation. *Climate Policy, 6*, 93–113.

Feenstra, R. C., and Hanson, G. H. (1996). Globalization, outsourcing, and wage inequality. *The American Economic Review, 86*(2), 240–245.

Fuss, S., Canadell, J. G., Peters, G. P., Tavoni, M., Andrew, R. M., Ciais, P., . . . Yamagata, Y. (2014). Betting on negative emissions. *Nature Climate Change, 4*(10), 850–853. doi: 10.1038/nclimate2392

IEA. (2005). *Industrial competitiveness under the European Union Emissions Trading Scheme*. Paris: IEA.

IEA. (2008). *World energy outlook 2008*. Paris: IEA.

IPCC. (2007a). *Climate change 2007: Synthesis report*. Paris: IPCC.

IPCC. (2007b). *Mitigation*. Contribution of Working Group III to the Fourth Assessment Report of the Intergovernmental Panel on Climate Change. (B. Metz, O. R. Davidson, P. R. Bosch, R. Dave, & L. A. Meyer, Ed.). Cambridge and New York: Cambridge University Press.

Jakob, M., and Marschinski, R. (2013). Interpreting trade-related $CO_2$ emission transfers. *Nature Climate Change, 3*(1), 19–23. doi: www.nature.com/nclimate/journal/v3/n1/abs/nclimate1630.html#supplementary-information

Jakob, M., Marschinski, R., and Hübler, M. (2013). Between a rock and a hard place: A trade-theory analysis of leakage under production- and consumption-based policies. *Environmental and Resource Economics, 56*(1), 47–72. doi: 10.1007/s10640–013–9638-y

Juergens, I., Barreiro-Hurlé, J., and Vasa, A. (2013). Identifying carbon leakage sectors in the EU ETS and implications of results. *Climate Policy, 13*(1), 89–109. doi: 10.1080/14693062.2011.649590

Kanemoto, K., Moran, D., Lenzen, M., and Geschke, A. (2014). International trade undermines national emission reduction targets: New evidence from air pollution. *Global Environmental Change, 24*(0), 52–59. doi: http://dx.doi.org/10.1016/j.gloenvcha.2013.09.008

Kanemoto, K., Lenzen, M., Peters, G. P., Moran, D. D., and Geschke, A. (2012). Frameworks for comparing emissions associated with production, consumption and international trade. *Environmental Science and Technology*, *46*, 172–179.

Kettner, C., Koppl, A., Schleicher, S., and Thenius, G. (2008). Stringency and distribution in the EU emissions trading scheme: First evidence. *Climate Policy*, *8*(1), 46–61.

Levinson, A., and Taylor, M. S. (2008). Unmasking the pollution Haven effect. *International Economic Review*, *49*(1), 223–254.

López, L.-A., Arce, G., and Zafrilla, J. (2014). Financial crisis, virtual carbon in global value chains, and the importance of linkage effects: The Spain – China case. *Environmental Science & Technology*, 48(1), 36–44. doi: 10.1021/es403708m.

López, L. A., Arce, G., and Zafrilla, J. E. (2013). Parcelling virtual carbon in the pollution haven hypothesis. *Energy Economics*, *39*, 177–186. doi: http://dx.doi.org/10.1016/j.eneco.2013.05.006

Martin, R., Muûls, M., de Preux, L. B., and Wagner, U. J. (2014). On the empirical content of carbon leakage criteria in the EU Emissions Trading Scheme. *Ecological Economics*, *105*, 78–88. doi: http://dx.doi.org/10.1016/j.ecolecon.2014.05.010

Monjon, S., and Quirion, P. (2011). Addressing leakage in the EU ETS: Border adjustment or output-based allocation? *Ecological Economics*, *70*, 1957–1971.

O'Rourke, D. (2014). The science of sustainable supply chains. *Science*, *344*(6188), 1124–1127. doi: 10.1126/science.1248526

Peters, G. P. (2008). From production-based to consumption-based national emission inventories. *Ecological Economics*, *65*(1), 13–23. doi: http://dx.doi.org/10.1016/j.ecolecon.2007.10.014

Peters, G. P. (2016). The "best available science" to inform 1.5 [deg]C policy choices. *Nature Climate Change*, *6*(7), 646–649. doi: 10.1038/nclimate3000 www.nature.com/nclimate/journal/v6/n7/abs/nclimate3000.html#supplementary-information

Peters, G. P., Davis, S. J., and Andrew, R. M. (2012). A synthesis of carbon in international trade. *Biogeosciences Discuss*, *9*(3), 3949–4023.

Peters, G. P., and Hertwich, E. (2008). CO_2 embodied in international trade with implications for global climate change. *Environmental Science & Technology*, *42*(5), 1401–1407.

Peters, G. P., Minx, J. C., Weber, C. L., and Edenhofer, O. (2011). Growth in emission transfers via international trade from 1990 to 2008. *Proceedings of the National Academy of Sciences*, *108*(21), 8903–8908. doi: 10.1073/pnas.1006388108

Reinaud, J. (2008a). *Climate policy and carbon leakage – impacts of the European emissions trading scheme on aluminium*. IEA Information Paper. Paris: IEA/OECD.

Reinaud, J. (2008b). *Issues behind competitiveness and carbon leakage – focus on heavy industry*. IEA Information Paper. Paris: IEA/OECD.

Sakai, M., and Barrett, J. (2016). Border carbon adjustments: Addressing emissions embodied in trade. *Energy Policy*, *92*, 102–110. doi: http://dx.doi.org/10.1016/j.enpol.2016.01.038

Sato, M., Neuhoff, K., Graichen, V., Schumacher, K., and Matthes, F. (2015). Sectors under scrutiny: Evaluation of indicators to assess the risk of carbon leakage in the UK and Germany. *Environmental and Resource Economics*, *60*(1), 99–124. doi: 10.1007/s10640-014-9759-y

Skelton, A. (2013). EU corporate action as a driver for global emissions abatement: A structural analysis of EU international supply chain carbon dioxide emissions. *Global Environmental Change*, *23*(6), 1795–1806. doi: http://dx.doi.org/10.1016/j.gloenvcha.2013.07.024

Steen-Olsen, K., Weinzettel, J., Cranston, G., Ercin, A. E., and Hertwich, E. G. (2012). Carbon, land, and water footprint accounts for the European Union: Consumption, production, and displacements through international trade. *Environmental Science & Technology*, *46*(20), 10883–10891. doi: 10.1021/es301949t

Steininger, K., Lininger, C., Droege, S., Roser, D., Tomlinson, L., and Meyer, L. (2014). Justice and cost effectiveness of consumption-based versus production-based approaches in the case of unilateral climate policies. *Global Environmental Change*, *24*, 75–87. doi: http://dx.doi.org/10.1016/j.gloenvcha.2013.10.005

Timmer, M. P., Dietzenbacher, E., Los, B., Stehrer, R., and de Vries, G. J. (2015). An illustrated user guide to the world input – output database: The case of global automotive production. *Review of International Economics*, *23*(3), 575–605.

UNEP. (2016). *The emissions gap report 2016*. Nairobi, Kenya: United Nations Environment Program.

Van Asselt, H., and Brewer, T. (2010). Addressing competitiveness and leakage concerns in climate policy: An analysis of border adjustment measures in the US and the EU. *Energy Policy*, *38*, 42–51.

Wagner, U., and Timmins, C. (2009). Agglomeration effects in foreign direct investment and the pollution Haven hypothesis. *Environmental & Resource Economics*, *43*(2), 231–256.

Wiedmann, T., and Barrett, J. (2013). Policy-relevant applications of environmentally extended MRIO databases – experiences from the UK. *Economic Systems Research*, *25*, 143–156.

Zhang, Y. (2012). Scale, technique and composition effects in trade-related carbon emissions in China. *Environmental and Resource Economics*, *51*(3), 371–389. doi: 10.1007/s10640-011-9503-9

# 14 An assessment of the effects of the new carbon tax in Chile

*Rocío Román, José M. Cansino and Manuel Ordóñez*

## Introduction

According to the Intergovernmental Panel on Climate Change (IPCC), human-induced contributions are evident, and it is extremely likely that the increase of anthropogenic greenhouse gas (GHG) emissions is the dominant cause of climate change (IPCC, 2014). Continued emissions of GHGs will likely cause a temperature increase and severe shifts in the climate system, amplifying the risks for all ecosystems on Earth (IPCC, 2014). This is why many scholars place the focus of their research on this topic, thanks to which there is a growing body of literature available (Gebre et al., 2014; Zhang and Da, 2015).

The aforementioned human-induced contributions to climate change are strongly linked to energy consumption and energy-related $CO_2$ emissions due to the high weight of fossil fuels in energy matrix. As energy consumption from fossil fuels has an anthropogenic origin, humans have the capacity to take action to reduce future climate risks through energy consumption saving. Such aspects have elevated the importance of this issue in public policy and environmental legislation (Fankhauser et al., 2015; Figallo, 2016).

From International Energy Agency statistics (IEA, 2016), energy related $CO_2$ emissions in Chile increased 178% for the 1990–2013 period, which is well above the world average (56%) for OECD-American countries (104%) and all OECD economies (9.4%). These emissions derived from fuel combustion only; therefore, they are linked to anthropogenic actions. Unless Chile's energy-related $CO_2$ emissions share only 0.2% of the total in the world; its percentage increase is 78.5% for the aforementioned period.

Recently (September 2015), within the framework of COP21 in Paris, Chile presented its Intended Nationally Determined Contribution (INDC) provided by the Government of Chile (2016). This document defines its commitment in the battle against climate change in terms of emission intensity (tons of $CO_2$ equivalent per unit of gross domestic product (GDP) in millions of CLP\$ 2011).

Chile's commitment is based on sectorial analyses and mitigation scenarios developed in conjunction with the Mitigation Actions Plans and Scenarios (MAPS) Chile project (Phase 2) (MAPS Chile, 2014), the National Greenhouse Gas Inventory results (1990–2010) and additional information provided by the

Ministries of Environment, Energy, Agriculture and Finance, as well as observations received during the Public Consultation of the Intended National Contribution (Government of Chile, 2010). MAPS Chile included a broad list of recommended policy measures including a carbon tax. This report also assessed economic impacts derived from proposed carbon tax by using a dynamic Computable General Equilibrium (CGE) model. However, no details of the CGE model were shown, so it appeared as a black box.

Finally, in September 2014, Chile's authorities approved a carbon tax which will be applied at the beginning of 2017 (Act 20.780) and is directly linked with commitments derived from Paris Agreement. This approved tax is rather dissimilar from the one included in MAPS Chile levied on fixed pollutant sources over 50 MWt of installed thermal capacity. Although Chile's carbon tax levies a set of pollutant emissions, the most relevant levy would be on $CO_2$ emissions. Legislative Act 20.780 establishes a quantity of US$5 per $CO_2$ ton emitted by a fixed source. It is expected that the revenue obtained will be US$168.1 million per year (Coronado, 2016).

In this chapter, Chile's tax reform is analyzed by considering this new carbon tax as an environmental Pigouvian tax. The research conducted deals with a hot topic of major concern, not only for scholars but also for policymakers, companies and all citizens.

The implementation of economic instruments such as carbon taxes leads to the internalization of $CO_2$ externality; an increase in energy prices could be expected to encourage manufacturing firms and households to adopt energy-saving technologies and practices with consequences for utilities. If an effective energy efficiency policy is to be pursued, then economic instruments providing a price signal to reduce energy demand should be applied (Tarancón et al., 2010). When energy prices fail to reflect the real cost of energy, consumers, utilities and companies under-invest in energy efficient-equipment.

In the field of energy policy and the battle against climate change, the two prevailing solutions to correct inefficiency are environmental taxes and pollution licenses or tradable permits. In both cases, policy measures seek to promote the internalization of externality costs by economic agents.[1] Pigouvian taxes constitute the basis for the first solution (Meade, 1952; Pigou, 1932; Scitovsky, 1954). The second solution finds its theoretical justification in emission trading schemes (Atkinson and Tietenberg, 1987; Coase, 1960; Dales, 1968; McGartland and Oates, 1985; Montgomery, 1972). This chapter focuses on the first solution type and therefore analyzes a relevant issue from the perspective of energy efficiency and the fight against climate change.

For this analysis, the Social Accounting Matrix (SAM) at purchase prices for Chile in 2013 (SAMCHL13) has been designed as detailed in section 2. SAMCHL13 serves as the database for a pricing model that includes the new tax.

The pricing model is an input-output (IO) methodology model introduced by Leontief (1946) to study the relationship between wages, profits and prices in the US economy of 1939. This methodology has been widely developed regarding Spain's domestic economy (Sancho, 1988; Roland-Holst and Sancho, 1995;

Llop, 2008 and more recently Tarancón et al., 2010). This model is an analytical method that is complementary to both the econometric approach (Labandeira and Labeaga, 2000) and the general equilibrium models developed in the field of environmental taxation by Goulder (1995), Bovenberg and Goulder (1996), Böhringer (2002), Kumbaroğlu (2003) and O'Ryan et al. (2005), at the international level by Fæhn et al. (2009) and André et al. (2005), Manresa and Sancho (2005), De Miguel-Vélez et al. (2009) and Labandeira et al. (2004) for the case of Spain.[2]

The aim of this chapter is to assess the impact of carbon tax in Chile on prices, tax revenues and private welfare measured trough the consumer purchase index. These results allow the uncertainty linked to possible impacts derived from the tax to be reduced. The resolution model, as well as the various simulations carried out, have resulted in the General Algebraic Modeling System (GAMS[3]) program, developed by Brooke et al. (1990) for the World Bank.

This chapter is structured as follows. After the introduction, details about the model are provided in section 2. The database used is shown in section 3. Section 4 provides the main results, while concluding remarks are offered in section 5.

## Methodology

### *The price model*

The price model is based on the SAM drafted by Chile for 2013 (SAMCHL13). This model indicates the 26 productive sectors where the 111 lines of business contemplated in Chile's National Accounts are grouped together. Table 14.A.1 in the Appendix details the aggregation criteria. Intermediate consumption is listed in each column as well as primary input for each productive sector used to produce its product. Constant yield is taken for granted. Likewise, each column indicates the net indirect taxes paid by economic agents when companies demand the goods and services needed and constitute the final demand. For this reason, when the various components defining the price model are combined, it is necessary to differentiate between the two types of prices. Moreover, the production prices for each productive sector are provided, as are the acquisition or final prices for each good produced.

In the price model, it is understood that economic sectors are interdependent, given that the sectors, in addition to primary input, use intermediate input from other sectors. Thus any variation in the prices of input, whatever the business activity, will impact not only on that business but also on the entire system, thus altering the prices of all components in all sectors. The result is a price structure that differs from the initial structure. Specifically, a price model is a useful tool for simulations in an economic system. With price models, analyses may be carried out – although there are limitations – regarding the effects that a variation in a given input (wages, taxes . . .) have on the prices of economic sector or on tax revenue.

Given that the production of a good involves the use of intermediate consumption (Manresa et al., 1988) and other production factors such as employment and capital, in SAMCHL13, the last two production factors are incorporated by the remuneration of workers and the gross operating surplus, respectively. When calculating a production price, in addition to the aforementioned production factors, taxes and distribution margins paid are included. Among the various taxes, one must mention the taxation of tobacco products and fuel, and other indirect taxes levied on products, with the net taxes on production and import duties.

The price model facilitates the estimation of unit costs for each of the goods manufactured by each business activity (Cardenete and Sancho, 2002). First of all, the technical coefficients resulting from dividing each intermediate consumption and the rest of the productive factors by the total for the production of each business activity are estimated. Upon multiplying each of these coefficients by their respective price, these are added, and considering the respective taxes and the distribution margins, the production price of the good is obtained. The production price $(p_j)$ of each good may be calculated using Eq (14.1):

$$p_j = \left(1+t_j\right)\left[\sum_{i=1}^{26} a_{ij} \cdot p_j + w \cdot l_j + r \cdot k_j + itc_j + ipr_j + mgr_j + \left(1+im_j\right) \cdot m_j\right], \quad (14.1)$$

where $t_j$, $itc_j$, $ipr_j$ e $im_j$ are the tax rates of net indirect taxes on products, on tobacco products and fuel, on production and import duties. The $a_{ij}$, $l_j$, $k_j$ y $m_j$ represent, respectively, the technical coefficients of intermediate consumption, the labor factor, the capital factor and imported goods; $w$ and $r$ are the unitary remuneration of labor and the capital; lastly, $mgr_j$ represents distribution margins.

The value of each parameter representing the technical coefficients was obtained from SAMCHL13. In the case of technical coefficients referring to intermediate consumption for each of the business activities, $a_{ij}$ is calculated as Eq (14.2):

$$a_{ij} = \frac{A_{ij}}{X_j}, \qquad (14.2)$$

where $A_{ij}$, is the element taken from the intermediate consumption matrix – in other words, the input consumption that sector $j$ makes from sector $i$ and $X_j$ is the total output for sector $j$.[4] In the case of the productive factor, $l_j$ has been calculated based on the following expression (14.3):

$$l_j = \frac{L_j}{X_j}, \qquad (14.3)$$

where $L_j$ are employee wages for sector $j$. For the productive factor $k_j$, the expression that follows has been used:

$$k_j = \frac{K_j}{X_j}, \qquad (14.4)$$

where $K_j$ is the gross operating surplus for sector $j$. Finally, the parameter $m_j$ has been calculated as follows:

$$m_j = \frac{M_j}{X_j}, \tag{14.5}$$

with $M_j$ being the imports made by sector $j$.

The tax rate for net indirect net taxes on intermediate products, on tobacco products and fuel, on production and import duties and with the technical coefficients, was obtained from SAMCHL13 using the expressions (14.6) to (14.9):

$$t_j = \frac{IP_j}{X_j - IP_j}, \tag{14.6}$$

$$itc_j = \frac{ITC_j}{X_j}, \tag{14.7}$$

$$ipr_j = \frac{IPR_j}{X_j}, \tag{14.8}$$

$$im_j = \frac{IM_j}{M_j}, \tag{14.9}$$

where the numerator represents the revenue in each business sector and the denominator its taxable income, which in the case of net indirect taxes is the total output minus indirect taxes on products paid by the sectors ($IP_j$). The tax base for production taxes and taxes on tobacco products and fuel have the total output for each sector as taxable income. In the case of import duties, taxable income corresponds to imports. The taxable rates obtained are not nominal rates established by the current legislation, but rather, an effective rate calculated by SAMCHL13. Finally, distribution margins are calculated by dividing the total for the margins paid in each sector and the total output, as shown in expression (14.10).

$$mgr_j = \frac{MGR_j}{X_j} \tag{14.10}$$

The purchase price is the result of adding the production price and distribution margins together with indirect taxes levied on finished products. The expression used to calculate the purchase price, $q_j$, is as follows:

$$q_j = \left(1 + iva_j\right).\left[p_j + mgdf_j\right], \tag{14.11}$$

where $iva_j$ is the net tax rate levied on finished products and applied as a percentage of the production price, and $mgdf_j$ represents distribution margins. Taxes are calculated as the quotient between the revenue and its tax base according to the SAMCHL13, using the following expression (14.12):

$$iva_j = \frac{IVA_j}{DF_j - IVA_j},$$    (14.12)

where $DF_j$, is the final demand. The parameter that represents the vector for distribution margins, $mgdf_j$, is obtained as follows:

$$mgdf_j = \frac{MG_j}{DF_j}.$$    (14.13)

The production price, the purchase price and the wage rate are endogenously obtained within the model. This is not the case with the unitary remuneration of capital, which is considered exogenous in the model.

For the remuneration of capital services, there is no benchmark index equivalent to what the Consumer Price Index (CPI) represents as a reference for salaries. This is the reason why, following Cardenete and Sancho (2002), this price is also considered exogenous in the model.

Regarding the wage rate, it adjusts to the evolution of consumer prices through the CPI, as this is the reference index that is usually used in collective bargaining for wage increases. Thus to calculate the wage rate, which, in turn, behaves as a final price variation index, the following expression is used (14.14):

$$w = \sum_{j=1}^{26} q_j \alpha_j,$$    (14.14)

where the wage rate, $w$, is a weighted average purchase price for the various goods produced by the productive sectors in which $\alpha_j$ is the weight used, which represents the proportion of goods consumption $j$ in relation to total private consumption.

Taking into account the aforementioned references – where the data provided by the SAMCHL13 are reproduced – the initial model uses unitary prices for both products as well as productive factors. Thus, upon performing simulations in the model to see the effects that certain measures have on prices, the analysis is much easier.

### Chile's carbon tax

Following a scheme similar to that of Cansino et al. (2007, 2016), in Chile, a carbon tax on $CO_2$ emissions in the atmosphere from fixed sources has been introduced into the model. In short, this refers to a tax such as the Chilean Carbon Tax. A sample description of this tax can be found in Coronado (2016). In practice, the productive sectors supporting the tax load are linked to the generation, transportation and distribution of electricity. The tax is levied on the goods produced by the electricity generation sector in an amount proportional to the value of each of the sectors it supplies. Thus the tax on emissions, determined by the rate (US$5 per $CO_2$ ton emitted) and the level of emissions, falls upon the electricity generation sector; this impacts on economic sectors with regard to the input needs of this sector. The effective tax rate for this model would be determined by dividing the amount calculated for each sector and its output level. This new tax is incorporated into the model at the same level as tax on production, as indicated in the expression (14.15):

$$p_j = \left(1+t_j\right)\left[\sum_{i=1}^{26} a_{ij} \cdot p_j + w \cdot l_j + r \cdot k_j + itc_j + ipr_j + ie_j + mgr_j + \left(1+im_j\right)\cdot m_j\right]. \quad (14.15)$$

Tax revenue would be the effective collection registered on Table IO. It is based on the effective rate, calculated as of the table, and not on nominal rates that appear in the law that regulates each of the taxes included in the model. The formula that allows the revenue from the various taxes to be calculated is detailed in expressions (14.17) to (14.20):

$$RIPRA = \sum_{j=1}^{26} t_j \left[\sum_{i=1}^{26} a_{ij} \cdot p_j + w \cdot l_j + r \cdot k_j + itc_j + ipr_j + ie_j + mgr_j + \left(1+im_j\right)\cdot m_j\right] X_j, \quad (14.16)$$

$$RITC = \sum_{j=1}^{26} itc_j \cdot X_j, \quad (14.17)$$

$$RIPR = \sum_{j=1}^{26} ipr_j \cdot X_j, \quad (14.18)$$

$$RIM = \sum_{j=1}^{26} im_j \cdot m_j \cdot X_j, \quad (14.19)$$

$$RIE = \sum_{j=1}^{26} ie_j \cdot X_j, \quad (14.20)\,(14.21)$$

where *RIPRA* is the revenue from taxes on net products; *RITC*, the revenue on tobacco products and fuel; *RIPR*, the revenue from taxes on production; *RIM*, the revenue from import duties; *RIE*, the revenue from the new Chilean carbon tax; *RIVA*, the revenue from taxes on products on final goods; $DF_j$, the net final demand of taxes for each of the sectors; and $XIP_j$, the total output of sector *j*. The total revenue derived is the expression (14.22):

$$RT = RIPRA + RITC + RIPR + RIM + RIE + RIVA. \quad (14.22)$$

### Private spending index

Changes in purchase prices as a result of a tax modification give rise to changes in household purchasing power and expenditure level. The gain or loss of consumers' can be measured following Cansino et al. (2016) through the so-called Private Spending Index (PSI). This index calculates the necessary variation in consumer expenditures to purchase the initial basket of goods and services, but at the new price. For this, Y is defined as the income used to purchase the original basket of goods and services, while $Y'$ is the income used to purchase the same basket of goods and services after the tax is introduced. The difference between the two incomes measures the change in household expenditure between the initial and the final situation.

$$PSI = Y - Y' = \sum_{j=1}^{26} q_j \cdot C_j - \sum_{j=1}^{26} q'_j \cdot C_j = \sum_{j=1}^{26} \left( q_j - q'_j \right) \cdot C_j, \qquad (14.23)$$

where $q_j$ and $q'_j$ are, respectively, the initial and final purchase price of the basket of goods and services, and $C_j$ is the basket of goods and services or consumption of the representative household. The PSI is the difference between $Y$ and $Y'$ – that is, the change in household expenditure after the tax has been introduced. A positive (negative) difference indicates that the final situation is better (worse) than the initial one – i.e. consumers will need a lesser (higher) income to purchase the same basket of goods and services, resulting in a higher (lower) level of household income.

## Data

SAMs initiated by Stone (1962) are used as the statistical support to build the economic models that facilitate the assessment of specific economic policies. SAM is represented by a square matrix that includes all of the monetary flows originating as a consequence of the transactions between the economic agents and the productive sectors, where each transaction has its own row and column in the matrix. The rows and columns are organized in an identical manner. In the SAM, each account is represented by a row $i$ and each column $j$, and it is agreed that the rows represent employment while the columns represent resources.

The SAM structure is flexible so as to allow for various construction forms to separate the accounts and sectors making it up. The degree of separation depends on the objective of the study and the availability of data. To draft SAM, four sub-matrices are needed: Intermediate Consumption Matrix, Primary Factor Matrix, Final Demand Matrix and the Closing Matrix.

The 2013 SAMs structure for Chile (SAMCHL13) contain 47 elements, of which 26 correspond to business activities. Details appear in Table 14.A.2 of the Appendix. The information to draft SAMCHL13 comes from the tables contained in the annual statistical yearbook titled "Cuentas Nacionales de Chile 2008–2015" published by the Central Bank of Chile. The yearbook tables contemplate 177 products and 111 business activities. Based on these tables for origin and destination, the Intermediate Consumer Matrix with the 111 business activities were created, following the D model, according to Eurostat (2008) terminology. This model establishes a fixed sales structure per product. Later, the 111 business activities are grouped into 26 productive sectors taken into consideration in this work. These tables have also been used to create the Primary Factor and Final Demand Matrices. Finally, to draft the Closing Matrix, the data was taken from the 2003–2014 integrated economic table, which was also published by the Central Bank of Chile (2016a).[5]

The data for the new carbon tax was undertaken based on the electricity generation data published by Chile's National Energy Commission. This institution publishes the generation of electricity for the *Sistema Interconectado Central* (SIC) and the *Sistema Interconectado Norte Grande* (SING), as well as emission factors for both systems. For 2013, the electricity generation data are 50,890.41 and 15,749.47 GWh for SIC and SING, respectively. The emission factors for these years and for both systems were 0.44 and 0.81 $tCO_2eq$/MWh, respectively. Therefore, the total emissions provoked by electricity generation in 2013 are 22,391,780 and 12,757,071 $tCO_2eq$, respectively (total amount is 35,148,851 $tCO_2eq$). If the tax rate is \$5/t and with a 2014 exchange rate of 495.31 CLP/\$ (Central Bank of Chile, 2016b), the total revenues expected are 87,047.89 million pesos.

## Results and discussion

As was expected, the new Chilean carbon tax provokes an inflationary impact either on production prices or on purchase prices in 2013. The details sector by sector are shown on Table 14.1. Higher impacts appear on the two sectors directly linked to electricity, thus evidencing that price model works properly. Together with these two sectors, the Cellulose and Copper Mining sectors are also important. In the case of Copper Mining, the result should be highlighted due to represents more than 10% of Chile's GDP.

There has been no impact on the housing services sector. The reason is that the relationship of this sector with all others in minimal. Specifically, the row (supplies to other sectors is null); it only has one supply and it is household consumption. On the other hand, the intermediate inputs only stem from five sectors (the other 21 are null), as well as most of the primary inputs (except capital-EBE) and net taxes on production.

Overall, the tax will spark a limited inflationary effect of 0.09%. Although small, the inflationary impact must be carefully assessed given that Chile's GDP has proven not to be very stable in the last ten years, to fluctuate between extreme values of 2.8% in 2009 and 7.82% in 2007. It has been estimated that the inflation rate for 2016 is 3.99% (Woldwide Inflation Data, 2016).

The last result shown by the model is linked to the impact of the new tax on private well-being. Once the new tax is applied, the Private Spending Index (PSI) is reduced in CLP \$ -65,808 M.

Together with the effect on prices, the new Chilean carbon tax also causes slight modifications in the relative weight of taxes in Chile. Table 14.2 shows the expected revenue for the first year that this new tax is applied (CLP \$ 87,048 M), thus slightly increase the relative weight of Value Aggregate Tax, decreasing the rest of indirect taxes, except, of course, the carbon tax.

Based on the above results, the impact of the new Carbon tax on Green House Gas (GHG) emissions can be estimated as follows: Firstly, the introduction of

*Table 14.1* Changes in production and purchase prices after the introduction of Carbon Tax in Chilean economy in 2013 (26 sectors).

| Productive sectors | Change in Production Prices | Change in Purchase Price |
|---|---|---|
| Agriculture, livestock & forestry | 0.03 | 0.02 |
| Fisheries | 0.03 | 0.03 |
| Copper mining | 0.16 | 0.16 |
| Other mining | 0.03 | 0.03 |
| Food, beverages & tobacco products | 0.03 | 0.03 |
| Textile, leather & footwear | 0.01 | 0.00 |
| Timber & furniture | 0.10 | 0.09 |
| Cellulose, paper & printing | 0.21 | 0.20 |
| Oil refineries | 0.01 | 0.01 |
| Chemical, rubber & plastic | 0.03 | 0.02 |
| Manufacturing of non-metal products | 0.04 | 0.04 |
| Basic metallurgy | 0.02 | 0.02 |
| Metal products, machinery & equipment and others | 0.01 | 0.01 |
| Generation of electricity | 1.70 | 1.70 |
| Transmission & distribution of electricity | 3.35 | 3.35 |
| Supply of gas, steam & water | 0.05 | 0.05 |
| Construction | 0.04 | 0.04 |
| Commerce | 0.06 | 0.06 |
| Restaurants & hotels | 0.04 | 0.04 |
| Transportation | 0.03 | 0.03 |
| Communications | 0.02 | 0.02 |
| Financial services | 0.03 | 0.03 |
| Entrepreneur services | 0.03 | 0.03 |
| Housing services | 0.00 | 0.00 |
| Personal services | 0.04 | 0.04 |
| Public administration | 0.06 | 0.06 |
| Average change | | 0.09 |

Source: Own elaboration.

*Table 14.2* Effects of Chilean Carbon Tax in tax revenues. Changes in the relative weight of taxes in 2013.

| Type of tax | Effects on revenue (millions of pesos) | | | Relative weight of taxes | |
|---|---|---|---|---|---|
| | Initial Situation | After Carbon Tax | Change | Initial Situation | After Carbon Tax |
| Tax on tobacco products & fuel | 1,694,838 | 1,694,838 | 0.0 | 11.3 | 10.9 |
| Value Aggregated Tax | 11,041,278 | 11,053,355 | 0.1 | 73.3 | 73.7 |
| Tax on production | 1,644,855 | 1,644,855 | 0.0 | 10.9 | 10.5 |
| Import duties | 682,719 | 682,719 | 0.0 | 4.5 | 4.4 |
| Tax on emissions | 0 | 87,048 | | 0.0 | 0.6 |
| **TOTAL** | **15,063,690** | **15,162,815** | 0.7 | | |

Source: Own elaboration

the Chilean Carbon tax causes a change in the production and purchase prices of every sector. Secondly, this change causes a shift in the household consumption that additionally provokes a variation in the sectoral output and in the energy consumption. Thirdly, the changes in the energy consumption of each sector is going to be used as a proxy for the change in sectoral output. Therefore, this information can be used for the estimation of GHG emissions changes in every sector after Carbon tax introduction.

For this analysis, should be recalculated the price changes after Carbon tax introduction of a new aggregation of productive sectors in order to adapt the sectors to the energy consumption sectors statistics.

The new sectors appear in Table 14.3; the impact of the new Carbon tax on production and purchase prices for the new sectoral aggregation was estimated.

Using the information offered by the Central Bank of Chile and the National Institute of Statistics (Banco Central de Chile and Instituto Nacional de Estadísticas, respectively) for the years 2012 and 2013, demand price-elasticities for the available sectors have been estimated. This price-elasticities have been assigned to the analyzed productive sectors. These elasticities appear in Table 14.4.

With the information contained in Tables 14.3 and 14.5, the change in the consumption demand of households in response to a change in the production and purchase prices has been estimated. Therefore, we assume that the same percentage change that happens in the households' consumption happens in the productive sectors' production. Additionally, we assume that this percentage change in the productive sectors' production provokes the same percentage change energy consumption of productive sectors. Therefore, the percentage change of households' consumption is considered a proxy of the percentage change of energy

*Table 14.3* Changes in production and purchase prices after the introduction of carbon tax in Chilean economy in 2013 (13 sectors)

| Economic sectors | Change in production prices | Change in purchase prices |
|---|---|---|
| Agriculture and Fisheries | 0.06 | 0.05 |
| Copper Mining | 0.12 | 0.12 |
| Other Mining | 0.02 | 0.02 |
| Cellulose, Paper and Printing | 0.17 | 0.16 |
| Oil Refineries | 0.01 | 0.01 |
| Chemical, Rubber and Plastic | 0.03 | 0.03 |
| Manufacturing of Non-metal Products | 0.06 | 0.05 |
| Basic Metallurgy | 0.02 | 0.02 |
| Other Industries and Others | 0.03 | 0.03 |
| Electricity | 1.86 | 1.88 |
| Supply of Gas, Steam and Water | 0.10 | 0.10 |
| Transportation | 0.04 | 0.04 |
| Commercial and Public | 0.05 | 0.06 |

Source: Own elaboration

*Table 14.4* Price-elasticity estimated and assigned to each sector

| Sector | Price-elasticities |
|---|---|
| Agriculture and Fisheries | −0.5 |
| Copper Mining | −1.1 |
| Other Mining | −1.1 |
| Cellulose, Paper and Printing | −1.1 |
| Oil Refineries | −1.1 |
| Chemical, Rubber and Plastic | −1.1 |
| Manufacturing of Non-metal Mineral Products | −1.1 |
| Basic Metallurgy | −1.1 |
| Other Industries and Others | −1.1 |
| Electricity | −3.5 |
| Supply of Gas, Steam and Water | −3.5 |
| Transportation | −4.8 |
| Commercial and Public | −4.8 |

Source: Own elaboration based on information from the Central Bank of Chile and its National Institute of Statistics

*Table 14.5* Change in energy consumption after the Chilean carbon tax is implemented in 2013

| Sector | Change in energy consumption (TCal) |
|---|---|
| Agriculture and Fisheries | −0.7 |
| Copper Mining | −48.3 |
| Other Mining | −1.4 |
| Cellulose, Paper and Printing | −42.1 |
| Oil Refineries | −1.7 |
| Chemical, Rubber and Plastic | −1.0 |
| Manufacturing of Non-metal Mineral Products | −1.8 |
| Basic Metallurgy | −0.5 |
| Other Industries and Others | −9.9 |
| Electricity | −168.5 |
| Supply of Gas, Steam and Water | −2.3 |
| Transportation | −205.2 |
| Commercial and Public | −46.1 |
| **TOTAL** | **−529.4** |

Source: Own elaboration

consumption of productive sectors. The estimation of the energy consumption changes in Chile in 2013 is shown in Table 14.5.

Finally, the change in GHG emissions measured in $CO_2$eq originating from the introduction of the carbon tax is calculated. This calculation was carried out in several steps.

To begin with, $CO_2$eq emissions for 2013 have to be estimated because the national inventory of emission in Chile only offers data up to 2010. The emissions for 2013 were estimated by applying the 2010 average rate for the full period. The emissions estimated for the available sectors (Table 14.6) showed no significant

*Table 14.6* Emissions, energy consumption and emissions factors by sectors of Chilean economy in 2013

| Sector | Emissions (Gg $CO_2eq$) | Energy consumption (Tcal) | Emission factors (Gg $CO_2eq$/Tcal) |
|---|---|---|---|
| Production of Electricity and Heat | 31,118 | 3,161 | 9.84 |
| Oil Refineries | 1,569 | 17,115 | 0.09 |
| Manufacturing Industry and Construction | 13,449 | 61,403 | 0.22 |
| Transportation | 23,611 | 93,909 | 0.25 |
| Production of Cement and Lime | 2,635 | 3,008 | 0.88 |
| Iron and Steel | 1,097 | 2,008 | 0.55 |
| Rest | 27,125 | 55,631 | 0.49 |
| **TOTAL** | **100,605** | **236,235** | **0.43** |

Source: Own elaboration

*Table 14.7* Emission factors assigned to each productive sector and GHG emissions avoided in Chilean economy in 2013

| Sector | Emissions factors (Tcal/ Gg $CO_2eq$) | Reduction of emissions (Gg $CO_2eq$) |
|---|---|---|
| Agriculture and Fisheries | 0.43 | 0 |
| Copper Mining | 0.43 | −21 |
| Other Mining | 0.43 | −1 |
| Cellulose, Paper and Printing | 0.22 | −9 |
| Oil Refineries | 0.09 | 0 |
| Chemical, Rubber and Plastic | 0.22 | 0 |
| Manufacturing of Non-metal Mineral Products | 0.88 | −2 |
| Basic Metallurgy | 0.55 | 0 |
| Other Industries and Others | 0.43 | −4 |
| Electricity | 9.84 | −1,659 |
| Supply of Gas, Steam and Water | 9.84 | −22 |
| Transportation | 0.25 | −52 |
| Commercial and Public | 0.43 | −20 |
| | | −1,790 |

Source: Own elaboration

difference from those published by the government of Chile in 2013 and that reached 109,908.8 Gg $CO_2eq$ (Government of Chile, 2016). Finally, the emission factors per unit of energy consumed are calculated considering the GHG emissions estimated for the available sectors for 2013 and with the information about the energy consumption of these sectors for 2013 provided by Government of Chile (2016).

The emission factors provided by Table 14.6 for some sectors allows us to assign them to the sectors analyzed in this research as is shown in Table 14.7. Additionally, with the information about the change in energy consumption for

*Table 14.8* Change in GHG emissions after the Chilean carbon tax introduction

| Sector | Reduction of emissions (Gg $CO_2eq$) |
|---|:---:|
| Agriculture and Fisheries | 0 |
| Copper Mining | −21 |
| Other Mining | −1 |
| Cellulose, Paper and Printing | −9 |
| Oil Refineries | 0 |
| Chemical, Rubber and Plastic | 0 |
| Manufacturing of Non-metal Mineral Products | −2 |
| Basic Metallurgy | 0 |
| Other Industries and Others | −4 |
| Electricity | −1,659 |
| Supply of Gas, Steam and Water | −22 |
| Transportation | −52 |
| Commercial and Public | −20 |
| TOTAL | −1,790 |

Source: Own elaboration

2013 (Table 14.5), and the emissions factors for all the sectors allow us calculating the $CO_2$ emissions that would be avoided in 2013 when the carbon tax is introduced in the Chilean economy. The data appears in Table 14.8 and shows a global savings of around 1,800 Gg $CO_2$eq.

## Concluding remarks

This chapter develops a price model to analyze the impact of the new carbon tax in Chile on prices, the revenue structure and private well-being. For this, the SAM for Chile in 2013 was calculated; the most recent year for which IO data are available. This is the first contribution of the chapter.

As expected, the major findings of the analysis reveal that the tax sparks a slight inflationary effect on the economy, which is particularly important in those sectors linked to electricity. The impact is also important for the Cellulous sector and for Copper Mining. Given the economic importance of this sector, it is foreseeable that the authorities in Chile establish compensation measures to retain the sector's competitiveness.

Although there is no consensus in the literature regarding the effectiveness of carbon taxes in the fight against climate change, it is a greatly used market based instrument. Specifically, it is coherent with the type of measures that could help achieve the commitments of Chile derived from its signing the Paris Agreement. Our results show a reduction of GHG emissions for 2013 of around 1,800 Gg $CO_2$eq.

It should be noted that the price model used is a linear general equilibrium model. Although this kind of model is perfectly valid when analyzing the effect on prices and revenues, it is more limited than an applied general equilibrium model, which allows the establishment of a comprehensive and complex network of relationships between the different economic agents, as well as the consideration of a greater number of macroeconomic variables. We might be cautious with results obtained. However, as an approximation to this network of interactions, the linear general equilibrium model provides enough insight into the effects that may result from a tax reform and later expand with the application of an applied general equilibrium model.

# Appendix

*Table 14.A.1* Correspondence of activities for Chile's national accounts, with the 26 sectors used to create SAMCHL13

| Input-output table sectors | National activity accounts |
|---|---|
| 1. Agriculture, livestock & forestry | 1. Annual crops (cereals and other) and forage |
| | 2. Vegetable crops and nursery crops |
| | 3. Vineyard crops |
| | 4. Other fruit groups |
| | 5. Cattle breeding |
| | 6. Pig breeding |
| | 7. Poultry farming |
| | 8. Other animal breeding |
| | 10. Forestry and logging |
| 2. Fisheries | 11. Aquaculture |
| | 12. Extensive fishing |
| 3. Copper mining | 15. Copper mining |
| 4. Other mining | 13. Extraction of coal |
| | 14. Extraction of crude oil and natural gas |
| | 16. Iron mining |
| | 17. Non-ferrous mining |
| | 18. Other mining and quarry operations |
| 5. Food, beverages & tobacco products | 19. Meat processing and preservation |
| | 20. Manufacturing of flour and fish oil |
| | 21. Fish and seafood processing and preservation |
| | 22. Vegetable processing and preservation |
| | 23. Production of oils |
| | 24. Production of dairy products |
| | 25. Manufacturing of milling products |
| | 26. Manufacturing of animal feed |
| | 27. Manufacturing of bakery products |
| | 28. Manufacturing of noodles and pasta |
| | 29. Manufacturing of other food products |
| | 30. Manufacturing of spirits and liqueurs |
| | 31. Production of wine |
| | 32. Manufacturing of beer |
| | 33. Manufacturing of non-alcoholic beverages |
| | 34. Manufacturing of tobacco products |

| Input-output table sectors | National activity accounts |
|---|---|
| 6. Textile, leather & footwear | 35. Manufacturing of textile products |
| | 36. Manufacturing of clothing |
| | 37. Manufacturing of leather and its products |
| | 38. Manufacturing of footwear |
| 7. Timber & furniture | 39. Sawmills and wood treatment |
| | 40. Manufacturing of wood products |
| | 62. Manufacturing of furniture |
| 8. Cellulose, paper & printing | 41. Manufacturing of cellulose |
| | 42. Manufacturing of paper and cardboard containers |
| | 43. Manufacturing of other paper and cardboard items |
| | 44. Printers and publishers |
| | 64. Recycling of waste and scrap |
| 9. Oil refineries | 45. Production of fuel |
| 10. Chemical, rubber & plastic | 46. Manufacturing of basic chemical substances |
| | 47. Manufacturing of paint and varnish |
| | 48. Manufacturing of pharmaceutical products |
| | 49. Manufacturing of toiletries and cosmetic products |
| | 50. Manufacturing of other chemical products |
| | 51. Manufacturing of rubber products |
| | 52. Manufacturing of plastic products |
| 11. Manufacturing of non-metal products | 53. Manufacturing of glass and glass products |
| | 54. Manufacturing of cement, lime and plaster/gypsum |
| | 55. Manufacturing of concrete and other non-metallic mineral products |
| 12. Basic metallurgy | 56. Basic iron and steel industries |
| | 57. Basic non-ferrous metal industries |
| 13. Metal products, machinery & equipment and others | 58. Manufacturing of metal products |
| | 59. Manufacturing of machinery and equipment for industrial and domestic use |
| | 60. Manufacturing of machinery and electric and electronic equipment |
| | 61. Manufacturing of transportation equipment |
| | 63. Other manufacturing industries |
| 14. Generation of electricity | 65. Generation of electricity |
| 15. Transmission & distribution of electricity | 66. Transmission of electricity |
| | 67. Distribution of electricity |
| 16. Supply of gas, steam & water | 68. Supply of gas and stream |
| | 69. Supply of water |
| 17. Construction | 70. Construction of residential buildings |
| | 71. Construction of non-residential buildings |
| | 72. Construction of civil engineering projects |
| | 73. Specialized construction activities |
| 18. Commerce | 74. Automobile industry |
| | 75. Wholesale commerce |
| | 76. Retail commerce |
| | 77. Repair of domestic fixtures |
| 19. Restaurants & hotels | 78. Hotels |
| | 79. Restaurants |

(Continued)

*Table 14.A.1* (Continued)

| Input-output table sectors | National activity accounts |
|---|---|
| 20. Transportation | 80. Railroad transportation |
| | 81. Other passenger terrestrial transportation |
| | 82. Highway cargo transportation |
| | 83. Pipeline transportation (gas ducts and oil ducts) |
| | 84. Maritime transportation |
| | 85. Air transportation |
| | 86. Other complementary transportation activities |
| | 87. Warehouse, storage activities and transportation agencies |
| 21. Communications | 88. Postage and messenger services |
| | 89. Cell phone |
| | 90. Land line and long distance telephones |
| | 91. Other telecommunication activities |
| 22. Financial services | 92. Financial intermediation |
| | 93. Insurance and reinsurance activities |
| | 94. Auxiliary financial services |
| 23. Entrepreneur services | 9. Support activities for agriculture and farming |
| | 95. Real estate activities |
| | 96. Machinery and equipment rentals |
| | 97. IT service activities |
| | 98. Judicial, accounting, research and development activities |
| | 99. Architectural, engineering and scientific activities |
| | 100. Publicity and market research |
| | 101. Other business support services |
| 24. Housing services | 102. Housing services |
| 25. Personal services | 104. Public education |
| | 105. Private education |
| | 106. Public health care |
| | 107. Private health care |
| | 108. Activities by social services and associations |
| | 109. Waste management |
| | 110. Recreational activities |
| | 111. Other service activities |
| 26. Public administration | 103. Public administration |

*Table 14.A.2* Accounts for SAMCHL13

| Account | Concept |
|---|---|
| 1–26 | Activity branch |
| 27 | Work |
| 28 | Capital |
| 29 | Property income |
| 30 | Taxes on tobacco products and fuel |
| 31 | Taxes on products from activity branches |
| 32 | Taxes on production |
| 33 | Import duties |

| Account | Concept |
|---------|---------|
| 34 | Profit margins for activity branches |
| 35 | Taxes on final demand added value |
| 36 | Profit margins final demand |
| 37 | Income tax |
| 38 | Social contributions |
| 39 | Social services and other ordinary transfers |
| 40 | Social transfers in kind |
| 41 | Homes |
| 42 | Private, non-profit institutions |
| 43 | Non-financial companies |
| 44 | Financial corporations |
| 45 | Public sector |
| 46 | Investment/ Savings |
| 47 | Exterior sector |

## Notes

1 Regulatory policies or direct control over polluting activities are another type of policy measure in this field.
2 The latter work integrates a micro-econometric model and a general equilibrium model.
3 The resolution program used by GAMS was MINOS.
4 The total output for sector *j* does not correspond to the total for employees and SAM resources, as these are not accounted for, nor are indirect taxes on products that constitute the final demand or distribution margins on those same products.
5 The SAM for Chile is available upon request.

## References

André, F. J., Cardenete, M. A., and Velázquez, E. (2005). Performing an environmental tax reform in a regional economy: A computable general equilibrium approach. *The Annals of Regional Science*, *39*(2), 375–392.

Atkinson, S. E., and Tietenberg, T. H. (1987). Economic implications of emissions trading rules for local and regional pollutants. *Canadian Journal of Economics*, 20, 370–386.

Böhringer, C. (2002). *Environmental tax differentiation between industries and households-implications for efficiency and employment: a multi-sector intertemporal CGE analysis for Germany*. ZEW Discussion Papers.

Bovenberg, A. L., and Goulder, L. H. (1996). Optimal environmental taxation in the presence of other taxes: general-equilibrium analyses. *The American economic review*, *86*(4), 985–1000.

Brooke, A., Kendrick, D., and Meeraus, A. (1990). *GAMS: A user's guide*. Redwood City, CA: The Scientific Press.

Cansino, J. M., Cardenete, M. A., Ordóñez, M., and Román, R. (2016). Taxing electricity consumption in Spain: Evidence to design the post-Kyoto world. *Carbon Management*, *7*(1–2), 93–104.

Cansino, J. M., Cardenete, M. A., and Roman, R. (2007). Regional evaluation of a tax on the retail sales of certain fuels through a social accounting matrix. *Applied Economics Letters*, *14*(12), 877–880.

Cardenete, M. A., and Sancho, F. (2002). Efectos económicos de variaciones de los impuestos indirectos sobre la economía de Andalucía. *Hacienda Pública Española, 162*(3), 61–78.

Central Bank of Chile. (2016a). *Cuadro Económico Integrado 2003–2014.* Santiago de Chile, Chile: Central Bank of Chile. Retrieved from www.bcentral.cl.

Central Bank of Chile. (2016b). *Cuentas Nacionales de Chile 2008–2015.* Santiago de Chile, Chile: Central Bank of Chile. Retrieved from www.bcentral.cl.

Coase, R. H. (1960). The problem of social cost. *The journal of Law and Economics, 56*(4), 837–877.

Coronado, E. (2016). *Impuesto chileno sobre emisiones a la atmósfera provenientes de fuentes fi jas (un estudio a la luz de la legislación española).* Instituto de Estudios Fiscales. Madrid.

Dales, J. H. (1968). *Pollution, property, and prices.* Toronto, Canada: University of Toronto Press.

De Miguel-Vélez, F. J., Flores, M. A. C., and Pérez-Mayo, J. (2009). Effects of the tax on retail sales of some fuels on a regional economy: A computable general equilibrium approach. *The Annals of Regional Science, 43*(3), 781–806.

Eurostat. (2008). *Eurostat manual of supply, use and input-output tables, methodologies and working papers.* Luxembourg: EU.

Fæhn, T., Gómez-Plana, A. G., and Kverndokk, S. (2009). Can a carbon permit system reduce Spanish unemployment? *Energy Economics, 31*(4), 595–604.

Fankhauser, S., Gennaioli, C., and Collins, M. (2015). The political economy of passing climate change legislation: Evidence from a survey. *Global Environmental Change, 35,* 52–61.

Figallo, E. (2016). Mexico's climate pledge: A credible commitment? *IIIEE Masters Thesis IMEN41 20162.* The International Institute for Industrial Environmental Economics. Sweden.

Gebre, S., Boissy, T., and Alfredsen, K. (2014). Sensitivity to climate change of the thermal structure and ice cover regime of three hydropower reservoirs. *Journal of Hydrology, 510,* 208–227.

Goulder, L. H. (1995). Environmental taxation and the "Double dividend:" A reader's guide. In Lans Bovenberg & Siibren Cnossen (eds.), *Public economics and the environment in an imperfect world.* Springer, New York, 277–313.

Government of Chile. (2010). *Letter to the UNFCCC Executive Secretary, 23th August.* Santiago de Chile, Chile: Ministry of Foreign Affairs, Government of Chile.

Government of Chile. (2016). *Chile's second biennial report on climate change.* Santiago de Chile, Chile: Government of Chile.

IEA. (2016). *Energy agency statistics.* International Energy Agency. Retrieved from www.iea.org

IPCC. (2014). *Climate change 2014: Mitigation of climate change.* Berlin, Germany: Intergovernmental Panel on Climate Change.

Kumbaroğlu, G. S. (2003). Environmental taxation and economic effects: A computable general equilibrium analysis for Turkey. *Journal of Policy Modeling, 25*(8), 795–810.

Labandeira, X., and Labeaga, J. M. (2000). Efectos de un impuesto sobre las emisiones de SO2 del sector eléctrico. *Revista de Economía Aplicada, 22,* 5–32.

Labandeira, X., Labeaga, J. M., and Rodríguez, M. (2004). Green tax reforms in Spain. *Environmental Policy and Governance, 14*(5), 290–299.

Leontief, W. (1946). Wages, profit and prices. *The Quarterly Journal of Economics, 61*(1), 26–39.

Llop, M. (2008). Economic impact of alternative water policy scenarios in the Spanish production system: An input – output analysis. *Ecological Economics*, *68*(1), 288–294.

Manresa, A., Polo, C., and Sancho, F. (1988). Una evaluación de los efectos del IVA mediante un modelo de producción y gasto de coeficientes fijos. *Revista Española de Economía*, *5*(1 Y 2), 45–64.

Manresa, A., and Sancho, F. (2005). Implementing a double dividend: Recycling ecotaxes towards lower labour taxes. *Energy Policy*, *33*(12), 1577–1585.

MAPS Chile. (2014). *Opciones de Mitigación para Enfrentar el Cambio Climático: Resultados de Fase 2*. Santiago de Chile, Chile: Ministerio del Medio Ambiente, Gobierno de Chile.

McGartland, A. M., and Oates, W. E. (1985). Marketable permits for the prevention of environmental deterioration. *Journal of Environmental Economics and Management*, *12*(3), 207–228.

Meade, J. E. (1952). External economies and diseconomies in a competitive situation. *The economic journal*, *62*(245), 54–67.

Montgomery, W. D. (1972). Markets in licenses and efficient pollution control programs. *Journal of Economic Theory*, *5*(3), 395–418.

O'Ryan, R., De Miguel, C. J., Miller, S., and Munasinghe, M. (2005). Computable general equilibrium model analysis of economywide cross effects of social and environmental policies in Chile. *Ecological Economics*, *54*(4), 447–472.

Pigou, A. C. (1932). *The economics of welfare*. London: Palgrave Macmillan.

Roland-Holst, D. W., and Sancho, F. (1995). Modeling prices in a SAM structure. *The Review of Economics and Statistics*, 77, (2), 361–371.

Sancho, F. (1988). Evaluación del Peso de la Imposición Indirecta en los Precios. *Hacienda Pública Española* (113), 159–164.

Scitovsky, T. (1954). Two concepts of external economies. *Journal of Political Economy*, *62*(2), 143–151.

Stone, R. (1962). *A social accounting matrix for 1960: A programme for growth*. London, UK: Chapman & Hall.

Tarancón, M. A., del Río, P., and Albinana, F. C. (2010). Assessing the influence of manufacturing sectors on electricity demand: A cross-country input-output approach. *Energy Policy*, *38*(4), 1900–1908.

Woldwide Inflation Data. (2016). Retrieved from http://es.inflation.eu/tasas-de-inflacion/chile/inflacion-historica/ipc-inflacion-chile.aspx

Zhang, Y.-J., and Da, Y.-B. (2015). The decomposition of energy-related carbon emission and its decoupling with economic growth in China. *Renewable and Sustainable Energy Reviews*, *41*, 1255–1266.

# 15 Paris-COP21 and carbon pricing

## Coordination challenges and carbon border measures: the case of the EU

*Jordi Roca, Paola Rocchi and Mònica Serrano*

## Introduction

The Paris Agreement negotiated during the 21st Conference of the Parties (COP21) is an important step forward in the effort to coordinate the fight against climate change at international level. In fact, the agreement constitutes the new global compromise to mitigate greenhouse gas (GHG) emissions reached after Kyoto. Anyway, while the Kyoto Protocol placed specific and legally binding obligations on industrialized nations to reduce their GHG emissions, in the Paris Agreement, each country determines its contribution through the so-called Intended Nationally Determined Contributions (INDCs). As a consequence, different countries set different goals and will likely implement different policies to reduce GHG emissions. In this perspective, there is a growing concern regarding a possible negative impact of these national or regional emissions reduction policies on competitiveness. Indeed, international trade intensifies the competitiveness problem since products that are produced in different countries might end up competing within the same market with a different treatment due to different policies, The analysis of possible solutions to this competitiveness problem has therefore become particularly important in the framework of the Paris-COP21 agreement. The aim of this chapter is to analyze and shed some light on this issue, looking more specifically to carbon border adjustment measures. The analysis focuses in particular on the European Union (EU), which is playing a leading role in the international effort to face climate change since the 1990s.

The chapter is structured as follows. Section 2 describes the challenges of finding a global solution to climate change, the importance of national and local actions, and the EU experience on carbon pricing so far. Then section 3 introduces carbon border adjustments as a possible solution to coordinate different carbon control initiatives. Section 4 focuses more in detail on the design of carbon border adjustments, proposing an exemplifying exercise applied to the EU. Finally, section 5 concludes the chapter.

## The challenge of Paris-COP21: global climate change and national actions

Climate change is a "global public bad" or, in other words, climate stability is a global common. Anyway, even if every country takes advantage from mitigation policies, there is no institution with the authority to globally implement these policies. Since the adoption of the United Nations Framework Convention on Climate Change (UNFCCC) in 1992, there have been attempts to internationally coordinate policies for reducing GHG emissions that contribute to climate change, but the results obtained so far have been very modest.

The Kyoto protocol signed in 1997 was an important step in climate change policy, but it was clearly insufficient to reduce world emissions. Indeed, the agreement was only partial, limiting only the amount of emissions of the most industrialized countries (the so-called Annex-B countries). Even if, at that moment, Annex-B countries' emissions represented more than a half of world emissions, the reduction imposed for the period of 2008–2012 was only about 5% of their total emissions (compared to the 1990 level). Moreover, the United States did not ratify the agreement, and some other countries exceeded their compromises. Finally, and even more importantly, the Copenhagen negotiations in 2009, which tried to follow up on the Kyoto Protocol through a more ambitious and inclusive agreement, completely failed.

In the COP21 celebrated in Paris in December 2015, a new global climate deal was adopted. The agreement requires all parties to set their INDCs to limit emissions in the next decades, but these national pledges have been fixed unilaterally, and experts suggest that they are insufficient to reach the global commitment of limiting global temperature rise to 2°C above pre-industrial levels[1] – not to mention the 1.5°C threshold considered a more adequate objective.[2] Moreover, these pledges are non-binding, and there is no guarantee that national countries will comply with their objectives (United Nations, 2015).

Several reasons may explain the failure to achieve a more ambitious and compulsory agreement, and to comply with it. The first one is the classical free-riding problem. Since there is no global authority able to impose a policy on climate change worldwide, some countries can try to benefit from other countries' efforts to reduce emissions, avoiding the costs of domestic emissions reduction. Secondly, even if different countries were ready to contribute to the reduction of their emissions, determining how to distribute the individual efforts is very complex, because the responsibility for present and – even more – for past emissions is extremely unequal. This distributive issue is very controversial and hampers the debate on climate change agreements. Finally, there are also other forces that hinder an international agreement on climate change. Important economic interests often lobby against climate change agreements (Godal and Holtsmark, 2001). Moreover, some social habits – such as the energy-intensive lifestyles of the wealthiest segments of the world population – go in a direction contrary to the emission control policies and are not easy to change.

In this framework, voluntary decisions to reduce GHG emissions taken by national governments, local authorities, and individual citizens acquire great importance. Ostrom (2009) supports the need of "a polycentric approach for coping with climate change". Without denying that a global agreement would be necessary, she recognizes that it is urgent – and possible – to adopt decentralized initiatives. Citizens might bear in mind the climate change problem when deciding their behaviours, and they might lobby local and national authorities to adopt climate change policies; as Sen emphasizes, human behaviour is complex, and in some contexts, people could voluntarily and significantly contribute to the provision of public goods (Sen, 1977). The same fulfilment of INDCs – and the possibility that they became more ambitious in the next years – depends on the voluntary adoption of policies at national level. To conclude, even if ambitious and compulsory international agreements would be better, without these agreements, there is also some scope for individual actions, especially when the actions to reduce GHG emissions frequently lead to local or national co-benefits (such as the reduction of local air pollution or less energy dependence on imports).

### Carbon pricing: experience and difficulties for national initiatives

There is broad consensus among economists that pricing carbon emissions at global level would be a key instrument to significantly reduce GHG emissions at a reasonable cost (Baranzini et al., 2017). One way to introduce carbon pricing would be a global tax whose revenues would be centrally collected and subsequently redistributed among countries – e.g. based on their demographic weight or any other criteria. Other alternatives to globally price carbon would be a harmonized tax applied and collected by the different countries, or a global emission allowances market. Anyway, regardless of the advantages of pricing carbon at the global level, the practical implementation of this instrument has never been in the agenda of international agreements, and it is not very realistic to expect that this will happen in the next future.

Although there is no a global carbon pricing, there is a significant and increasing number of carbon pricing experiences at regional and national level. Moreover, many INDCs include proposals for emission trading systems (ETS) and/or carbon taxes. According to a World Bank report, carbon pricing instruments – including explicit carbon taxes and ETS – covered about 13% of annual global GHG emissions in 2016, while in 2005, this figure was only about 4%. The plan to introduce a national ETS in China in 2017 would considerably increase the number of emissions affected by carbon pricing (The World Bank and ECOFYS, 2016).

Even if these advances are important, the introduction of carbon pricing is very partial, uncoordinated, and in most cases, prices are very low. Indeed, as suggested in the same World Bank report, three quarters of covered GHG emissions are affected by prices lower than US$10 per ton of $CO_2$ – approximately 9.5 € per ton of $CO_2$ ($€/tCO_2$) – (The World Bank and ECOFYS, 2016, p. 3). Another recent OECD report (OECD, 2016) – which analyzes the "effective carbon rates" in 41 OECD and G20 countries and covers 80% of world energy use and carbon emissions[3] – concludes again most parts of GHG emissions (around 60%) are unpriced, and pricing is very unequal between sectors and countries. According to this report, only 10% of GHG emissions are priced at an effective carbon rate equal or exceeding 30 $€/tCO_2$, suggesting that 30€ is a "low end estimate of the climate damage they ($CO_2$ emissions) cause" (OECD, 2016, p. 15). Other authors recommend than the carbon price should be no less than US$100 – approximately 95 €/tCO$_2$ – (Van Den Bergh and Botzen, 2014).

The unilateral non-global application of mitigation policies, and especially the implementation of carbon taxes and auctioned ETS, is subject to two main inter-connected problems. One problem is the loss of competitiveness compared to other countries that do not apply similar policies. A second problem is the carbon leakage. In this case, the emissions reduction induced by the climate change policies could be partially, completely, or even more than compensated because some production processes could be moved to other countries that do not apply similar policies. These problems also explain why many carbon taxes experiences have been characterized by a more favourable treatment for energy-intensive sectors open to external competition, moving the policy away from the strict application of the "polluter pay principle" and reducing the effectiveness of the taxes (Baranzini and Carattini, 2014; Ekins and Speck, 1999).

### Carbon pricing experience in the European union

The use of taxation as one of the key elements of the EU climate change policy has been debated in EU institutions since the early 1990s (Padilla and Roca, 2004). In 1992, the European Commission (EC) presented a directive proposal for implementing an "ecotax" on energy products (European Commission, 1992). The tax was not conceived as an EU own resource, but as a harmonized minimum energy tax applied by all member countries. The proposal recommended a minimum harmonized tax of mixed type, taxing the different forms of energy according to their energy content and according to the CO$_2$ emissions emitted in their use. The proposal exempted most renewable energies. Since the EU requires the unanimity for any initiative affecting taxes, the 1992 EC proposal was not implemented due to some countries' veto. In 1995, the EC came up with a new directive (European Commission, 1995) with similar proposal but longer transition periods. The directive failed again because of the opposition of some countries. While the CO$_2$ tax at the EU level was blocked, since the early 1990s, some individual countries decided to apply explicit carbon taxes to energy uses; the most relevant cases are Denmark, Finland, and Sweden. Anyway these countries apply much lower taxes to some industrial activities due to competitiveness concerns, resulting in a very different effective taxation for different activities (Eurostat, 2003).

Although all the EU attempts to introduce a carbon tax failed so far, also in 1992, the European Council approved a first taxation on mineral oils and natural gas (European Council, 1992) to harmonize minimum rates across member countries. The European Energy Taxation Directive (ETD) successively approved in 2003 (European Council, 2003) governs the current regime of energy taxation. This directive fixes minima tax rates on the use of energy products that countries must take into account when enacting their national implementations. Compared to the previous legislation, the ETD widens the scope of taxation to more energy products, distinguishes between motor fuels and other uses of energy products, and increases the minimum rates. Anyway, the minima for non-motor fuel use are still very low. Moreover, it includes a complex system of reductions and exemptions for the industries that are highly dependent on energy products.

In 2003, the EU also introduced a new important economic tool for emissions control: the EU-ETS (European Parliament and European Council, 2003). The tool consists of a system of "cap and trade": a total amount of allowances to emit a tone of $CO_2$ are distributed across the economic unities falling under the regulatory regime; allowances can be used or traded. Thus the total emissions are set politically, but the market determines the final distribution of emissions across several economic unities. Compared to carbon tax, in this case, the policy fixes the limit to the quantity of emissions, and the price is the result of the demand for emissions permits.

The 2003 EU directive on ETS established two initial phases for the market: 2005–2007 and 2008–2012. Initially, the allowances were basically freely distributed based on historical emissions (grandfathering) to most parts of large industrial installations belonging to sectors that emit most GHGs (power plants, steel factories, oil refineries, paper mills, and glass and cement installations).[4] The first phase was considered as an experimental phase. Even though the market was very active and prices were initially high, a decreasing trend in the allowance prices made it clear that the supply of allowances were too high. Finally, the prices completely collapsed at the end of 2007.[5] In the first months of the second phase, permits were traded at a price of 20–25 €/t$CO_2$ or even more, but the economic crisis dramatically decreased the demand for allowances and their prices.

In the current phase three (2013–2020), some changes have been introduced. Now auctioning is the default method for allocating allowances: it is applied to the electric utility sector and progressively to manufacturing industry (in 2013, manufacturing industry received 80% of its allowances for free, but the proportion of free permits should decrease to 30% in 2020).[6] The main justification of the different treatment between electric sector and other sectors is to safeguard the competitiveness of industries covered by the EU-ETS. In fact, the issue of avoiding leakage and protecting competitiveness of some sectors included in ETS is in constant debate in the EU.[7]

Anyway, in phase three, carbon prices have remained very low. Using the words of Ellerman et al. (2016), "as phase III started in 2013, the prices paid to emit carbon was less than €5 [/t$CO_2$], not the €30 [/t$CO_2$] or more (. . .) that was generally expected at that time" (p. 103). At the time of this writing (December 2016), the situation is the same even though there are many political debates on how to keep allowances' prices higher (see Figure 15.1). Low carbon prices are a barrier to obtain a sufficient return for many investments in low-carbon alternatives.

Meanwhile, the EC has made a further attempt to reform the tax on energy products, trying once again to introduce a carbon tax for non-ETS. In fact, in 2011, the EC proposed a new version of the European ETD (European Commission, 2011) to reform energy taxes. To strengthen the environmental nature of this instrument, the EC proposed three changes compared to the current legislation. First, the proposal fixed higher minimum rates. Second, as the 1992 proposal, it suggested a tax with two components: a component based on the energy content

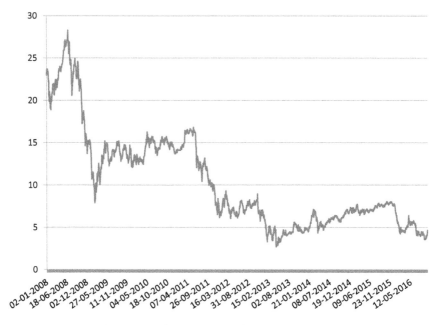

*Figure 15.1* EU-ETS: Average of daily closing price. Unit: €/tCO$_2$

Source: Own elaboration from CO$_2$ prices from SendeCO$_2$ (http://sendeco2.com/).

of any energy products and a component based on the carbon emitted equivalent to 20 €/tCO$_2$ that only applies to enterprises not affected by ETS. Third, the proposal tried to limit reductions and exemptions, removing, for example, unjustified favoured treatment for certain fossil fuels, such as diesel and coal. Nonetheless, the European Parliament did not support the EC's proposal, and the 2003 directive continues in force.

Once again, the failure in applying the reform is due to the unanimity requirement for fiscal issues in an EU where countries have very different economic structures, interests, and priorities. Among the reasons to block the reform, one of the important worries expressed by some countries' representatives was the concern about competiveness impact (Euractiv, 2012). The worries on the competitiveness are more clearly a critical issue when one considers that these concerns have been crucial to the failure of the reform, although there is no clear evidence that the reform would have had a major impact on prices. In Rocchi et al. (2014), using a multiregional input-output price model, we simulate the effect that the 2011 ETD reform would have had on prices if it were implemented in the EU countries. Using data from the year 2008, we assume that countries would have adapted their taxes to the new minimum proposed and that they would have maintained the existing taxes if these were already higher than the minimum. We find that, expressed as an increase in price consumer index, the impacts would have only been between 0.12% (Sweden) and 1.91% (Bulgaria).[8]

In short, looking at carbon policies in the EU, on the one hand, the EU has been a leader in proposals and initiatives on carbon pricing, as the 1992 and 1995 "ecotax" proposals and the introduction of the world most important ETS show. However, on the other hand, the current situation of carbon pricing in EU is far from being sufficiently effective. The minimum energy taxes are low and do not include an explicit carbon component and the ETS – that was presented as the flagship of the EU climate policy (Vlachou and Pantelias, 2014) – has been characterized by very low prices during the last years.

In the framework of the Paris-COP21 agreement, the EU presented its INDC, adopting the objective of reducing GHG emissions by 40% in 2030 (in comparison with 1990 level) with the perspective of reducing emissions by 80%–95% in 2050 (also compared to 1990).[9] To assure this reduction is not easy, and an effective carbon pricing would be a key tool for the EU climate change policy. Anyway, the greater the carbon tax is, the more challenging the problem of competitiveness becomes and some solutions are needed to address it.

## A possible solution: carbon border adjustment

Different carbon pricing initiatives or different carbon prices might arise a problem related to international trade flows. In fact, they imply a different treatment to domestic and foreign imported products that compete in the same market, and they might cause competitiveness losses and emission leakage. The concern for these negative effects has fuelled the debate on border adjustment measures, which consist in also applying a carbon price on the products imported by the region that is domestically pricing carbon emissions. The objective of these measures is leveling the carbon playing field between domestic and foreign countries when these countries apply different emissions reduction policies.

In the case of adopting a carbon tax, the way to achieve this objective would be introducing a carbon border tax adjustment (CBTA) – a tariff on imports imposed by countries implementing carbon taxes. Through a CBTA, the products imported by a country imposing a carbon tax would also be taxed according to their carbon intensity. Meanwhile, to level the carbon playing field abroad also, the goods that are exported to countries without emissions regulation should be exempted or refunded from the domestic carbon tax to avoid competitive disadvantages for domestic firms (Mattoo et al., 2009).

CBTA has also been raised as complementary measure to also avoid losses of competitiveness in the case of ETS proposals.[10] However, since allowances prices in an ETS change depending on allowances demand, it would be difficult to fix CBTA rates. Moreover, if permits – or part of them – are freely distributed, a CBTA could be considered discriminatory. Thus, in the case of ETS, it seems more adequate to ask importers to purchase emissions permits when importing goods (Kuik and Hofkes, 2010), which would be a measure probably even more complex to apply than a CBTA(Persson, 2010).

There are different possible designs of a CBTA.[11] We consider two of them. The first one consists of taxing imports, taking into account their embodied emissions – i.e. the emissions generated abroad in producing the imported goods. The second one consists on taxing imports according to the emissions that would be generated in the importing country to produce domestically the imported goods in all the phases of production; we call this alternative the "avoided emissions" design.

We can compare these two alternatives based on different criteria. One of them is their political feasibility in the framework of the World Trade Organization (WTO) rules. Even if these rules require legal interpretation and the debate on the use of import tariffs for environmental purposes is quite complex, it seems clear that the avoided emissions approach is more clearly compatible with WTO rules: the imported goods would be treated identically irrespective of the country of origin. For instance, any ton of steel would pay the same. In contrast, the application of the embodied emissions design is more controversial because it means to apply different tariffs depending on the production methods of the different countries (Hillman, 2013); the acceptability of this design would require applying an environmental exception to the general principles of WTO (as required by article XX of WTO, 1994).

Other criterion of comparison is the ease of implementation in terms of data requirement. Data access remains one of the several practical challenges of all CBTA designs, but under this perspective, the avoided emissions design is also clearly superior because it does not require data on emissions from foreign countries (Persson, 2010). Taking into account that exporting countries are not interested in revealing this information (a problem of asymmetric information), and considering the complex value chains in a globalized world, it would be extremely difficult to obtain these embodied emissions data.[12]

Finally, other criterion of comparison is the environmental impact. Under this criterion, the design based on embodied emissions would be more effective because it discriminates, taking into account if foreign production techniques are more or less polluting.

## Comparing different CBTA designs: the case of the EU

In this section, we present a comparison between two CBTA designs: the embodied emissions approach and the avoided emissions approach. We consider the EU as a case study due to its pioneering role in proposing explicit carbon taxes. We simulate and compare two hypothetical CBTAs designs that the EU could implement to balance a domestic carbon tax.

In particular, we assume that the EU decides to implement a domestic carbon tax of 20 €/tCO$_2$ applied to all domestic emissions. This tax level was the tax rate for the non-ETS sectors proposed, but not approved, by the EC to reform the European ETD (European Commission, 2011; Rocchi et al., 2014). As described in section 2.1 of this chapter, this rate would be a very moderate one. Anyway, our main interest is not the specific tariffs obtained for each design, but instead the comparison between the two designs. Moreover, the analysis can be expressed in a general form for any tax level $t$, multiplying the results of our simulation for

$t/20$. So, as an example, for a carbon tax equal to 40€, the tariffs would double compared to our results.

We assume the EU applies tariffs to all manufactured goods imported from non-EU countries. These tariffs are equivalent to 20 €/tCO$_2$ on embodied or avoided emissions depending on the design. This level of tariffs can be justified when other countries do not have carbon taxes at all (certainly the dominant situation), or alternatively assuming that the other countries are refunding their carbon taxes to exporters. We omit from the analysis agricultural products and raw materials. In fact, for many products belonging to these categories, import is the only way to provide these products to the European market. Moreover, we consider CBTA as a system of tariffs exclusively applied to products physically imported and thus not affecting services.

Since we assume that the EU implements a carbon tax on all domestic emissions, the fiscal load charged on a domestic good would be related not only to the direct pollution that a sector emits to make it but also to the emissions contained in the inputs used to produce it, because the sectors producing the inputs would also be subject to the same tax. So if a border tax aims to apply the same treatment to foreign products, it has to account for the input structure and the input emissions content.

### Emissions accounting and tariffs

To introduce the two methods used, let us consider an example. Assume the EU imports a car from Japan. This car has been produced using glass imported from Russia and pneumatics produced in China. A CBTA based on the emissions embodied in a car considers not only emissions in Japan but also emissions in Russia and China for producing inputs used in the car production. Alternatively, CBTA based on the emissions avoided in the EU by importing the car considers the emissions that the EU would emit producing the car and also the glass and the pneumatics; thus, we propose to take into account avoided emissions in the case that the car and all the inputs were produced in the EU (abating region).

To compute emissions embodied in imports we use an environmentally extended multi-region input-output (EE-MRIO) model, formally described in the Appendix. Using information about all inter-sector, inter-country deliveries and emissions by sector, the model permits to compute the emissions contained in one extra unit produced by any sector, accounting not only for the direct emissions of that sector but also for the emissions contained in its inputs, in the inputs required to produce its input, and so on. Then we re-allocate emissions by sector to emissions by product, taking into account that each sector can produce different products and that any product can actually be produced by different sectors. Finally, we obtain the CBTA tariffs by multiplying the carbon tax rate $t$ that the region is applying to domestic products times the emissions per monetary unit of imported product.

For the second simulation, we need to calculate the amount of emissions that would have been contained in a good produced in the EU, with the technology available domestically. Anyway, we need to define what "domestic technology" means. In fact, it can be the case that the EU goods are produced in different ways. Following the previous example, let us assume that some cars in the EU are produced using glass and pneumatics produced in the same EU (domestic inputs), but other cars might be produced using imported glass and domestic pneumatics, or imported pneumatics and domestic glass, or glass and pneumatics both imported from abroad. Determining how many emissions are avoided importing a car could be ambiguous depending on which one of the four cases we consider. One possibility would be to estimate the average emissions generated producing cars in the EU. This would be possible applying the EE-MRIO model to EU products, as it is usually suggested in literature. Anyway, we think this approach is not the more adequate one because it does not completely "level the carbon field". This is the reason why, to compute avoided emissions, we apply the environmentally extended single-region input-output (EE-IO) model. This method uses the so-called domestic technology assumption (DTA) and permits the computation of the emissions generated in the EU in the case that the car and all the inputs were produced in the EU (see the Appendix for a formal description of the EE-IO model).

Since input-output data are expressed in monetary terms, when the DTA is used to compute avoided emissions, an important issue related to the units considered arises, as it is extensively shown in the pioneering work of Arto et al. (2014). Using data in monetary terms, when we calculate the emissions applying the DTA, we actually estimate the emissions produced by making the imported goods with the domestic technology, but we consider the value of imported goods instead of the physical quantities imported. Due to differences in prices among countries, it can be the case that the monetary value of imports would correspond to a different monetary value if the products imported were produced domestically. Or, in other terms, to calculate the emissions that would have been produced to make domestically all the products imported is important to adjust for the level of prices, or to deflate the value of imports in order to account for international price differences. So we compute emissions avoided by trade applying the "physical DTA" adjusting for price differences across countries. The Appendix explains in detail how deflators are computed and why it is important to use the highest possible data disaggregation to avoid biases in the deflators obtained.

Also, in this second simulation, we finally compute tariffs, multiplying the emissions content of each product for the tax level $t$ implemented in the EU. Anyway, in this case we need to apply the deflators also to the tariffs obtained. To explain why this last deflation is needed, let us continue with the previous example. Let us assume that the EU fixes a domestic carbon tax rate $t$ equal to 20 €/tCO$_2$. Let us also assume that emissions to produce a car in the EU are equal to 0.5 tons of CO$_2$ per thousand € produced. So the carbon tax applied to the EU car would be equal to 0.01 per monetary unit (a 1% tax). If the price of the EU car is 10,000 €, the tax applied to each car is 100 €. A CBTA on avoided emissions applies to foreign products the same fiscal treatment as to domestic products. In our example, this means imposing a tariff equal to 100 € on each car imported from abroad. If the price of a Japanese car is 5,000 €, the tariff per monetary unit is 2% instead of 1%. So we apply a deflator per each product and each foreign country to express tariffs per monetary units.

All the analysis described earlier requires three main data, which are MRIO tables, $CO_2$ emissions data, and international trade data in physical and monetary units. The databases used are described in the Appendix.

### Embodied emissions versus avoided emissions: the comparison of two CBTAs

Table 15.1 shows results at a product level, comparing tariffs based on embodied emissions and tariffs based on avoided emissions.[13] The table analyzes the results obtained for the most affected countries: China, Indonesia, India, Russia, and Taiwan.

Generally, the most affected products are the energy-intensive products such as "other non-metallic mineral products", "basic metals", and "fabricated metal products". Even if these are the most affected products under both designs, there is a clear difference between rates based on embodied emissions and rates based on avoided emissions.[14] This reflects important differences in the production processes used in these countries compared to the average technology available in the EU. In the embodied emissions designs, for these most affected products and countries, a moderate carbon tax of 20 €/t$CO_2$ would imply tariffs higher than 6% or even two-digit tariffs. For China, India, and Russia, one of the main reasons for these high rates is a highly carbon polluting electricity sector. For very few products, tariffs based on avoided emissions would be higher than tariffs on embodied emissions, and this manly regards Indonesian products.

Energy-intensive products remain the most affected products also looking at the less affected countries that are Australia, Brazil, Canada, Japan, and United States (see Table 15.2).

In fact, for these products, the average rate would be higher than 2% in all the 14 non-EU countries. Also, for the less affected countries, in general, tariffs computed on embodied emissions are higher, although there are more cases where the opposite is true, such as for "textiles" imported from Brazil and Canada, or "leather and leather products" imported from Australia and Brazil. The most interesting case is Brazil, where tariffs under a system on avoided emissions would be higher for the most part of products considered.

Tax rates applied to different products provide a measure of the impact that CBTA would have. Anyway, its effect would depend also on the volume of goods imported in the EU from abroad. Figure 15.2 also takes into account trade volume showing the ten products-countries, over the 308 analyzed, mostly affected by a CBTA system based on embodied emissions: the total effect of the policy corresponds to the area of each column, computed as the tax rates (represented by the width of the column) multiplied by the total value imported in the EU (represented by the height of the column).

The main result is that seven out of ten products would be imported from China that alone would sustain roughly 30% of the policy's effect. The ranking of these

Table 15.1 CBTA rates for the most affected non-EU countries, 2009. Unit: percentage

| WIOD product | China | | Indonesia | | India | | Russia | | Taiwan | |
|---|---|---|---|---|---|---|---|---|---|---|
| | EE | AE | EE | AE | EE | AE | EE | AE | EE | AE |
| Food products and beverages | 2 | 0.6 | 0.9 | 1.8 | 3.7 | 0.8 | 2.2 | 1.7 | 1.5 | 1.2 |
| Tobacco products | 2 | 0.5 | 0.9 | 3.8 | 3.7 | 3 | 2.2 | 1 | 1.5 | 0.8 |
| Textiles | 2.8 | 2.1 | 3.8 | 2.5 | 3.8 | 1.6 | 2.6 | 2 | 2.7 | 1.5 |
| Wearing apparel | 2.8 | 1.5 | 3.8 | 1 | 3.8 | 1.4 | 2.6 | 0.8 | 2.7 | 1.7 |
| Leather and leather products | 2.1 | 2.6 | 1.8 | 1 | 2.3 | 1.1 | 2.7 | 1.4 | 1.6 | 1.4 |
| Wood and products of wood and cork | 2.9 | 0.9 | 1.6 | 0.6 | 5.1 | 0.7 | 3.3 | 1.3 | 1.5 | 0.4 |
| Pulp, paper and paper products | 3.9 | 0.5 | 2.8 | 0.6 | 5.3 | 0.6 | 3.1 | 0.7 | 2.6 | 0.3 |
| Printed matter and recorded media | 3.9 | 1.9 | 2.8 | 2.6 | 5.3 | 2.3 | 3.1 | 0.7 | 2.6 | 0.8 |
| Coke, refined petroleum products | 5.1 | 1.2 | 1.6 | 1.7 | 4.9 | 1.8 | 5.4 | 2 | 3.4 | 1.9 |
| Chemicals, chemical products | 5.5 | 2.5 | 2.2 | 8.1 | 5.1 | 2.4 | 9.5 | 3.3 | 3.8 | 1.6 |
| Rubber and plastic products | 4.2 | 1.4 | 2.1 | 1.1 | 4.5 | 1.3 | 4.5 | 0.7 | 2.3 | 0.9 |
| Non-metallic mineral products | 10.1 | 7.6 | 12.3 | 6.1 | 12.9 | 4.7 | 12.8 | 7.8 | 12.3 | 4.2 |
| Basic metals | 6.4 | 1.7 | 6.7 | 0.5 | 8.3 | 1.7 | 10.3 | 1.3 | 4.2 | 1.3 |
| Fabricated metal products | 6.2 | 3.2 | 6.7 | 2.3 | 7.8 | 3 | 10.3 | 3 | 4.2 | 2.9 |
| Machinery and equipment nec | 4 | 1.7 | 1.5 | 1.3 | 4.5 | 1.4 | 4.5 | 1.2 | 1.8 | 1.1 |
| Office machinery and computers | 3.3 | 0.7 | 0 | 1.4 | 3.8 | 1.1 | 4.3 | 0.3 | 1.7 | 0.4 |
| Electrical machinery | 3.3 | 1.2 | 1.8 | 1 | 4.2 | 1.3 | 4.3 | 1.1 | 1.7 | 0.5 |
| Radio, television and comm. eq. | 3.3 | 1.4 | 1.8 | 0.7 | 3.8 | 2.2 | 4.3 | 0.8 | 1.7 | 0.7 |
| Medical and optical instruments | 3.3 | 4.2 | 1.8 | 0.8 | 4 | 1.9 | 4.3 | 0.2 | 1.7 | 1.6 |
| Motor vehicles, trailers | 3.3 | 1.6 | 1.3 | 0.8 | 4.1 | 0.9 | 3.4 | 1 | 1.7 | 0.9 |
| Other transport equipment | 3.3 | 1.1 | 1.3 | 2.2 | 4.5 | 1.5 | 3.4 | 3.1 | 1.7 | 0.9 |
| Furniture | 3.3 | 1.6 | 2.1 | 1.6 | 2.9 | 0.9 | 4.1 | 0.7 | 1.9 | 1.2 |

Note: Rates based on embodied emissions (EE) and on avoided emissions (AE).
Source: Own elaboration

Table 15.2 CBTA rates for the less affected non-EU countries, 2009. Unit: percentage

| WIOD product | Australia | | Brazil | | Canada | | Japan | | United States | |
|---|---|---|---|---|---|---|---|---|---|---|
| | EE | AA | EE | AA | EE | AA | EE | AA | EE | AA |
| Food products and beverages | 1.1 | 1 | 0.7 | 1.6 | 1 | 0.5 | 0.6 | 0.3 | 1.4 | 0.9 |
| Tobacco products | 1.1 | 0.8 | 0.7 | 2.3 | 1 | 0.4 | 0.6 | 1.4 | 1.4 | 0.9 |
| Textiles | 1.2 | 0.7 | 0.6 | 1.2 | 1.2 | 1.5 | 0.8 | 0.5 | 1.5 | 0.8 |
| Wearing apparel | 1.1 | 0.7 | 0.6 | 1 | 1 | 0.4 | 0.8 | 0.2 | 1.4 | 0.7 |
| Leather and leather products | 1.1 | 1.8 | 0.5 | 0.9 | 0.9 | 0.9 | 0.7 | 0.3 | 1.4 | 1.1 |
| Wood and products of wood and cork | 1.2 | 0.8 | 0.5 | 0.8 | 1.1 | 0.9 | 0.9 | 0.2 | 1.8 | 0.6 |
| Pulp, paper and paper products | 1.1 | 0.7 | 0.7 | 0.8 | 1.1 | 0.7 | 0.9 | 0.1 | 1.3 | 0.5 |
| Printed matter and recorded media | 1 | 0.6 | 0.7 | 0.5 | 1 | 0.4 | 0.9 | 0.3 | 1.1 | 0.5 |
| Coke, refined petroleum products | 2.1 | 10.2 | 1.4 | 2.8 | 3.4 | 3.2 | 1.7 | 1.8 | 2.3 | 2.9 |
| Chemicals, chemical products | 2 | 1 | 1.1 | 3.5 | 2.2 | 1.3 | 1.6 | 0.4 | 1.9 | 0.8 |
| Rubber and plastic products | 1.5 | 0.5 | 0.8 | 0.7 | 1.2 | 0.8 | 1.1 | 0.4 | 1.4 | 0.4 |
| Non-metallic mineral products | 4.1 | 1.4 | 3.2 | 3.6 | 2.9 | 4.4 | 3.7 | 0.7 | 4.9 | 1.3 |
| Basic metals | 2.2 | 0.5 | 1.6 | 1.1 | 2 | 0.3 | 1.9 | 0.6 | 1.9 | 0.9 |
| Fabricated metal products | 2.6 | 1 | 1.6 | 1.9 | 1.9 | 1.1 | 1.9 | 0.9 | 1.9 | 0.7 |
| Machinery and equipment nec | 1.7 | 0.5 | 0.8 | 1.1 | 1.1 | 0.4 | 0.9 | 0.5 | 1 | 0.5 |
| Office machinery and computers | 0.9 | 0.2 | 0.8 | 0.4 | 1 | 0.3 | 0.9 | 0.3 | 0.7 | 0.4 |
| Electrical machinery | 1.3 | 0.2 | 0.8 | 1.3 | 1 | 0.2 | 0.9 | 0.3 | 0.7 | 0.2 |
| Radio, television and comm. eq. | 1.4 | 0.7 | 0.8 | 1.3 | 1 | 0.4 | 0.9 | 0.7 | 0.7 | 0.6 |
| Medical and optical instruments | 1.3 | 0.3 | 0.8 | 1.2 | 1 | 0.5 | 0.9 | 0.5 | 0.7 | 0.4 |
| Motor vehicles, trailers | 1.2 | 0.4 | 0.7 | 0.7 | 1 | 0.6 | 0.9 | 0.5 | 1.1 | 0.5 |
| Other transport equipment | 1.2 | 1 | 0.7 | 0.6 | 1 | 0.9 | 0.9 | 0.6 | 1.1 | 0.8 |
| Furniture | 1.3 | 0.2 | 0.6 | 8.7 | 1 | 0.4 | 1 | 0.4 | 0.9 | 0.7 |

Note: Rates based on embodied emissions (EE) and on avoided emissions (AE).
Source: Own elaboration

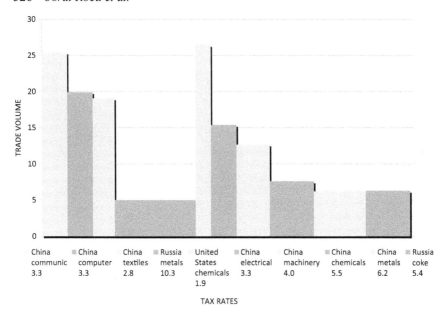

*Figure 15.2* Products most affected by CBTA on embodied emissions, 2009. Unit: trade volume in billions of €. Tax rates in percentage

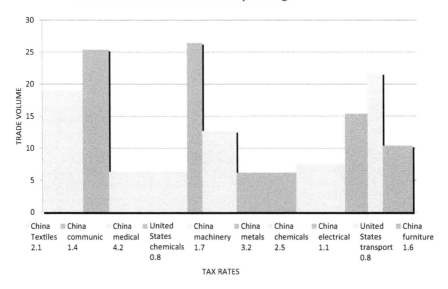

*Figure 15.3* Products most affected by CBTA on avoided emissions, 2009. Unit: trade volume in billions of €. Tax rates in percentage

products seems to be more related with the volume of trade than the severity of the rates imposed: the three most affected products, for example, would not be energy-intensive products, but "radio, television, and communication equipment"; "office machinery and computers"; and "textiles". For the CBTA, based on avoided emissions, although the impact in absolute terms would be different, the ranking of the most affected products would change only partially (see Figure 15.3). One reason is that, as previously described, the policy impact relies a lot more on the volume of trade than on the severity of the tariffs imposed.

## Final remarks: the climate policy after Paris-COP21 agreement and the future of carbon taxes

Some experts celebrated the Paris-COP21 agreement as a historical step in the fight against climate change, while others denounced its great shortcomings. The future is open. We do not know if most countries will respect and strength their mitigation plans – as the objective of maintaining emissions in a non-very dangerous trend would require – or if, on the contrary, many national plans will be missed.[15]

According to Paris-COP21 strategy, individual countries decide their emissions objective and their mitigation policies. Thus, in the short term, there is no perspective regarding introducing some type of carbon pricing at the global level. In the best scenario, many countries will implement ambitious policies to reduce carbon emissions and carbon pricing might have an important role as a tool to reduce the costs of controlling emissions. If national initiatives strongly advance, we might think of some type of carbon pricing convergence to a great club of countries or even at global level. Facing this possible advance, many difficulties and oppositions arise; one of them is that non-global advances in carbon pricing could imply competitiveness and emissions leakage problems. As is already happening, it is very likely that carbon pricing proposals and initiatives will increase in the future and that the debate over carbon border adjustments will grow.

To contribute to the debate on the future of carbon pricing in the Paris-COP21 framework, the chapter provides first a description of the trajectory that the EU has followed so far with regard to carbon pricing policies. Then, due to the leading role the EU has taken since the 1990s, the chapter considers the EU as a case study to compare two different designs of a carbon border tax (embodied emissions and avoided emissions) in order to add information to the debate on carbon border adjustments. The exercise we proposed focuses on the carbon tax that is the simplest way of applying the polluter pays principles. However, we are aware that, probably, there will be more initiatives to create emission allowances markets than carbon taxes. In any case, these initiatives also foster the debate on carbon adjustment measures and require some accountability of emissions for imported products, thus our outcomes remain relevant.

We conclude that design matters a lot in terms of implied tariffs. The practical difficulties of implementation of both designs are also very different, being much lower in the avoided emissions design. We can also of other designs that could considerably reduce these difficulties as limiting the CBTA only to the most energy-intensive products and/or defining some standards of emissions for the different products (perhaps based in the best available technology concept).

# Appendix

## The EE-MRIO and EE-IO models

To compute emissions embodied in imports we use an EE-MRIO model. Let us consider a world consisting of $c$ countries, each composed by n sectors.[16] Matrix X represents the inter-country, inter-sector deliveries in the world, where its element $x_{ij}^{rs}$ shows the amount of output from sector $i$ in country $r$ consumed as intermediate input by sector $j$ in country $s$. Matrix **A** represents the world input structure, where each element $a_{ij}^{rs}$ is obtained as $a_{ij}^{rs} = x_{ij}^{rs} / x_i^r$, $x_i^r$ being the total output of sector $i$ in country $r$. A permits us to define the Leontief inverse $\mathbf{L} = (\mathbf{I} - \mathbf{A})^{-1}$, where any element $l_{ij}^{rs}$ reveals additional direct and indirect output that sector $i$ of county $r$ produces for an additional monetary unit of sector $j$ in country $s$. An EE-MRIO adds information on emission intensity $e_i^r$ obtained from dividing total emissions by sector over total output produced by each sector. Using this additional information, we compute $\mathbf{G} = \hat{\mathbf{e}}\mathbf{L}$, where any element $g_{ij}^{rs}$ reveals the emissions that sector $i$ of country $r$ produces for an additional unit of sector $j$ in country $s$. Then we re-allocate emissions by sector to emissions by product, taking into account that each sector can produce different products and that any product can actually be produced by different sectors. So we use a rectangular matrix **U** of dimension $[(n \times c) \times (m \times c)]$ to link the information at a sector level to different products m. **U** is a diagonal block matrix, where $u_{ik}^{rs}$ shows the share of product $k$ of country $s$ produced by sector $i$ in country $r$. Emissions embodied in any product is obtained as a $(m \times c)$-dimensional vector $\tilde{\mathbf{e}}$ equal to $\tilde{\mathbf{e}} = \mathbf{i}'\mathbf{GU}$, with **i** being one's vector of appropriate dimensions. Finally, we obtain the CBTA $\boldsymbol{\tau}$ by multiplying the carbon tax rate $t$ that the region is applying to domestic products times the emissions per monetary unit of imported product. For emissions embodied in imports, we have $\boldsymbol{\tau} = t\tilde{\mathbf{e}}$.

The method needed to compute avoided emissions is EE-IO model, applying the so-called DTA. Through this model, we calculate the amount of emissions that would have been contained in a domestic product if all its inputs were produced domestically, with the technology available domestically in region $R$. So emissions by sector per unit of output are represented by $\mathbf{G}_{\mathbf{R}} = \hat{\mathbf{e}}_{\mathbf{R}}\mathbf{L}_{\mathbf{R}}$, where $\mathbf{e}_{\mathbf{R}}$ is the vector of emission intensities for region $R$ and $\mathbf{L}_{\mathbf{R}}$ is the Leontief inverse derived from the matrix of total input coefficients $\mathbf{A}_{\mathbf{T}}$ of the region that includes domestic and imported inputs. As before, emissions by product are calculated as

$\tilde{\mathbf{e}}_{\mathbf{R}} = \mathbf{i'}\mathbf{G}_{\mathbf{R}}\mathbf{U}_{\mathbf{R}}$, where $\mathbf{U}_{\mathbf{R}}$ is a ($n \times m$) matrix showing the share of any product $k$ produced by any sector $i$ of the region. We finally deflate the value of imports in order to account for international price differences.

## Computation of deflators

For MRIO and environmental data, we use the database made available by the WIOD project since April 2012 and updated in November 2013 (Timmer et al., 2015). For MRIO tables, the study considers the information contained in the world input output tables and international supply and use tables (WIOT-ISUT). These data refer to 27 European counties, 13 other major countries in the world, and all the remaining regions aggregated in a single "rest of the world" region. In particular, we use the symmetrical world input-output table at factor prices (disaggregated in 35 economic sectors) and the international supply-and-use table at current prices (with information on 59 products). For $CO_2$ emissions data, we use the environmental accounts made available by WIOD. This satellite accounts have the same sector breakdown and geographical coverage as the WIOT-ISUT series. For our simulation, we use data from 2009, being the more recent year with data on emissions available in WIOD.

Finally, we use data on international trade from the database COMEXT made available by Eurostat (Eurostat, 2015). This database contains statistics collected by member states on merchandise trade among EU countries and between member states and global partners. Data are expressed in monetary terms (euro) as well as in physical term (kilograms). In particular, among all data available, we use the information for the 14 non-European countries available in WIOD too and information on 217 products.

## Dataset

To compute tariffs based on avoided emissions, the analysis has to consider that usually the same product produced in different countries has different prices. We consider the EU as a single region. We compute the emissions that the EU would generate in order to domestically produce the goods imported – that is, the avoided emissions. Computing avoided emissions through the domestic technology assumption, we need to apply a deflator for each product and each country to take into account international differences in prices. The deflators are also applied to the final tax rates obtained since tariffs are a tax on quantity imported that should not depend on international price differences. The deflator $d_k^r$ of product k that the EU imports from country r is equal to the ratio between the domestic price of k in the EU and the price of the same good produced abroad and imported by the EU, $d_k^r = p_k^s / p_k^r$, with s being the EU.

We obtain data on prices from the COMEXT database (Eurostat, 2015), which contains information on imports/exports to/from the EU in both monetary and physical terms. We obtain the prices of the imported product $p_k^r$ by dividing the value of a product imported in the EU from a foreign country over its quantity. Regarding the domestic price of the EU product $p_k^s$, we compute the price of the products exported from EU, and we assume that the prices of products exported from EU are the same as the domestic price of EU products, because data in physical terms are available only for international trade flows.

By using data in monetary and physical terms from COMEXT, the prices obtained are those implicit in the COMEXT database. As the deflators are then applied to WIOD import data, we assume that prices in the two databases are the same.[17] There are two reasons for using data in monetary and physical terms from COMEXT. First, the database records imports in "cost, insurance, and freight" (CIF) prices and exports in "free on board" (FOB) prices. Also, as the WIOD uses CIF and FOB prices, assuming that prices are the same seems to be realistic. Second, using data in monetary terms from COMEXT has a further advantage as data are more disaggregated than in the WIOD. We use information for 217 COMEXT products to compute the deflators for the 22 WIOD products on which the analysis is focused.

Using aggregated data could cause a bias in the deflators computed, just because the relative weight of different sub-products belonging to the same aggregate category is different. Let us consider a simplified numerical example in which the EU exports and imports two different manufactured food products, yogurt, and wine, with a non-EU country. Let us also assume that while the European yogurt exported is twice as expensive as the imported yogurt ($P_y^E = 4P_y^I = 2$), the price of a bottle of wine is the same ($P_W^E = P_W^I = 10$). Finally, let us imagine that Europe exports 10 units of yogurt and 10 bottles of wine ($Q_y^I = 10$, $Q_w^E = 10$), and imports 50 units of yogurt and 10 bottles of wine (($Q_y^E = 50$, $Q_w^I = 10$). The values of exported and imported goods are thus $V_y^E = 40, V_y^E = 100, V_y^I = 100, V_w^I = 100$. If data on the available values and quantities are disaggregated, by dividing the values over the quantities of yogurt and wine exported and imported, we obtain the original prices, and the deflators obtained are equal to two for yogurt and one for wine. If data on values and quantities for the two products are aggregated (($V^E = 140, V^I = 200, Q^E = 20, Q^I = 60$), we obtain a price for the unique good exported ($P^E = 7$) and a price for the unique product imported ($P^I = 3.3$) based on the relative weight of each product, resulting in a deflator equal to 2.1, which will be greater than the highest deflator obtained with disaggregated data.

Therefore, to compute a deflator for each WIOD product, we compute the prices of imports and exports with the highest disaggregation possible using COMEXT data, and we then aggregate in a single price for each WIOD category, weighting the prices for the quantities imported. In the previous numerical example, we would obtain an "adjusted" aggregated price of export $P^E_{\text{adjusted}}$ equal to 5, an "adjusted" aggregated price of import $P^I_{\text{adjusted}}$ equal to 3.3, and a deflator equal to 1.5.[18] Formally, the adjusted prices are computed as follows in (15.A.1) and (15.A.2):

$$P^E_{adjusted} = \frac{P_y^E * Q_y^I + P_w^E * Q_w^I}{Q_y^I + Q_w^I} = 5 , \tag{15.A.1}$$

$$P^I_{adjusted} = \frac{P_y^I * Q_y^I + P_w^I * Q_w^I}{Q_y^I + Q_w^I} = 3.3 . \tag{15.A.2}$$

# Notes

1 A report form the United Nations Environment Programme (UNEP) analyses the implications of the INDCs committed of 146 countries accounting for around 90% of global GHG emissions. The report estimates the gap between these INDCs and their estimated world emission trajectory compatible with staying below 2°C above pre-industrial levels. It concludes that "submitted contributions are far from enough and the emission gap in both 2025 and 2030 will be very significant" (UNEP, 2015, p. xxii). In the words of a OECD report, "mitigation pledges submitted by individual countries in the lead up to COP21 are not sufficient to limit temperatures increases to below 2°C but instead are more likely to put the world in a pathway leading to a temperature increase of about 3°C" (OECD, 2016, p. 26).

2 The 1.5°C objective has been defended not only for many ONGs. Also, the official UNFCCC website considers this objective when describing the Paris Agreement: "The Paris Agreement's central aim is to strengthen the global response to the threat of climate change by keeping a global temperature rise this century well below 2 degrees Celsius above pre-industrial levels and to pursue efforts to limit the temperature increase even further to 1.5 degrees Celsius" (http://unfccc.int/paris_agreement/items/9485.php).

3 The report includes not only explicit carbon taxes and ETS but also specific energy taxes that are in fact the main component in pricing carbon emissions.

4 The EU ETS affects less than a half of total EU GHG emissions.

5 In this first phase, allowances could not be accumulated (banked) for being used in 2008 or after. During the second phase – and following years – the banking of allowances was permitted. Ellerman et al. (2016) provide an excellent synthesis of the ETS experience during the first two phases and during the beginning of phase three.

6 See information from the European Commission (http://ec.europa.eu/clima/policies/ets/allowances/index_en.htm).

7 See information from the European Commissionn (http://ec.europa.eu/clima/policies/ets/allowances/leakage/index_en.htm).

8 The estimate can be considered as the maximum potential impact on final prices.

9 See http://www4.unfccc.int/submissions/INDC/Published%20Documents/Latvia/1/LV-03-06-EU%20IN DC.pdf. The reduction for 2030 is not so much ambitious as it would seem if we take into account that the EU GHG emissions in 2014 were nearly 25% lower than 1990 emissions (http://ec.europa.eu/eurostat/statistics-explained/index.php/Greenhouse_gas_emission_statistics).

10 In 2009, the US government submitted a proposal to implement an emissions trading mechanism, the American Clean Energy and Security Act (American House of Representatives, 2009). Although ultimately the act was not approved, the proposal included border adjustment as a competitiveness measure to ensure the equal distribution of costs in the absence of an international agreement limiting emissions.

11 The debate on the possible designs also applies in the case of allowances purchased by importers in an ETS. Anyway, from now on we focus the analysis exclusively on CBTA.

12 In any design, the difficulties of applying a CBTA could be reduced – but not avoided – limiting the CBTA to the products potentially more affected by loss of competiveness.

13 A caveat must be considered concerning the emissions related to international transport. In fact, emissions associated with international transport are included in the data used, but IO data is only permitted to calculate one average technology for each good produced by each country, while they are not permitted to distinguish between the emissions contained in a good produced in one country and sold in the same country, and the emissions contained in the same good sold abroad. This implies that the analysis could be underestimating embodied emissions and overestimating avoided emissions.

14 Observe that tariffs based in avoided emissions are also different for different countries; the reason is that these tariffs are not expressed by physical unity but for unity of value and prices are different in different countries.
15 The results of 2016 presidential elections in the United States do not invite optimism at all.
16 Matrices are indicated by bold, upright capital letters; vectors by bold, upright lower case letters; and scalars by italicized lowercase letters. Vectors are columns by definition so that row vectors are obtained by transposition, indicated by a prime. A diagonal matrix with the elements of any vector on its main diagonal and all other entries equal to zero is indicated by a circumflex.
17 An alternative method would be to use data in monetary terms from the WIOD. This implies directly finding the prices of the WIOD database, but assuming that the quantities recorded in the two databases are the same.
18 An alternative way would be, inversely, to adjust the import price for the quantities exported. We choose the first alternative because the deflators obtained are then applied to adjust products imported by the EU.

# References

American House of Representatives. (2009). *American Clean Energy and Security Act H.R.2454.*

Arto, I., Roca, J., and Serrano, M. (2014). Measuring emissions avoided by international trade: Accounting for price differences. *Ecological Economics, 97*, 93–100.

Baranzini, A., and Carattini, S. (2014). *Taxation of emissions of greenhouse gases.* In *Global Environmental Change* (pp. 543–560). Dordrecht, The Netherlands: Springer.

Baranzini, A., van den Bergh, J. C. J. M., Carattini, S., Howarth, R., Padilla, E., and Roca, J. (2017). *Carbon pricing in climate policy: Seven reasons, complementary instruments, and political-economy considerations*: WIREs Climate Change. e462. doi: 10.1002/wcc.462. West Sussex, United Kingdom: John Wiley & Sons Ltd (in press).

Ekins, P., and Speck, S. (1999). Competitiveness and exemptions from environmental taxes in Europe. *Environmental and Resource Economics, 13*(4), 369–396.

Ellerman, A. D., Marcantonini, C., and Zaklan, A. (2016). The European Union emissions trading system: Ten years and counting. *Review of Environmental Economics and Policy, 10*(1), 89–107.

Euractiv. (2012). *Parliament shoots down commission's energy tax plan.* Retrieved from www.euractiv.com/sustainability/meps-deal-blow-commission-energy-ne-ws-512275

European Commission. (1992). Proposal for a council directive introducing a tax on carbon dioxide emissions and energy. COM (92) 226 final, June 30. Brussels, Belgium: EU.

European Commission. (1995). Amended proposal for a council directive introducing a tax on carbon dioxide emissions and energy. COM (95) 172 final, May 10. Brussels, Belgium: EU.

European Commission. (2011). Proposal for a Council Directive amending Directive 2003/96/EC restructuring the Community framework for the taxation of energy products and electricity. COM (2011) 169, March 8. Brussels, Belgium: EU.

European Council. (1992). Council Directive 92/81/EEC of 19 October 1992 on the harmonization of the structures of excise duties on mineral oils. 92/81/EEC, October 19. Brusels, Belgium: EU.

European Council. (2003). Council directive restructuring the Community framework for the taxation of energy products and electricity. 2003/96/EC, October 27. Brusels, Belgium: EU.

European Parliament and European Council. (2003). Directive 2003/87/EC of the European Parliament and of the Council of 13 October 2003 establishing a scheme for greenhouse gas emission allowance trading within the Community and amending Council Directive 96/61/EC. 2003/87/EC, October, 13. Brusels, Belgium: EU.

Eurostat. (2003). Energy taxes in the nordic countries- does the polluter pay? National Statistics offices in Norway, Sweden, Finland and Denmark, Final Report. Luxembourg EU.

Eurostat. (2015). EU Trade since 1988 by CPA_2002 (DS-056992). Luxembourg: EU.

Godal, O., and Holtsmark, B. (2001). Greenhouse gas taxation and the distribution of costs and benefits: the case of Norway. *Energy Policy*, *29*(8), 653–662.

Hillman, J. (2013). Changing climate for carbon taxes: Who's afraid of the WTO? *German Marshall Fund of the United States Climate and Energy Paper Series*.

Kuik, O., and Hofkes, M. (2010). Border adjustment for European emissions trading: Competitiveness and carbon leakage. *Energy Policy*, *38*(4), 1741–1748.

Mattoo, A., Subramanian, A., Van Der Mensbrugghe, D., and He, J. (2009). *Reconciling climate change and trade policy*. World Bank Policy Research Working Paper 5123.

OECD. (2016). *Effective carbon rates: Pricing $CO_2$ through taxes and emissions trading-systems*. Paris, France: OECD Publishing.

Ostrom, E. (2009). A polycentric approach for coping with climate change. Policy Research Working Paper, Background Paper to the 2010 World Development Report.

Padilla, E., and Roca, J. (2004). The proposals for a European tax on $CO_2$ and their implications for intercountry distribution. *Environmental and Resource Economics*, *27*(3), 273–295.

Persson, S. (2010). Practical aspects of border carbon adjustment measures: Using a trade facilitation perspective to assess trade costs. *Issue Paper* (Vol. 13). International Centre for Trade and Sustainable Development (ICTSD) Geneva, Switzerland.

Rocchi, P., Serrano, M., and Roca, J. (2014). The reform of the European energy tax directive: Exploring potential economic impacts in the EU27. *Energy Policy*, *75*, 341–353.

Sen, A. K. (1977). Rational fools: A critique of the behavioral foundations of economic theory. *Philosophy & Public Affairs*, *6*(4), 317–344.

Timmer, M. P., Dietzenbacher, E., Los, B., Stehrer, R., and de Vries, G. J. (2015). An illustrated user guide to the world input – output database: The case of global automotive production. *Review of International Economics*, *23*(3), 575–605.

United Nations. (2015). *Synthesis report on the aggregate effect of the intended nationally determined contributions*. Conference of the Parties, Twenty-first session, Paris, 30 November to 11 December 2015. United Nations, Framework Convention on Climate Change (https://unfccc.int/resource/docs/2015/cop21/eng/07.pdf).

UNEP. (2015). The emissions gap report 2015. Nairobi, Kenya: United Nations Environment Program

Van Den Bergh, J. C. J. M., and Botzen, W. J. W. (2014). A lower bound to the social cost of $CO_2$ emissions. *Nature Climate Change*, *4*(4), 253–258.

Vlachou, A., and Pantelias, G. (2014). The EU's emissions trading system. *Cambridge Journal of Economics*, *38*, 127–152.

The World Bank and ECOFYS. (2016). *Carbon pricing watch 2016*. Washington, DC: The World Bank Retrieved from http://hdl.handle.net/10986/24288

WTO. (1994). *General agreement on tariffs and trade*. World Trade Organization (https://www.wto.org/english/docs_e/legal_e/legal_e.htm#GATT94).

# 16 Revisiting Japanese carbon footprint studies

*Yosuke Shigetomi, Keisuke Nansai, Kayoko Shironitta, and Shigemi Kagawa*

## Introduction

The Paris Agreement, aimed at keeping global temperatures of the year 2100 within 2°C of those before the Industrial Revolution, was adopted at the Conference of Parties (COP 21) held in December 2015. The agreement sets a new international framework involving all nations, including economically developing nations, to strive for reduction of greenhouse gases (GHG) in a coordinated manner. When the Japanese government ratified the Paris Agreement on November 8, 2016, it undertook a commitment to have domestic GHG emissions of 2030 that will be 26% lower than those of 2013, in line with a Nationally Determined Contribution (NDC) (Prime Minister of Japan and His Cabinet, 2016b). Japan, an industrial nation with heavy manufacturing industries and information technology industries as its economic backbone, emitted the fifth largest carbon dioxide ($CO_2$) emission amount worldwide in 2015 (IEA, 2015). For COP3 of the Kyoto Protocol held in December 1997, Japan set a target of 6% emissions reduction compared with 1990. It achieved that goal during the first commitment period (2008–2012). Territorial emissions of Japan in recent years, however, have been far from the targets set out in the Paris Agreement for Japan (Greenhouse Gas Inventory Office of Japan, 2016). Partially explaining that background, the shutdown of nuclear power plants after the Great East Japan Earthquake in 2011 and the consequent increased imports of fossil fuels have cast a long shadow on Japanese aspirations. Therefore, attainment of the Paris Agreement targets will require technological innovations such as new energy and low-carbon technologies (e.g. electric vehicles) – an energy mix centered on expansion of renewable energy and carbon dioxide capture and storage (CCS). However, from the viewpoints of energy costs and energy security assurance, low-carbon measures depending entirely upon technical aspects of the energy supply side entail large risks (McLellan et al., 2013). For Japan, with particularly poor energy resources, it is extremely important to undertake emissions reduction efforts that involve transformation of the energy demand side (consumer side). Earlier research by Hertwich (2005b, 2011) and by the Working Group III (WG3) of the Fifth Assessment Report (AR5) by the Intergovernmental Panel on Climate Change (i.e. IPCC AR5 WG3 Chapter 9.3) has identified the importance of demand-side roles for climate change mitigation.

With increased importance of overviewing life-cycle environmental burdens associated with production activities from the consumer side, consumption-based accounting has been proposed as a tool to quantify environmental burdens generated by supply chains through which consumers purchase goods and services (Barrett et al., 2013; Davis and Caldeira, 2010; Hertwich and Peters, 2009; IPCC AR5 WG3, 2014; Lenzen et al., 2004; Peters, 2008; Peters and Hertwich, 2006, 2008; Peters et al., 2011; Wiedmann, 2009). Consumption-based accounting is based on the concept of "consumer responsibility" with respect to conventional "producer responsibility" by which $CO_2$ generated by the production of energy, goods, and services is attributed to the producer (Munksgaard and Pedersen, 2001). As an earlier case study, Munksgaard et al. (2000) analyzed direct and indirect $CO_2$ emissions induced by household consumption demand in Denmark during 1966–1992. From that study, they reported, "Danish consumers are responsible for the global environmental consequences of their consumption." Based on the results of that study, Munksgaard and Pedersen (2001) pointed out the necessity of expanding the accounting of $CO_2$ emissions to include $CO_2$ embodied in imported non-energy goods. Subsequently, the quantification of consumption-based environmental burdens has been used widely in the form of "environmental footprints" (Hoekstra and Wiedmann, 2014). Environmental footprints have been used for analyses of diversified environmental issues such as water resources (Feng et al., 2011), land utilization (Weinzettel et al., 2013), biodiversity (Lenzen et al., 2012), mineral resources (Wiedmann et al., 2015), health effects of air pollutants (Takahashi et al., 2014; Nagashima et al., 2016), chemical substance pollution (Koh et al., 2016), and nitrogen (Oita et al., 2016), as well as GHG ($CO_2$) (Hertwich and Peters, 2009). Moreover, in recent years, mapping of global environmental footprints on the earth (spatial footprints) has been attempted (Kanemoto et al., 2016; Moran and Kanemoto, 2016a, 2016b).

Although much room remains for discussion of how emission responsibilities are to be shared between producers and consumers (Lenzen et al., 2007; Rodrigues and Domingos, 2008), consumption-based GHG emissions – that is, carbon footprints of consumption (Wiedmann and Minx, 2008), present numerous benefits from a political perspective. For instance, Wiedmann (2009) indicated that consumption-based accounting complements conventional production-based accounting by revealing all drivers of GHG emissions associated with consumption and then referred to the other benefits related to international climate policies. Peters (2008) and Peters and Hertwich (2008) demonstrated that because consumption-based emissions of economically developed nations are more involved with global emissions than production-based (territorial) emissions of a few countries, consumption-based accounting can be expected to increase emissions mitigation options for economically developed nations and can facilitate cleaner production through international mitigation schemes such as clean development mechanisms (CDM). Furthermore, Kanemoto et al. (2014) argued that the Kyoto Protocol jurisdiction could grow from 28% of the fastest-growing flows to 80% of them if the same Kyoto signatories set targets based on consumption-based accounting in addition to production-based accounting.

Given that academic background, this chapter will "revisit" earlier studies related to carbon footprints of Japan. Next, we present connections between their findings and contributions, and emissions reduction targets of the Paris Agreement. Finally, we discuss the policy vision for accomplishment of the Japanese NDC of the Paris Agreement using footprint information.

## Lessons from past Japanese carbon footprint studies

### Carbon leakage and carbon footprint of Japan

Carbon footprint studies of Japan's final demand using input-output analysis were developed based on analytical methods used to quantify embodied energy consumption, which were vigorously pursued in the 1980s. Those studies started from the beginning of the 1990s just as the world was alerted to the looming danger of climate change (Imura et al., 1994; Kondo et al., 1998; Moriguchi et al., 1993a, 1993b; Yoshioka et al., 1991; Yoshioka et al., 1992). As Nansai (2009) has summarized, Japan has a detailed input-output table comprising approximately 400 intermediate sectors, by which estimation of embodied $CO_2$ emissions by sector and its database compilation have been promoted extensively. For instance, Nansai, Kagawa, Kondo, Tohno, et al. (2013) estimated not only embodied emission intensities related to $CO_2$ emissions originating and not originating from energy production, but also embodied intensities for energy consumption, nitrogen oxides ($NO_x$), sulfur oxides ($SO_x$), and suspended particulate matter in Japan in 1995. Information about these intensities, distributed to the public via a web page called "Embodied Energy and Emission Intensity Data for Japan Using Input-Output Tables (3EID)" (Nansai and Moriguchi, 2013), was used widely not only for life-cycle inventory data for academic studies but also for estimation of the direct and indirect environmental burdens associated with corporate activities in the form of Corporate Social Responsibility (CSR).

Identification of Japan's carbon leakage using such embodied intensity started in the 1990s. Kondo et al. (1998) demonstrated that embodied $CO_2$ emissions induced by exports from Japan exceeded those by imports from foreign countries until 1985 under domestic technology assumptions. This tendency reversed in 1990. In other words, their results indicate that carbon leakage of Japan existed already during 1985–1990. Hondo et al. (1997) attempted to ascertain a more realistic value of indirect emissions to foreign nations using a hybrid approach (Suh and Huppes, 2005; Suh et al., 2004) by which $CO_2$ emissions obtained from the process-based, life-cycle assessment (LCA) data were applied to Japan's major imported goods such as fossil fuels and mineral resources. Today, the reliability of carbon leakage identification is improved considerably because of the utilization of a multi-regional input-output (MRIO) model (Lenzen et al., 2004; Leontief et al., 1985; Moran and Wood, 2014; Tukker and Dietzenbacher, 2013; Wiedmann, 2009; Wiedmann et al., 2011), which has developed remarkably in recent years. As a Japanese example, Nansai, Kagawa, et al. (2012) estimated the carbon footprint of Japan in 2005 as 1,675 Mt-$CO_2$eq using a global link input-output model (GLIO) (Nansai, Kagawa, Kondo, and Suh, 2013; Nansai et al., 2009; Nansai, Kagawa, Kondo, Tohno, et al., 2013; Nansai, Kondo, et al., 2012). Nansai, Kondo, et al. (2012) revealed that 541 Mt-$CO_2$eq of emissions originate in foreign nations. Therefore, consumption-based emissions exceeded production-based emissions by as much as 18%. The breakdown of the carbon footprint by final demand is 61% from household consumption, 9.3% from government expenditures, 25.1% from fixed capital formation, and 4.3% from other sources. The results confirm the necessity of policies promoting low-carbon household consumption (Nansai, Kondo, et al., 2012).

In addition, the development of interregional MRIO for Japan (Hasegawa, 2009) has facilitated analyses of carbon footprints and carbon leakage occurring in the 47 domestic prefectures considering the structure of emissions at the regional level (Hasegawa et al., 2015).

### *Supply chain carbon management of industries*

Input-output analysis has been applied to the calculation of carbon footprints related to individual technologies and industries. With regard to power generation technology in Japan, Hondo (2005) estimated the carbon footprint per unit of electricity generation for nine power generation systems including thermal power (coal, oil, liquefied natural gas, and liquefied natural gas combined cycle), nuclear power, hydropower, geothermal power, wind power, and solar photovoltaic power. Those carbon footprints per unit of electricity generation were determined using hybrid LCA technique. They were ascertained by incorporating the direct emissions from power generation in process-based LCA with indirect emissions associated with plant construction in IO-LCA. Results revealed that thermal power generation produces a much larger contribution to the carbon footprint than other power generation systems (Hondo, 2005).

In Japan, the steel industry and the automobile industry, respectively, rank second (World Steel Association, 2015) and third worldwide in terms of production volume (IOMVM, 2015). Both are, therefore, regarded as the core of Japan's national economy. Carbon footprint analyses have specifically examined the respective supply chains of these major industries. To assess carbon footprints of automobiles and tailpipe air pollutant emissions ($NO_x$, hydrocarbon, carbon monoxide), Kagawa et al. (2011) investigated the influences during 1990–2000 of extending and shortening the product lifetime of automobiles by one year. Results demonstrated that, when the lifetime of automobile products was extended one year during the period, the estimated carbon footprint of automobiles was reduced, even though older automobiles have lower fuel efficiency than newer automobiles. Furthermore, Kagawa et al. (2013) verified effects of so-called eco-car policy subsidies aimed at encouraging consumers to replace their old automobiles with fuel-saving new ones (Ministry of Land, Infrastructure, Transport and Tourism, Japan, 2012). They applied cost-benefit analyses based on the environmental benefits (lower carbon footprint of automobiles) and government expenses associated with policy implementation. Ohno et al. (2016) reported the respective national carbon footprints produced during the production of alloys of steel (chrome, nickel, manganese, molybdenum) consumed in Japan, indicating the importance of technical support for nations playing important roles in the utilization of these metals.

## Carbon footprint of lifestyle

The importance of the contributions of household consumption to the carbon footprint of a nation, as shown by Nansai, Kagawa, et al. (2012), is common particularly to Japan and other economically developed nations (Hertwich, 2005b, 2011; Hertwich and Peters, 2009). In addition, the household carbon footprint is strongly correlated with consumer lifestyles. In-depth studies of household carbon footprints have been conducted from the beginning of 2000 by incorporating input-output tables with a consumer expenditure survey (CES), with emphasis on the age of the household head and income distribution (Chitnis et al., 2014; Girod and de Haan, 2009, 2010; Jones and Kammen, 2011; Kerkhof, Benders, et al., 2009; Kerkhof, Nonhebel, et al., 2009; Kronenberg, 2009; Peters and Hertwich, 2006; Reynolds et al., 2015; Weber and Matthews, 2008; Wiedenhofer et al., 2016; Wier et al., 2001). Some studies have assessed the household carbon footprint from similar perspectives in Japan. Abe et al. (2002) estimated carbon footprints by household size and household head age for households with two or more people using the CES of Japan and the input – output table of 1990. M. Nakamura and Otoma (2004) highlighted features of household footprints based on household attributes by income class, gender, and age. Shigetomi et al. (2016) specifically examined differences of lifestyles according to household income. They identified carbon footprints per person by income quintile in 2005 with particular attention to increase in expenditures because of differences in the number of household members (Chitnis et al., 2014; Girod and De Haan, 2010; OECD, 2008).

In preference to present state analyses, some studies have examined the influences of consumer lifestyle changes upon the household carbon footprint. Takase et al. (2005) formulated three scenario analyses related to lifestyle changes: (1) modal shift from passenger automobiles to electric trains or buses, (2) longer-term use of electric appliances, and (3) shifting from eating at home to dining out. Then they quantified the carbon footprints and landfill consumption under those scenarios while considering the life cycle up to the disposal stage for each scenario using a waste input-output (WIO) model (S. Nakamura and Kondo, 2002). Moreover, they measured rebound effects (Druckman et al., 2011; Hertwich, 2005a) associated with increases of income and the consequent presumed changes in lifestyle. Nansai et al. (2007) estimated optimal consumption patterns to minimize each environmental footprint (carbon, energy, waste, air pollutants) associated with household consumption. Nansai et al. (2008) extended the study by adding other footprints (chemical, water pollutants) and considering the increment of footprints induced by fixed capital formation necessary for goods and services supplied to households. Results showed the respective optimal consumption patterns to minimize the different footprints while maintaining current GDP (Nansai et al., 2008). Furthermore, they scrutinized which commodities should be reduced preferentially to minimize all the footprints and which commodities should be commonly reduced for the footprints. Kawajiri et al. (2015) predicted an amount of money that is actually savable by expenditure items from a questionnaire survey administered on the Internet and presented quantitative rebound effects of the carbon footprint induced by that amount of saving.

### Future projection of household carbon footprints

One study has been introduced to analyze influences on the carbon footprint in the future while regarding changes in household consumption structure. Earlier studies that projected the long-term outlook of consumption-based GHG emissions (Barrett and Scott, 2012) and emissions associated with household consumption (Chitnis et al., 2012; Girod et al., 2014; Kronenberg, 2009) are few compared with the numerous studies that have estimated future production-based emissions (O'Neill et al., 2010). Yoshikawa et al. (2009) conducted regression estimation of future demand by household attributes according to an economic scenario based on demographic trends, the Special Report Emissions Scenarios (SRES) of IPCC, and temperature rise. Using the estimated future household demand, they conducted scenario analyses of carbon footprints associated with domestic supply chains and landfill consumption induced by households. For 2005–2035, Shigetomi et al. (2014) analyzed the influences of an aging society with fewer children on household carbon footprints in light of future demographic trends, the CES, and the embodied emissions intensity calculated using GLIO. This study used mathematical programming to resolve an inconsistency between the CES and the final demand of the household consumption expenditure sector on the input-output table – i.e., differences arising from the social accounting matrix (SAM) (Schreyer, 2013). Results of Yoshikawa et al. (2009) and Shigetomi et al. (2014) indicate marked increases in indirect emissions, such as those produced by medical services, attributable to changes in household composition, as represented by an increase in single-person households and households headed by elderly people. This trend is generally consistent with carbon footprint trends in economically developed nations such as the United Kingdom, the United States, the Netherlands, and Denmark during 1990–2000 (Hertwich, 2011), which appears to be a common issue among many economically developed nations into the future.

The common limitation of both studies is that they did not fully incorporate consideration of future changes expected in various technologies, domestic industrial structures, and global supply chain structures. To elucidate these changes, direct emission intensity by industrial sector and the Leontief inverse matrix should be estimated. Nevertheless, future estimations of these two factors based on precise evidence are extremely difficult. In addition, influences of the most recent social and economic policies on the future carbon footprint have not been addressed. Forecasting carbon footprints is therefore expected to show improved accuracy by virtue of those future trends.

# Discussion

## *Importance of climate policy design considering carbon footprints*

Production innovation and consumption transformation in the Japanese economy will be indispensable for the considerable degrees of carbon footprint reduction necessary to realize climate change mitigation. Innovation of production systems is expected to include the practical realization of CCS as well as the mass introduction of clean energy such as solar power and hydropower, in addition to promotion of low-carbon technologies such as those for electric vehicles. In Japan, nuclear power generation has long served as the keystone of low-carbon policies. However, after the Great East Japan Earthquake of March 2011, various discussions have been put forth over the benefits, shortcomings, and future challenges of resuming the use of nuclear power plants (McLellan et al., 2013; Moriguchi, 2014). Superiority of nuclear power generation against global warming is still remarkable if considered merely from a life-cycle GHG point of view (Hondo, 2005). However, health risks and economic losses caused by nuclear power plant disasters might be extremely serious and might be incomparable with hazards posed by other types of generation systems. This new realization underscores the difficulty of establishing a low-carbon society in Japan from the use of any single technology as conventional nuclear power generation. At the same time, that realization highlights the responsibilities of producers, which must grasp every reasonable opportunity for the step-by-step reduction of carbon footprints based on knowledge of their own structure of supply-chain GHG emissions. One example of such efforts is the quantification of carbon footprints with emphases on product lifetime improvement and extension of the duration of use. Overviewing product supply chains is expected to facilitate the design of GHG reduction policies that are balanced with economic benefits (Kagawa et al., 2013; Kagawa et al., 2011; Nishijima, 2016).

Under the international schemes of Scope 3 (WRI and WBCSD, 2011), organization carbon footprint (ISO, 2013), organization environmental footprint (European Commission, 2012), accounting, and disclosure are being conducted from supply-chain emission information related to all business activities, but by individual product. For further promotion of these schemes, roles of institutional investors, who are major shareholders, as well as consumers as "customers", are attracting attention in recent years. In Japan, the Government Pension Investment Fund, the world's largest institutional investor, signed the United Nations Principles for Responsible Investment in 2015. This movement to socially responsible investment is increasingly enhancing the value of environment-social-governance information disclosure by business enterprises. Some studies have pointed out that, to exert influence on consumer behavior, the producer side must foster its own environmental literacy (Leire and Thidell, 2005; Rex and Baumann, 2007). Disclosure of environmental information by producers should play a role in transforming consumer behaviors and improving dialogue with institutional investors. It should not merely remain as a one-way information service.

Innovation from consumption can derive from the transformation of lifestyles and the institutional design supporting it. Many consumers are already well aware that conserving electricity and restricting the use of private automobiles can suppress GHG emissions, but consumers must be informed about their many emissions reduction alternatives which are closely lifestyle related. One idea is to highlight differences of the carbon footprints between dining out and eating at home. If a person gets one idea, then it can be an opportunity for that person to review the frequency of restaurant use in a similar manner to those of electricity conservation and restricted use of private automobiles. For the Kyoto Protocol, for attainment of the reduction commitment, the Japanese government had been enlightening consumers and business operators. It provided policy support in terms of decarbonization. The catchphrase of "team minus 6%" was used, but no definite sectoral target for GHG reduction was given. However, the identification of household footprints has revealed that the contribution of food and energy use to the total carbon footprint is large for low-income groups and that of passenger cars and public transportation, and dining out become remarkably larger as annual income increases (Shigetomi et al., 2016). Therefore, footprint reduction opportunities differ depending on consumer attributes. That fact underscores for the necessity of creating a framework to assess footprints at the individual level ultimately, and to detect opportunities for reducing GHG emissions effectively.

Presentation of carbon footprint information is expected to be useful to suppress rebound effects and to identify reduction opportunities for consumers. Regarding an example in Japan, Takase et al. (2005) suggested that modal shift to public transportation and long-term use of electric appliances, which might seem to result in low carbonization at first glance, will eventually cause rebound effects through increased income because of changes in such lifestyles. Construction of a framework that teaches consumers examples of typical rebound effects in an easy-to-understand manner is a politically important issue to lead consumer lifestyles to steady support of a low carbon society. Related to this, Kawajiri et al. (2015) developed the "Rebound Matrix," which can be used to check which expenditure item should be preferred for reduction of the net carbon footprint increase attributable to a consumer's conservation activities.

### Importance of the climatic-economic-resource policy nexus

By 2030, Japan has agreed to meet the Paris Agreement target of achieving domestic GHG emissions that are 26% lower than those of 2013 – i.e., 367 Mt-$CO_2$eq. The present cabinet also established as the keystone of its economic policy an economic growth strategy based on "A Society in Which All Citizens Are Dynamically Engaged," aimed at cessation of Japan's aging society with its lower birthrate and inducement of increased incomes (Prime Minister of Japan and His Cabinet, 2016a). This policy includes achievement of 600 trillion Japanese yen GDP, recovery of the birthrate to 1.8, and enhancement of the social security system for double-income households, which are intended to resolve current difficulties confronting Japan such as an escape from a decline in the number of children, labor force improvement, and the movement of women into society. Seen as countermeasures against global warming, however, household expenditures are expected to increase because of an increase in the number of household members, with double-income households, thereby boosting GHG emissions (M. Nakamura and Otoma, 2004; Shigetomi et al., 2016; Yoshikawa et al., 2009). According to an estimate by Shigetomi et al. (2014), if the aging society with lower birthrates in Japan continues at present trends (2005), the household carbon footprint in 2030 would be smaller, at 46.5 Mt-$CO_2$eq, than that in 2005. Of that result, reduction in domestic emissions would account for 30.7 Mt-$CO_2$eq. In terms of 2013 level, this figure cannot even approach the reduction targets of the Paris Agreement. Moreover, if economic policy succeeds and incomes and birthrates are increased, then this small amount of reduction would be offset quickly, thereby increasing emissions. In other words, for attainment of Paris Agreement goals, considerable reduction efforts are unavoidable if one assumes the successful implementation of economic policy. Demand for commodities that will be induced by recovery of the birthrate and increases in double-income households should be anticipated carefully. Moreover, policy support should be given to induce technological improvements that mitigate the carbon footprints of the identified commodities. Now is the time to reconsider how an environmental input-output analysis can contribute to policy collaboration producing synergetic effects on global warming policy and economic policy while avoiding the trade-offs between them.

As another issue, results of footprint studies indicate the importance of cooperation with resource policy, such as the Circular Economy policy currently discussed in Europe (Ellen MacArthur Foundation, 2014). Some low-carbon technologies require the use of critical metals such as rare-earth metals, for which instability of the resource supply is a concern (Graedel et al., 2015). This looming instability presents the possibility that global warming policy based on the mass introduction of such technologies might increase the vulnerability of one nation, depending greatly on resource availability (European Commission, 2010; National Research Council, 2008). In recent years, some studies have started to assess quantitative and qualitative risks of resource supplies from a consumption-based accounting viewpoint (Nansai et al., 2015; Nansai et al., 2014; Nansai et al., 2017; Shigetomi et al., 2015; Tisserant and Pauliuk, 2016). The nexus between resource policy and economic policy should be noted too. Lifestyle changes resulting from income growth might act as a contributing factor that expands critical metal footprints in Japan, perhaps exceeding the expected increase of carbon footprints (Shigetomi et al., 2016). Identification of such trade-offs among low-carbon, economic, and resource policies should be conducted further such that the progress of one policy might not hinder the others.

Lastly, we refer to the nexus to Sustainable Development Goals (SDGs) by the United Nations that officially came into effect in 2016 (UN, 2015). Countermeasures for GHG reduction should not sacrifice the 17 targets specified in SDGs. The SDGs are specific in that they encompass social impacts such as poverty, starvation, inequality, educational problems, and the like in addition to environmental problems. It is readily inferred that consideration of common ground between climate change policy and resource policy alone is insufficient. Studies of footprint measurements using input-output analysis have been developed to assess social effects (Alsamawi et al., 2015; Alsamawi, Murray, and Lenzen, 2014; Alsamawi, Murray, Lenzen, et al., 2014; Gómez-Paredes et al., 2016; Gómez-Paredes et al., 2015; McBain, 2015; Simas et al., 2014; Simas et al., 2015). Their results suggest that Japanese climate change policy must integrate the viewpoint of social footprints, and overcome diverse trade-offs among economic, social, and environmental goals. In the future, Japan ought to lead pioneering work in support of international collaboration, such as the Paris Agreement and SDGs, through implementation of those ambitious policies.

## Acknowledgments

This research was supported in part by JSPS Grants-in-Aid for Scientific Research (A) (Nos. 26241031 and 16H01797) and a JSPS Grant-in-Aid for Research Activity Start-up (No. 16H07072).

## References

Abe, J., Miura, S., and Tonooka, Y. (2002). Study on the characteristics of CO emissions caused by family life based on the LCA database. *Journal of Architecture, Planning & Environmental Engineering*, 551, 93–98.

Alsamawi, A., McBain, D., Murray, J., and Geschke, A. (2016). Social impacts of international trade on the Chinese transport sector. *Journal of Industrial Ecology*, 20(3) 603–610.

Alsamawi, A., Murray, J., and Lenzen, M. (2014). The employment footprints of nations. *Journal of Industrial Ecology*, *18*(1), 59–70. doi: 10.1111/jiec.12104

Alsamawi, A., Murray, J., Lenzen, M., Moran, D., and Kanemoto, K. (2014). The inequality footprints of nations: A novel approach to quantitative accounting of income inequality. *PLoS ONE*, *9*(10), e110881.

Barrett, J., Peters, G. P., Wiedmann, T. O., Scott, K., Lenzen, M., Roelich, K., and Le Quéré, C. (2013). Consumption-based GHG emission accounting: A UK case study. *Climate Policy*, *13*(4), 451–470.

Barrett, J., and Scott, K. (2012). Link between climate change mitigation and resource efficiency: A UK case study. *Global Environmental Change*, *22*(1), 299–307.

Chitnis, M., Sorrell, S., Druckman, A., Firth, S. K., and Jackson, T. (2014). Who rebounds most? Estimating direct and indirect rebound effects for different UK socioeconomic groups. *Ecological Economics*, *106*, 12–32.

Chitnis, M., Druckman, A., Hunt, L. C., Jackson, T., and Milne, S. (2012). Forecasting scenarios for UK household expenditure and associated GHG emissions: outlook to 2030. *Ecological Economics*, *84*, 129–141.

Davis, S. J., and Caldeira, K. (2010). Consumption-based accounting of $CO_2$ emissions. *Proceedings of the National Academy of Sciences*, *107*(12), 5687–5692.

Druckman, A., Chitnis, M., Sorrell, S., and Jackson, T. (2011). Missing carbon reductions? Exploring rebound and backfire effects in UK households. *Energy Policy*, *39*(6), 3572–3581.

Ellen MacArthur Foundation. (2014). *Towards the circular economy: Accelerating the scale-up across global supply chains* (Vol. 64). Geneva, Switzerland: World Economic Forum Reports.

European Commission. (2010). *Critical raw materials for the EU; the Ad-Hoc working group on defining critical raw materials*: Brussels, Belgium.

European Commission. (2013). *Organisation Environmental Footprint (OEF) guide.* Ispra, Italy: Institute for Environment and Sustainability.

Feng, K., Chapagain, A., Suh, S., Pfister, S., and Hubacek, K. (2011). Comparison of bottom-up and top-down approaches to calculating the water footprints of nations. *Economic Systems Research, 23*(4), 371–385.

Girod, B., and de Haan, P. (2009). GHG reduction potential of changes in consumption patterns and higher quality levels: Evidence from Swiss household consumption survey. *Energy Policy, 37*(12), 5650–5661.

Girod, B., and De Haan, P. (2010). More or better? A model for changes in household greenhouse gas emissions due to higher income. *Journal of Industrial Ecology, 14*(1), 31–49.

Girod, B., van Vuuren, D. P., and Hertwich, E. G. (2014). Climate policy through changing consumption choices: Options and obstacles for reducing greenhouse gas emissions. *Global Environmental Change, 25*, 5–15.

Gómez-Paredes, J., Yamasue, E., Okumura, H., and Ishihara, K. N. (2015). The labour footprint: A framework to assess labour in a complex economy. *Economic Systems Research, 27*(4), 415–439.

Gómez-Paredes, J., Alsamawi, A., Yamasue, E., Okumura, H., Ishihara, K. N., Geschke, A., and Lenzen, M. (2016). Consuming childhoods: An assessment of child labor's role in Indian production and global consumption. *Journal of Industrial Ecology, 20*(3), 611–622.

Graedel, T., Harper, E., Nassar, N., Nuss, P., and Reck, B. K. (2015). Criticality of metals and metalloids. *Proceedings of the National Academy of Sciences, 112*(14), 4257–4262.

Greenhouse Gas Inventory Office of Japan. (2016). *National GHG inventory report of Japan 2016.* Tsukuba, Japan: National Institute for Environmental Studies.

Hasegawa, R. (2009). An examination of estimation methods employed for determining $CO_2$ emissions at the prefectural level in Japan. J. 15. *Applied Input – Output Analysis, 15*, 1–20.

Hasegawa, R., Kagawa, S., and Tsukui, M. (2015). Carbon footprint analysis through constructing a multi-region input – output table: A case study of Japan. *Journal of Economic Structures, 4*(1), 1–20.

Hertwich, E. G. (2005a). Consumption and the rebound effect: An industrial ecology perspective. *Journal of Industrial Ecology, 9*(1–2), 85–98.

Hertwich, E. G. (2005b). Life cycle approaches to sustainable consumption: A critical review. *Environmental Science & Technology, 39*(13), 4673–4684.

Hertwich, E. G. (2011). The life cycle environmental impacts of consumption. *Economic Systems Research, 23*(1), 27–47.

Hertwich, E. G., and Peters, G. P. (2009). Carbon footprint of nations: A global, trade-linked analysis. *Environmental Science & Technology, 43*(16), 6414–6420.

Hoekstra, A. Y., and Wiedmann, T. O. (2014). Humanity's unsustainable environmental footprint. *Science, 344*(6188), 1114–1117.

Hondo, H. (2005). Life cycle GHG emission analysis of power generation systems: Japanese case. *Energy, 30*(11), 2042–2056.

Hondo, H., Tonooka, Y., and Uchiyama, Y. (1997). Environmental burdens associated with production activities in Japan using an input-output table. *Socio-Economic Research Center, Reo. No. Y, 97017*, 1–35.

IEA. (2015). *Energy agency statistics*. International Energy Agency. Retrieved from www.iea.org

Imura, H., Moriguchi, Y., Shiratsuchi, H., and Sakai, T. (1994). Study of the export – import pertinent to the international balance of environmental loads trade of goods and services. *Journal of Environmental Sciences*, *7*(3), 225–236.

IOMVM. (2015). *2014 production statistics*. International Organization of Motor Vehicle Manufactures. Retrieved from www.oica.net/category/production-statistics/2014-statistics/

IPCC AR5 WG3. (2014). *Climate change 2014: Mitigation of climate change*. Berlin, Germany: Working Group III contribution to the fifth assessment report of the intergovernmental panel on climate change.

ISO. (2013). ISO/TS 14067. Greenhouse gases. Carbon footprint of products. Requirements and guidelines for quantification and communication. Geneva, Switzerland: International Organization for Standardization.

Jones, C. M., and Kammen, D. M. (2011). Quantifying carbon footprint reduction opportunities for US households and communities. *Environmental Science & Technology*, *45*(9), 4088–4095.

Kagawa, S., Nansai, K., Kondo, Y., Hubacek, K., Suh, S., Minx, J., . . . Nakamura, S. (2011). Role of motor vehicle lifetime extension in climate change policy. ACS Publications. *Environmental Science & Technology*, 45(4), 1184–1191.

Kagawa, S., Hubacek, K., Nansai, K., Kataoka, M., Managi, S., Suh, S., and Kudoh, Y. (2013). Better cars or older cars? Assessing $CO_2$ emission reduction potential of passenger vehicle replacement programs. *Global Environmental Change*, *23*(6), 1807–1818.

Kanemoto, K., Moran, D., and Hertwich, E. G. (2016). Mapping the carbon footprint of nations. *Environmental Science & Technology*, *50*(19), 10512–10517.

Kanemoto, K., Moran, D., Lenzen, M., and Geschke, A. (2014). International trade undermines national emission reduction targets: New evidence from air pollution. *Global Environmental Change*, *24*, 52–59.

Kawajiri, K., Tabata, T., and Ihara, T. (2015). Using a rebound Matrix to estimate consumption changes from saving and its environmental impact in Japan. *Journal of Industrial Ecology*, *19*(4), 564–574.

Kerkhof, A. C., Benders, R. M., and Moll, H. C. (2009). Determinants of variation in household $CO_2$ emissions between and within countries. *Energy Policy*, *37*(4), 1509–1517.

Kerkhof, A. C., Nonhebel, S., and Moll, H. C. (2009). Relating the environmental impact of consumption to household expenditures: an input – output analysis. *Ecological Economics*, *68*(4), 1160–1170.

Koh, S., Ibn-Mohammed, T., Acquaye, A., Feng, K., Reaney, I., Hubacek, K., . . . Khatab, K. (2016). Drivers of US toxicological footprints trajectory 1998–2013. *Scientific Reports*, 6(1), 39514.

Kondo, Y., Moriguchi, Y., and Shimizu, H. (1998). $CO_2$ emissions in Japan: Influences of imports and exports. *Applied Energy*, *59*(2), 163–174.

Kronenberg, T. (2009). The impact of demographic change on energy use and greenhouse gas emissions in Germany. *Ecological Economics*, *68*(10), 2637–2645.

Leire, C., and Thidell, Å. (2005). Product-related environmental information to guide consumer purchases – a review and analysis of research on perceptions, understanding and use among Nordic consumers. *Journal of Cleaner Production*, *13*(10), 1061–1070.

Lenzen, M., Moran, D., Kanemoto, K., Foran, B., Lobefaro, L., and Geschke, A. (2012). International trade drives biodiversity threats in developing nations. *Nature*, *486*(7401), 109–112.

Lenzen, M., Murray, J., Sack, F., and Wiedmann, T. O. (2007). Shared producer and consumer responsibility – theory and practice. *Ecological Economics, 61*(1), 27–42.

Lenzen, M., Pade, L.-L., and Munksgaard, J. (2004). $CO_2$ multipliers in multi-region input-output models. *Economic Systems Research, 16*(4), 391–412.

Leontief, W., Duchin, F., and Szyld, D. B. (1985). New approaches in economic analysis. *Science, 228*, 419–423.

McBain, D. (2015). Is social footprinting relevant to industrial ecology? *Journal of Industrial Ecology, 19*(3), 340–342.

McLellan, B. C., Zhang, Q., Utama, N. A., Farzaneh, H., and Ishihara, K. N. (2013). Analysis of Japan's post-Fukushima energy strategy. *Energy Strategy Reviews, 2*(2), 190–198.

Ministry of Land; *Infrastructure; Transport and Tourism; Japan.* (2012). Retrieved from www.mlit.go.jp/jidosha/jidosha_fr1_000008.html

Moran, D., and Kanemoto, K. (2016a). Identifying species threat hotspots from global supply chains. *Nature Ecology & Evolution, 1*, 0023. doi: 10.1038/s41559–016–0023. Retrieved from www.nature.com/articles/s41559-016-0023#supplementary-infor mation

Moran, D., and Kanemoto, K. (2016b). Tracing global supply chains to air pollution hotspots. *Environmental Research Letters, 11*(9), 094017.

Moran, D., and Wood, R. (2014). Convergence between the Eora, WIOD, EXIOBASE, and OpenEU's consumption-based carbon accounts. *Economic Systems Research, 26*(3), 245–261.

Moriguchi, Y. (2014). An overview: Consequences of accidents in Fukushima Daiichi nuclear power plant – state of pollution, responses and future challenges. *Energy and Resources, 35*(2), 81–86.

Moriguchi, Y., Kondo, Y., and Shimizu, H. (1993a). Analysing the life cycle impacts of cars: The case of $CO_2$. *Industry and Environment,* 16(1/2), 42–45.

Moriguchi, Y., Kondo, Y., and Shimizu, H. (1993b). Estimation of $CO_2$ emission in Japan by sector and by origin. *Energy and Resources, 14*(1), 32–41.

Munksgaard, J., and Pedersen, K. A. (2001). $CO_2$ accounts for open economies: Producer or consumer responsibility? *Energy Policy, 29*(4), 327–334.

Munksgaard, J., Pedersen, K. A., and Wien, M. (2000). Impact of household consumption on CO 2 emissions. *Energy Economics, 22*(4), 423–440.

Nagashima, F., Kagawa, S., Suh, S., Nansai, K., and Moran, D. (2016). Identifying critical supply chain paths and key sectors for mitigating primary carbonaceous $PM_{2.5}$ mortality in Asia. *Economic Systems Research,* 29(1), 105–123.

Nakamura, M., and Otoma, S. (2004). Analysis of $CO_2$ emission originating from household consumption, taking attributes of families into account. *Environmental Science (Japan),* 17(5), 389–401.

Nakamura, S., and Kondo, Y. (2002). Input-output analysis of waste management. *Journal of Industrial Ecology, 6*(1), 39–63.

Nansai, K. (2009). Chapter 31: Environmental input-output database building in Japan. In S. Suh (Ed.), *Handbook of input-output economics in iIndustrial ecology* (pp. 653–688). Dordrecht, The Netherlands: Springer.

Nansai, K., Inaba, R., Kagawa, S., and Moriguchi, Y. (2008). Identifying common features among household consumption patterns optimized to minimize specific environmental burdens. *Journal of Cleaner Production, 16*(4), 538–548.

Nansai, K., Kagawa, S., Kondo, Y., and Suh, S. (2013). Chapter 8: Simplification of multiregional input – output structure with a global system boundary: global link input – output model (GLIO). In J. Murray & M. Lenzen (Eds.), *The sustainability practitioner's guide to multiregional input – output analysis.* Champaign, Illinois, United States: Common Ground.

Nansai, K., Kagawa, S., Kondo, Y., Suh, S., Inaba, R., and Nakajima, K. (2009). Improving the completeness of product carbon footprints using a global link input – output model: The case of Japan. *Economic Systems Research, 21*(3), 267–290.

Nansai, K., Kagawa, S., Kondo, Y., Suh, S., Nakajima, K., Inaba, R., . . . Terakawa, T. (2012). Characterization of economic requirements for a "carbon-debt-free country". *Environmental Science & Technology, 46*(1), 155–163.

Nansai, K., Kagawa, S., Kondo, Y., Tohno, S., and Suh, S. (2013). Chapter 19: Estimating global environmental impacts of goods and services produced in Japan using a global link input – output model (GLIO). In J. Murray & M. Lenzen (Eds.), *The sustainability practitioner's guide to multiregional input – output analysis.* Champaign, Illinois, United States: Common Ground.

Nansai, K., Kagawa, S., and Moriguchi, Y. (2007). Proposal of a simple indicator for sustainable consumption: classifying goods and services into three types focusing on their optimal consumption levels. *Journal of Cleaner Production, 15*(10), 879–885.

Nansai, K., Kondo, Y., Kagawa, S., Suh, S., Nakajima, K., Inaba, R., and Tohno, S. (2012). Estimates of embodied global energy and air-emission intensities of Japanese products for building a Japanese input – output life cycle assessment database with a global system boundary. *Environmental Science & Technology, 46*(16), 9146–9154.

Nansai, K., and Moriguchi, Y. (2013). *Embodied energy and emission intensity data for Japan using input–output tables (3EID): For 2005 IO table.* Retrieved from www.cger. nies.go.jp/publications/report/d031/index. html. Tsukuba, Japan: Japanese National Institute for Environmental Studies

Nansai, K., Nakajima, K., Kagawa, S., Kondo, Y., Shigetomi, Y., and Suh, S. (2015). Global mining risk footprint of critical metals necessary for low-carbon technologies: The case of neodymium, cobalt, and platinum in Japan. *Environmental Science & Technology, 49*(4), 2022–2031.

Nansai, K., Nakajima, K., Suh, S., Kagawa, S., Kondo, Y., Takayanagi, Y., and Shigetomi, Y. (2017). The role of primary processing in the supply risks of critical metals *Economic Systems Research*, doi:10.1080/09535314.2017.1295923.

Nansai, K., Nakajima, K., Kagawa, S., Kondo, Y., Suh, S., Shigetomi, Y., and Oshita, Y. (2014). Global flows of critical metals necessary for low-carbon technologies: The case of neodymium, cobalt, and platinum. *Environmental Science & Technology, 48*(3), 1391–1400.

National Research Council. (2008). *Minerals, critical minerals, and the US economy*, Washington DC, USA: National Academies Press.

Nishijima, D. (2016). Product lifetime, energy efficiency and climate change: A case study of air conditioners in Japan. *Journal of Environmental Management, 181*, 582–589.

O'Neill, B. C., Dalton, M., Fuchs, R., Jiang, L., Pachauri, S., and Zigova, K. (2010). Global demographic trends and future carbon emissions. *Proceedings of the National Academy of Sciences, 107*(41), 17521–17526.

OECD. (2008). *Growing unequal? Income distribution and poverty in OECD countries.* Paris, France: OECD.

Ohno, H., Matsubae, K., Nakajima, K., Nansai, K., Fukushima, Y., and Nagasaka, T. (2016). Consumption-based accounting of steel alloying elements and greenhouse gas emissions associated with the metal use: The case of Japan. *Journal of Economic Structures, 5*(1), 28.

Oita, A., Malik, A., Kanemoto, K., Geschke, A., Nishijima, S., and Lenzen, M. (2016). Substantial nitrogen pollution embedded in international trade. *Nature Geoscience*, *9*(2), 111–115.

Peters, G. P. (2008). From production-based to consumption-based national emission inventories. *Ecological Economics*, *65*(1), 13–23.

Peters, G. P., and Hertwich, E. G. (2006). The importance of imports for household environmental impacts. *Journal of Industrial Ecology*, *10*(3), 89–109.

Peters, G. P., and Hertwich, E. G. (2008). Post-Kyoto greenhouse gas inventories: Production versus consumption. *Climatic Change*, *86*(1), 51–66.

Peters, G. P., Minx, J. C., Weber, C. L., and Edenhofer, O. (2011). Growth in emission transfers via international trade from 1990 to 2008. *Proceedings of the National Academy of Sciences*, *108*(21), 8903–8908.

Prime Minister of Japan and His Cabinet. (2016a). *The Japan's plan for dynamic engagement of all citizens* [Press release]. Retrieved from www.kantei.go.jp/jp/singi/ichioku-soukatsuyaku/pdf/plan2.pdf

Prime Minister of Japan and His Cabinet. (2016b). *Statement by the Prime Minister on the acceptance of the Paris agreement* [Press release]. Retrieved from http://japan.kantei.go.jp/97_abe/statement/201611/1219866_11019.html

Rex, E., and Baumann, H. (2007). Beyond ecolabels: What green marketing can learn from conventional marketing. *Journal of Cleaner Production*, *15*(6), 567–576.

Reynolds, C. J., Piantadosi, J., Buckley, J. D., Weinstein, P., and Boland, J. (2015). Evaluation of the environmental impact of weekly food consumption in different socio-economic households in Australia using environmentally extended input – output analysis. *Ecological Economics*, *111*, 58–64.

Rodrigues, J., and Domingos, T. (2008). Consumer and producer environmental responsibility: Comparing two approaches. *Ecological Economics*, *66*(2), 533–546.

Schreyer, P. (2013). *Social accounting matrix and microdata: new areas of research*. Paper presented at the 21st International Input-Output Conference & the Third Edition of the International School of Input-Output Analysis, Kitakyushu, Japan.

Shigetomi, Y., Nansai, K., Kagawa, S., and Tohno, S. (2014). Changes in the carbon footprint of Japanese households in an aging society. *Environmental Science & Technology*, *48*(11), 6069–6080.

Shigetomi, Y., Nansai, K., Kagawa, S., and Tohno, S. (2015). Trends in Japanese households' critical-metals material footprints. *Ecological Economics*, *119*, 118–126.

Shigetomi, Y., Nansai, K., Kagawa, S., and Tohno, S. (2016). Influence of income difference on carbon and material footprints for critical metals: The case of Japanese households. *Journal of Economic Structures*, *5*(1), 1.

Simas, M., Golsteijn, L., Huijbregts, M., Wood, R., and Hertwich, E. (2014). The "Bad Labor" footprint: Quantifying the social impacts of globalization. *Sustainability*, *6*(11), 7514.

Simas, M., Wood, R., and Hertwich, E. (2015). Labor embodied in trade. *Journal of Industrial Ecology*, *19*(3), 343–356. doi: 10.1111/jiec.12187

Suh, S., and Huppes, G. (2005). Methods for life cycle inventory of a product. *Journal of Cleaner Production*, *13*(7), 687–697.

Suh, S., Lenzen, M., Treloar, G. J., Hondo, H., Horvath, A., Huppes, G., . . . Moriguchi, Y. (2004). System boundary selection in life-cycle inventories using hybrid approaches. *Environmental Science & Technology*, *38*(3), 657–664.

Takahashi, K., Nansai, K., Tohno, S., Nishizawa, M., Kurokawa, J.-I., and Ohara, T. (2014). Production-based emissions, consumption-based emissions and consumption-based health impacts of $PM_{2.5}$ carbonaceous aerosols in Asia. *Atmospheric Environment*, *97*, 406–415.

Takase, K., Kondo, Y., and Washizu, A. (2005). An analysis of sustainable consumption by the waste input-output model. *Journal of Industrial Ecology*, *9*(1–2), 201–219.

Tisserant, A., and Pauliuk, S. (2016). Matching global cobalt demand under different scenarios for co-production and mining attractiveness. *Journal of Economic Structures*, *5*(1), 4.

Tukker, A., and Dietzenbacher, E. (2013). Global multiregional input – output frameworks: An introduction and outlook. *Economic Systems Research*, *25*(1), 1–19.

UN. (2015). *Sustainable development goals*. Retrieved from https://sustainabledevelop ment.un.org/topics/sustainabledevelopmentgoals

Weber, C. L., and Matthews, H. S. (2008). Quantifying the global and distributional aspects of American household carbon footprint. *Ecological Economics*, *66*(2), 379–391.

Weinzettel, J., Hertwich, E. G., Peters, G. P., Steen-Olsen, K., and Galli, A. (2013). Affluence drives the global displacement of land use. *Global Environmental Change*, *23*(2), 433–438.

Wiedenhofer, D., Guan, D., Liu, Z., Meng, J., Zhang, N., and Wei, Y.-M. (2016). Unequal household carbon footprints in China. *Nature Climate Change*, 7(1), 75–80

Wiedmann, T. O. (2009). A review of recent multi-region input – output models used for consumption-based emission and resource accounting. *Ecological Economics*, *69*(2), 211–222.

Wiedmann, T. O., and Minx, J. (2008). A definition of "carbon footprint". *Ecological Economics Research Trends*, *1*, 1–11.

Wiedmann, T. O., Wilting, H. C., Lenzen, M., Lutter, S., and Palm, V. (2011). Quo Vadis MRIO? Methodological, data and institutional requirements for multi-region input – output analysis. *Ecological Economics*, *70*(11), 1937–1945.

Wiedmann, T. O., Schandl, H., Lenzen, M., Moran, D., Suh, S., West, J., and Kanemoto, K. (2015). The material footprint of nations. *Proceedings of the National Academy of Sciences*, *112*(20), 6271–6276.

Wier, M., Lenzen, M., Munksgaard, J., and Smed, S. (2001). Effects of household consumption patterns on $CO_2$ requirements. *Economic Systems Research*, *13*(3), 259–274.

World Steel Association. (2015). *Steel statistical yearbook*. Brussels, Belgium: World Steel Association.

WRI and WBCSD (2011). Corporate value chain (Scope 3) accounting and reporting standard—supplement to the GHG Protocol Corporate Accounting and Reporting Standard, World Resources Institute and World Business Council for Sustainable Development, Retrieved from http://www. ghgprotocol.org/files/ghgp/public/Corporate-Value-Chain-Accounting-Reporing-Standard_041613.pdf

Yoshikawa, N., Amano, K., and Shimada, K. (2009). Analysis of environmental load related to household consumption considering climate change and household characteristics *Journal of Life Cycle Assessment, Japan*, *5*(2), 252–261.

Yoshioka, K., Hayami, H., and Ikeda, A. (1991). Input – output tables for environmental analysis: Processes and significance of the compilation. *Innovationand I/O Technique*, *2*(3), 14–24.

Yoshioka, K., Hayami, H., Ikeda, A., and Suga, M. (1992). Application of environmental input – output tables: $CO_2$ emission associated with production activity and its factors. *Innovation and I/O Technique*, *3*(4), 31–41.

# 17 The socioeconomic and environmental impacts of fossil fuels subsidies reduction and renewable energy expansion in China

*Liang Dong, Jingzheng Ren,*
*João F. D. Rodrigues and Arnold Tukker*

## Background

For a long time, China has faced the contradiction between the extensive mode of economic growth and the restriction of resources and environment, which significantly challenges the nation's sustainable development (BP, 2011; Dong, Fujita, et al., 2016). Particularly for the energy sector, it is well known that China's current energy structure is coal-based dominant, with low proportions of renewable energy, which brings about a great challenge on climate change and other issues (Dong, Liang, et al., 2016; H. Liu and Liang, 2013; L. Liu et al., 2011). It was reported that China has become not only the powerhouse of the economy but also the largest energy consumer and $CO_2$ emitter (Dong and Liang, 2014), with surging consumption of fossil fuels in the past decades (Figure 17.1). As a result, we realize that coordinating development of the environment and economy, optimizing the industrial structure and transforming the economic growth mode are of critical importance for China's sustainable development (Li Li and Yonglei, 2012).

Especially in the "post-Paris era", how to deepen China's reform on the energy policies to forward more efficient low-carbon transformation has become a gigantic topic for China (H.-Y. Yu and Zhu, 2015). From the technical perspective, China has already adopted a series of energy conservation and pollutants reduction, as well as stimulation on renewable energy for years. The national "12th Five-Year Plan" (FYP) (for 2011 to 2015) and mid-long-term planning (for the year up to 2020) proposed the goals of energy saving and emission mitigation. Chinese government aims to reduce the energy intensity by 16% up to 2015 and the $CO_2$ emission per unit GDP by 40%–45% compared to the level of 2005 by 2020 (Lo and Wang, 2013; X. Yu and Qu, 2013; X. Zhang et al., 2013). However, apart from pure technological issues, market measures also deserve significant attention so as to forward the transformation.

From a "push" and "pull" perspective, two measures are critical. First of all, via energy efficiency enhancement and market reform, it is critical to push to reduce fossil fuels consumption (Hong et al., 2013). Among the series of policies of this point, fossil fuel subsidies reform is one important concern, especially for

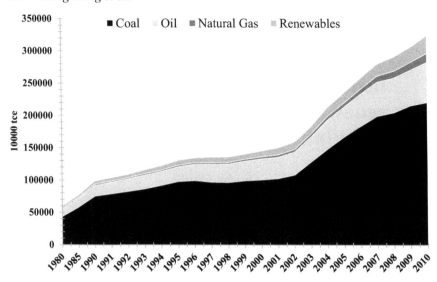

*Figure 17.1* China's surging energy consumption and its structure from 1980 to 2010

Note: Renewables include nuclear energy and renewable energy

Source: China Energy Statistical Yearbook

developing countries such as China. From the theory of energy economics, energy subsidies lower the end price and, as a result, encourage the fossil fuels consumption and hereby impede the environment (De Moor, 2001; IEA, 1999; UNEP, 2008b). From this point, proper energy subsidies reform would be an effective way to mitigate the rebound effect and further make the energy efficiency measures more efficient, thus finally achieving a co-benefit in terms of environmental benefit and economic benefit (as subsidies are a budget load) (OECD, 2005). Therefore, to see how fossil fuel subsidies reform can generate multiple impacts on China's energy system and economy will be of significance.

Secondly, renewable energy (REE) promotion is regarded as one of the most effective measures to pull the realization of the aforementioned national targets[3] (F. Wang et al., 2010) through adjusting the coal-dominent consumption structure in China The government is making REE development a key focus of its national FYP and is paving a strong support and regulatory policy framework for fostering REE deployment (Ming et al., 2013; F. Wang et al., 2010; Xingang et al., 2012). The milestone policies include, but are not limitted to, "China's Landmark Renewable Energy Law (REL)", implemented in 2006 and revised in 2009, which is the umbrella policy for guiding the development of REE. "Guidance Catalogue of the Renewable Energy Industry", implemented in 2006 by National Development and Reform Commission (NDRC), is used to guide policymaking and investments in the area of R&D. "Medium to Long-Term Plan for Renewable Energy Development in China (2007–2020)", implemented in 2007, sets specific targets for the REE up to 2010. "Strategic Emerging Industries Development Guidelines

(2010–2020)", released directly by the State Council in 2010 under the background of global financial crisis in 2009, releases the guidelines to develop seven "strategic emerging industries" (SEIs) which were expected to drive the country's economic growth and to eventually account for 15% of China"s overall GDP by 2020. Renewable energy industry (REEI) is one of the seven SEIs (Becker and Fischer, 2013; Huang et al., 2012; Zeng et al., 2013). Under this circumstance, the REEI in China is rapidly developing.

It is highlighted that one merit of promoting REEI is the generation of "green jobs", which according to the definitiion from UNEP (UNEP, 2008a), refers to the employment generated by the industries related to environmental protection and sustainable development, such as works on the ecosystem and biodiversity protection, works contributing to energy consumption reduction and resources saving and works on waste management (Energy and Climate Change Sustainable Development Commission, 2009). From this regard, it is understandable that promoting REEI will generate "green jobs", considering REE is "clean energy" and will reduce the consumption of "dirty" coals. However, it is also noted that, with promotion of REEI, not only will new "green jobs" be created but also job loss due to the shrink of fossil fuel industries, such as the closing down of small-scale, coal-fired power plants (Cai et al., 2011). As a result, to evaluate the merits and trade-offs of REE expansion, better policymaking is necessary.

With this circumstance, this chapter aims to assess the socioeconomic and environmental impacts of fossil fuel subsidies reform and REE expansion in China and to explore the co-benefits that may emerge from the complex interactions of energy, environment and economy systems. A hybrid physical input and monetary output model (HPIMO) with integrated sectors (electricity sectors and sectors of the rest of the economy) is constructed based on the Chinese 2007 national input-output table (IOT), additional material and energy flow analysis (MEFA) and life-cycle analysis (LCA) data of sector-level energy mix inventories, emissions and employment. The model allows us to analyze the interactions between the different sectors and to calculate the impacts on the whole supply-demand chains of the simulated energy subsidies reform and renewables sector expansion. Impacts in terms of employment (socioeconomic), saving on the budget (economic), $CO_2$ and air pollutants ($SO_2$ and $NO_x$) mitigation (environmental) effects are evaluated. Business-as-usual (BAU) scenario (no reform on fossil subsidies and a baseline renewable energy projection in 2007) as well as fossil subsidies reform scenario and renewable energy scenarios in 2015 are designed to investigate the insights for policy implications. To our best knowledge, few studies addressed such topics before, hence our analysis will be critical to informing policymakers to better design low-carbon policies and to promote a sustainable pathway for China.

The remainder of this chapter is organized as follows: after this introduction section, section 2 reviews the related literature; sections 3 describes the methods and data; section 4 and section 5 overview the fossil fuels subsidies in China and its scale, as well as the development of renewable energy in China; section 6 presents and discusses the analysis and results; and, finally, section 7 draws the conclusions and implications.

## Literatures Review

### *Mitigate rebound effects via subsidies reform*

By lowering the market price of fossil fuels, energy subsidy was one driver of the rebound effect, especially for developing countries such as China (Li H., et al., 2011a). Some early studies and insights on the rebound effect and the estimation of energy savings were presented in Khazzoom (1980). Since then, the rebound effect has been widely studied in various sectors (manufacturing, transport, etc.) (Bentzen, 2004; Li Li and Yonglei, 2012; Matos and Silva, 2011), including the empirical studies in developed and developing regions and/or countries (e.g. the United Kingdom, Hong Kong, China) (Barker et al., 2007; Freire-González, 2010; Mizobuchi, 2008; Ouyang et al., 2010; H. Wang, Zhou, Zhou, et al., 2012); applications of various modeling approach for evaluating the rebound effects, including econometric method; [31] and partial[34] and general equilibrium models (Grepperud and Rasmussen, 2004). As for China, most case studies focused on the direct rebound effect in certain sectors [29, 34] (H. Wang, Zhou, and Zhou, 2012). However, although subsidies research is critical to the rebound effect due to their inner connection, to date there have been few studies innovatively linked to them. It was highlighted that integrating energy efficiency measures and energy policy tools was an important way to mitigate the rebound effect (Maxwell et al., 2011); therefore, considering the interaction of energy subsidies and the rebound effect was necessary and important to proper policymaking.

With this background, this chapter used a co-benefit approach to link the topic of energy subsidies reform and the rebound effect, choose China as the case study to make a quantified analysis on how the fossil energy subsidies reform would contribute to the mitigation of the rebound effect and applied an improved HPIMO.

### *Green jobs*

As explained in the introduction section, the research on green jobs attracted more and more attention after the 2008 financial crisis. Two methods were the mainstream to quantify the impacts of employments. The first was input-output analysis (IOA), which was able to take into account the indirect employment impact of the industry on other relevant sectors throughout the life-cycle process (Lehr et al., 2012; Llera Sastresa et al., 2010; Wei et al., 2010). The second was the process analytical approach, which directly estimated the number of job creation results, usually in the form of employment per units of installation volume. Compared with IOA, the analytical approach was simple and clear, but ignored the indirect employment caused by the multiplier effect and the impact of the inter-sector transfer on the macro-economy (Kievani et al., 2010; Lee et al., 2008; Methipara et al., 2008; Pollin and Wicks-Lim, 2008).

Compared with international research, the domestic studies were rather few. Our previous works (Hong and Liang, 2011) designed indicators and applied life-cycle process analysis to green jobs creation from wind power industries, which laid a foundation for the data and future model integration. But on the whole, the related research in China lacks comprehensive evaluation methodology development and empirical research on green jobs.

With this circumstance, this chapter takes the co-benefit benefit as the cut-in point, integrating the index and the input-output model to investigate the environmental benefits of REE expansion and the related impacts on employment. We analyze the co-benefit and green jobs to link these two hot topics together. Furthermore, this chapter will provide innovation on the evaluation method via the indicators' design and construction of the hybrid input-output model. With case studies on wind and solar energy industries, the qualitative and quantitative results will offer critical insights to the policymakers in China.

### Co-benefits

The term "co-benefits" was first proposed by IPCC TAR (Intergovernmental Panel on Climate Change Third Assessment Report) to indicate that one could get extra effects from one technological or policy implementation (Bollen et al., 2009; Shrestha and Pradhan, 2010; J. Zhang and Wang, 2011). As a systematical approach to achieve multiple targets, it has been gradually adopted into the environment and energy policies fields. The core of the "co-benefit" approach is that the atmospheric pollutants (e.g., sulfur dioxide and other acidic gases) and greenhouse gas (GHG) sources are basically the same, which is fossil fuel combustion. Traditional pollutant assessment policies focus on only one aspect, the lack of comprehensive assessment on the synthetic effects of two or more kinds of gas emission reduction. Therefore, the "co-benefit" approach has attracted more and more attention nowadays (Rive, 2010; Rive and Aunan, 2010; Van Vuuren et al., 2006).

In this study, we defined the co-benefit from a physical perspective that indicates that one option could reduce pollutants and/or save energy and/or make money/societal benefits while also reducing $CO_2$ emissions and/or the other air pollutants. In particular, the two topics we focused on can both generate co-benefits. a) Fossil energy subsidies reform could not only reduce the governmental budget and the distortion of energy market (monetary issues) but also reduce the energy consumption and related emissions. The removal of the price gap and the reduction of energy consumption would contribute to the mitigation of the rebound effect. As a result, the co-benefit was achieved. b) REE expansion could not only contribute to low-carbon effects but also generate "green jobs" as socioeconomic benefits. In this way, a co-benefit is gained.

The added value of GHG mitigation has become a hotspot of international and domestic research. Emerging studies highlighted that reduction of air pollutants not only offered environmental benefits but also generated significant socioeconomic bonus – e.g. it improved the regional environmental quality; reduced $SO_2$, $NO_x$ and $PM_{2.5}$ at the same time (Chae, 2010; Mao et al., 2012); increased health benefits (He et al., 2010; D. Zhang et al., 2012); and reduced cost (economic benefits) for climate change and environmental protection (Barker, 1993; McKinley et al., 2005).

In recent years, more domestic studies focused on the quantitative research on the socioeconomic benefits from GHG mitigation. The highlighting studies included, but were not limited to, the study by the Center for Environmental and Economic Policy Studies of the Ministry of Environmental Protection and the Norwegian Economic Analysis Center, which presented research that stated, if positive and effective GHG reduction measures were adopted, China would have a synergistic emission reduction potential from 1 to 6 million tons of $SO_2$ per year. The additional health benefits would reduce the deaths by 9,000 to 48,000 cases, equal to 30 billion CNY of health benefits (Hu et al., 2004). The study on Beijing by Tsinghua University showed that the co-benefit measures were able to reduce 10.5 million tons of $CO_2$ and enable access to 1.38 billion CNY in health benefits (Liping Li and Zhou, 2009). But in general, there have still been few co-benefit studies focused on green jobs, such as the ones generated by REEI.

## *Input-output analysis*

The input-output model (IO model) is a mature and powerful tool, which enables the effective presentation of the interactions between different sectors of national and regional economies, developed by Leontief (1905–1999) in 1936. From the unit perspective, it could be divided into a monetary input-output model, a physical input-output model and a hybrid model (Giljum and Hubacek, 2009; Holub and Schnabl, 1985).

Compared with a traditional monetary input-output model, a hybrid input-output model can be an effective tool for stimulating different energy and environmental implications. Compared with material flow analysis, the hybrid input-output model has advantages in calculating the inherent relationship between material flows and economic flows, reflecting the interconnection between sectors (Liang et al., 2010). Compared with LCA, which focuses on the technology level, input-out model fits the analysis on the meso-level, and the data is more available in China (Xu, 2010; Xu et al., 2008).

A number of previous works about using input-output models in environmental study fields have been done, but few focus on the energy policies topic. Here we construct an improved HPIMO to assess how certain energy policies could contribute to energy saving and pollutant mitigations, which could be contribute to application tools. In such a revised hybrid model, for the inputs, the energy resources were presented in standardized energetic units, the output was presented in monetary units and air pollutants were presented in mass units. The model could quantitatively represent the correlations between economic sectors by monetary input-output table (MIOTs), thus presenting the interactions between the environmental and the economic systems. In this way, the performance of the system, in terms of environmental and economic, could be simulated and interpreted by changing those parameters according to the scenarios' settings.

## Methods and data

Several terminologies or conceptions and methodologies were applied in this paper. This section will clarify their interconnection under the general analytical framework of this study.

### *Co-benefit indicators*

The co-benefits of fossil fuel subsidies reform mainly generate subsidies reform that could dismiss the price gap of energy products, thus reducing the final demand of relative sectors and finally reducing the consumption and related emissions. Such reduction could be seen as a mitigation of the rebound effect. To evaluate the co-benefit, we propose two indicators.

One co-benefit is $CO_2$ emissions reduction per unit of monetary saving ($tCO_2$/CNY), which means the amount of $CO_2$ emission that could be reduced at the same time one unit of money is saved.

The second co-benefit indicates energy savings per unit of monetary savings (tce/CNY), which represents the amount of energy that could be saved at the same time one unit of money is saved.

From the two proposed indicators, we could identify how subsidies' reform could contribute to the mitigation of the rebound effect (save energy) and at the same time save money; it is a co-benefit. As to the energy consumption, a life-cycle perspective (consumption in the whole supply chain) could be considered via the hybrid input-output model.

As to the renewable energy expansion, we want to mainly investigate its environmental benefits as well as the impacts on employments so as to verify its contribution to green jobs generation. For this sake, the corresponding indicators are designed as follows:

Jobs creation per unit of installation (person/MW): jobs creation is calculated from IOA, including the direct and indirect jobs generated through the REEI supply chain.

Emissions reduction per unit of installation (ton/MW): considers $CO_2$ and air pollutants ($SO_2$ and $NO_x$).

### *HPIMO model*

To help to quantify supply-chain impacts in a life-cycle perspective and to support scenario analysis, a hybrid input-output model is constructed. On the basis of previous works about using input-output models in environmental study fields[12, 62, 64, 65, 66], here we construct an improved HPIMO, which also can be seen as hybrid LCA approach, to assess how environmental and energy policies could contribute to energy saving and pollutants mitigations.

In detail, firstly, based on China's 2007 national IO table and according to the sector and energy consumption features, we integrate 42 sectors into 7 sectors named First Industry-AGR, Mining Industry-MIN, Manufacturing-MANUFCT,

Power Sector-PS, Construction Sector-CON, Transport Sector-TRAN and Service Sector-SERV. To further conduct modeling on the employment impacts of renewable energy (here the focuses are wind power and solar PV), the power sector is divided into four sub sectors named Coal-Fired Power Generation-PG, Wind Power-WIND, Solar Power-SOLAR and All Others-OTHER. The process data is gained via on-site survey to the main companies as well as the industrial reports. In this way, the direct energy consumption matrix can be gained accordingly. Based on process analysis and life-cycle inventory data, we can further compile the sectorial pollutants inventory as well as the jobs engaged (detail was presented in our previous works)[46] (Hong Li et al., 2011) and therefore gain the emissions matrix. Material and energy inventory for each sector is gained, and the monetary IOA will provide the consumption coefficient matrix between the sectors. In this way, we can link monetary flows with physical flows.

Finally, the energy inputs include 13 fuel types, with a ton coal equivalent (tce) – the official unit in Chinese statistics. Employment is in person or 10,000 persons, and pollutants include $CO_2$, $SO_2$ and $NO_x$ (highlighted as the main contributors to acid rain and climate change, and the national control target pollutants in which $CO_2$ controls targets on intensity and the other two targets on the amount of control).

Table 17.1 shows the structure of the constructed China national HPIMO model. The $n \times n$ matrix $M$ indicates monetary interactions among sectors. The $m \times n$ matrix $E$ indicates physical energy interactions among sectors. The $n \times 1$ column vectors of $Y$ and $X$ indicate final demand and total output of each sector in monetary form. The $n \times k$ matrix $P$ indicates the pollutants emissions in each sector.

*Table 17.1* Structure of the hybrid physical input monetary output model

| Monetary input | | Intermediate monetary output sector 1. . . . n | Final demand | Total output | Pollutants emissions |
|---|---|---|---|---|---|
| | | | Y | X | P |
| **Intermediate monetary input** | 1 | A | $Y_1$ | $X_1$ | $P_{11}$ |
| | . . . | | . . . | . . . | . . . |
| | n | | $Y_n$ | $X_n$ | $P_{kn}$ |
| **Added value** | V | | | | |
| **Total monetary output** | X | | | | |
| **Physical energy input** | | Physical input distribution | | | |
| **Energy resource** | 1 | E | | | |
| | . . . | | | | |
| | m | | | | |
| **Employment** | 1 | J | | | |
| | . . . | | | | |
| | q | | | | |

The definitions of direct monetary consumption matrix $A$, Leontief's inverse matrix $(I - A)^{-1}$ and the row balances are kept consistent with previous studies (Leontief, 1936; Li H., et al., 2011b).[61,63] The row balances equations are shown next:

$$AX + Y = X, \tag{17.1}$$
$$X = (I - A)^{-1}Y. \tag{17.2}$$

The $m \times n$ matrix $E$ denotes the energy intensity among sectors. The $n \times k$ matrix $P$ denotes the pollutants emissions intensity among sectors. Relationships between total energy consumption and final demand, as well as pollutants emission and final demand, are shown in the following equations, respectively:

$$D = EX = E(I - A)^{-1}Y, \tag{17.3}$$
$$W = PX = P(I - A)^{-1}Y, \tag{17.4}$$
$$Z = JX = J(I - A)^{-1}Y. \tag{17.5}$$

$D$ denotes the total or cumulative energy consumption. $W$ denotes the total or cumulative pollutants emissions. $Z$ denotes the total jobs creation. Based on this, sectorial energy consumption, emissions and jobs generation can be calculated via the change of final demand.

For the inputs, the energy resources were presented in standardized energetic units and employment was presented in person units. The output was presented in monetary units, and air pollutants were presented in mass units. The model could quantitatively represent the correlations between economic sectors by MIOTs, thus shaping the connections between the environmental system and the economic system.

## Data

The main data sources are the first-hand survey data on energy prices and tax information (for the sake of calculation on subsidies). The detailed data source can refer to our past works[12,46,67] (Hong Li et al., 2011). As to the employment number in key REEI, we get the manufacturing-related data (e.g. employment for each manufacturing process) based on the survey as well as the technical reports. The detailed data source can also be found in our past work.[3,46]

## Fossil energy subsidies and their reform in China

### Fossil fuel subsidies in China and the scale

Fossil energy subsidies reform could not only save the governmental budget and reduce the distortion of the energy market (monetary issues) but also reduce the energy consumption and related carbon emissions as a result of environmental benefits. The removal of the price gap and ensuing energy consumption reduction would contribute to the mitigation of the rebound effect, realizing economic and environmental gains.

Calculating the scale of subsidies is the foundation for the next step in the evaluation. The detailed calculation could be referenced in our previous work.[12,46,67,68] The main concern is to calculate the price gap (it is seen as the gap between the real price of fossil fuels considering their environmental externality and the market prices, which is seen as the disturbed prices) for each fuel type. In theory, subsidy rate equates to the ratio between the price gap and the reference price. According to the market and tax information via survey, we calculate four categories of energy resources called coal, oil, natural gas and electricity. Table 17.2 summarizes the price gap and consumption for different energy products in China in 2007.

Based on the price-gap approach and the results in Table 17.2,[12,46,67,68] the fossil energy subsidies scale in 2007 is calculated and shown in Table 17.3.

According to Table 17.3, China's total fossil energy subsidies in 2007 accounted for 582.0 billion CNY (76.6 billion USD). (IEA, 2008) estimated that China's energy subsidies were about 300 billion CNY (including electricity subsidies) in 2007, which was a bit lower than our results. The main reason was due to different views of the coal price mechanism and the selection of reference prices.

### Subsidies reform and the price change

Subsidies reform mainly considers the removing or reducing of subsidies, which will change the energy price. Here the economic method is applied to trace such supply-demand changes. This chapter uses the constant elasticity inverse

*Table 17.2* Price gap and consumption of energy products of China, 2007

| Energy products | End-use prices | Reference prices | Price-gap | Consumption |
|---|---|---|---|---|
| **Coal (CNY per ton)** | | | | |
| Steam coal | 480.3 | 500.7 | 20.4 | 1.33 billion tons |
| Coal contract | 285.0 | 306.0 | 21.0 | 0.76 billion tons |
| **Oil products (CNY per ton)** | | | | |
| Gasoline | 6464.1 | 7652.5 | 1188.4 | $5552.5 \times 10^4$ tons |
| Diesel | 5548.2 | 7105.9 | 1557.8 | $12466.4 \times 10^4$ tons |
| Fuel oil | 3526.7 | 4088.1 | 561.4 | $1932.2 \times 10^4$ tons |
| Aviation kerosene | 5106.7 | 6893.7 | 1787.0 | $45.3 \times 10^4$ tons |
| **Natural gas (CNY per m³)** | | | | |
| Industry | 2.47 | 3.41 | 0.94 | 50.9 billion m³ |
| Resident | 2.15 | 3.41 | 1.26 | 13.3 billion m³ |
| Public service | 2.09 | 3.41 | 1.32 | 5.3 billion m³ |
| **Electricity (CNY per KWh)** | | | | |
| Resident | 0.49 | 1.03 | 0.54 | 362.27 billion KWh |

*Table 17.3* Calculation for fossil energy subsidies scale of China, 2007

| Energy products | Subsidies scale (billion CNY) | Average subsidies rate |
|---|---|---|
| **Coal** | **43.0** | **6.46%** |
| **Oil products** | **271.8** | **19.52%** |
| *Gasoline* | *65.9* | *15.53%* |
| *Diesel* | *194.3* | *21.92%* |
| *Fuel oil* | *10.8* | *13.73%* |
| *Aviation kerosene* | *0.8* | *25.92%* |
| **Natural gas** | **71.6** | **35.46%** |
| **Electricity** | **195.6** | **52.43** |
| **Total (billion CNY)** | **582.0** | – |

*Table 17.4* Price change of different energy resources after removing the subsidies

| Energy sources | Subsidy rate | Price elasticity | Price change after removing the subsidies |
|---|---|---|---|
| Coal | 6.46% | −0.35 | +6.37% |
| Oil | 19.52% | −0.27 (Transportation) | +18.26% |
| | | −0.19 (Industry) | +18.98% |
| Natural gas | 23.56% | −0.31 | +20.42% |
| Electricity | 52.43% | −0.16 | +46.55% |

demand function to calculate the impacts of removing the subsidies on energy consumption.

$$q = P^{\varepsilon}, \tag{17.6}$$
$$\Delta q = Q_0 - Q_1, \tag{17.7}$$

where
$q$ is the energy consumption;
$\varepsilon$ is the long-term demand elasticity; and
$\Delta q$ stands for the change in consumption after removing the subsidies.

$Q_0$ and $Q_1$ are the quantity before and after removing the price gap, respectively.

With the aforementioned methods, the subsidies scale estimates and price elasticity, how the price will change after removing the subsidies can be calculated. The results are listed in Table 17.4. The price elasticity follows our previous work.[12]

## Overview of the development of China's renewable energy

There are several key points to developing renewable energy, including abundant REE sources, considerable demand, integrated policies and policy effectiveness.

As for China, there are both advantages and disadvantages. The former includes the following: (1) China has abundant renewable resources, shown in Figure 17.2. The estimated REE potential is up to $42.50 \times 10^8$ tce, even more than the total China's energy demand up to 2015 (about 35 to $40 \times 10^8$ tce). (2) Both international and domestic situations call for the rapid development of renewables. The use and investment of REE sources has been expanding rapidly in recent years, and this trend is set to continue, which would provide large markets and beneficial environments for REE development. The disadvantage is that renewable technologies are not as mature as fossil energy technologies, thus compared to traditional fossil fuels, prices are higher, which makes renewables relatively less competitive in the market. In order to encourage the development of REE, the government policy is the initial power to overcome such disadvantages. In addition, China has vast regional disparity, which further affects the local REEI development. Thus designing the most appropriate policy system at the local level is significantly important.

After 2005, a series of REE promotion policies were implemented, and now the REE is undergoing a surge of development in China (Figure 17.3). By 2010, China was the biggest entity in terms of new financial investment in REEI (Figure 17.4), especially for wind power and solar power; the development ratio is

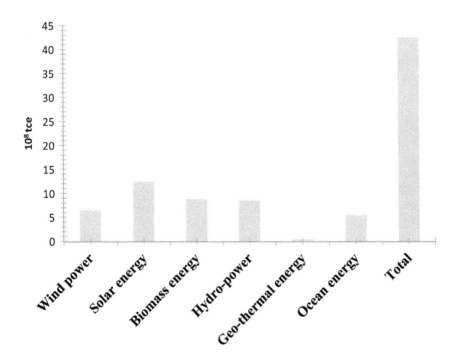

*Figure 17.2* Resource potential of REE, $10^8$ tce

Source: Research of China's mid-long-term renewables development strategy, Chinese Academy of Engineering, 2009

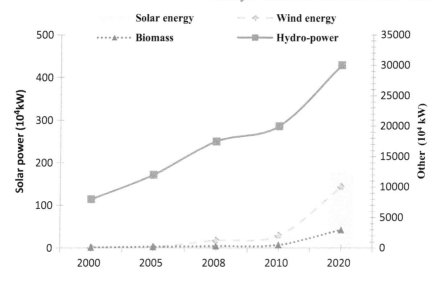

*Figure 17.3* China's REE development status (data for 2020 is the national target)

Source: http:// www.eri.org.cn/

very high. Wind and solar power generate large added value through industrial chains, thus they are the most emerging REE currently in China.

## Analysis and discussions

### *Analysis of fossil subsidies reform in China*[1]

Via the price elasticity, the final demand change can be investigated under the subsidies reform (according to the market equilibrium theory, when removing the price gap, the market price will increase and, as a result, final demand will be reduced, further reducing the physical input of energy in specific sectors). The changes to final demand are summarized in Table 17.5. With the change in final demand, the related environmental impacts can be simulated with the built HPIMO model.

The simulation results of the HPIMO model are shown in Figure 17.5. The results showed that by removing energy subsidies, the coal, oil, natural gas and electricity would be reduced by 17.74, 13.47, 3.64 and 15.82 million tce, respectively.

As to the co-benefit indicators, they are as follows ($CO_2$ emissions reduction could be calculated based on the emissions coefficients of different energy types):

- the total $CO_2$ emissions reduction is 77.60 million tons;
- monetary saving per unit of $CO_2$ emissions reduction is 7500 CNY/t$CO_2$; and
- monetary savings per unit of energy savings is 11502 CNY/tce.[2]

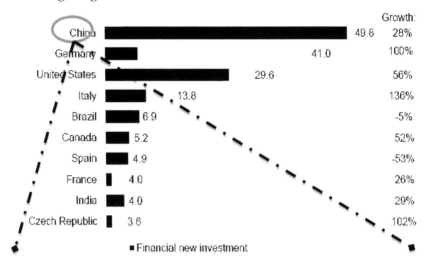

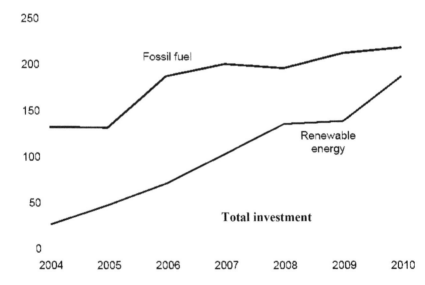

*Figure 17.4* China's financial investment for REE and the comparison with fossil fuel
(unit: billion USD)

Source: Bloomberg New Energy Finance, UNEP

### Analysis of renewable energy expansion

The case study on renewable energy expansion focuses on wind power and solar
energy, according to their importance in the REEI development in China as well
as the integratity of their industrial chains (lead to data availability). We further
apply the model to simulate the employment change. As basic data input, the

*Table 17.5* The change to final demand of each sector

| Sectors | Change to final demand |
|---------|------------------------|
| A | 0 |
| B | −1.45% |
| C | −1.45% |
| D | −6.47% |
| E | −11.21% |
| F | −11.21% |

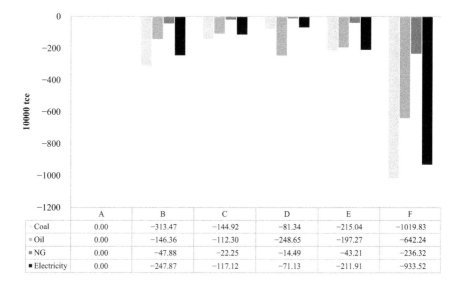

|  | A | B | C | D | E | F |
|--|----|----|----|----|----|----|
| Coal | 0.00 | −313.47 | −144.92 | −81.34 | −215.04 | −1019.83 |
| Oil | 0.00 | −146.36 | −112.30 | −248.65 | −197.27 | −642.24 |
| NG | 0.00 | −47.88 | −22.25 | −14.49 | −43.21 | −236.32 |
| Electricity | 0.00 | −247.87 | −117.12 | −71.13 | −211.91 | −933.52 |

*Figure 17.5* Simulation result of HPIMO model

Note: A to F present First Industry-AGR; Mining Industry-MIN, Manufacturing-MANUFCT, Construction Sector-CON, Transport Sector-TRAN and Service Sector-SERV. As subsidies of electricity (second energy comes from the power sector) are one of the key subsidies in China, electricity subsidies are considered and the impact of the power sector is not included (their product-electricity is allocated to other sectors).

employment of each sector in 2007 is presented in Figure 17.6. Wind sector and solar sector contributes to 550,000 and 200,000 employees, repectively.

*Scenarios*

The next step is to build scenarios. It is well known that China promotes five-year national planning policies (FYP), thus we select 2007 as a benchmark year and 2015 (the end of the twelfth FYP) as the scenario year. The scenarios include the following:

- Scenario-1: BAU: considering common technological advancement (e.g. energy efficiency enhancement), industrial structure adjustment and energy

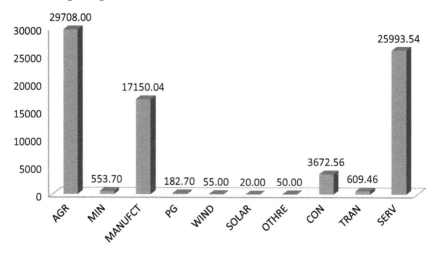

*Figure 17.6* Employment in each sector in 2007, 10,000 person

conservation and pollutants reduction policies (according to national target), no expansion on REE.

- Scenario-2: Wind power expansion (WPE): promote the wind power expansion.
- Scenario-3: Solar power expansion (SPE): promote the solar power expansion.
- Scenario-4: Comprehensive expansion scenario (CES): promote both the wind power and solar power expansion.

*Parameters setting*

Based on the national industries development policies and technological reports, the parameters are set for scenarios (Table 17.6). The change in final demand for each sector can be seen as the result of economic growth, while the change in energy consumption per unit of GDP (energy efficiency) is a result of technologies development (Table 17.7).

*Analytical results*

Based on the earlier scenarios and related parameter settings, socioeconomic and environmental impacts of REE expansion is simulated. Energy consumption and emissions in BAU scenario are illustrated in Figure 17.7. In general, with industrial structure adjustment, technologies advancement and energy conservation and emissions reduction, the emissions per unit of economic outcome will be reduced, but with the economic scale expansion, the total amount will still increase. As a result, extra countermeasures are needed.

Analytical results of wind energy expansion and solar energy expansion are presented in Figure 17.8 and 17.9, respectively. They highlight, in the WPE scenario

*Table 17.6* Parameters setting for BAU scenario

| Sector | Final demand change | Change of energy consumption per unit of GDP |
|---|---|---|
| AGR | 107.19% | −5% |
| MIN | 100.00% | −20% |
| MANUFCT | 150.00% | −20% |
| PG | 163.02% | −6%[a] |
| WIND | 100.00% | −0% |
| SOLAR | 100.00% | −0% |
| OTHER | 100.00% | −0% |
| CON | 150.00% | −20% |
| TRAN | 180.00% | −10% |
| SERV | 200.00% | −10% |

Note: [a] As to the power sector, it refers to electricity supply energy consumption (according to national energy conservation and emission reduction standards).

*Table 17.7* Parameters setting for renewable energy expansion scenarios

| Sector | Final demand under WPE | Final demand under SPE | Final demand under CES | Change of energy consumption per unit of GDP |
|---|---|---|---|---|
| AGR | 107.19% | 107.19% | 107.19% | −5% |
| MIN | 100.00% | 100.00% | 100.00% | −20% |
| MANUFCT | 150.00% | 150.00% | 150.00% | −20% |
| PG | 161.93% | 162.34% | 145.43% | −6% |
| WIND | 217.01% | 100% | 217.01% | −0% |
| SOLAR | 100% | 487.12% | 487.12% | −0% |
| OTHER | 100% | 100% | 168.89% | −0% |
| CON | 150.00% | 150.00% | 150.00% | −20% |
| TRAN | 180.00% | 180.00% | 180.00% | −10% |
| SERV | 200.00% | 200.00% | 200.00% | −10% |

Note: Power industry twelfth FYP; twelfth FYP for energy conservation and emission reduction in the power sector, China Electricity Council, 2010

in 2015, the reductions of fossil fuels consumption $CO_2$, $SO_2$ and $NO_x$ emissions amount to 77.57 million tce, 206.13 million ton, 242.60 thousand ton and 25.40 thousand ton, respectively. Regarding the SPE scenario in 2015, reductions of fossil fuels consumption $CO_2$, $SO_2$ and $NO_x$ emissions amount to 48.63 million tce, 129.22 million ton, 152.10 thousand ton and 15.90 thousand ton, respectively. Via both developing wind and solar energy in 2015, reductions in fossil fuels consumption $CO_2$, $SO_2$ and $NO_x$ emissions amount to 126.20 million tce, 335.35 million ton, 394.72 thousand ton and 41.40 thousand ton, respectively (Figure 17.10). In summary, significant environmental benefits were achieved.

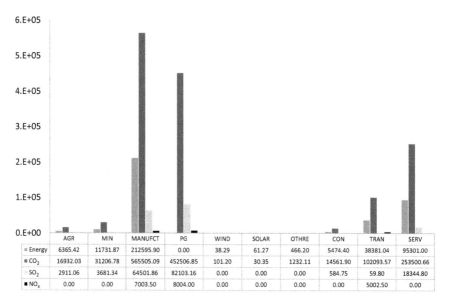

| | AGR | MIN | MANUFCT | PG | WIND | SOLAR | OTHRE | CON | TRAN | SERV |
|---|---|---|---|---|---|---|---|---|---|---|
| ▦ Energy | 6365.42 | 11731.87 | 212595.90 | 0.00 | 38.29 | 61.27 | 466.20 | 5474.40 | 38381.04 | 95301.00 |
| ▪ $CO_2$ | 16932.03 | 31206.78 | 565505.09 | 452506.85 | 101.20 | 30.35 | 1232.11 | 14561.90 | 102093.57 | 253500.66 |
| $SO_2$ | 2911.06 | 3681.34 | 64501.86 | 82103.16 | 0.00 | 0.00 | 0.00 | 584.75 | 59.80 | 18344.80 |
| ▪ $NO_x$ | 0.00 | 0.00 | 7003.50 | 8004.00 | 0.00 | 0.00 | 0.00 | 0.00 | 5002.50 | 0.00 |

*Figure 17.7* Results of BAU in 2015

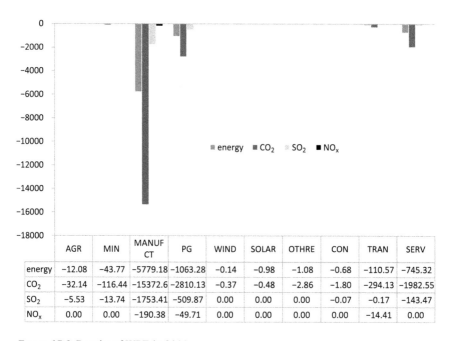

| | AGR | MIN | MANUFCT | PG | WIND | SOLAR | OTHRE | CON | TRAN | SERV |
|---|---|---|---|---|---|---|---|---|---|---|
| energy | −12.08 | −43.77 | −5779.18 | −1063.28 | −0.14 | −0.98 | −1.08 | −0.68 | −110.57 | −745.32 |
| $CO_2$ | −32.14 | −116.44 | −15372.6 | −2810.13 | −0.37 | −0.48 | −2.86 | −1.80 | −294.13 | −1982.55 |
| $SO_2$ | −5.53 | −13.74 | −1753.41 | −509.87 | 0.00 | 0.00 | 0.00 | −0.07 | −0.17 | −143.47 |
| $NO_x$ | 0.00 | 0.00 | −190.38 | −49.71 | 0.00 | 0.00 | 0.00 | 0.00 | −14.41 | 0.00 |

*Figure 17.8* Results of WPE in 2015

Note: For energy and $CO_2$, the unit is 10,000 tce/ton; for $SO_2$ and $NO_x$, the unit is 100 ton

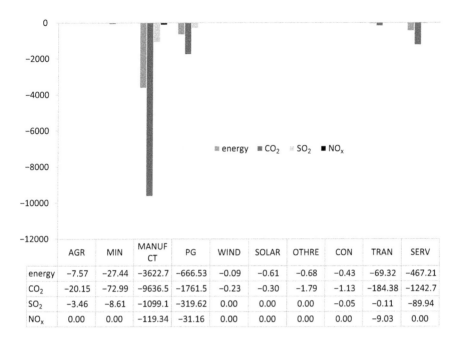

| | AGR | MIN | MANUF CT | PG | WIND | SOLAR | OTHRE | CON | TRAN | SERV |
|---|---|---|---|---|---|---|---|---|---|---|
| energy | −7.57 | −27.44 | −3622.7 | −666.53 | −0.09 | −0.61 | −0.68 | −0.43 | −69.32 | −467.21 |
| CO₂ | −20.15 | −72.99 | −9636.5 | −1761.5 | −0.23 | −0.30 | −1.79 | −1.13 | −184.38 | −1242.7 |
| SO₂ | −3.46 | −8.61 | −1099.1 | −319.62 | 0.00 | 0.00 | 0.00 | −0.05 | −0.11 | −89.94 |
| NOₓ | 0.00 | 0.00 | −119.34 | −31.16 | 0.00 | 0.00 | 0.00 | 0.00 | −9.03 | 0.00 |

*Figure 17.9* Results of SPE in 2015

Note: For energy and $CO_2$, the unit is 10,000 tce/ton; for $SO_2$ and $NO_x$, the unit is 100 ton

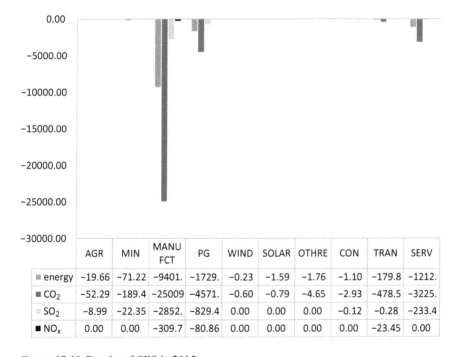

| | AGR | MIN | MANU FCT | PG | WIND | SOLAR | OTHRE | CON | TRAN | SERV |
|---|---|---|---|---|---|---|---|---|---|---|
| energy | −19.66 | −71.22 | −9401. | −1729. | −0.23 | −1.59 | −1.76 | −1.10 | −179.8 | −1212. |
| CO₂ | −52.29 | −189.4 | −25009 | −4571. | −0.60 | −0.79 | −4.65 | −2.93 | −478.5 | −3225. |
| SO₂ | −8.99 | −22.35 | −2852. | −829.4 | 0.00 | 0.00 | 0.00 | −0.12 | −0.28 | −233.4 |
| NOₓ | 0.00 | 0.00 | −309.7 | −80.86 | 0.00 | 0.00 | 0.00 | 0.00 | −23.45 | 0.00 |

*Figure 17.10* Results of CES in 2015

Note: For energy and $CO_2$, the unit is 10,000 tce/ton; for $SO_2$ and $NO_x$, the unit is 100 ton

Apart from the industrial structure adjustment, technology advancement and energy conservation and emissions reduction implications, how wind and solar energy expansion will impact employment is analyzed and summarized in Figures 17.11 and 17.12. The results highlight that, by 2015, promoting the wind energy expansion will contribute to jobs creation by 507.10 thousand persons, while promoting solar energy expansion will increase employment by 631.10 thousand persons, respectively. The employment benefits of renewable energy expansion not only come from direct job generation but also benefits from the whole industrial chain from a life-cycle perspective. For example, the wind energy expansion will pull the related high-end equipment manufacturing industry, which also belongs to the seven "strategic emerging industries" to be promoted by the Chinese government by 2020. From this point, the expansion of REEI will strongly pull the industrial transformation in China.

Finally, co-benefits indicators are analyzed and summarized in Table 17.8. Simulated by the HPIMO model, the impact of employment can be seen as a change in the whole life cycle (both direct and indirect impacts). Results highlight that, to increase one MW wind energy will reduce $CO_2$, $SO_2$ and $NO_x$ emissions by 3680.98 ton, 4.33 ton and 0.45 ton, respectively, while also increasing jobs by about nine; to increase one MW solar energy will reduce $CO_2$, $SO_2$ and $NO_x$ emissions by 6153.29 ton, 7.24 ton and 0.76 ton, respectively, while increasing jobs by about 30. Obvious co-benefits are realized.

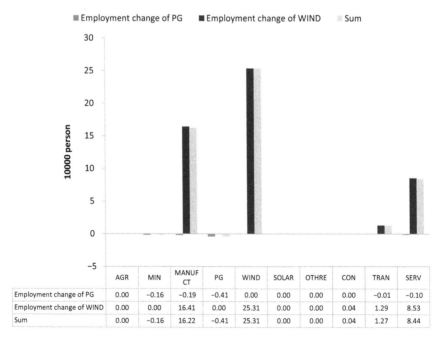

|  | AGR | MIN | MANUF CT | PG | WIND | SOLAR | OTHRE | CON | TRAN | SERV |
|---|---|---|---|---|---|---|---|---|---|---|
| Employment change of PG | 0.00 | −0.16 | −0.19 | −0.41 | 0.00 | 0.00 | 0.00 | 0.00 | −0.01 | −0.10 |
| Employment change of WIND | 0.00 | 0.00 | 16.41 | 0.00 | 25.31 | 0.00 | 0.00 | 0.04 | 1.29 | 8.53 |
| Sum | 0.00 | −0.16 | 16.22 | −0.41 | 25.31 | 0.00 | 0.00 | 0.04 | 1.27 | 8.44 |

*Figure 17.11* Employments change in WPE in 2015

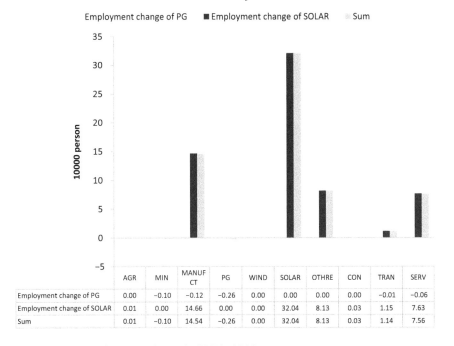

Employment change of PG   ■ Employment change of SOLAR   ▨ Sum

| | AGR | MIN | MANUF CT | PG | WIND | SOLAR | OTHRE | CON | TRAN | SERV |
|---|---|---|---|---|---|---|---|---|---|---|
| Employment change of PG | 0.00 | −0.10 | −0.12 | −0.26 | 0.00 | 0.00 | 0.00 | 0.00 | −0.01 | −0.06 |
| Employment change of SOLAR | 0.01 | 0.00 | 14.66 | 0.00 | 0.00 | 32.04 | 8.13 | 0.03 | 1.15 | 7.63 |
| Sum | 0.01 | −0.10 | 14.54 | −0.26 | 0.00 | 32.04 | 8.13 | 0.03 | 1.14 | 7.56 |

*Figure 17.12* Employments change in SPE in 2015

*Table 17.8* Co-benefits of renewable energy expansion in 2015

| Co-benefit indicators | Unit | WPE2015 | SPE2015 |
|---|---|---|---|
| Job creation per unit of installation | person/MW | 9.05 | 30.05 |
| $CO_2$ reduction per unit of installation () | ton/MW | 3680.98 | 6153.29 |
| $SO_2$ reduction per unit of installation | ton/MW | 4.33 | 7.24 |
| $NO_x$ reduction per unit of installation | ton/MW | 0.45 | 0.76 |

## Conclusions and implications

### *Main conclusions*

For the sake of pursuing low-carbon countermeasures in the context of China, this chapter evaluated the socioeconomic and environmental impacts of fossil fuel subsidies reform and REE expansion in China and explored the co-benefits. A HPIMO with integrated sectors (electricity sectors and sectors of the rest of the economy) was constructed based on the Chinese 2007 national IOT, which enabled us to analyze the interactions between the different sectors and to calculate the impact on the whole supply-demand chains. The impact in terms of employment (socioeconomic), saving on the budget (economic), $CO_2$ and air pollutants ($SO_2$ and $NO_x$) mitigation (environmental) effects were evaluated.

In regard to the fossil fuels reform, simulation results showed that removing energy subsidies would cause the prices of coal, oil, natural gas and electricity to increase by 6.37%, 18.62%, 20.42% and 46.55%, respectively; furthermore, the physical total consumption of coal, oil, natural gas and electricity would be reduced by 17.74, 13.47, 3.64 and 15.82 million tce, respectively. The co-benefit of reducing the budget as well as reducing energy consumption and related $CO_2$ emissions was achieved.

Regarding the REE expansion, significant co-benefits in terms of environmental benefits and social benefits (employments generation) were achieved. In summary, by promoting the set scenario of wind energy expansion by 2015, $CO_2$, $SO_2$ and $NO_x$ emissions were reduced by 3680.98 ton, 4.33ton and 0.45ton per unit of MW installation, respectively. Meanwhile, around nine jobs per unit of MW were generated; by promoting the set scenario of solar energy expansion by 2015, $CO_2$, $SO_2$ and $NO_x$, emissions were reduced by 6153.29 ton, 7.24 ton and 0.76 ton per unit of MW installation, respectively. This generated about 30 jobs per unit of MW.

Compared with general technology advancement, industrial structure adjustment and environmental regulation, wind energy expansion by 2015 was able to reduce energy consumption and emissions of $CO_2$, $SO_2$ and $NO_x$ by 77.57 million tce, 206.13 million tons, 242.60 thousand tons and 25.40 thousand tons, respectively. Meanwhile, 507.10 thousand jobs were created in the whole economic system. Expansion of solar energy by 2015 reduced fossil fuels consumption $CO_2$, $SO_2$ and $NO_x$ emissions by 48.63 million tce, 129.22 million tons, 152.10 thousand tons and 15.90 thousand tons, respectively. Meanwhile, it created 631.10 thousand jobs in the whole economic system. Co-benefit indicators effectively present the multiple benefits of such energy implications. In the methodological perspective, the application of IOA helps to quantify the accumulative effects in the whole life-cycle of the industrial chain.

### *Policy implications*

Based on the aforementioned analytical results, critical policy implications were proposed and discussed:

- Energy subsidies reform should not only focus on its environmental effects but also the comprehensive social-economic matters, such as how it would have affected the macro-economy, households living and the interconnection of each industry. To support such decision making, a relative modeling approach and indicators are needed. This study lays a good foundation for these future concerns.
- Removing subsidies will result in better policy effects by cooperating with the measures of second distribution of the saved money and the other policies as environmental taxes. Particularly, this study verified the significant co-benefits of REE expansion; hence the transfer of fossil fuels subsidies to REE subsidies should be considered and well designed.

- Not only co-benefits but also trade-offs should be considered. Our results not only reveal job creation through the expansion of wind and solar energy industries but also because of their pull effect on the whole supply chain. This also highlights that somehow job loss will be caused by some negative impacts on traditional industries, such as coal-fired power generation. To reduce such impacts, employment transfer and secondary training are of importance.
- Finally, this chapter applies IOA to quantify the environmental and employment impact of promoting REE industries by 2015. However, in the methodological perspective, IOA has its limits in regard to data resolution as well as the reflection of the market equilibrium and products' diversity because of the assumption that the ratio of outputs to inputs is constant and factor prices are also constant. Such methods' limit the future concerns of improvement, including but not limited to, improving the inventory database of REE industries via on-site surveys so that the estimation of employment and industrial data are more accurate, integrating with the equilibrium model to better analyze the market system and developing a dynamic simulation tool to support public policy making.

## Acknowledgement

This research was supported by the project "Smart Industrial Parks (SIPs) in China: Towards Joint Design and Institutionalization", which has been co-funded by NWO – Netherlands Organisation for Scientific Research and MOST – Ministry of Science and Technology of China (NWO no. 467–14–003, MOST no. 2015DFG62270).

## Notes

1 The detail analysis regarding this part of the study refers to our publication 12.
2 Tce-ton coal equivalent. 1 tce = 29.27 GJ.

## References

Barker, T. (1993). Secondary Benefits of Greenhouse Gas Abatement: The Effects of a UK Carbon/Energy Tax on Air Pollution', Energy-Environment-Economy Modelling Discussion Paper No.4, Department of Applied Economics, University of Cambridge, Cambridge.
Barker, T., Ekins, P., and Foxon, T. (2007). The macro-economic rebound effect and the UK economy. *Energy Policy*, *35*(10), 4935–4946.
Becker, B., and Fischer, D. (2013). Promoting renewable electricity generation in emerging economies. *Energy Policy*, *56*, 446–455.
Bentzen, J. (2004). Estimating the rebound effect in US manufacturing energy consumption. *Energy Economics*, *26*(1), 123–134.
Bollen, J., Brink, C., Eerens, H., and Manders, T. (2009). *Co-benefits of climate policy* (pp. 1–75). The Netherlands: Netherlands Environmental Assessment Agency.
BP. (2011). BP world energy statistics 2011. BP p.l.c., London, United Kingdom.

Cai, W., Wang, C., Chen, J., and Wang, S. (2011). Green economy and green jobs: Myth or reality? The case of China's power generation sector. *Energy*, *36*(10), 5994–6003.

Chae, Y. (2010). Co-benefit analysis of an air quality management plan and greenhouse gas reduction strategies in the Seoul metropolitan area. *Environmental Science & Policy*, *13*(3), 205–216.

De Moor, A. (2001). *Towards a grand deal on subsidies and climate change.* Paper presented at the Natural Resources Forum.

Dong, L., Fujita, T., Dai, M., Geng, Y., Ren, J., Fujii, M., . . . Ohnishi, S. (2016). Towards preventative eco-industrial development: an industrial and urban symbiosis case in one typical industrial city in China. *Journal of Cleaner Production*, *114*, 387–400.

Dong, L., and Liang, H. (2014). Spatial analysis on China's regional air pollutants and CO 2 emissions: emission pattern and regional disparity. *Atmospheric Environment*, *92*, 280–291.

Dong, L., Liang, H., Gao, Z., Luo, X., and Ren, J. (2016). Spatial distribution of China's renewable energy industry: Regional features and implications for a harmonious development future. *Renewable and Sustainable Energy Reviews*, *58*, 1521–1531.

Energy and Climate Change Sustainable Development Commission. (2009). *Green jobs for Wales, 2009*. Wales: Energy and Climate Change Sustainable Development Commission in Wales.

Freire-González, J. (2010). Empirical evidence of direct rebound effect in Catalonia. *Energy Policy*, *38*(5), 2309–2314.

Giljum, S., and Hubacek, K. (2009). Conceptual foundations and applications of physical input-output tables. In *Handbook of input-output economics in industrial ecology* (pp. 61–75). Edited by: Sangwon Suh. Springer. Berlin, Germany.

Grepperud, S., and Rasmussen, I. (2004). A general equilibrium assessment of rebound effects. *Energy Economics*, *26*(2), 261–282.

He, K., Lei, Y., Pan, X., Zhang, Y., Zhang, Q., and Chen, D. (2010). Co-benefits from energy policies in China. *Energy*, *35*(11), 4265–4272.

Holub, H., and Schnabl, H. (1985). Qualitative input-output analysis and structural information. *Economic Modelling*, *2*(1), 67–73.

Hong, L., and Liang, D. (2011). Promoting green employment and enhancing the eco-efficiency of the industry: An empirical study based on wind energy industry. *Journal of Peking University (Philosophy & Social Sciences)*, *1*, 017.

Hong, L., Liang, D., and Di, W. (2013). Economic and environmental gains of China's fossil energy subsidies reform: A rebound effect case study with EIMO model. *Energy Policy*, *54*, 335–342.

Hu, T., Tian, C., and Li, L. (2004). Influence of co-benefit on policy in China. *Environmental Protection*, *9*, 56–58.

Huang, C., Su, J., Zhao, X., Sui, J., Ru, P., Zhang, H., and Wang, X. (2012). Government funded renewable energy innovation in China. *Energy Policy*, *51*, 121–127.

IEA. (1999). World energy outlook insights, looking at energy subsidies: Getting the prices right. Paris, France: International Energy Agency.

IEA. (2008). *World energy outlook 2008*. Paris, France: IEA.

Khazzoom, J. D. (1980). Economic implications of mandated efficiency in standards for household appliances. *The Energy Journal*, *1*(4), 21–40.

Kievani, R., Tah, J. H., Kurul, E., and Habanda, H. (2010). *Green jobs creation through sustainable refurbishment in the developing countries*. International Labor Organization (ILO). Geneva, Switzerland.

Lee, K. T., Weeks, G., and Hardcastle, A. (2008). *Green economy jobs in Washington state*. Washington, DC: Washington State Employment Security Department, Washington State University.

Lehr, U., Lutz, C., and Edler, D. (2012). Green jobs? Economic impacts of renewable energy in Germany. *Energy Policy*, *47*, 358–364.

Leontief, W. W. (1936). Quantitative input and output relations in the economic systems of the United States. *The Review of Economic Statistics*, 18(3), 105–125.

Li, H., Dong, L., and Duan, H. (2011a). A study on the comprehensive evaluation and optimization of renewable energies development in China. *Resources Science*, *33*(3), 1–10.

Li, H., Dong, L., and Xie, M. (2011b). A study on the comprehensive evaluation and optimization of how removing gas and electricity subsidies would affect households' living. *Economic Research Journal*, *2*, 009.

Li, L., and Yonglei, H. (2012). The energy efficiency rebound effect in China from three industries perspective. *Energy Procedia*, *14*, 1105–1110.

Li, L., and Zhou, G. (2009). Don't neglect the co-benefit of pollution mitigation. *Journal of Environmental Protection*, *434*(24), 36–38.

Liang, S., Wang, C., and Zhang, T. (2010). An improved input – output model for energy analysis: A case study of Suzhou. *Ecological Economics*, *69*(9), 1805–1813.

Liu, H., and Liang, D. (2013). A review of clean energy innovation and technology transfer in China. *Renewable and Sustainable Energy Reviews*, *18*, 486–498.

Liu, L., Liu, C.-X, and Sun, Z.-Y. (2011). A survey of China's low-carbon application practice – opportunity goes with challenge. *Renewable and Sustainable Energy Reviews*, *15*(6), 2895–2903.

Llera Sastresa, E., Usón, A. A., Bribián, I. Z., and Scarpellini, S. (2010). Local impact of renewables on employment: Assessment methodology and case study. *Renewable and Sustainable Energy Reviews*, *14*(2), 679–690. doi: http://dx.doi.org/10.1016/j.rser.2009.10.017

Lo, K., and Wang, M. Y. (2013). Energy conservation in China's Twelfth Five-Year Plan period: Continuation or paradigm shift? *Renewable and Sustainable Energy Reviews*, *18*, 499–507.

Mao, X., Yang, S., Liu, Q., Tu, J., and Jaccard, M. (2012). Achieving $CO_2$ emission reduction and the co-benefits of local air pollution abatement in the transportation sector of China. *Environmental Science & Policy*, *21*, 1–13.

Matos, F. J., and Silva, F. J. (2011). The rebound effect on road freight transport: Empirical evidence from Portugal. *Energy Policy*, *39*(5), 2833–2841.

Maxwell, D., Owen, P., McAndrew, L., Muehmel, K., and Neubauer, A. (2011). Addressing the rebound effect, a report for the European Commission DG Environment. *European Commission DG ENV*.

McKinley, G., Zuk, M., Höjer, M., Avalos, M., González, I., Iniestra, R., . . . Reynales, L. M. (2005). *Quantification of local and global benefits from air pollution control in Mexico City. Environmental Science & Technology*, *39*(7), 1954–1961.

Methipara, J., Sauer, A., and Elles, C. (2008). *Jobs from renewable energy and energy efficiency* (C. Werner, Ed.). Washington, DC: Environmental and Energy Study Institute.

Ming, Z., Kun, Z., and Jun, D. (2013). Overall review of China's wind power industry: Status quo, existing problems and perspective for future development. *Renewable and Sustainable Energy Reviews*, *24*, 379–386.

Mizobuchi, K. (2008). An empirical study on the rebound effect considering capital costs. *Energy Economics*, *30*(5), 2486–2516.

OECD. (2005). *Environmentally harmful subsidies: Challenges for reform*. Paris, France: OECD.

Ouyang, J., Long, E., and Hokao, K. (2010). Rebound effect in Chinese household energy efficiency and solution for mitigating it. *Energy*, *35*(12), 5269–5276.

Pollin, R., and Wicks-Lim, J. (2008). *Job opportunities for the green economy: A state-by-state picture of occupations that gain from green investments.* Amherst: Political Economy Research Institute, University of Massachusetts.

Rive, N. (2010). Climate policy in Western Europe and avoided costs of air pollution control. *Economic Modelling, 27*(1), 103–115.

Rive, N., and Aunan, K. (2010). Quantifying the air quality cobenefits of the clean development mechanism in China. *Environmental Science & Technology, 44*(11), 4368–4375.

Shrestha, R. M., and Pradhan, S. (2010). Co-benefits of $CO_2$ emission reduction in a developing country. *Energy Policy, 38*(5), 2586–2597.

UNEP. (2008a). *Green jobs: Towards decent work in a sustainable, low-carbon world.* Paris, France: United Nations Environment Programme.

UNEP. (2008b). Reforming energy subsidies: Opportunities to contribute to the climate change agenda. Paris, France: United Nations Environment Programme.

Van Vuuren, D., Cofala, J., Eerens, H., Oostenrijk, R., Heyes, C., Klimont, Z., . . . Amann, M. (2006). Exploring the ancillary benefits of the Kyoto Protocol for air pollution in Europe. *Energy Policy, 34*(4), 444–460.

Wang, F., Yin, H., and Li, S. (2010). China's renewable energy policy: Commitments and challenges. *Energy Policy, 38*(4), 1872–1878.

Wang, H., Zhou, D., Zhou, P., and Zha, D. (2012). Direct rebound effect for passenger transport: empirical evidence from Hong Kong. *Applied Energy, 92*, 162–167.

Wang, H., Zhou, P., and Zhou, D. (2012). An empirical study of direct rebound effect for passenger transport in urban China. *Energy Economics, 34*(2), 452–460.

Wei, M., Patadia, S., and Kammen, D. M. (2010). Putting renewables and energy efficiency to work: How many jobs can the clean energy industry generate in the US? *Energy Policy, 38*(2), 919–931.

Xingang, Z., Jieyu, W., Xiaomeng, L., and Pingkuo, L. (2012). China's wind, biomass and solar power generation: What the situation tells us? *Renewable and Sustainable Energy Reviews, 16*(8), 6173–6182.

Xu, M. (2010). Development of the physical input monetary output model for understanding material flows within ecological – economic systems. *Journal of Resources and Ecology, 1*(2), 123–134.

Xu, M., Zhang, T., and Allenby, B. (2008). How much will China weigh? Perspectives from consumption structure and technology development. *Environmental Science & Technology, 42*(11), 4022–4028.

Yu, H.-Y., and Zhu, S.-L. (2015). Toward Paris: China and climate change negotiations. *Advances in Climate Change Research, 6*(1), 56–66.

Yu, X., and Qu, H. (2013). The role of China's renewable powers against climate change during the 12th Five-Year and until 2020. *Renewable and Sustainable Energy Reviews, 22*, 401–409.

Zeng, M., Li, C., and Zhou, L. (2013). Progress and prospective on the police system of renewable energy in China. *Renewable and Sustainable Energy Reviews, 20*, 36–44.

Zhang, D., Tang, S., Lin, B., Liu, Z., Zhang, X., and Zhang, D. (2012). Co-benefit of poly-crystalline large-scale photovoltaic power in China. *Energy, 41*(1), 436–442.

Zhang, J., and Wang, C. (2011). Co-benefits and additionality of the clean development mechanism: An empirical analysis. *Journal of Environmental Economics and Management, 62*(2), 140–154.

Zhang, X., Wu, L., Zhang, R., Deng, S., Zhang, Y., Wu, J., . . . Wang, Y. (2013). Evaluating the relationships among economic growth, energy consumption, air emissions and air environmental protection investment in China. *Renewable and Sustainable Energy Reviews, 18*, 259–270.

# Index